UCLA FORUM IN MEDICAL SCIENCES
NUMBER 29
SERIES EDITOR: MARY A. B. BRAZIER
University of California, Los Angeles

Neurobiology of Higher Cognitive Function

Edited by

ARNOLD B. SCHEIBEL
UNIVERSITY OF CALIFORNIA, LOS ANGELES

ADAM F. WECHSLER
WADSWORTH VETERANS ADMINISTRATION MEDICAL CENTER

THE GUILFORD PRESS
New York   London

UCLA FORUM IN MEDICAL SCIENCES

EDITORIAL BOARD

Mary A. B. Brazier, *Editor-in-Chief*

Library of Congress Cataloging-in-Publication Data
Neurobiology of higher cognitive function / edited by Arnold B. Scheibel, Adam F. Wechsler
  p. cm. — (UCLA forum in medical sciences; no. 29)
  Based on a meeting held Mar. 20–23, 1988 in the UCLA Conference Center at Lake Arrowhead.
  Includes bibliographical references.
  ISBN 0-89862-425-8
  1. Cognition—Physiological aspects—Congresses.
  2. Neurophysiology—Congresses. 3. Neuropsychology—Congresses.
  I. Scheibel, Arnold B. II. Wechsler, Adam F. III. Series.
  [DNLM: 1. Brain—physiology—congresses. 2. Cognition—physiology—congresses. 3. Neurobiology—congresses. W3 U17 no. 29 / WL 102 N494522 1988]
  QP395.N49 1990
  153.4—dc20
  DNLM/DLC
for Library of Congress   89-23636
                                                                CIP

UCLA FORUM IN MEDICAL SCIENCES

MARY A. B. BRAZIER, Editor

1. *Brain Function: Cortical Excitability and Steady Potentials; Relations of Basic Research to Space Biology.* Ed. Mary A. B. Brazier, 1963.
2. *Brain Function: RNA and Brain Function. Memory and Learning.* Ed. Mary A. B. Brazier, 1964.
3. *Brain and Behavior: The Brain and Gonadal Function.* Eds. Roger A. Gorski and Richard E. Whalen, 1966.
4. *Brain Function: Speech, Language, and Communication.* Ed. C. Carterette, 1966.
5. *Gastrin.* Ed. Morton I. Grossman, 1966.
6. *Brain Function: Brain Function and Learning.* Eds. Donald B. Lindsley and Arthur A. Lumsdaine, 1967.
7. *Brain Function: Aggression and Defense. Neural Mechanisms and Social Patterns.* Eds. Carmine D. Clemente and Donald B. Lindsley, 1967.
8. *The Retina: Morphology, Function, and Clinical Characteristics.* Eds. Bradley R. Straatsma, Raymond A. Allen, Frederick Crescitelli, and Michael O. Hall, 1969.
9. *Image Processing in Biological Science.* Ed. Diane M. Ramsey, 1969.
10. *Pathophysiology of Congenital Heart Disease.* Eds. Forrest H. Adams, H. J. C. Swan, and V. E. Hall, 1970.
11. *The Interneuron.* Ed. Mary A. B. Brazier, 1969.
12. *The History of Medical Education.* Ed. C. D. O'Malley, 1970.
13. *Cardiovascular Beta Adrenergic Responses.* Eds. Albert A. Kattus, Jr., Gordon Ross, and Rex N. MacAlpin, 1970.
14. *Cellular Aspects of Neural Growth and Differentiation.* Ed. Daniel C. Pease, 1971.
15. *Steroid Hormones and Brain Function.* Eds. Charles Sawyer and Roger A. Gorski, 1971.
16. *Multiple Sclerosis: Immunology, Virology, and Ultrastructure.* Eds. Frederick Wolfgram, George Ellison, Jack Stevens, and John Andrews, 1972.
17. *Epilepsy: Its Phenomena in Man.* Ed. Mary A. B. Brazier, 1973.
18. *Brain Mechanisms in Mental Retardation.* Eds. Nathaniel A. Buchwald and Mary A. B. Brazier, 1975.

DEDICATION: DR. AUGUSTUS S. ROSE

On June 25, 1989, the world of neurology was saddened by the death of one of its giants, Dr. Augustus S. Rose. In addition to his illustrious career as chairman of the Department of Neurology at UCLA and as distinguished physician at the Wadsworth Veterans Administration Medical Center, Dr. Rose was the founder and first chairman of the National Scientific Advisory Board of the John Douglas French Foundation for Alzheimer's Disease Research.

Dr. Rose's warm support and encouragement were instrumental in the publication of a previous volume in the UCLA Forum in Medical Sciences, *The Biological Substrates of Alzheimer's Disease*. His support continued with the publication of the present volume, which the editors would like to dedicate to his undying memory.

CONTRIBUTORS TO THIS VOLUME

JACKSON BEATTY, PhD   Department of Psychology and Brain Research Institute, University of California, Los Angeles, Los Angeles, California

JASON W. BROWN, MD   Department of Neurology, New York University Medical Center, New York, New York

DAVID F. CAWTHON, MD   Department of Neurological Surgery, University of Washington, Seattle, Washington

JEFFREY M. CLARKE, MA   Department of Psychology, University of California, Los Angeles, Los Angeles, California

MARIAN CLEEVES DIAMOND, PhD   Department of Physiology and Anatomy, University of California, Berkeley, Berkeley, California

JOAQUIN M. FUSTER, MD, PhD   Department of Psychiatry and Biobehavioral Sciences and Brain Research Institute, University of California, Los Angeles, Los Angeles, California

ALBERT M. GALABURDA, MD   Dyslexia Neuroanatomical Laboratory, Charles A. Dana Research Institute, Department of Neurology, Beth Israel Hospital and Harvard Medical School, Boston, Massachusetts

DARREN R. GITELMAN, MD   Department of Biological Psychiatry, Brain Imaging Division, New York State Psychiatric Institute, and Departments of Psychiatry, Neurology, and Radiology, College of Physicians and Surgeons, Columbia University, New York, New York

ERIC HALGREN, PhD   Department of Psychiatry and Brain Research Institute, University of California, Los Angeles, Los Angeles, California; Epilepsy Center, Wadsworth Veterans Administration Hospital, West Los Angeles, California

STEVEN A. HILLYARD, PhD   Department of Neurosciences, University of California, San Diego, La Jolla, California

ETTORE LETTICH, REEGT   Department of Neurological Surgery, University of Washington, Seattle, Washington

GEORGE R. MANGUN, PhD   Department of Neurosciences, University of California, San Diego, La Jolla, California

GEORGE A. OJEMANN, MD   Department of Neurological Surgery, University of Washington, Seattle, Washington

JÖRG J. PAHL, MD, FCP(SA)   Division of Nuclear Medicine and Biophysics, Department of Radiological Sciences, University of California, Los Angeles, Los Angeles, California; present address: Department of Psychiatry, The University of Iowa College of Medicine, Iowa City, Iowa

DEEPAK N. PANDYA, MD   Edith Nourse Rogers Memorial Veterans Administration Hospital, Bedford, Massachusetts; Department of Anatomy and Neurology, Boston University School of Medicine, and Harvard Neurological Unit, Beth Israel Hospital, Boston, Massachusetts

ISAK PROHOVNIK, PHD   Department of Biological Psychiatry, Brain Imaging Division, New York State Psychiatric Institute, and Departments of Psychiatry, Neurology, and Radiology, College of Physicians and Surgeons, Columbia University, New York, New York

GLENN D. ROSEN, PHD   Dyslexia Neuroanatomical Laboratory, Charles A. Dana Research Institute, Department of Neurology, Beth Israel Hospital and Harvard Medical School, Boston, Massachusetts

ARNOLD B. SCHEIBEL, MD   Departments of Anatomy and Psychiatry and Brain Research Institute, University of California, Los Angeles, Los Angeles, California

JOHN SCHLAG, MD   Department of Anatomy and Cell Biology and Brain Research Institute, University of California, Los Angeles, Los Angeles, California

MADELEINE SCHLAG-REY, PHD   Department of Anatomy and Cell Biology and Brain Research Institute, University of California, Los Angeles, Los Angeles, California

GORDON F. SHERMAN, PHD   Dyslexia Neuroanatomical Laboratory, Charles A. Dana Research Institute, Department of Neurology, Beth Israel Hospital and Harvard Medical School, Boston, Massachusetts

BRANDALL SUYENOBU, MA   Department of Psychology, University of California, Los Angeles, Los Angeles, California

ADAM F. WECHSLER, MD   Department of Neurology, Wadsworth Veterans Administration Medical Center, Los Angeles, California

SANDRA F. WITELSON, PHD   Departments of Psychiatry, Psychology, and Biomedical Sciences, McMaster University, Hamilton, Ontario, Canada

EDWARD H. YETERIAN, PHD   Edith Nourse Rogers Memorial Veterans Administration Hospital, Bedford, Massachusetts; Department of Psychology, Colby College, Waterville, Maine

ERAN ZAIDEL, PHD   Department of Psychology and Brain Research Institute, University of California, Los Angeles, Los Angeles, California

PREFACE

For the better part of three decades, the UCLA Forum in Medical Sciences has provided a vigorous platform on which investigators could meet and compare ideas on some of the most intriguing medical problems of the time. The range of topics examined over this period has been a remarkably broad one, although not surprisingly (from our point of view at least) a majority have concerned themselves with some aspect of the brain and nervous system.

Inherent in the structure of the Forum series, as initially conceived by Dean Sherman Mellinkoff, was the bringing together of distinguished extramural investigators with those members of our faculty who were signally involved in a research field of contemporary interest. "The editing and publication of such meetings . . . periodically held at UCLA seemed . . . to be one small part of an answer to a large need accentuated by the information explosion." Clearly, the explosive information load of 1962 has become a tidal wave today, and with the logarithmic increment in active investigators and the maturation of international transportation, the theme-oriented research conference is commonplace.

Nevertheless, we like to think that there continues to be something special about our UCLA Forum conferences. They represent more than an ongoing record of the intellectual passions of the time. With their core of UCLA faculty members, they also reflect research areas to which UCLA has made significant contributions—a record, in a sense, of its involvement in the conceptual issues of the day and of the university's investment in the future.

The present symposium dealing with neurobiological substrates of higher cognitive function addresses a group of issues of enormous complexity. With the unbelievable growth of knowledge about molecular genetics and membrane and cell biology, it has become possible to ask profound questions about basic biological mechanisms. With these new reductionist methods, it is difficult to resist biting continuously deeper into questions that would have been beyond our grasp even 5 years ago. But biological systems, and the brain above all others, operate in hierarchical modes, and the kinds of sophisticated perceptual and behavioral activity that represent higher cognitive function in action, especially in primates and man, seems almost disarticulated from the concepts and methods of the new breed of "basic brain sciences." We believe that this apparent disarticulation reflects primarily our ignorance and that confident monism is actively replacing the ambivalent dualisms of the recent past. But what kind of evidence can be marshaled to support increasingly powerful intuitive notions that the entire range of mental life is "imminent" in brain structure and function?

This conference provides documentation to support our suppositions that such data are becoming available. Powerful new minimally invasive techniques such as PET, SPECT, and MRI have begun to show us the living brain *in situ* and in action. The already classical methods of electroencephalography, evoked potential, and microelectrode physiology have been refined to provide exciting insights into processes underlying higher cognitive function. Quantitative studies of neural field and structure, macro and micro, when related to individual behavior, talent, and circumstance, are providing fascinating glimpses of the brain–mind correlates we seek.

Unlike previous UCLA Forum conferences, we chose to hold this one at some distance from the university campus. The UCLA Conference Center at Lake Arrowhead in early spring provided the quiet 2½-day setting in which our little group of investigators could talk, listen, and think together. The facilities were excellent, and the Arrowhead staff was sensitive to our needs. A group process quickly developed in this almost ideal place, and local faculty and visitors enjoyed the kind of interaction that seldom comes in busier conference settings. We are personally grateful to the staff of the Brain Research Institute, and particularly to Joyce Fried and Jody Spillane, who worked so hard to make everything seem effortless. And we are indebted to the Dean's Office of the UCLA School of Medicine, the John Douglas French Foundation for Alzheimer's Disease Research, and the UCLA Brain Research Institute, whose financial support made this conference possible.

Publication of this volume also marks the retirement of Dr. Mary A. B. Brazier as Editor-in-Chief of the UCLA Forum series. For almost three decades Mollie was the moving spirit in this enterprise, taking personal interest in the selection of each topic, in the development and maturation of each conference, and in the publication of the proceedings. She took executive responsibility for a significant number of these volumes and her very special imprimatur will remain. All of us who have worked with her share gratitude for her leadership and her insistence on the highest possible standards for the series.

Arnold B. Scheibel
Adam F. Wechsler

CONTENTS

CONTENTS

MORPHOLOGICAL CORTICAL CHANGES AS A CONSEQUENCE OF LEARNING AND EXPERIENCE

MARIAN CLEEVES DIAMOND, PhD
University of California, Berkeley

INTRODUCTION

When I asked leading Berkeley astronomer and Nobel Laureate Charles Townes, "Which is more complex, the 100 billion stars in our galaxy or the 100 billion nerve cells in the 3-pound mass within our heads?" he answered without hesitation, "The brain." "For, after all," I responded, "it is only the brain that can interpret our galaxy." And it is only the brain that can interpret its own cognizance.

Since this volume deals with the neurobiological substrates of higher cognitive functions, we need to ask, "What are the biological substrates of the brain, and what is meant by higher cognitive functions?" We know that it is nerve cells interacting with glial cells that learn by acquiring knowledge and in turn exhibiting higher cognitive functions, including the capacity for reasoning and understanding. It is these cells and their chemical interrelationships that possess an aptitude for grasping truths, facts, and meanings.

Often we ask ourselves, "What is intelligence?" One answer could be "the ability to use knowledge derived from reason and to profit by mistakes." An extensive vocabulary exists to help us elaborate on intelligence, including words such as sound, bright, good judgment, natural quickness to understand, speed of integration of thought, astute, clever, apt, discerning, and shrewd—all adjectives describing higher cognitive processing.

Most of these words refer to the end results produced by cerebral cortical as well as other cellular interactions within the brain. I have spent my professional life studying the cerebral cortex because I thought that if I have only 100 years on this earth why not accept the challenge offered by examining the structures and functions of this unique, intriguing mass of tissue concerned with higher cognitive functions. But if one tackles such a task, then as many variables as possible need to be considered. These include differences among sexes, hemispheres, ages, regions, cellular types, membrane adaptations, neurotransmitters, vascular roles, plasticity, and so forth. This chapter addresses some of these variables and offers the results showing morphological changes in the rat cerebral cortex as a consequence of a specific learning paradigm versus a broader form of experiential enrichment.

1

Cortical Changes Caused by Maze Learning

This experiment was designed to study the effects on cerebral cortical structure induced by gradually increasing the complexity of a learning experience. Dr. Kay Kerker Malkasian, while working in our laboratory many years ago, divided 10 pairs of 71-day-old female Long–Evans rats accordingly: one was given formal maze training with food as a reward, and the other served as a nontrained control (Kerker, 1968). The control animal was placed in a simple maze with only one barrier for the same length of time as the maze-trained animal, but no food reward was offered. Yet both rats in a pair were food deprived for several hours before being placed in the mazes.

Methods

The 1-month period of maze training was divided into 10 days of pretraining and 22 days of formal training. During pretraining, the rat explored the maze, a box 76 × 76 × 10 cm, for 30 minutes per day with only one barrier between the start and the goal box. During formal training, a series of barriers, each more complex than the last, were placed in the maze. At the beginning of the experiment, the barrier patterns were comparable to those used in the original Hebb–Williams maze. However, since the rats appeared to learn these challenges very easily, an additional complex series of barriers was established, offering seven new patterns of increasing difficulty. Figure 1 shows the placement of the barriers for the last maze the rats had to solve.

For the simple patterns, the rats had about 45 minutes to run the maze correctly; with the more difficult patterns, the time was severely shortened to 15 to 20 minutes. The period spent in the food-filled goal box was also shortened to 15 to 20 seconds. To indicate that learning and memory had taken place, the rats were tested the following day and showed a decrease in running time and made fewer errors. To illustrate that the rats in each pair were not differentially

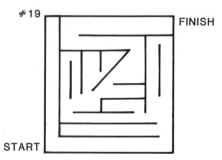

Figure 1. The floor plan of the barriers used in the most complex pattern in the modified Hebb–Williams maze, maze number 19.

hindered by the eating conditions, body weights were recorded at the termination of the experiment, and no significant differences were found.

In order to collect brain samples, the pentobarbital anesthetized rats were perfused with normal saline followed by 10% formol-saline. Transverse, 10-μm paraffin-embedded sections of the frontal, somatosensory, and occipital cortex were stained with Windle's thionine method (Windle, Rhines, & Rankin, 1943).

Cortical thickness was measured on microslide-projected images as mentioned in our other publications (Diamond, Lindner, & Raymond, 1967). In addition, in the lateral portion (area 39) of the section designated as the occipital cortical sample, measurements of neuronal nuclear diameter and area were made with the aid of a camera lucida at a magnification of 1,000X (Figure 2).

Only those nuclei with a clear nuclear membrane and a well-defined nucleolus were measured. The longest and narrowest dimensions of the nucleus were measured with a millimeter rule and divided by 2,000 to obtain nuclear diameter. To determine nuclear area, the virtual image of the nucleus was drawn on millimeter graph paper. The number of squares (each square was 1 mm) within the projected image was counted and divided by 1,000 to obtain nuclear area.

Results

The results from comparing the cortical thickness of the trained versus the nontrained littermates revealed significant differences in the thickness of area 39,

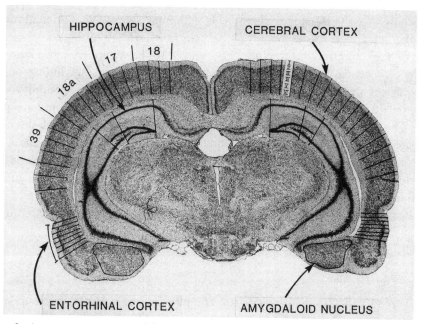

Figure 2. A transverse section of the rat brain taken at the level of the posterior commissure to indicate the position of area 39 where the cortical increases were found as a consequence of learning the Hebb–Williams maze.

with the trained being greater than the nontrained by 6% ($p < .025$). From the measurements of the nucleus, we learned that the nuclear diameter was 8% greater ($p < .05$) in the trained than in the nontrained, whereas the nuclear area displayed an even greater difference, 17% ($p < .02$). Again it was the trained animal that had the larger nuclear area. No significant morphological changes were noted in the frontal, somatosensory, or occipital cortex under these conditions.

Our preliminary results clearly indicate that when rats learn to solve a specific maze task, certain cerebral cortical nerve cells change their dimensions, as noted by cortical thickness and neuronal nuclear dimensions in area 39. These results need to be replicated, but for the present they offer significant information regarding cerebral plasticity as a consequence of problem-solving activity in the form of goal-oriented maze learning. In this chapter, I am using only our data to compare enriched environmental effects with those of specific learning tasks because our methods of sampling the brains were similar for both types of experiments.

Cortical Changes Caused by Enriched, Standard Colony, and Impoverished Environments

Methods

For these experiments, some animals were exposed to an abundant supply of objects with which they could interact. In other words, the rats had an unhindered opportunity to explore the objects without a specific goal orientation. The enriched condition for the male Long–Evans rats before weaning (i.e., before 26 days of age) consisted of three mothers living with three pups each in a large cage (70 × 70 × 42 cm) and having access to objects or "toys," including ladders, wheels, and small mazes. Enrichment for young, postweaned, or adult animals included 12 rats living together in the same large-sized cage with similar types of toys. The impoverished preweaned animals included one mother with three pups in a small cage (34 × 20 × 20 cm) without toys. For the postweaned or adult rats, the impoverished condition consisted of one rat living alone in a small cage (as above) with no toys. The standard colony condition consisted of three rats in a small cage (as above) with no toys. All animals had free access to food and water in a 12:12 light:dark cycle (Diamond, 1988; Krech, Rosenzweig, & Bennett, 1960).

Results

CORTICAL THICKNESS

Table 1 indicates the percentage differences in cortical thickness found in the brains of enriched versus impoverished animals living in their respective conditions for varying periods of time and at various ages. Only the results from the medial occipital cortex are shown because it is this area (area 18) that changes

TABLE 1
PERCENT DIFFERENCES IN MEDIAL OCCIPITAL CORTICAL DEPTHS
BETWEEN ENVIRONMENTALLY ENRICHED AND IMPOVERISHED RATS

Duration in days	Ages	Percent differences	Number of EC > IC (pairs)	p
1	60–61	0.7	10/24	N.S.
4	60–64	2.9	17/24	.01
4	26–30	3.7	15/20	.001
7	25–32	3.8	19.5/22	.001
15	25–40	7.1	22/23	.001
30	25–55	6.6	25/30	.001
30	60–90	6.7	45.5/50	.001
80	25–105	7.9	22/22	.001
80	105–185	5.0	13/18	.05
160	25–185	3.0	16/22	.05
		Total	205/255	
	Total minus the 1-day group		195/231	

Note. From M. C. Diamond, 1976. Anatomical brain changes induced by environment. In L. Petrinovich & J. L. McGaugh (Eds.), *Knowing, thinking and believing* (pp. 215–239). New York: Plenum Press. Copyright 1976 by Plenum Press. Reprinted by permission.

most consistently with these types of environmental conditions. It is clear from examining the table that at every duration, except for the 1-day group, the brains showed responses to the environmental conditions. As large a change is noted at 15 days as at 30 days. However, it is important to indicate that although the differences created by exposing rats from 26 to 30 days of age and from 60 to 64 days of age were the same, a 4% difference, the factors responsible for these differences were not. In later experiments, we used the standard colony animals in the design. That is, we compared the enriched animals with those in the standard colony and the impoverished animals with those in the standard colony. With these comparisons, we learned that in the very young rats (26 to 30 days), the changes in cortical thickness for the 4-day period were caused primarily by impoverishment, but in the adult rats (60 to 64 days), the differences were caused by both enrichment and impoverishment. Here age was a very important factor. Separating the animals from their mothers directly into impoverishment proved very detrimental to cortical development, and only a small amount of our enrichment effect was noted. If, on the other hand, the animals had lived three to a cage after weaning until 60 days of age and were then placed in their respective environments, impoverishment became even more marked and the effects of enrichment more clearly manifest. The reduced environmental effect found in the animals exposed between 25 and 185 days was related to the fact that the toys were not changed during this period except during cleaning. Therefore, no new varieties of stimuli were offered during this 160-day period.

As has been mentioned several times previously, we have learned that cortical thickness changes are caused by many structural alterations in the neuron (e.g., soma, nucleus, dendrites, spines, and synapses), in the number of glial cells, in size of capillaries, in protein, acetylcholinesterase, cholinesterase, hexokinase, etc. (Table 2 shows some of these changes.) Therefore, once we noted that these factors were responsible for the cortical thickness changes, this measure became our most commonly used indicator of cortical responses to the environment.

CELL COUNTS

To examine the cellular changes that result from differential experience, initially cell counts per microscopic field were taken. The enriched animals had fewer neurons per field, which we interpreted as indicating more neuropil in the enriched than in the nonenriched brains; thus, the somata were more widely separated from each other (Diamond, Krech, & Rosenzweig, 1964). It has been shown that in a single cortical column there are twice as many neurons in the visual cortex as in other cortical areas. Such a great quantity of nerve cells makes it difficult to differentiate individual layers, but by using the number of microme-

TABLE 2
Effects of Differential Experience on Occipital Cortex
(Differences between Littermates of S_1 Strain in
EC or IC from 25 to 105 Days of Age)

Measure	Difference	p	Number of EC > IC
Weight	6.1	<.001	106/141
Depth	6.3	<.001	36/41
Total protein	7.9[a]	<.001	25/32
Total AChE	2.3	<.01	83/140
Total ChE	10.2	<.001	77.5/98[b]
Total hexokinase	6.9[c]	<.01	17/21
Number of neurons	−3.1	N.S.	7/17
Number of glia	14.0	<.01	12/17
Perikaryon cross section	13.4	<.001	11.5/13[b]

Note. From E. L. Bennett, M. R. Rosenzweig, & M. C. Diamond, 1970. Effects of experience on brain and behavior. In W. L. Byrne (Ed.), *Molecular approaches to learning and memory* (pp. 55–89). New York: Academic Press. Copyright 1970 by Academic Press. Reprinted by permission.

[a]Weight difference 7.0% in these experiments.
[b]Fractional value indicates tied score.
[c]Weight difference 5.5% in these experiments.

ters that reportedly designate each layer, we could plot the distribution of neurons through the thickness of the visual cortex. The greatest differences between the enriched and impoverished nerve cell counts on an initial and replication experiment were found in layers II, III, and IV. Apparently these outer layers, which are the last to develop phylogenetically and embryologically, retain their plasticity more than the lower layers after the cortex has reached its peak during morphological development. The lower layers also show changes, but these are not as consistent or as large as those in the upper layers. In measuring neuronal soma and nuclear size, again the upper layers show the greatest changes, and alterations in the size of these structures are also noted in all layers.

I have only once observed a mitotic figure in a nerve cell in the postnatal cerebral cortex of a 3-day-old kitten but never in a rat cortex. As anticipated, no increase in nerve cell bodies was noted, but glial cells were greater in number in the brains of enriched than of nonenriched animals. In fact, it was the oligodendroglia that showed the most significant increases (Diamond et al., 1966). The specific functions of these cells that were demanding an increase is not clear, since several activities are attributed to oligodendroglia. In the central nervous system, they form myelin, the amount of which is directly related to the speed of impulse conduction. This function might be affected by an enriched experiential condition. Oligodendroglia are also found closely adjacent to neuronal somata and blood capillaries, probably carrying out some metabolic roles, but their specific role in these positions is not clear at present. Oligodendrocytes possess insulin receptors, which affect their glucose uptake (Clarke, Boyd, Kappy, & Raizada, 1984). That oligodendrocytes are in some way interacting with the immune system is well documented (Merrill et al., 1984), but again the precise interrelationships are not well known. In other words, these cells have many roles, any one of which could be influenced by the increased input brought to the cerebral cortex as a consequence of a stimulating living condition.

INDIVIDUAL LINE COMPARISONS

Another question that concerned us was whether individual columns of cortical cells (ranging in size from 200 to 1,000 μm) were affected more than others. We did not measure precise columns, but our method of sampling cortical thickness allowed us to include areas encompassing several columns. By comparing individual lines through the thickness of the cortex throughout a complete area such as area 18, we were able to determine in a general manner whether some columns were more affected than others. The results indicated that all of area 18 was increasing approximately equally with enrichment and decreasing equally with impoverishment. A 4-day exposure to the experimental conditions, from 60 to 64 days of age, showed significant changes, but experimental conditions between 60 and 90 days produced even greater results (Diamond, 1988).

DENDRITIC BRANCHING AND SPINE MEASURES

Measuring the differences between individual lines over a considerable area of the cortex and finding that the whole area changed by the environmental conditions provided credence for quantifying the dendritic branches of nerve cells through this entire area. By using the Scholl method, dendrites were measured on nerve cells from rats 112 days of age (base line) and from those in enriched or standard colony conditions from 112 to 142 days of age. The greatest increases were noted in the third- and fourth-order dendrites, with both of the 142-day-old groups having more dendrites than the 112-day-old animals (Uylings, Kuypers, Diamond, & Veltman, 1978). The sixth-order dendrites were shown to increase in length in rats exposed to enriched or standard colony environments from 600 to 630 days of age (Connor, Melone, Yuen, & Diamond, 1981). Here were two examples of dendritic plasticity as a consequence of experiential environment. Other laboratories have also shown dendritic adaptability (Greenough, Volkmar, & Juraska, 1973).

Initial spine counts on the enriched and impoverished animals' brains were carried out many years ago in collaboration with Albert Globus (Globus, Rosenzweig, Bennett, & Diamond, 1973). The results of these studies indicated that there were more spines per dendrite in the enriched animals' brains than in those of the impoverished animals. A later study (Connor, Diamond, & Johnson, 1980) reported that in older animals experiencing either impoverished or standard colony conditions from 600 to 630 days of age, it was the "nubbin" spine (head dimension similar to neck) that was greater in number in the impoverished compared to the standard. The enriched condition had more "lollipop" spines (head dimension greater than neck) than the standard. Several investigators speculate that the "nubbin" spine is a degenerating one and thus might be predicted to be greater in number in old, isolated animals.

RIGHT VERSUS LEFT HEMISPHERIC DIFFERENCES

All of our morphological measurements have indicated changes in the nerve cell dimensions at every level as a consequence of the amount of input into the cerebral cortex. But now we ask, "Do these different kinds of environmental inputs affect the cells in one hemisphere more than in another?" From measuring cortical thickness in both right and left hemispheres in representative sections from the frontal, parietal, and occipital cortex of male Long–Evans rats, we have found that, for the most part, the hemispheres are affected equally. The most significant increases in thickness are seen in the occipital cortical sample (Diamond et al., 1987).

Most of the previously reported studies were carried out on the brains from male animals. For future reference in studying male and female brains during various environmental inputs and learning situations, the data on cell counts in right and left hemispheres may prove useful. From the report of McShane et al. (1988), the male rat has more neurons and glial cells in the sample from right cortical area 39 than in a similar sample from the left hemisphere. The female shows the opposite results, with more neurons and glial cells in the left area 39 than in the right. These cell counts coincide nicely with the right and left cortical thickness differences in the Long–Evans male and female rats.

CONCLUSION

In conclusion, our studies have illustrated the fact that not only can different amounts of environmental input alter the structure of the cerebral cortex, but complex maze learning can also change cortical morphology. We have found that area 18, a known visual association area, changes most readily with enriched or impoverished living conditions. The reason for this event is not yet known. In the animals solving complex maze patterns for a food reward, it is area 39, a multisensory integrating area, that shows the significant increases in neuronal dimensions when compared to a nontrained control. The environmental studies have been replicated many times. If the learning experiments can also be successfully replicated, then chemists and molecular biologists might focus on these two areas to throw further light on the differences between specific learning versus environmental stimulation or deprivation conditions. At present, we are finding cellular changes only in well-known structures. No new types of glial cells or synapses have been identified with our experimental paradigm. As we have said before, even though we have come a long way, the search for understanding the interaction of the neurobiological substrates of higher cognitive functions in the mammalian cerebral cortex has still only just begun.

REFERENCES

Bennett, E. L., Rosenzweig, M. R., & Diamond, M. C. (1970). Effects of experience on brain and behavior. In W. L. Byrne (Ed.), *Molecular approaches to learning and memory* (pp. 55–89). New York: Academic Press.

Clarke, D. W., Boyd, F. T., Jr., Kappy, M. S., & Raizada, M. K. (1984). Insulin binds to specific receptors and stimulates 2-deoxy-D-glucose uptake in cultured glial cells from rat brain. *Journal of Biological Chemistry, 259,* 11672–11675.

Connor, J. R., Diamond, M. C., & Johnson, R. E. (1980). Aging and environmental influences on two types of dendritic spines in the rat occipital cortex. *Experimental Neurology, 70,* 371–379.

Connor, J. R., Melone, J., Yuen, A., & Diamond, M. C. (1981). Terminal segment length of dendrites in aged rats: An environmentally induced response. *Experimental Neurology, 73,* 827–830.

Diamond, M. C. (1976). Anatomical brain changes induced by environment. In L. Petrinovich & J. L. McGaugh (Eds.), *Knowing, thinking and believing* (pp. 215–239). New York: Plenum Press.

Diamond, M. C. (1988). *Enriching heredity.* New York: The Free Press.

Diamond, M. C., Greer, E. R., York, A., Lewis, D., Barton, T., & Lin, J. (1987). Rat cortical morphology following crowded-enriched living conditions. *Experimental Neurology, 96,* 241–247.

Diamond, M. C., Krech, D., & Rosenzweig, M. R. (1964). The effects of an enriched environment on the histology of the rat cerebral cortex. *Journal of Comparative Neurology, 123,* 111–120.

Diamond, M. C., Law, F., Rhodes, H., Lindner, B., Rosenzweig, M. R., Krech, D., & Bennett, E. L. (1966). Increases in cortical depth and glia numbers in rats subjected to enriched environment. *Journal of Comparative Neurology, 128,* 117–126.

Diamond, M. C., Lindner, B., & Raymond, A. (1967). Extensive cortical depth measurements and neuron size increases in the cortex of environmentally enriched rats. *Journal of Comparative Neurology, 131,* 357–364.

Globus, A., Rosenzweig, M. R., Bennett, E. L., & Diamond, M. C. (1973). Effects of differential experience on dendritic spine counts in rat cerebral cortex. *Journal of Comparative and Physiological Psychology, 82,* 175–181.

Greenough, W. T., Volkmar, F. R., & Juraska, J. M. (1973). Effects of rearing complexity on dendritic branching in frontolateral and temporal cortex of the rat. *Experimental Neurology, 41,* 371–378.

Kerker, K. (1968). *The effect of Hebb-Williams maze training on the morphology of the adult female rat brain.* Senior thesis, University of California, Berkeley.

Krech, D., Rosenzweig, M. R., & Bennett, E. L. (1960). Effects of environmental complexity and training on brain chemistry. *Journal of Comparative Physiological Psychology, 53,* 509–519.

McShane, S., Glaser, L., Greer, E. R., Houtz, J., Tong, M. F., & Diamond, M. C. (1988). Cortical asymmetry—a preliminary study: Neurons–glia, female–male. *Experimental Neurology, 99,* 353–361.

Merrill, J. E., Kutsunai, S., Mohlstrom, C., Hofman, F., Groopman, J., & Golde, D. W. (1984). Proliferation of astroglia and oligodendroglia in response to human T-cell derived factors. *Science, 244,* 1428–1430.

Uylings, H. B. M., Kuypers, K., Diamond, M. C., & Veltman, W. A. M. (1978). The effects of differential environments on plasticity of dendrites of cortical pyramidal neurons in adult rats. *Experimental Neurology, 62,* 658–677.

Windle, W., Rhines, R., & Rankin, J. (1943). A Nissl method using buffered solutions of thionin. *Stain Technology, 18,* 77–86.

DISCUSSION

ADAM WECHSLER: Have you been able to determine whether the enriched rats show greater abilities than the impoverished rats? In other words, could you see developing a new experiment to find out whether or not the enriched cortex or the impoverished cortex really represents a significant asset or liability as far as their functional activity is concerned?

MARIAN DIAMOND: Thank you, Adam. Since we are not psychologists, we have not done behavioral studies, but many other laboratories have, and they have shown that the rats that have lived in the enriched environments run a better maze than those that have lived in the impoverished environment. Not all mazes, but most mazes. So they are utilizing this enlarged cortex to benefit them in solving problems.

JASON BROWN: I just wondered if you try to disambiguate the effects of novelty in an enrichment device, switching from one enriched environment to another so they're constantly confronted with novel stimuli because an initially novel stimulus and an enriched environment very quickly become old hat.

DIAMOND: Yes, we do change the toys. This is what we've learned. First we just thought having the toys present for an 80-day period was adequate, but it's certainly not. They have to be changed at least twice a week to maintain those brain changes, and what the students are trying now is to change the toys every day. Many pediatricians are asking me to please try overstimulation, because they are concerned about young mothers today who want brilliant children and are accordingly bombarding their babies with new toys. My next experiment is to have the toys changed every hour during the night while the rats are most active and see if we find a ceiling effect. Will the cortex stop at 7% or 8%, or will we find that the animals will just retract completely as some babies do if you give them too much stimulation? In such cases they just retreat, sleep, and become colicky. So we don't know what the effects with our rats will be with overstimulation. (Recent information from our latest experiments informs us that too much stimulation does *not* change the cortex as much as our usual enrichment.)

ERAN ZAIDEL: I have a couple of questions. First, with regard to simultaneous changes, do you ever find that one area increases but another decreases? In other words, could there be some reciprocal relationship between areas?

DIAMOND: I think this could occur. What we need to do is study this problem more carefully. We have the data to do this, area by area. So far it appears that the same areas that increase with enrichment also decrease with impoverishment. The second question has to do with some possibly critical period. Could it be that if you get some changes in the cortex from enrichment or impoverishment, and if you get them at a certain age, subsequent experiences may have a larger or smaller effect? We have not yet done an experiment in which we enrich, then let them sit for a while, then put them back into enrichment and see whether we bring the cortex back up to where it was originally or even take it beyond where it was. However, we have found that at every age we can change the cortex. We have done this with the prenatal animal and have found that when the female is pregnant and in enrichment, her pups' cortices have increased dimensions. We have shown we can change the preweaned brain, the young adult, and the middle-aged. Even our 900-day-old animals' cortices are larger from the enriched than from the impoverished, so the plasticity is there once those dendrites are formed.

GLENN ROSEN: I also have a couple of questions. The first one refers to the cell counts. The thing that struck me was that they pattern exactly the kind of findings you've shown in asymmetry and thickness, so would you go out on a limb and say that different asymmetries would be caused by differences in cell numbers on the two sides?

DIAMOND: We now have data that show in the male right cerebral cortex there are more neurons per unit area than in the left. In the female it is the left cortex that has more neurons per unit area than the right.

ROSEN: O.K., and the other question was, when you showed that wonderful slide at the beginning with the different effects depending on the age of stimulation and the amount of stimulation, were these animals sacrificed at a given age?

DIAMOND: As you saw, we had some that were in environments from 25 to 55 days of age, so we sacrificed at 55 days of age. We had some that were in environments for 25 to 105, so we sacrificed at 105 days of age. Yes, they were being sacrificed at different ages.

ROSEN: Then what would you expect would happen if you sacrificed all these animals at, let's say, 180 days of age? Would you see a decrease in thickness because they're going back to another environment?

DIAMOND: Very definitely. We find that the longer they're in the environment, the longer the change persists. It's definitely correlated with the length of time of exposure to enrichment. We do see that the cortex decreases when the animals are removed from enrichment. But as we mentioned earlier, we don't yet know, if we put them back into enrichment after they have been removed for an extended period, whether we can bring the cortex back to that level or take it even beyond with subsequent stimulation.

ROSEN: Can I just ask one more? What is the long-term consequence of enrichment if after they're finished with the enrichment you get an increase in all these parameters? If you take them away, they decrease, but are there long-term changes in the brain?

DIAMOND: That's a favorite question too. I wonder, when you grow a spine, and you lose it, does it disappear to be reabsorbed within the membrane or have we changed the molecular configuration of the membrane at the site of reabsorption so that when stimulation comes along again the spine is going to redevelop more rapidly? We don't have an answer.

DESIGN AND ANALYSIS
OF COGNITIVE IMAGING EXPERIMENTS

DARREN R. GITELMAN, MD, and ISAK PROHOVNIK, PhD
New York State Psychiatric Institute and
College of Physicians and Surgeons, Columbia University

INTRODUCTION

The mapping of brain regions associated with cognitive activity is a time-honored neuroscientific tradition. From the fanciful attempts of Franz Joseph Gall to chart individual feelings on the skull and underlying cerebral cortex to the systematic studies of Hughlings Jackson, Wernicke, Broca, Brodmann, Kraepelin, Penfield, and countless others, there has been continued interest in the attempt to localize the functions of the mind to different areas of the brain (Kandel, 1985; Andreasen, 1988). Previous work has made use of animal models through autoradiography, histological techniques, and electrical mapping; in humans, investigations at autopsy and intraoperative examination of both focal lesions and areas of stimulation have added to our knowledge of localization. These techniques, although contributing significantly to our present understanding of the brain, suffer from several limitations; animal models tell us little about human cognitive and emotional functions; postmortem human studies do not allow direct observation of function and are often confounded by the effects of aging, prior medication usage, and medical illnesses (Andreasen, 1988).

Over the last 20 years, the advent of functional brain-imaging technology has overcome many of these previous problems. By providing correlations of observable behavior with anatomy in a manner that allows simultaneous visualization of functionally related areas, these methods reveal an integrated approach to understanding cerebral structure and function. With the new tools now available, precise physiological information can be obtained; it is possible to image not only cortical blood flow but subcortical as well as cortical changes in metabolism, perfusion, blood volume, pH, local hematocrit, and neurotransmitter–receptor systems down to a spatial resolution of 3–4 mm.

Acknowledgments: Preparation of this chapter was aided by research grants from the National Institutes of Health (AG 05433), the Jean and Louis Dreyfus Foundation, and the Mental Illness Foundation.

In light of these technological advances, brain imaging should be more than a tool for cerebral cartography; it has the power to provide objective testing for new theories of cerebral operation. To date, however, although experiments have provided an elegant confirmation of established doctrines, they have not yet contributed to new explanations of cortical and subcortical operation. Nevertheless, the reverification of well-described theories has provided the necessary neuropsychiatric validation for these techniques (Wood, 1980). Thus it remains for us to design appropriate experiments using these methods to their fullest advantage. Unfortunately, the procedures are not easily accessible, the experiments are expensive, and the methodological complexity has increased concomitantly with observational power.

The present chapter is therefore intended as a starting point to help investigators design powerful and cost-effective brain-imaging protocols. We briefly summarize imaging theory and technology, relevant cerebral physiology, basic principles of experimental imaging design, and conclude by discussing one promising statistical method of analysis.

PHYSIOLOGICAL FOUNDATIONS

Functional imaging provides cerebral physiological data that are thought to reflect either ongoing neuronal activation and information processing or the "state" of neuronal interconnections and sensitivity to activation. Almost a century ago, Roy and Sherrington (1890) first suggested that local chemical products of cerebral metabolism controlled vascular tone, and thus assessment of local cerebral blood flow could be used to image information processing. Although the molecular mechanisms of cerebrovascular control remain largely unknown, the coupling among neuronal activity, metabolism, and blood flow is a founding principle in cognitive imaging technology. The brain, containing almost no energy reserves, is set against a background of constant energy utilization (and therefore constant demand for substrate supply) in order to maintain its tremendous rates of chemical and electrical activity. Although these relationships may be altered by certain pathological conditions (e.g., acute stroke) (Fieschi, Battistini, & Lenzi, 1978; Lenzi, Frackowiak, & Jones, 1982), and recent work demonstrates more complex linkages among blood flow, oxygen consumption, and glucose utilization than previously realized (Fox, Raichle, Mintun, & Dence, 1988), its principle remains robust: brain work involves utilization of energy; measurement of the consumption of substrates (glucose and oxygen) or their transport (cerebral perfusion) reflects local activity.

In a similar fashion, neuroreceptor and transmitter imaging provides data on neuronal connections, functional sensitivity, and possible sites of pharmacological manipulation, all pertinent to theories of cognitive operation. Finally, imaging of *in vivo* protein synthesis, although not showing changes with acute neuronal stimulation (Bustany et al., 1983), may be able to demonstrate the longer-term effects of a variety of stimuli and disease states. In contrast, techniques such as measurement of cerebral blood volume (CBV) and pH, although no less "dynamic" than the methods mentioned above, have not yet proved relevant to answering cognitive dilemmas and therefore are not discussed further in this chapter.

Cognitive brain imaging relies on the interface between nuclear medicine and tracer kinetics. Although a full discourse on tracer kinetic theory is beyond the scope of this chapter, several of its principles bear review as a basis for comprehending functional imaging principles.

All cellular and thereby whole-organ functions are founded on a multitude of chemical reactions. As previously noted, the brain depends on reactions involved with the maintenance and generation of cellular energy. In addition, those reactions subserving neurotransmitter release and reception provide the mechanisms of data transmission within the brain and at its interfaces with the rest of the body. Thus measurements of the rates of these various reactions provide an estimate of brain activity and function. Furthermore, if correlated both spatially within the brain and temporally with behavior, these activity estimates demonstrate cerebral areas involved in the generation of a particular action or thought process.

Rates of all chemical reactions can theoretically be determined by measuring either the disappearance of one or more of the reactants or the production of one or more of the products. The use of tracers is based on labeling one of the reactants so that the basic kinetics of the reaction remains unaltered while quantification of either the disappearance of a precursor or the formation of a product is facilitated (Sokoloff & Smith, 1983). In functional brain imaging, radioactive tracers are advantageous for several reasons. (1) Their high signal-to-noise ratio allows reliable detection with the use of minute chemical quantities. (2) Because isotopes usually behave in a chemically equivalent fashion, the addition of labeled compounds does not commonly affect the kinetics of a particular reaction. (3) Gamma photons, at the energies currently employed in imaging, penetrate tissues easily, thereby allowing detection outside the intact, living organism.

The use of radioactive tracers also introduces several complications into the measurement of cerebral physiology. These include (1) the need for isotopic specific activity, (2) isotopic effects on reaction rate, and (3) dissemination of labeled molecules to nonrelevant reactions (Sokoloff & Smith, 1983). Further details can be found in a comprehensive text. A basic understanding of tracer kinetics is germane to the design of all cognitive imaging studies and is particularly relevant in cases of new labels, techniques, or ligands.

TECHNOLOGICAL CHOICES

The design of cogent functional imaging experiments is probably best conceived as a series of questions that may be applied toward the planning of any imaging study. The initial questions are the following:

1. What are the technologies of measurement, their theories of operation, advantages, and disadvantages?
2. What are the methodologies of measurement, their correspondence to cerebral physiology, advantages, and disadvantages?
3. Given a particular cerebral function of interest, what should be measured (i.e., a synthesis of questions 1 and 2)?

Obviously, such questions are faced by those who confront the luxury of choice, having access to more than one technique. It is also obvious that the answers to each of these questions by itself could fill a chapter if not an entire book. We therefore limit this discussion to brief descriptions and explanations of the techniques involved. Further information on particular techniques can be obtained through the bibliography at the end of this chapter.

Brain imaging that provides *in vivo* physiological data can be performed by two general methods involving detection and mapping of (1) electromagnetic fields or (2) emitted gamma photons from externally administered isotopes. A third technique, stable xenon CT/CBF scanning, provides spatial resolution equivalent to conventional CT but has not been used for cognitive studies: it suffers from limited access, high radiation exposure, neurological side effects, excessive sensitivity to motion, and suboptimal signal-to-noise ratio, although some of these limitations have been reduced significantly with the newer-generation CT scanners (Yonas, Gur, Latchaw, & Wolfson, 1987).

Anatomic imaging technology as represented by MRI and CT scanning, although providing the highest *in vivo* spatial resolution, provides no information on changes either primary or secondary to cognitive activation. These methods are therefore not reviewed here.

Electromagnetic mapping is done with a computerized version of the EEG and allows analysis of both spontaneous EEG and event-related potentials. In addition, direct registration of magnetic (as opposed to electrical) fields, although still in its infancy, promises to enhance spatial resolution. These topics are addressed in other chapters.

Gamma photon imaging may be performed by the measurement of either single photon emissions or dual photon emissions resulting from positron annihilations. The single-photon techniques include [133]xenon rCBF nontomographic imaging ([133]Xe rCBF) and single-photon-emission computed tomography (SPECT), whereas the dual-photon technique is positron emission tomography (PET).

For the purposes of comparison, Table 1 presents greatly simplified and approximate current technological capabilities and costs of each functional imaging technique. Note that technological advances in this field are occurring constantly, and considerations may be very different in the near future.

The [133]Xe rCBF technique employs a series of collimated NaI detectors (from 2 to 256) arranged around the head so as to view cortical areas of interest. Xenon may be administered either as a gas by inhalation or dissolved in saline and

TABLE 1
TECHNOLOGICAL CAPABILITIES AND COSTS OF FUNCTIONAL IMAGING METHODS

	Technique		
	Xenon rCBF	SPECT	PET
Cost/study (approximate)	$300	$800	$3,000
Resolution (FWHM [mm])	20–30	6–20	5–12
Radiation exposure	Lowest	Moderate	Variable
Rapid repetition of studies	Easy	Difficult	Variable
Physiology	Perfusion	Perfusion, some receptors	Perfusion, metabolism (O_2, glucose), many receptors
Portable	Yes	No	No
Ancillary needs	Nurse/technician	Nurse/technician, ?others (see PET)	Nurse/technician, chemist, cyclotron
Display	Planar	Tomographic	Tomographic
Quantitative	Yes	Only with xenon	Usually, given assumptions

Note. All categories and specifications have been simplified for the purposes of comparison. Because technological advances in this field are occurring constantly, considerations may be very different in the near future.

given by intravenous or intracarotid injection. Studies require only 11 minutes to perform (under certain circumstances only 2–3 minutes), and dosimetry is quite favorable with this technique; typical absorbed doses per procedure are 4.2 mrad whole body and gonad and 33 mrad to the lung (the critical organ). These low absorbed dose levels coupled with the very short biological half-life of xenon allow repeated studies within subjects without fear of excessive radiation exposure (Atkins et al., 1980). As is discussed below, the "within-subject" experimental design results in greater statistical power for a given experiment.

Resolution, however, is poor with the [133]Xe rCBF method because of hemispheric cross talk, Compton scattering, intrinsic detector limitations, and planar display (Lassen, 1988). The typical 32-detector setup provides only 20–30 mm full width at half maximum (FWHM) planar resolution. (A 256-detector machine provides 10-mm FWHM planar resolution, but it is not clear that the improvement provides sufficient additional information to justify its substantial additional cost.) Although the mathematical models of this technique are optimized for estimates of tissue perfusion, there is evidence to suggest that other information (compartment size, relative tissue weight, and CBV approximation) can be extracted as well (D. R. Gitelman, I. Prohovnik, L. Coté, & S. Hilal, unpublished observations). In addition, because the technique is noninvasive and technologically straightforward, portable machines are available, allowing measurements to be made in practically any patient care area. This method is the least expensive, best documented, and most easily quantitated. Although it typically provides only cortical perfusion levels, it may be the most effective method for display of cortical regional patterns of activity.

SPECT imaging, like the ^{133}Xe rCBF technique, detects single photons. However, the detector system is adjusted to view the brain through different angles during the scanning process (e.g., circular, rectilinear) and produces tomographic pictures using CT-scanning-type algorithms. Thus, cortical as well as subcortical structures can be examined. SPECT units comprise a wide spectrum of available technologies, from the venerable rotating Anger camera to dedicated multidetector systems. The resolution is quite good with these latter systems, approaching 6–8 mm FWHM. The technique is limited, relative to PET imaging, by a lack of available biological radiopharmaceuticals, as it requires compounds labeled with single-gamma photon emitters (e.g., ^{99m}Tc, ^{123}I, ^{133}Xe) for detection. Studies of cognition with the SPECT technique have therefore been restricted to an assessment of tomographic rCBF, using ^{123}I-iodoamphetamine (^{123}I-IMP) and more recently ^{99m}Tc-hexamethylpropyleneamine oxime (^{99m}Tc-HMPAO), and limited muscarinic neuroreceptor imaging using ^{123}I-3-quinuclinidyl-4-iodobenzilate (^{123}I-QNB) (Maurer, 1988). As the chemistry of single-photon emitters becomes better described, more biological ligands will probably become available. In addition, some of the newer machines are capable of detecting gamma photons produced as a result of positron annihilation, albeit without coincidence counting. This may allow the use of a wider range of labels including ^{18}F-fluorodeoxyglucose (^{18}F-FDG) and ^{18}F-dopamine (^{18}F-DOPA) without the necessity of an on-site cyclotron. SPECT imaging also possesses the theoretical capability of simultaneous multilabel experiments using multiple window settings on the detector unit. Although SPECT technology may never achieve the biochemical flexibility, sensitivity, or resolution of PET, its future capabilities may not be far afield, and it promises to be a more cost-effective solution (Maurer, 1988).

PET imaging provides the most biological flexibility and highest tomographic resolution, but it is the most expensive and complex of the imaging technologies available today. This system detects by coincidence counting the two gamma photons produced simultaneously and at approximately 180° to each other following the emission and annihilation of a positron. With the current state of technology, coincidence detection allows finer localization and higher spatial resolution than are achievable by single-photon devices alone. With appropriate reconstruction algorithms, fast-response detector crystals, and well-designed electronics, spatial resolution to 3–4 mm FWHM is achievable with some experiments. However, positrons travel an average finite distance before annihilation (e.g., 2 mm for ^{18}F and 8 mm for ^{15}O), resulting in definite theoretical limitations to resolution depending on the isotope employed (Martin & Brust, 1985). The versatility of this technique results from the practically limitless ability to label biological molecules with such positron emitters as ^{11}C, ^{15}O, ^{13}N, and ^{18}F. However, substantial disadvantages arise from this same flexibility in terms of cost and personnel requirements. An on-site cyclotron is necessary to produce ^{15}O, ^{13}N, and ^{11}C with physical half-lives that range from 2 to 20 minutes, respectively. (With its 109-minute half-life, ^{18}F may be shipped from a nearby cyclotron.) Added to the cyclotron costs are those of a laboratory for on-site synthesis of biological compounds as well as a multitude of support personnel. Other difficulties include split-second scheduling when using ^{15}O, the long biological half-life of ^{18}F-FDG, and long scan times required with some molecules. PET technology is likely to remain the most powerful of all techniques but, given its high costs, technological complexity, and methodological constraints, will probably be fully accessible to only a few investigators.

METHODOLOGICAL CHOICES

How should an investigator evaluate the relative merits of perfusion, glucose consumption, oxygen utilization, protein synthesis, and various receptor ligands in evaluating a specific cognitive function? Certainly, accessibility sometimes provides the answer: if a PET is not available, $CMRo_2$, protein synthesis, and many receptors cannot be imaged. If a cyclotron is not on site, only glucose metabolism can be assessed with FDG. What if all are available?

Questions of experimental design must incorporate a knowledge of what can be measured into how best to assess a particular cerebral function. Therefore, if a study is of a pilot or exploratory nature, then techniques should be used that are rapid, low cost, nonspecific (but sensitive), and permit repeated measures within subjects; both ^{133}Xe rCBF and SPECT imaging fulfill these requirements. Further considerations will be dictated by desired resolution (spatial and temporal), physiological coupling, cognitive challenge conditions, and homogeneity of the study population.

How the assessed parameter corresponds to the cerebral physiology of interest is an important observation and may significantly affect interpretation of the brain physiology under study. For example, Fox et al. (1988) showed that although energy utilization at rest could be reflected by both oxygen uptake and glucose consumption, the precise match between these two parameters, formerly considered to be constant, could be altered by normal physiological neural activity. In addition, CBF was shown to remain closely coupled to $CMR_{GLUCOSE}$ but not $CMRo_2$. Thus, diverse imaging methodologies examining the same cortical function may show the investigator different, complementary, or equivalent aspects of the parameter under study. It is therefore necessary to understand and specify the conditions of measurement, especially when comparing data between studies. Also, because the relationships between the measured and functional parameters may change under a variety of conditions, it is vital to assess continued correspondence with each new experimental paradigm.

An investigator must consider the spatial and/or temporal resolution required to see the physiology of interest. As noted by Wood (1980), cognitive imaging technologies usually represent a compromise between spatial and temporal resolution (a cognitive uncertainty principle, as it were). Yet this tradeoff also helps to minimize the overwhelming and nearly uninterpretable quantity of data that would be generated if *in vivo* techniques were available with the temporal resolution of electrical mapping and the spatial resolution of electron microscopy. Although this example is extreme, it points to the need for carefully matching attainable resolution to the task at hand. Thus, PET and SPECT provide high-resolution tomographic images, but rCBF techniques may provide a better overall view of cortical tissue alone that is free from partial-volume effects.

Information pertaining to spatial resolution requirements may be available through the use of several methods. For a functional example, the intraoperative stimulation work of Ojemann, Cawthon, and Lettich (this volume) has examined language processing. Object naming critically depends on the activity of one or more temporoparietal cortical surface areas, 1–1.5 cm^2 in size, with sharp borders extending no more than 1–2 mm. These sites are most often located on gyral surfaces rather than in the depths of sulci. Areas not critical for performance but participating nonetheless extend for several centimeters around the critical regions, possibly with tonic excitation proximally and tonic inhibition peripherally. Table 2 shows several CNS structures and their approximate largest physical

TABLE 2
BRAIN STRUCTURE MEASUREMENTS

Structure	Page no.	Length (mm)	Width (mm)
Superior frontal gyrus	11	12.4	22.2
Precentral gyrus	15	27.3	13.6
Broca's area	19	22.7	6.1
Thalamus	23	31.9	10.4
Head of the caudate	29	27.6	7.7
Globus pallidus	29	25.3	5.4
Lenticular nuclei	31	27.4	13.7
Red nucleus	33	9.7	6.1
Septal area	33	14.0	1.7
Subthalamic nucleus	33	8.6	3.7
Lateral amygdaloid nucleus	37	4.3	1.5
Locus coeruleus	37	1.9	1.7
Mammillary nucleus	37	5.5	3.4

Note. A sampling of brain structure measurements (mm) from axial cadaver head sections. Measurements were made from photographs that included a centimeter scale and appeared in the atlas by Schnitzlein and Murtagh (1985), *Imaging Anatomy of the Head and Spine*. We attempted to measure the largest possible dimensions of each listed structure as it was shown in a series of sections; however, actual sizes will vary between subjects. Page numbers refer to the page in the atlas on which the measured structure appears.

dimensions on axial sections of cadaver brains. Functional activation may involve all, some, or none of a specific cerebral structure. It is apparent that the assessment of areas less than 20 mm on a side or in a subcortical location will dictate the use of SPECT or PET technology.

As for temporal resolution, all imaging methods integrate cerebral events over time periods lasting from 1 to 120 minutes as a function of the tracer and imaging equipment employed: ^{133}Xe rCBF is able to observe events lasting only 2–3 minutes (Wood, 1980), whereas PET imaging of CMRGLUCOSE may require not only 30–40 minutes of stimulation after injection, but also image acquisition lasting 5–10 minutes per tomographic cut (Kessler et al., 1983). CMRO$_2$ imaging is perhaps the fastest technique and can take as little as 1 minute per tomographic slice (Raichle, 1985). Finally, the temporal resolution of SPECT imaging falls in an intermediate range (Lassen, Andersen, & Vorstrup, 1986). Thus, the events to be observed as well as stimulation procedures utilized must be temporally coherent with the particular imaging methodology and tracer used for each experiment.

Experimental Design Principles

One major problem in the analysis of cognitive imaging data is the nature and magnitude of experimental noise or variability. This variability is often not created by measurement error or technological unreliability. It reflects true biological variation, which is most apparent in the resting state wherein subjects are "loose" from experimental control (Wood, 1980). In addition, the anatomy of the human brain is highly individual: physiological functions may appear to be variably distributed over equivalent anatomy. As an example, the differences in location of cortical sites critical for object naming have been extensively described by Ojemann et al. (this volume). Strikingly, these sites show marked alteration not only with regard to location within a given gyrus but also to completely different lobar locations between subjects. On isolated images, these cortical sites could therefore appear as unrelated areas; how are we to interpret such results? Perhaps the most powerful concept of experimental imaging design is the use of challenge procedures (i.e., cerebral manipulation through behavioral or pharmacological stimulus conditions). Challenge procedures allow the subtraction of control-state data from images obtained during cerebral stimulation. The resulting activation patterns can enhance image interpretation and functional localization by (1) reducing variance in the face of similar functional activation means and (2) deconfounding relevant from nonrelevant cognitive processes (e.g., controlling for motor and sensory aspects of a memory process under scrutiny). Statistical reliability is therefore enhanced through uniformity in experimental condition. The examples below illustrate behavioral and pharmacological challenge conditions for several techniques.

Posner, Petersen, Fox, and Raichle (1988) used PET studies during word reading to provide evidence for localization of cerebral processing on visual, phonological, and semantic codes of presented words. For example, PET images using rapid CBF sampling were generated while subjects were either (1) repeating presented words or (2) repeating assigned tasks for each presented word (e.g., "pound" for "hammer"). The former condition ostensibly provided equivalent motor and sensory activation to the latter and, on subtraction, was able to demonstrate those brain areas involved with semantic processing. Other challenge conditions in this experiment included word-versus-nonsense pattern presentation for showing visual codes and rhyming word pairs versus separately presented words for showing phonological activation. In this manner, cerebral processing of words was separated and localized to different functional areas depending on the encoded information of interest.

Another example comes from Weinberger, Berman, and Illowsky (1988), who carried out a series of experiments using ^{133}Xe rCBF and a cognitive task that had previously been shown to activate the dorsolateral prefrontal cortex (DLPFC) in normal humans. Schizophrenic patients, however, failed to show activation of the DLPFC with this task, suggesting physiological dysfunction in this cortical area. Further specificity was achieved by showing that schizophrenics were able to activate other cortical regions similarly to normals during alternate challenge conditions (Weinberger, Berman, & Zec, 1986; Berman, Illowsky, & Weinberger, 1988). These experiments demonstrate the utility of selecting challenge procedures with definitive effects on circumscribed cognitive networks. Cognitive imaging could then be used both to define effects in normals and to assay the dysfunctional aspects in patients. Experiments of this type can provide localization of normal cognitive functions while pointing to areas in need of further investigation in the presence of an abnormality.

As a final example, Honer, Prohovnik, Smith, and Lucas (1988), in a study of ^{133}Xe rCBF, gave scopolamine to young adults as a pharmacological challenge condition versus the resting (unmedicated) state. After administration of scopolamine, the subjects manifested an acute decline in long-term memory coupled with flow reductions in primarily frontal regions. The sites of these perfusion deficits suggested a linkage between muscarinic cholinergic pathophysiology and disease states producing similar frontal rCBF deficits and disturbances of cognitive function (e.g., Pick disease, bilateral electroconvulsive therapy). Furthermore, the scopolamine-induced frontal flow deficits were clearly distinct from the characteristic parietotemporal reductions seen in Alzheimer disease (AD) and indicated that scopolamine-generated dementia was probably an inadequate model for AD.

Table 3 briefly summarizes the challenge conditions discussed in the text. It is apparent that with the appropriate choice of assessed physiology, control condition, and challenge stimulus, it is possible to localize sites of normal processing, dysfunctional areas associated with specific disease states, sites of pharmacological action, and changes in cerebral physiology associated with cognitive activation. New challenge conditions will certainly continue to reveal new aspects

TABLE 3

COGNITIVE IMAGING TECHNOLOGY AND CORTICAL CHALLENGE PROCEDURES

Technology	Physiology	Subjects	Control[a]	Challenge	Results[b]	Reference
133Xe rCBF	rCBF	No CNS lesions	Rest	Digit-span backward	Increased global flow with cognition	Ingvar & Risberg (1967)
133Xe rCBF	rCBF	Normal and schizophrenic	Rest	Simple matching Wisconsin card sort	No regional rCBF differences Schizophrenic did not activate DLPFC	Weinberger et al. (1986)
133Xe rCBF	rCBF	Normal	Rest	Scopolamine	Regional cortical drug effects	Honer et al. (1988)
PET	CMRo₂	Normal	Fixation Words Words	Single words Usage assignment Rhyming words (aloud)	Sites of visual word coding Sites of semantic word coding Sites of phonological word coding	Posner et al. (1988)
PET	CMRo₂, rCBF, and CMRGLU	Normal	Resting	Flashing pattern	Physiological coupling relationships	Fox et al. (1988)

Note. This table presents, in abbreviated format, the various challenge procedures discussed in the text. Obviously only a small and noncomprehensive sample of the total work in the literature is reported here. The table illustrates functional assessments based on the observed physiology and challenge procedure(s) employed. The work of Ingvar and Risberg (1967) is included as a historical reference. In cases with multiple challenge conditions, repetitious data were left blank to enhance visual clarity, and the missing values are identical to those listed above within each study.

[a]Control and challenge conditions are matched across each line for the total specified subject population in the preceding column. Detailed explanations of each condition can be found in the original reference.

[b]Results refers to the functional assessment obtained from each imaging procedure for the control and challenge conditions on that particular line. As in *a*, this included the entire specified subject population.

of cognitive functioning. The reader is referred to the bibliography for further examples. The works of Kosslyn (1987, 1988), in particular, discuss a novel approach to the separation of cognitive functions, and this paradigm may lend itself well to the design of powerful imaging studies.

Design principles of cognitive imaging are summarized below, and the initial technical choices are presented in abbreviated algorithmic format in Figure 1. The algorithm and subsequent discussion assume all technologies are readily available, although this will usually not be the case.

1. Choose the cerebral physiology of interest. Under most conditions CBF can substitute for CMR and may prove considerably less expensive. Receptor studies are probably best performed on well-described, homogeneous populations and require the use of PET or SPECT technology.

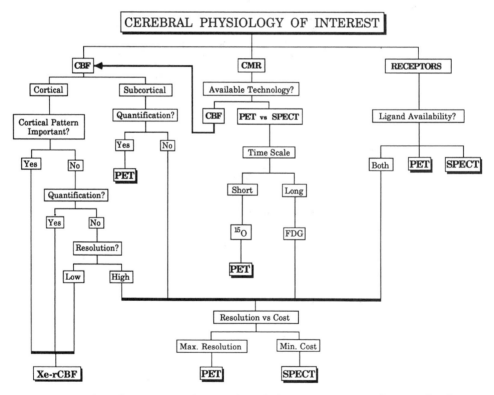

Figure 1. An algorithmic approach to technical choices in imaging design. This figure represents an abbreviated program for the selection of imaging techniques and includes only the most widely used physiological methods (e.g., protein synthesis is not included). In regard to CBF, the cortical pattern refers to display of the whole cortex proper in one image, as would be seen with [133]Xe rCBF. Quantification refers to the need for absolute as opposed to relative measured values. High resolution implies the use of tomographic technology in this algorithm, although there does exist a high-resolution (256-detector) machine for performing [133]Xe rCBF. Other decision points are self-explanatory or referred to in the text.

2. Define the need for cortical or subcortical assessment. For cortical assessment alone, [133]XE rCBF can display cortical perfusion values for an entire hemisphere simultaneously and may provide the best general view of the cortex alone.

3. Define the temporal and spatial resolution needed for the cognitive function to be imaged.

4. Define the need for absolute quantification versus obtaining relative values. (Quantification will be most important when global values are expected to change, with little or no alteration in the regional pattern.)

5. Groups should be matched for cognitive ability, medication status, disease severity, etc.

6. Be cognizant of biological variability and statistical power.

7. The experimental design should include repeated measures as well as challenge and control conditions with identifiable and subtractable components.

8. Always consider the cost–benefit ratio.

This last condition, although not yet discussed, is an important fact of experimental imaging design. More expensive, higher-resolution technology will not provide better answers to poorly formulated questions. The importance of assessing cognitive function in a general manner before proceeding to local analysis cannot be overstressed. Thus, a cost–benefit ratio includes not only a strict measurement of dollars per millimeter resolution (Figure 2) but also

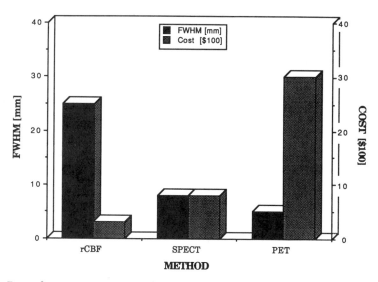

Figure 2. Procedure costs versus resolution in millimeters, FWHM, for each of the three functional imaging techniques. These parameters should never be the only indications on which imaging decisions are based but may provide a guide when other considerations are equal.

whether by increasing technical and analytical complexity, answers will be provided that could not have been obtained more simply.

DATA ANALYSIS

Having performed a proper experiment, the investigator is likely to be confronted with a bewildering array of dependent measures with associated complexity in mathematical analysis and/or anatomic resolution. For instance, rCBF data may be analyzed by one or more of three common physiological models, each resulting in as many as 10 possible variables (various tissue compartment estimates) for each of 32 cortical regions. Similarly, a high-resolution tomographic image may contain as many as 128×128 pixels for a single measured variable. Such considerations are usually not encountered in anatomic (static) imaging (i.e., CT or MRI), as the data are rarely quantified and are not subject to dynamic manipulation. In the case of static imaging, a human observer identifies abnormal patterns of signal intensity within defined anatomic structures. Functional cognitive imaging examines cortical structures in relation to both anatomy and physiology. Furthermore, the dynamic links between neuronal structures are (1) not static at the functional level and (2) largely unknown.

The sheer size of the dependent variable matrix is an imposing task for classical statistics. In addition, the data commonly violate basic assumptions of distribution and independence. Neural networks and the models that describe also demonstrate unpredictable and complex interrelationships. Thus, even though the experiment may have a rigorous, classic, and even simple design, the statistical analysis is likely to be difficult.

Although practiced in the past, it is no longer considered legitimate to conduct multiple t-test analyses. Univariate analysis of variance (ANOVA) designs are also inadequate in most circumstances for large numbers of related variables. Classical statistics, in this circumstance, offers only multivariate analysis of variance (MANOVA) as a solution. Although MANOVA techniques are superior to alternatives and satisfy several important statistical considerations, their greatest drawback lies in interpretational difficulties. Consider a relatively simple design of three conditions by two hemispheres by 10 regions of interest in each hemisphere, with the result of interest lying in the interaction. Given a significant interaction, the investigator knows that at least one of the 20 regions will show significant changes as a function of the experimental condition. However, deciphering this $3 \times 2 \times 10$ matrix to identify the relevant contrasts is a daunting task. Furthermore, even if the matrix is analyzed, the end result is a list of regions that may change in the same direction, opposite directions, or independently.

An ideal statistical technique for imaging analysis, which has long been sought after, would provide a comprehensive solution consisting of identifiable networks of regions that change coherently as a function of conditions or classifying variables. We discuss one such solution recently proposed by Móeller,

Strother, Sidtis, and Rottenberg (1987). Although still too recently developed to have allowed independent verification and experience, this approach, termed the subprofile scaling model (SSM), may be an optimal analytic technique. The following discussion is based on our limited experience with this analysis.

The SSM is essentially a principal-component technique, and as such, it might have been subject to known limitations of these methods, namely, a tendency to enforce structure on weak data interrelationships and a lack of traditional inferential significance testing. However, as currently performed, the SSM is blind to design structure, thus alleviating or eliminating these weaknesses. The SSM can be used on all data, combining groups, conditions, and hemispheres into one array. In addition, factors isolated by the SSM can be subjected to traditional ANOVA or discriminant analysis techniques, thus providing significance testing and a strong test of construct validity. For instance, one of the factors could discriminate between conditions, another the right from left hemisphere, and a third between patients and controls. In this way, SSM actually provides richer information than just the cognitive activation results.

Since the SSM is blind to experimental structure, it does not capitalize on random variation as does discriminant analysis. However, by providing multifactorial results, it imparts insights not available through traditional techniques. Each derived factor provides a network of coherent regions rather than a list of independent regions. The regions of interest (ROIs) with high loading in a factor demonstrate a high degree of covariance under the relevant conditions and truly represent a network. Although the SSM is still under testing by several groups, it is a highly promising method of analysis.

COMMENT

The technology available today for visualizing the working brain was unimaginable as recently as 20 years ago. Unfortunately, its complexity and costs are equally astounding. Current experiments have the potential of being much more revealing, but the pressure to justify each experimental investment is also more acute.

The combination of powerful technology, testable theories, and rigorous design should result in significant breakthroughs in our understanding of brain function. One last point noted by Wood (1980) reflects on the interdisciplinary nature of this technology. Input from neurologists, neuroscientists, psychologists, psychiatrists, radiologists, physicists, chemists, and statisticians will be necessary to provide basic tools and new testable theories for functional imaging technology. No one source can provide the technical and theoretical concepts necessary for continued rigorous experimental cognitive imaging design and execution. We hope this chapter will provide an introduction to the field and encourage not only reference to the literature but also interdisciplinary collaboration with other investigators and in this manner a more rational use of brain-imaging resources.

REFERENCES

Andreasen, N. C. (1988). Brain imaging: Applications in psychiatry. *Science, 239,* 1381–1388.

Atkins, H. L., Robertson, J. S., Croft, B. Y., Tsui, B., Susskind, H., Ellis, K. J., Loken, M. K., & Treves, S. (1980). Estimates of radiation absorbed doses from radioxenons in lung imaging. *Journal of Nuclear Medicine, 21,* 459–465.

Berman, K. F., Illowsky, B. P., & Weinberger, D. R. (1988). Physiological dysfunction of dorsolateral prefrontal cortex in schizophrenia: IV. Further evidence for regional and behavioral specificity. *Archives of General Psychiatry, 45,* 616–622.

Bustany, P., Henry, J. F., Sargent, T., Zarifian, E., Cabanis, E., Collard, P., & Comar, D. (1983). Local brain protein metabolism in dementia and schizophrenia: *In vivo* studies with ^{11}C-L-methionine and positron emission tomography. In W. D. Heiss & M. E. Phelps (Eds.), *Positron emission tomography of the brain* (pp. 208–211). New York: Springer-Verlag.

Fieschi, C., Battistini, N., & Lenzi, G. L. (1978). Circulatory and metabolic aspects of cerebral ischemia in experimental animals and in men. *European Neurology, 17*(Suppl.1), 31–34.

Fox, P. T., Raichle, M. E., Mintun, M. A., & Dence, C. (1988). Nonoxidative glucose consumption during focal physiologic neural activity. *Science, 241,* 462–464.

Honer, W. G., Prohovnik, I., Smith, G., & Lucas, L. R. (1988). Scopolamine reduces frontal cortex perfusion. *Journal of Cerebral Blood Flow and Metabolism, 8,* 635–641.

Ingvar, D. H., & Risberg, J. (1967). Increase of regional cerebral blood flow during mental effort in normals and in patients with focal brain disorders. *Experimental Brain Research, 3,* 195–211.

Kandel, E. R. (1985). Brain and behavior. In E. R. Kandel & J. H. Schwartz (Eds.), *Principles of neural science* (2nd ed., pp. 3–12). New York: Elsevier.

Kessler, R.M., Clark, C. M., Buchsbaum, M. S., Holcomb, H., Margolin, R. A., Cappeletti, J., Channing, M., vanKammen, D. P., King, A. C., Johnson, J., & Manning, R. G. (1983). Regional correlations in patterns of glucose use in patients with schizophrenia and normal subjects during mild pain stimulation. In W. D. Heiss & M. E. Phelps (Eds.), *Positron emission tomography of the brain* (pp. 196–200). New York: Springer-Verlag.

Kosslyn, S. M. (1987). Seeing and imagining in the cerebral hemispheres: A computational approach. *Psychological Review, 94*(2), 148–175.

Kosslyn, S. M. (1988). Aspects of a cognitive neuroscience of mental imagery. *Science, 240,* 1621–1626.

Lassen, N. A. (1988). Basic principles of CBF measurement by xenon-133 and external recording by multiple stationary detectors. In S. Knezevic, V. A. Maximilian, Z. Mubrin, I. Prohovnik, & J. Wade (Eds.), *Handbook of regional cerebral blood flow* (pp. 25–36). Hillsdale, NJ: Lawrence Erlbaum Associates.

Lassen, N. A., Andersen, A. R., & Vorstrup, S. (1986). Cerebral blood flow tomography using gamma-emitting radioisotopes. In J. Wade, S. Knezevic, V. A. Maximilian, Z. Mubrin, & I. Prohovnik (Eds.), *Impact of functional imaging in neurology and psychiatry* (pp. 44–53). London: John Libbey.

Lenzi, G. L., Frackowiak, R. S. J., & Jones, T. (1982). Cerebral oxygen metabolism and blood flow in human cerebral ischemic infarction. *Journal of Cerebral Blood Flow and Metabolism, 2*(3), 321–335.

Martin, J. H., & Brust, J. C. (1985). Imaging the living brain. In E. R. Kandel & J. H. Schwartz (Eds.), *Principles of neural science* (2nd ed., pp. 259–283). New York: Elsevier.

Maurer, A. H. (1988). Nuclear medicine: SPECT comparisons to PET. *Radiologic Clinics of North America, 26*(5), 1059–1074.

Móeller, J. R., Strother, S. C., Sidtis, J. J., & Rottenberg, D. A. (1987). Scaled subprofile model: A statistical approach to the analysis of functional patterns in positron emission tomographic data. *Journal of Cerebral Blood Flow and Metabolism, 7*(5), 649–658.

Posner, M. I., Petersen, S. E., Fox, P. T., & Raichle, M. E. (1988). Localization of cognitive operations in the human brain. *Science, 240,* 1627–1631.

Raichle, M. E. (1985). Measurement of local brain blood flow and oxygen utilization using oxygen 15 radiopharmaceuticals: A rapid dynamic imaging approach. In M. Reivich & A. Alavi (Eds.), *Positron emission tomography* (pp. 241–247). New York: Alan R. Liss.

Roy, C. S., & Sherrington, C. S. (1890). On the regulation of the blood supply of the brain. *Journal of Physiology, 11,* 85–108.

Schnitzlein, H. N., & Murtagh, F. R. (1985). *Imaging anatomy of the head and spine.* Baltimore: Urban & Schwarzenburg.

Sokoloff, L., & Smith, C. (1983). Biochemical principles for the measurement of metabolic rates *in vivo.* In W. D. Heis & M. E. Phelps (Eds.), *Positron emission tomography of the brain* (pp. 2–18). New York: Springer-Verlag.

Weinberger, D. R., Berman, K. F., & Illowsky, B. P. (1988). Physiological dysfunction of dorsolateral prefrontal cortex in schizophrenia, II. A new cohort and evidence for a monoaminergic mechanism. *Archives of General Psychiatry, 45,* 609–615.

Weinberger, D. R. Berman, K. F., & Zec, R. F. (1986). Physiologic dysfunction of dorsolateral prefrontal cortex in schizophrenia: I. Regional cerebral blood flow evidence. *Archives of General Psychiatry, 43,* 114–124.

Wood, F. (1980). Theoretical, methodological, and statistical implications of the inhalation rCBF technique for the study of brain–behavior relationships. *Brain and Language, 9*(1), 1–8.

Yonas, H., Gur, D., Latchaw, R., & Wolfson, S. K. (1987). Stable xenon CT/CBF imaging: Laboratory and clinical experience. *Advances and Technical Standards in Neurosurgery, 15,* 4–37.

BIBLIOGRAPHY

Heiss, W. D., & Phelps, M. E. (Eds.). (1983). *Positron emission tomography of the brain.* New York: Springer-Verlag.

Kandel, E. R., & Schwartz, J. H. (Eds.). (1985). *Principles of neural science* (2nd ed.). New York: Elsevier.

Knezevic, S., Maximilian, V. A., Mubrin, Z., Prohovnik, I., & Wade, J. (Eds.). (1988). *Handbook of regional cerebral blood flow.* Hillsdale, NJ: Lawrence Erlbaum Associates.

Lassen, N. A., & Perl, W. (1979). *Tracer kinetic methods in medical physiology.* New York: Raven Press.

Magistretti, P. L. (Ed.). (1983). *Functional radionuclide imaging of the brain.* New York: Raven Press.

Reivich, M., & Alavi, A. (Eds.). (1985). *Positron emission tomography.* New York: Alan R. Liss.

Wade, J., Knezevic, S., Maximilian, V. A., Mubrin, Z., & Prohovnik, I. (Eds.). (1986). *Impact of functional imaging in neurology and psychiatry.* London: John Libbey.

DISCUSSION

ARNOLD SCHEIBEL: May I use the chairman's prerogative to make a few comments even though Dr. Prohovnik knows the literature a lot better than I do? Coleman and Buell showed compensatory growth of basilar dendrites in the normal aging population, and we have shown that in presenile Alzheimer patients there is unexpected and explosive dendritic growth. Carrying this just a little bit further, we were fascinated by what you said about the observation that, early on, the Alzheimer patient shows this hypertrophied vascular response, but later in the disease this response vanishes. In our own laboratory, we have found that one of the characteristics of advanced Alzheimer disease is the complete disappearance of the perivascular neural plexus on all the capillaries in the affected areas. The presumption might be that you need this innervation for this vascular response.

ADAM WECHSLER: Actually I have two questions. I'm not sure that I understood you completely, but if I did, you said that the age-matched controls did not show that compensatory response of the Alzheimer patient. Did you take the elderly subjects out to the ninth or perhaps even the 10th decade to see whether, at that extreme, you could get a compensatory response in the aged? The other question is whether you had an opportunity to study a group of unusually gifted individuals, let's say mathematicians, to see whether, compared to a normal control group, you might see less of a physiological demand and perhaps even less cortical blood flow than you would in a normal subject?

ISAK PROHOVNIK: Regarding the first question, neither we nor anyone else studied people who were 90 or 100 years old, but there is an entity called age-associated memory impairment or benign senescent forgetfulness, and those may be nearly the equivalent of such people. But we have just started those studies and don't have answers yet. Regarding the other question, neither we nor anybody else has ever studied extremely gifted people to see what happens. You are suggesting analogy to trained athletes and their basal metabolic rate. I find it very hard to believe that the analogy between brain and myocardium will extend that far, although it's not impossible. I agree with you that one would predict that brilliant mathematicians might have extremely low blood flow at rest, perhaps, and only small increases on equivalent tests. It hasn't been done yet.

JOAQUIN FUSTER: These deficits in delayed matching are also consistent with frontal deficits. I notice that some of your pictures show a decrement in activation in frontal areas. Could it be that they are responsible for it?

PROHOVNIK: I'm glad that you asked this question. This is a very big issue, and I'll be happy to tell you more afterwards. Alzheimer disease is supposedly a disease of the cholinergic system. There is a very powerful hypothesis that Alzheimer disease is caused by problems in the nucleus basalis of Meynert. So we wanted to see whether a cholinergic antagonist would create in normal subjects a cognitive pattern similar to that of Alzheimer patients and thus confirm the possibility of a cholinergic deficit. However, the effect of muscarinic cholinergic antagonism on cerebral blood flow is fascinating: scopolamine, without touching the parietal or temporal lobes, turns off the prefrontal lobe and frontotemporal areas. At the same time it creates a transient amnesia, which some people say is similar to Alzheimer disease, although other people contest that. But this is identical to what bilateral ECT does, which is also associated with transient amnesia and also turns off the frontal lobes. For this reason we're beginning to suspect that the cholinergic involvement in Alzheimer disease is indeed related to some memory components that are more associated with the frontal type of disease than the parietal. You're correct.

JACKSON BEATTY: A comment and two questions. At the AAAS meeting there was a report from the University of California at Irvine psychiatry department on PET scans in normal individuals performing a continuous performance task and Raven's progressive matrices, showing an inverse correlation between glucose utilization and quality of performance on Raven's test. That may speak to the issue that you raised there. Now the two questions. One is, are the original data on normal individuals and cerebral blood flow compromised by data gathered over the last 5 years, and the second has to do with the resolution of the problem of ventilation versus injection techniques.

PROHOVNIK: I'm sorry, I didn't understand the first question.

BEATTY: The first question is—you were reporting data from the 1970s through the early 1980s in normals that seemed to be very exciting and then said that you were disheartened later but had the data . . .

PROHOVNIK: No, the data still stand. My disillusionment lay in the possibility of applying such data to the clinical setting. The data still stand and are probably correct in normal 25-year-old subjects. The problems only start when you try to interpret what a schizophrenic brain or a demented brain will do with the same kind of tests. That was the problem. Was the other one about inhalation and injection?

BEATTY: Do you have to use a carotid injection?

PROHOVNIK: No, nowadays, of course, we don't. Not in the States, at least. Some places still use carotid injection. Nowadays it's inhalation or I.V. It's much simpler. It's safer. It's a wonderful method for that.

JÖRG PAHL: I think your data on Alzheimer disease are very, very interesting. What I'd like to ask you is this. Recently there have been some reports indicating that blood flow and metabolism in certain situations don't correlate. Would you comment on that? The second thing is: could you again explain why in Alzheimer disease we do have neuronal loss. What method can be used *in vivo* to show that this does occur?

PROHOVNIK: The tight coupling between blood flow and metabolism was always a fundamental credo of the field. It was always part of our bible. And although there was no evidence, everybody always assumed that the flow increases were secondary to metabolic demand and that they therefore would occur later in time. Additionally, in terms of magnitude, the metabolic changes should be more sensitive and more accurate than the flow changes, which are after all only a response to that. But 4 years ago the St. Louis group of Raichle, Fox, and others started reporting data that showed the opposite. In other words, blood flow increased before the metabolic shift. Other recent studies now seem to support this. I think it's an important discovery, suggesting that something is going on there that we don't understand. For all practical purposes it doesn't matter, because for those kinds of studies, we don't care about the few milliseconds of delay between the one and the other. But in terms of the fundamental physiology involved, I think that's a very exciting question, and we still don't have an answer to that.

As to your second question, there are two ways in functional imaging to separate gray and white matter. One is simply to push spatial resolution to the limit. If you have excellent resolution in your PET or SPECT, you can center your region of interest on an area that is "pure gray" or "pure white." It will never be exactly pure, but it will be predominantly gray or white. The other method is based on knowing they are perfused at totally different rates and have different characteristics. Then you can build the physiological model, which will mathematically separate the tissue into gray and white matter, and that's what was done in this case. When you do that, you not only derive the perfusion in each compartment but also the relative size, magnitude, and weight of each compartment. Using that, we have shown that in this particular problem, there is a relative loss of gray matter in Alzheimer disease, which correlates positively with clinical severity, but much more dramatically so in the presenile variant than in the senile type. There is some loss of gray matter in normal aging, and some senile Alzheimer patients appear to be similar to elderly controls. It's the young ones, the patients who get Alzheimer disease at age 50 or so, who have a dramatic loss of gray matter, but that loss is not accentuated in the parietal–temporal area where we might otherwise see flow perfusion problems.

SCHEIBEL: Until about 40 to 45 years ago, an accepted way to attempt to improve cerebral circulation after a CVA was through a stellate ganglion block. About the time I was in medical school it was decided that this was almost useless, and it became fashionable to believe that CO_2 was really the only effective dilator of the vascular bed. I think one of the most exciting discoveries of the last 10 years has been the finding that the parenchyma of the brain controls, to some extent, its own vascularity, and so we obviously have several mechanisms operating. This leads to the notion that one can prepare a certain cortical bed for the things that are to happen there simply by the brain "set." It makes good sense, and I find this extremely exciting. Any other questions for the speaker?

JOHN SCHLAG: I have both a comment and a question, and they come from another discipline. I think that there is a basic assumption inherent in these beautiful results, and that is that an area that is utilized in a particular performance should be activated. One of the troubles is that, at least for us neurophysiologists, when we are recording the activity of the neurons in that region, it's not evident that the neuronal firing rates in that region correlate with the increase of metabolic activity in that region. I remember some results of Evarts, for instance, that indicated that there are some cells that are regularly activated and some cells that are inhibited. There are approximately 33% in each group, and this is the kind of result we sometimes find, and I think that Joaquin is going to agree with that. Maybe the selection of the units from which we are recording is not ideal, and we are not seeing all varieties of activity but are selecting only a skewed sample. Perhaps we'll have to discuss the relationship between this measurement of metabolism as expressed by physical circulation and the reactivity of neurons during the performance. What counts is the exchange of information, and information corresponds as much to inhibition as to excitation. There is no reason to have an increase of metabolic activity.

PROHOVNIK: I think you're right. There's no question that we know of many cells that do their work by inhibition. We know of inhibitory neurotransmitters, and we also know that what we're measuring when we measure general metabolism or blood flow is a final common pathway, which is the net result of several preceding very complicated stages. However, inhibition is also an active process that requires energy utilization, so that if you think of a very simple neural network with just two neurons, when the target neuron is being inhibited, it may utilize less energy, and therefore in terms of blood flow, metabolism will be lower. But the cell that generates the presynaptic activity, whether it sends inhibitory or excitatory information, will always require energy to send that information. So in this sense, the positive relationship between neural activity and energy utilization is maintained at the source but not necessarily at the target of the information. I agree that it's a fundamental problem. I would also suggest that so much data have been gathered over the last two decades or so that there is no longer any question that when the brain performs cognitive activity it utilizes energy. This means you have increases of metabolism and blood flow. As a general phenomenon there may be some exceptions, and I think that's what you are talking about. In some regions under some circumstances we may see phenomena opposite to what we're used to. But the general principle still stands.

ERAN ZAIDEL: Just to follow this up, do you see any way of teasing those two apart with techniques like the one you've described?

PROHOVNIK: You mean, in humans, *in vivo*?

ZAIDEL: Ideally, yes.

PROHOVNIK: I think not. Like everybody else we do audioradiography, and we now have a resolution approaching something on the order of 100 μm or so in simple work and better than that in some specialized setups. In animals, we could look for that. But, in humans . . .

ZAIDEL: Depth electrodes or something like that?

PROHOVNIK: No, well, yes and no. The problem is that electrical information is very different from metabolic information. That's the problem of interpreting EEGs. The EEG was introduced in 1929. Today in 1988 we still have no idea what the EEG is or where it comes from. This is what you were alluding to. When you look at the electrical activity of a single cell, you may well see a decrease of activity. The information code consists of a reduced frequency rather than elevated frequency. That is complicated, and we have no way, and I don't think we will ever have a way, in the human to measure metabolism and blood flow or any other energy common pathway with the resolution sufficient to do that. MRI spectroscopy, for example, can show the energy balance of small regions by clinical standards; small regions meaning a couple of millimeters. But by standards of electrophysiology and neurophysiology, those are still huge collections of networks. I don't think that we will be able to do that.

POSITRON EMISSION TOMOGRAPHY IN THE STUDY OF HIGHER COGNITIVE FUNCTIONS

JÖRG J. PAHL, MD, FCP(SA)
University of California, Los Angeles

INTRODUCTION

Neuropsychological and electrophysiological investigations in normal subjects and split-brain patients have led to rapid advances in our understanding of how the brain functions. Neuroimaging has become an integral part of this neuroscience revolution by demonstrating the anatomical, biochemical, and physiological substrates underlying human cognitive functions. These studies emphasize the intricate nature and inherent interdependence of individual brain systems that participate in cognition.

Music, visual scenes, and tactile sensations are complex sensory stimulation patterns that are comprised of primary variables. Stimulus repetition rates and other physical stimulus parameters individually affect neuronal firing rates. Specific stimulus characteristics such as color composition and light intensity preferentially activate neurons in specific brain areas. Information exchange within and between discrete cerebral regions is, however, necessary for analysis of these various elementary stimuli. The final recognition and interpretation of resultant stimulus patterns as, for instance, a painting by Picasso or a checkerboard pattern is accomplished by comparing such processed information with stimulus patterns that have previously been encoded in memory.

Fuster (1989) describes such information processing as occurring in a hypothetical network consisting of two broad categories of neuronal populations and the connections linking them. The first neuronal population, which is located in the primary cortical areas, is activated by the physical characteristics of the stimulus. The second population consists of neurons of the association cortices that represent the attributes the stimulus has acquired by experience.

Acknowledgments: This research was supported in part by National Institutes of Health grant PO1-NS-15-654, National Institute of Mental Health grant RO1 MH 37916-AC03-76-SF0012, and Department of Energy grant DE-AC03-76-SF0012. I am indebted to John C. Mazziotta, MD, PhD, Jeffrey L. Cummings, MD, and Nancy C. Andreasen, MD, PhD for critical comments; L. Griswold and W. Wilson for preparing the illustrations; R. Sumida and C. Whitt for technical assistance; and K. Burrows, K. Engbar, and M. Chang for preparing the manuscript. Present address for Jörg J. Pahl: Department of Psychiatry, The University of Iowa College of Medicine, Iowa City, Iowa.

Brain maps acquired with functional imaging modalities picture the brain at work. They are based on the central assumption that cerebral blood flow and metabolism are coupled and reflect neuronal function, a relationship that was first demonstrated by Roy and Sherrington in 1890. Initial techniques were capable of quantifying global cerebral blood flow only but were eventually replaced by methods that measured and depicted regional flow. Lassen, Ingvar, and Skinhoj's report in *Scientific American* (1978) represents an excellent overview of these pioneering regional cerebral blood flow (rCBF) studies. The authors describe the use of cortical probes and radioactive xenon-133 gas in mapping rCBF changes in appropriate cortical areas after visual, auditory, and tactile cognitive challenge.

Two-dimensional cortical probes have recently been complemented by three-dimensional imaging techniques that include positron emission tomography (PET) and single-photon-emission computed tomography (SPECT). PET represents the most elegant and precise functional imaging technique presently available. Phelps and Mazziotta (1985) have demonstrated PET's ability to measure discrete alterations in physiological and biochemical variables that accompany mental work and external sensory stimulation. PET offers distinct advantages over cortical probes as a functional brain-imaging modality since it represents both cortical and subcortical activation patterns as high-resolution three-dimensional regional functional landscapes.

Modern image analysis techniques greatly increase the information content of functional brain images. Fox et al. (1986) have used image subtraction techniques in conjunction with PET to detect and display discrete foci of activation. They were able to visualize regions of interest (ROI) that lay well below the resolving power of their PET camera, a phenomenon that they have compared to visual hyperacuity. Thus, 3-mm activation foci were detected using PET cameras with an in-plane resolution of 18 mm at full width half maximum (FWHM).

The generation and meaningful interpretation of qualitative and quantitative neurobehavioral PET images are based on a thorough appreciation of the technological aspects of PET, the inherent underlying variability of brain structure and function, and the effects of changing stimulus parameters on such function. Thus, stimulation paradigms have to be carefully devised to maximize the brain's response to stimulation in discrete ROIs. Primary stimulus variables (repetition rate, etc.), stimulus presentation mode (i.e., mon- or binaural stimulation), and the subject's cognitive strategy must all be examined for the individual effects each may have on the final image.

Both intra- and intersubject comparisons of regional quantitative PET data are heavily dependent on accurate identification of cerebral structures using anatomical localization schemes that are known to differ in their ability to map brain function to standard anatomical areas such as are represented in Brodmann architectonic maps.

PET studies have shown that regional cerebral function is characterized by considerable variability in health and disease. Gur et al. (1982) and Kuhl, Metter, Riege, and Phelps (1982) have shown that age, sex, and handedness are personal attributes that may contribute to such intersubject variability. Brain-mapping studies have great potential for answering intriguing questions about such inter-subject differences. They can also be used to explore brain plasticity and functional reorganization that occur during brain maturation and after hemispherec-tomies and other brain resections. This overview describes the present status of positron emission tomography in the study of normal cognition.

Principles of Positron Emission Tomography

Higher cognitive functions result in neuronal activation and concomitant dynamic alterations in regional cortical and subcortical physiological and bio-chemical variables. The major PET components that are needed to measure such variables accurately include a cyclotron for the production of radioisotopes, a PET camera to acquire and reconstruct the cross-sectional concentration of the isotope, valid tracer kinetic models, and anatomical localization schemes to quantify such images.

Radiotracer choice is important in the design of research protocols that study component parts of complex cognitive functions sequentially in a single setting. The advantage of oxygen-15 (^{15}O) over ^{18}F-fluorodeoxyglucose (^{18}FDG) lies in the former isotope's short half-life ($t_{1/2}$ ^{15}O = 2 minutes; ^{18}F = 109 minutes). This both improves temporal resolution and allows cognitive studies to be divided into 8–10 subsections that can be examined at 10-minute intervals. Paradigms using ^{18}FDG as a radiotracer are generally repeated after a 10-hour delay (or for practical purposes the next day) to allow sufficient decay of the ^{18}F isotope.

Present-generation PET cameras produce functional brain images in stan-dard transverse, coronal, and sagittal views with an in-plane and axial resolution of 6 mm. Improved scanner resolution allows accurate visualization of multiple small cortical and subcortical structures including the hippocampus, parahippo-campus, and thalamic nuclei. Magnetic resonance imaging (MRI), event-related potentials, and other electrophysiological measurements can be combined with PET, thereby adding further spatial and temporal detail to such studies.

A major aim of stimulation paradigms has been to determine the anatomical substrates of specific cortical processes. These studies are complicated by the presence of brain asymmetries, intersubject regional anatomical variability, and intersubject variation in cognitive processing. Thus, considerable time and effort have been spent in developing methods that take into account the abovemen-tioned anatomical factors and allow accurate regionalization and quantification of PET images.

The different anatomical localization schemes have recently been reviewed by Mazziotta and Koslow (1987). Regions of interest have been transcribed by some investigators onto PET images from templates derived from standard anatomic atlases. Patient scans have also been regionalized by using information gained from the subject's own x-ray CT or MRI. Fox, Perlmutter, and Raichle have used stereotactic methods to identify regions of interest using computer programs that potentially eliminate investigator interaction totally. Studies now under way are examining the feasibility of electronically superimposing MRI and PET scans, thus using the inherently superior anatomical detail of the MRI image to define accurately PET ROIs. These methods are expected to improve the quantification of the functional images. They may also result in the semiautomatic analysis of PET images.

Finally, it is important for PET scientists to understand the assumptions and limitations that underlie tracer kinetic methods used to convert regional isotope concentrations (as detected by the PET scanner) into physiological and biochemical units (i.e., glucose utilization in mg/100 g/min).

RESTING AND BASELINE STATES

Sequential increases in stimulus complexity result in a progressive increase in cerebral blood flow and metabolism above a reference state that can vary from total or partial sensory deprivation through increasing levels of sensory stimulation. The resting, unstimulated state is usually characterized by minimal external sensory stimulation in an awake, relaxed subject who is not engaged in mental or motor activity. Ambient conditions during such studies consist of diffuse dim lighting and low noise levels mainly caused by PET camera operations (Figure 1). Ingvar (1979) has described a "hyperfrontal" resting cerebral blood flow pattern (prefrontal 30% greater than hemispheric mean; frontal flow higher than parietal lobe flow; temporal lobe flow the lowest) in such resting subjects using the intracarotid xenon-133 method. The significance of the hyperfrontal pattern remains unknown. Anxiety, emotional factors, and intent to act may all underlie this phenomenon.

Mazziotta and Phelps (1984a), in a study of the resting state, demonstrated cortical and subcortical left–right metabolic symmetry in normal subjects in the eyes- and ears-open condition and during states of partial sensory deprivation (eyes patched or ears plugged). More complete sensory deprivation states (eyes patched and ears plugged) resulted in metabolic asymmetries (left greater than right; magnitude 3–7%) in the inferior frontal, perisylvian, and lateral occipital cortices.

Controlled baseline states have been devised by some investigators to reduce the effects of anxiety and thinking on isotope uptake during the PET procedure. Reivich, Gur, and Alavi (1983) have, for instance, shown that anxiety increases the glucose metabolic rate in the posterior fronto-orbital and middle frontal regions. Uncontrolled thinking represents brain work and therefore also affects blood flow and metabolism. A possible disadvantage of controlled baseline states is that they may activate the targeted regions of the investigation. Thus, there is no easy

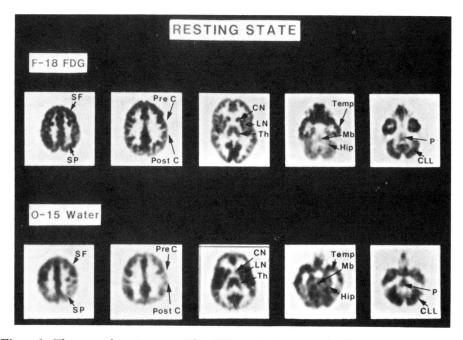

Figure 1. The normal resting state. This PET study depicts two different individuals who were both examined in the eyes- and ears-open state. The cortical ribbon and subcortical structures are clearly visible. Note that the resolution of the [18]FDG image is slightly better than that of the [15]O scan. SF, superior frontal cortex; SP, superior parietal cortex; Pre C, precentral gyrus; Post C, postcentral gyrus; CN, caudate nucleus; LN, lenticular nucleus; Th, thalamus; Temp, temporal lobe; Mb, midbrain; Hip, hippocampus; P, pons; CLL, cerebellar cortex.

solution to the problem of choosing the baseline state. Ideally, a controlled baseline task should activate the same regions as the experimental activation task, apart from the ones specific to the experimental task. This goal is, however, difficult to achieve in reality.

FUNCTIONAL ACTIVATION

Functional activation of the brain results in increased energy demand that is mainly met by oxidative metabolism of glucose under nonfasting conditions. The sodium pump is the major determinant of the cell's energy demands during neuronal activity. Ackermann, Finch, Babb, and Engel (1984) have shown that neuronal inhibition results in greater energy utilization than actual neuronal firing. Yarowsky, Crane, and Sokoloff (1985) have shown that, following neuronal stimulation, glucose utilization increases predominantly at synapses in the neuropil, where the surface-to-volume ratio is much greater than that of the cell body. Areas showing increased cerebral blood flow and metabolism in PET images thus predominantly reflect regions of synaptic activity rather than the localization of cell bodies, whose energy needs are relatively low during activation. The subcellular region of primary energy utilization becomes an important issue in the interpretation of functional PET images when cell bodies and nerve endings are located in different structures that comprise part of a single functional unit.

PRIMARY STIMULUS VARIABLES

Alterations in primary stimulus variables, including stimulus intensity, quality, duration, and repetition rate, may result in profound effects on neuronal activity in primary cortical areas. Few PET examinations have used paradigms that systematically vary such parameters. The study by Fox et al. (1986) illustrates the importance of such investigations. They examined the effect on visual cortex cerebral blood flow of increasing the stimulus rate during reversed checkerboard visual stimulation. Cerebral blood flow varied systematically with stimulus rate, increasing to a maximum at a reversal frequency of 7.8 Hz.

The activation of secondary cortical association areas by music and visual scenes may also be highly dependent on the composition of primary stimulus variables that comprise complex stimulus patterns.

PARADIGM DESIGN

Paradigm design is heavily influenced by the half-life of the isotope used. Initial PET investigations of cognitive function were primarily [18]FDG studies. They were characterized by considerable variability in local cerebral responses to sensory stimulation. The following PET- and patient-related factors may have been responsible for the high degree of variability: long half-life of [18]FDG (109 minutes) resulted in the necessity of separating baseline and stimulation studies by at least 10 hours and usually by a day; image planes acquired in the second study often did not accurately match those of the first despite the use of identical external landmarks during head positioning; local cerebral metabolism could have been affected during the relatively long 40-minute [18]FDG isotope uptake period by individual differences in response habituation. Fox and Raichle (1984) observed a significant response decrement within 10 to 20 minutes after the start of stimulation when using [18]FDG.

Numerous factors have helped to improve the validity and to decrease the variability of newer PET studies. These include increased scanner sensitivity and resolution because of technical advances in PET camera design. Newer multislice scanners are capable of sampling 15 planes simultaneously and have eliminated the need for repositioning the patient's head during most studies. Thus, the plane of imaging is kept constant between studies. Improved anatomical localization schemes allow accurate definition and sampling of regions of interest within and between subjects. Investigators have substituted [15]O for [18]FDG in their stimulation experiments. The short half-life of ^{15}O (2 minutes) has enabled the investigators to repeat studies at 10-minute intervals. The limited radiation exposure for ^{15}O allows 8–10 studies to be performed in a single research setting. Habituatory effects are unlikely to occur during the short performance time (40–60 seconds) of a typical ^{15}O H_2O bolus study.

Hierarchical research protocols have been used to examine the effects of progressively increasing stimulus complexity. These studies have selected ^{15}O to study individuals 8 to 10 times during a single experimental setting. Image analysis subtraction techniques used in combination with such designs determine the relative contribution of each increase in stimulus complexity to the variable being measured (i.e., cerebral blood flow, metabolism).

ACTIVATED BRAIN

Visual Stimulation

Phelps, Kuhl, and Mazziotta (1981) have studied the effect on cerebral glucose metabolism of increasing visual stimulus complexity. The baseline state consisted of eyes closed and patched. This state of visual deprivation, which reflects spontaneous neuronal firing, resulted in a slight decrease in metabolic rate. Subjects were initially stimulated with white light. The small response above baseline, 12% for the primary visual cortex and 6% for the association visual cortex, was ascribed to the fact that light intensity discrimination occurs primarily in the lateral geniculate body and superior colliculus.

In a second experiment subjects were stimulated with an alternating black and white checkerboard pattern (2 cycles/second) that inherently includes information on moving edges, spatial frequency, and light intensity. The primary visual cortex responded with a 2.4-fold increase, and the association visual cortex was increased 4.4-fold over baseline. Individuals were finally subjected to a complex visual scene from a park that led to the greatest increase in metabolic rate (primary visual cortex 45%; association visual cortex 59%) above base line, with the association visual cortex increasing at a faster rate than the primary visual cortex as the visual scene complexity increased. Primary stimulus characteristics, including increased rate of stimulation with increasing stimulus complexity, may be partly responsible for increased metabolic rates found during stimulation with such highly structured visual patterns (Figure 2).

Roland and Skinhoj (1981) have shown that extrastriate cortical areas are activated by visual discrimination tasks in man. They used a paradigm in which test subjects had to indicate their response verbally while discriminating between two ellipses of identical area but different shape. Regional cerebral blood flow responses indicated that the posterior superior parietal cortex analyzed spatial characteristics of the visual information that had been extracted by the visual cortical areas.

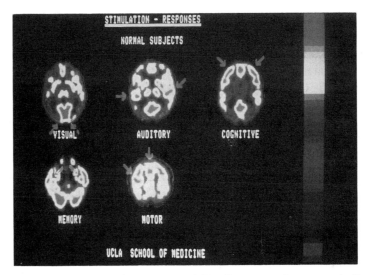

Figure 2. The activated brain. This composite PET illustration shows metabolic responses in appropriate cortical regions during visual, auditory, and mental (cognitive) stimulation of the brain. Memory and motor tasks lead to increased glucose utilization rates (arrowed areas) in the corresponding hippocampal and motor areas. Radiotracer, [18]FDG.

Auditory Stimulation

Auditory activation paradigms have presented individuals with verbal and nonverbal stimuli mon- and binaurally to examine the effects of stimulus characteristics and side of presentation on the cerebral response. Reivich et al. (1979), in a pioneering study, presented six subjects monaurally with a factual story to either right ($n = 3$) or left ear ($n = 3$), with resultant 20% to 25% increases in the glucose utilization rate of the entire right temporal lobe regardless of the side of stimulation. Greenberg et al. (1981) subsequently reported a study of two groups of seven subjects. Each heard either a meaningful factual story or a nonmeaningful (foreign language) story presented monaurally; the same right-greater-than-left temporary asymmetry was found regardless of the ear stimulated.

Mazziotta, Phelps, Carson, and Kuhl (1982) studied the effect of monaural and binaural verbal and nonverbal auditory stimuli on regional glucose metabolism. Verbal stimuli (Sherlock Holmes story) were presented to either left or right ear in the monaural stimulation paradigm. These monaural verbal stimuli produced diffuse metabolic changes in the left hemisphere and bilateral activations of the transverse and posterior temporal lobes. The nonverbal stimuli consisted of the Seashore measures of musical talents, a two-part test composed of a tonal memory test and a timbre test. The monaural nonverbal stimulation with chords demonstrated bilateral parietotemporal activations and diffuse right-greater-than-left frontotemporal asymmetries. Tone sequence pairs presented monaurally produced asymmetries that differed by the subject's analysis strategy. Non-analytical, musically naive subjects had right-greater-than-left frontotemporal asymmetries, whereas analytically or musically sophisticated subjects had an absence of right-greater-than-left relative hypermetabolism and demonstrated left-greater-than-right temporal asymmetries. Binaural presentation of a factual story and music produced diffuse bilateral activations of the temporal and frontal cortices. These results demonstrate that metabolic responses to auditory stimuli are determined by the content of the stimulus and the analysis strategy of the subject rather than by the side of stimulation.

Somatosensory Stimulation

The majority of the initial studies of the somatosensory system have also been limited to ^{18}FDG metabolic studies. Greenberg et al. (1981) showed that unilateral light brushing (2–3 Hz) of the fingers and hand resulted in a proportionately greater contralateral than ipsilateral metabolic response (9 ± 10.2% asymmetry) in the somatosensory postcentral cortex. The activation occurred in the appropriate hand region of the sensory homunculus. Reivich et al. (1983) have reported pilot studies in which light unilateral brush stroking of the face and lip was performed and showed asymmetric labeling in the most ventral portions of the parietal cortex.

More recent studies have selected ^{15}O to map focal neuronal activity in the somatosensory cortex. Fox, Burton, and Raichle (1987) used vibratory stimulation in eight normal volunteers with ^{15}O. They found well-defined zones of increased CBF in regions of the postrolandic cortex that corresponded with the site of cutaneous stimulation.

Motor System

Roland, Meyer, Shibasaki, Yamamoto, and Thompson (1982) used ^{77}Kr inhalation and unilateral ballistic finger movements to measure rCBF responses of the motor system. Results demonstrated contralateral increases in regional cerebral blood flow as compared to the ipsilateral side for the somatosensory cortical representation of the hand area (23.3 ± 2.3% contralateral, 0.5 ± 1.6% ipsilateral) and the globus pallidus (20.1 ± 2.7% contralateral, 10.0 ± 2.8% ipsilateral). Bilateral increases in regional cerebral blood flow were reported for the supplementary motor cortex (30%), premotor cortex (10%), parietal opercula (9%), paracentral cortex (20%), putamen (15%), caudate (11–15%), and thalamus (10%).

More recently, Mazziotta and Phelps (1984b) demonstrated differences in the sites of increased local cerebral metabolic rates of glucose utilization (LCMRGLC) using two different motor tasks. Novel finger movement tasks caused increases in LCMRGLC in the contralateral sensorimotor cortex (18.6 ± 3.9%). Overlearned tasks (repeated signature writing), while resulting in a cortical response of similar distribution and magnitude, in addition produced bilateral metabolic rate increases in the striata ($19.0 \pm 10.2\%$ contralateral, $18.3 \pm 8.4\%$ ipsilateral to the moving hand).

Mental Work

Roland, Eriksson, Stone-Elander, and Widen (1987) studied the effect of mental work on regional cerebral blood flow and oxidative metabolism of the brain. Subjects were required to image a specific route visually in familiar surroundings. Results were compared with a baseline study that showed that local cerebral blood flow was linearly correlated with oxygen metabolism (regional cerebral metabolic rate for oxygen consumption, $rCMRo_2$). The specific mental imagery raised the oxidative metabolic rate in 25 homotypical cortical areas. Active regions were located in the superior and lateral prefrontal cortex and the frontal eye fields. The greatest response appeared in the posterior superior lateral parietal cortex and the posterior superior medial parietal cortex in the precuneus.

Subcortically, metabolism increased in the neostriatum and posterior thalamus. Regional cerebral blood flow increased proportionally in these active fields and structures. Thus, a dynamic coupling of regional cerebral blood flow and oxidative metabolism was observed during the physiological activation. The authors concluded that the posterior medial and lateral parietal cortices could be classified as remote visual association areas participating in the generation of visual images of spatial scenes from memory. The posterior thalamus was assumed to participate in the retrieval of such memories.

Language

Language functions are distributed widely throughout both cerebral hemispheres. Extensive postmortem, neuropsychological, and electrophysiological investigations have been performed to define their anatomical substrates. Broca and Wernicke were the first to demonstrate that lesions of the dominant hemispheres were most likely to result in aphasia. Geschwind and Levitsky (1968) produced further anatomical evidence for hemispheric specialization of language functions by noting that the dominant hemisphere's planum temporale was larger than that of the opposite side.

The contribution of the nondominant hemisphere to language has been more controversial. Although older studies have tended to deemphasize its role, newer investigations have shown that it is the hemisphere that is primarily responsible for prosodic and pragmatic aspects of language.

The last decade has been marked by research into functional characteristics of speech production and language comprehension. Neuropsychological, electrophysiological, and, more recently, neuroimaging techniques have been used to explore individual differences in anatomical substrates that underlie the individual language functions.

PET and SPECT, combined with ^{15}O, xenon-133, and other short-lived radiotracers, are particularly relevant to this avenue of research. These techniques offer distinct advantages over postmortem studies and structural imaging modalities (x-ray CT and MRI) for the investigator who is interested in determining the relative contributions of individual cerebral regions of both hemispheres to normal (and pathological) language communication.

Cortical probes and the xenon-133 technique were used initially to visualize the living human brain in normal individuals and stroke patients during speech production and comprehension. These CBF measurements demonstrated an important finding: functional abnormalities were typically more extensive in the brains of stroke patients than the anatomical lesions seen either at postmortem or on x-ray CT.

The original PET investigations confirmed the earlier impression gained with cortical probes that functional brain abnormalities affected larger cortical areas than did structural lesions. These studies also demonstrated poor overall correlation between individual symptoms and metabolic abnormalities as seen on the PET scan. It became increasingly apparent to investigators that complex language functions had to be dissected into component parts to allow a more meaningful interpretation of functional studies.

Petersen, Fox, Posner, Mintun, and Raichle (1988) pioneered such a hierarchical paradigm by combining PET with the ^{15}O-labeled water bolus technique, allowing them to identify brain regions active during single-word processing. Their study was also designed to determine the relative validity of the cognitive and clinical neurological models for word processing. The cognitive model proposes that visual and auditory presentations of words result in the activation of separate modality-specific codes with access in parallel to shared articulatory and semantic codes. This model differs from the neurological one, which proposes serial word processing with subsequent transfer of the visual input into an auditory-based code that represents the final articulatory and semantic output.

Six to 10 blood flow scans were obtained by these authors in each subject during successive visual or auditory presentation of words. Subtraction image analysis techniques were then used to determine the relative contribution of each new stimulus to overall regional changes in CBF. The study demonstrated that distinct visual and auditory cortical regions are involved in single-word processing and that they have independent access to supramodel articulatory and semantic systems. These findings were in agreement with the parallel cognitive rather than the serial visual-to-auditory word-processing model.

NORMAL SUBPOPULATIONS

Cognitive functions are dependent on postnatal maturation of cortical and subcortical structures. Huttenlocher, deCourten, Garey, and Van Der Loos (1982) have shown that such normal brain development is characterized by initial overproduction and subsequent elimination of excessive neurons, synapses, and dendritic spines. These mechanisms form the basis for plasticity and functional specialization of the brain.

Chugani, Phelps, and Mazziotta (1987) have complemented Huttenlocher's histological studies with a series of PET examinations of the living human brain in which they have mapped changing rates of glucose utilization as a function of age in children. The investigations have shown that these metabolic findings closely reflect the cortical and subcortical maturation process. They have also demonstrated that absolute values for LCMRGLC are low at birth and rapidly rise to reach adult values by 2 years. Furthermore, LCMRGLC rates continue to rise and reach their highest values at 3 to 4 years. These high rates are maintained until approximately 9 years, when they begin to decline, and reach adult rates again by the latter part of the second decade.

Chugani et al. (1987) have also described a temporal pattern for the maturation of individual brain regions that closely parallels their functional development. Thus, 5-week-old infants had the highest LCMRGLC values in their sensorimotor cortex, thalamus, brainstem, and cerebellar cortex. By 6 to 8 months, LCMRGLC had increased in frontal and dorsolateral occipital cortical regions.

Children with normal milestones demonstrated distinctive metabolic patterns, which differed unequivocally from those of age-matched mentally retarded children. The latter were characterized by a failure to show the expected initial increase (and subsequent decline) in regional glucose utilization rates. These investigations emphasize the need for functional maturation to occur before the brain is able to engage in cognition.

PET has been used to study the effect of aging, sex, and brain size on the fully developed brain during resting conditions and after activation. Studies of normal aging have yielded contradictory results. Kuhl et al. (1982) reported a 26% decline in mean glucose utilization rates between the ages of 18 and 78 years. Not all laboratories have reported age-related declines in cerebral blood flow and metabolism. Thus, Duara et al. (1984) failed to replicate an age-related decline in oxidative metabolism in 40 healthy men aged 21 to 83 years. The inclusion of, for instance, preclinical Alzheimer disease subjects in "normal aged" populations may explain why the two studies differed.

Blood flow and metabolic rate per unit volume of tissue have been found to vary inversely with brain size across species. Smaller brains have higher neuronal packing densities and correspondingly higher rates of cerebral blood flow and metabolism. This finding has recently been extended to humans by Hatazawa, Brooks, DiChiro, and Bacharach (1987). The authors reported an inverse correlation between brain size and cerebral metabolic rate. It is unknown whether previously observed sex differences in cerebral metabolic rates are also related to this inverse correlation. Baxter et al. (1987), who reported 19% higher metabolic rates in women than men, partly attributed their results to the performance of PET scans at a time of high estrogen levels.

Conclusions

Man's ability to think, communicate, and create and appreciate visual art and music differentiates him from the lower species. Neuroscientists have until recently employed postmortem, neuropsychological, and electrophysiological methods to define anatomic substrates for these and less complex cognitive functions. The recent addition of *in vivo* brain-imaging techniques to the more established research methodologies has led to substantial advances in our understanding of how the brain works.

Interdisciplinary research groups comprised of psychiatrists, neurologists, neuropsychologists, and brain-imaging specialists have cooperated with basic neuroscientists to develop novel approaches to brain imaging. Paradigms have been designed that promise to unravel the complex interactions of specific brain regions that underlie the execution of intricate brain tasks. Advances in radiotracer synthesis and PET camera design have recently allowed scientists to characterize such cognitive functions in both physiological and chemical terms.

Innovative hierarchical PET research paradigms have determined the anatomical and functional substrates that underlie word processing. The studies, as outlined above, repudiate the commonly held notion that visual-to-auditory encoding is necessary for word processing to occur. This is but one example of how neuroimaging is being used to test cognitive information-processing models. The combination of state-of-the-art high-resolution PET cameras with short-lived radiotracers also opens up the possibility of identifying where specific components of a cognitive task are being processed in the brain.

The discipline of functional brain imaging is still in its infancy. PET has, for instance, been available to this field for a little less than a decade. Despite this fact, PET has proven its ability to accurately visualize the living human brain during the execution of such diverse tasks as writing, speaking, and thinking. The potential of PET and related functional imaging modalities for unraveling the brain's cognitive functions seems promising indeed.

REFERENCES

Ackermann, R. F., Finch, D. M., Babb, T. L., & Engel, J., Jr. (1984). Increased glucose metabolism during long-duration recurrent inhibition of hippocampal pyramidal cells. *Journal of Neuroscience, 4,* 251–264.

Baxter, L. R., Jr., Mazziotta, J. C., Phelps, M. E., Selin, C. E., Guze, B. H., & Fairbanks, L. (1987). Cerebral glucose metabolic rates in normal human females versus normal males. *Psychiatry Research, 21,* 237–245.

Chugani, H. T., Phelps, M. E., & Mazziotta, J. C. (1987). Positron emission tomography study of human brain functional development. *Annals of Neurology, 22,* 487–497.

Duara, R., Grady, C., Haxby, J., Ingvar, D., Sokoloff, L., Margolin, R. A., Manning, R. G.,

Cutler, N. R., & Rapoport, S. I. (1984). Human brain glucose utilization and cognitive function in relation to age. *Annals of Neurology, 16,* 702–713.

Fox, P. T., Burton, H., & Raichle, M. E. (1987). Mapping human somatosensory cortex with positron emission tomography. *Journal of Neurosurgery, 67,* 34–43.

Fox, P. T., Mintun, M. A., Raichle, M. E., Miezin, F. M., Allman, J. M., & Van Essen, D. C. (1986). Mapping human visual cortex with positron emission tomography. *Nature, 323,* 806–809.

Fox, P. T., & Raichle, M. E. (1984). Stimulus rate dependence of regional cerebral blood flow in human striate cortex, demonstrated by positron emission tomography. *Journal of Neurophysiology, 51,* 1109–1120.

Fuster, J. M. (1989). *The prefrontal cortex* (2nd ed., pp. 189–190). New York: Raven Press.

Geschwind, N., & Levitsky, W. (1968). Human brain: Left–right asymmetries in temporal speech region. *Science, 161,* 186–187.

Greenberg, J. H., Reivich, M., Alavi, A., Hand, P., Rosenquist, A., Rintelmann, W., Stein, A., Tusa, R., Dann, R., Christman, D., Fowler, J., MacGregor, B., & Wolf, A. (1981). Metabolic mapping of functional activity in human subjects with the [^{18}F]fluorodeoxyglucose technique. *Science, 212,* 678–680.

Gur, R. C., Gur, R. E., Obrist, W. D., Hungerbuhler, J. P., Younkin, D., Rosen, A. D., Skolnick, B. E., & Reivich, M. (1982). Sex and handedness differences in cerebral blood flow during rest and cognitive activity. *Science, 217,* 659–661.

Hatazawa, J., Brooks, R. A., DiChiro, G., & Bacharach, S. L. (1987). Glucose utilization rate versus brain size in humans. *Neurology, 37,* 583–588.

Huttenlocher, P. R., deCourten, C., Garey, L. J., & Van Der Loos, H. (1982). Synaptogenesis in human visual cortex: Evidence for synapse elimination during normal development. *Neuroscience Letters, 33,* 247–252.

Ingvar, D. H. (1979). "Hyperfrontal" distribution of the cerebral grey matter flow in resting wakefulness; on the functional anatomy of the conscious state. *Acta Neurologica Scandinavica, 60,* 12–25.

Kuhl, D. E., Metter, E. J., Riege, W. H., & Phelps, M. E. (1982). Effects of human aging on patterns of local cerebral glucose utilization determined by the [^{18}F]fluorodeoxyglucose method. *Journal of Cerebral Blood Flow and Metabolism, 2,* 163–171.

Lassen, N. A., Ingvar, D. H., & Skinhoj, E. (1978). Brain function and blood flow. *Scientific American, 239,* 62–71.

Mazziotta, J. C., & Koslow, S. H. (1987). Assessment of goals and obstacles in data acquisition and analysis from emission tomography: Report of a series of international workshops. *Journal of Cerebral Blood Flow and Metabolism, 7,* S1–S3.

Mazziotta, J. C., & Phelps, M. E. (1984a). Human sensory stimulation and deprivation: Positron emission tomographic results and strategies. *Annals of Neurology, 15(Suppl.),* S50–S60.

Mazziotta, J. C., & Phelps, M. E. (1984b). Positron computed tomography studies of cerebral metabolic responses to complex motor tasks. *Neurology, 34(Suppl. 1),* 116.

Mazziotta, J. C., Phelps, M. E., Carson, R. E., Kuhl, D. E. (1982). Tomographic mapping of human cerebral metabolism: Auditory stimulation. *Neurology, 32,* 921–937.

Petersen, S. E., Fox, P. T., Posner, M. I., Mintun, M., & Raichle, M. E. (1988). Positron emission tomographic studies of the cortical anatomy of single-word processing. *Nature, 331,* 585–589.

Phelps, M. E., Kuhl, D. E., & Mazziotta, J. C. (1981). Metabolic mapping of the brain's response to visual stimulation: Studies in humans. *Science, 211,* 1445–1448.

Phelps, M. E., & Mazziotta, J. C. (1985). Positron emission tomography: Human brain function and biochemistry. *Science, 228,* 799–809.

Reivich, M., Greenberg, J., Alavi, A., Christman, D., Fowler, J., Hand, P., Rosenquist, A., Rintelmann, W., & Wolf, A. (1979). The use of the [^{18}F]fluorodeoxyglucose technique for mapping of functional neural pathways in man. *Acta Neurologica Scandinavica, 60(Suppl. 72)*, 198–199.

Reivich, M., Gur, R., & Alava, A. (1983). Positron emission tomographic studies of sensory stimuli, cognitive processes and anxiety. *Human Neurobiology, 2*, 25–33.

Roland, P. E., Eriksson, L., Stone-Elander, S., & Widen, L. (1987). Does mental activity change the oxidative metabolism of the brain? *Journal of Neuroscience, 1*, 2373–2389.

Roland, P. E., Meyer, E., Shibasaki, T., Yamamoto, Y. L., & Thompson, C.J. (1982). Regional cerebral blood flow changes in cortex and basal ganglia during voluntary movements in normal human volunteers. *Journal of Neurophysiology, 48*, 467–480.

Roland, P. E., & Skinhoj, E. (1981). Extrastriate cortical areas activated during visual discrimination in man. *Brain Research, 222*, 166–171.

Yarowsky, P., Crane, A., & Sokoloff, L. (1985). Metabolic activation of specific postsynaptic elements in superior cervical ganglion by antidromic stimulation of external carotid nerve. *Brain Research, 334*, 330–334.

DISCUSSION

MARIAN DIAMOND: With both verbal and memory tasks, the occipital cortex appeared very active. Would you care to comment on that please?

JÖRG PAHL: I think the question was whether this was a primary visual area or secondary visual area. The other question had to do with whether the patient had his eyes open during the procedure.

JASON BROWN: On either your eyes-open, eyes-closed, ears-open, ears-closed, resting scans, what is your test–retest reliability on multiple or serial scanning? In some of our C11 PET work at NYU we find very poor test–retest reliability on the resting scans, but fortunately on some of our activation or perturbation studies we can do two scans in the same day, and we find very good correlation between the two scans.

PAHL: I think the primary variable there is when you retest your patient. Do you retest the patient on the same day within a couple of hours, or do you retest the patient about 2 days later? The retest scan under resting conditions is always much better the closer you do it to the first time. I think that the kind of variability you have in the resting state is on the order of 8–12%, which is not a small percentage. I think that that would improve with the new anatomical localization scans with better resolution.

SANDRA WITELSON: Continuing on this point, and in a way picking up on something that you mentioned, I wonder whether you would consider that the poor test–retest reliability in the resting condition could be because you don't really control the cognitive activity of the individual, whereas in the activation task, at least you know you've put in a particular stimulus or required a particular task. In some of the PET scans Dr. Steve Garnett has been doing with colleagues at McMaster University, we have considered this as a possible explanation for the low test–retest reliability.

PAHL: May I say, "Are you a psychologist?"

WITELSON: Yes.

PAHL: I think that is a very important point. Bob Ackermann, who is just across the way from me, always points out that it's extremely important to control the base line whether resting or otherwise. This has been one of the major problems with functional brain imaging in general. What do we mean by hypo- or hyperfrontality as seen in the resting state? You're quite right. The morbid patient, more than the normal subject, would have a lot going on in his brain, which could activate a lot of structures.

ISAK PROHOVNIK: I think the issue of reproducibility in measurement is complicated but not as bad as that. What do we actually mean by measurement error when we deal with something as sensitive as this system? Basically, all modern imaging methods are very good, very reliable. The measurement error, strictly defined, that is attributable to the physics and the mechanics and the electronics, independent of the organism, is minimal. I think that here we're mixing biological variability with measurement error. I would agree that the reproducibility of resting studies is something on the order of 10–20%, but that is not measurement error. That is true variability of brain function, which is not at all surprising. The problem is not how to eliminate that, because that is actually one of the things we want to study. I think what Sandra is proposing is probably impossible. I doubt that we will ever truly be able to maintain a normal conscious human being in a steady state psychologically speaking or even physiologically speaking for 20 minutes. Alternatively, I think we're damaging ourselves by improving resolution, and that is something that has to be addressed at some point. You mentioned SPECT resolution of about 10 to 17 mm. We actually have a machine with a 7-mm resolution, just like the PET, and I regret that. I insist on addressing a question to Dr. Ojemann here about what a brain really looks like. If we do succeed in bringing our resolution down to 5 mm, I think we will be in a position where we will be unable to do any group studies, because patients will be totally different from each other. If you want to do language studies, you will find activation at totally different points of the brain, and that will all be true, but when you average all the groups, you'll get minimal or zero fix because the activation events occur at so widely different areas, functionally speaking. I don't know how to solve this, but I think that is part of the reason for both the variability and small cognitive effects.

ARNOLD SCHEIBEL: George, do you have an answer to that?

GEORGE OJEMANN: At the 1-cm level of resolution, variability in language localization between patients is already so large that much information is going to be lost averaging across cases.

PAHL: I agree with you that increased resolution is not necessarily a good thing. You can image 30 planes, and you can use 60 planes in one patient, with 15 regions of interest per side. You get into extremely complex statistics, etc. The improved resolution, I think, is very important for the smaller structures, and if you went, for instance, into an area that is particularly important, something like the thalamus where you have motor nuclei, the pulvinar, etc., resolution there is very important. Resolution of 5 mm versus resolution of 10 mm means a lot because in motor tasks, for instance, the VL and VA nuclei can be selectively activated. You don't see this if your regional interest encompasses the whole thalamus.

SCHEIBEL: It has taken physics 50 years to come to terms with the problems of quantum dynamics, and now it seems that we in biology are going to have to face our own uncertainty problems. Adam, one more question.

ADAM WECHSLER: From the standpoint of a clinical neurologist, I find it a little disturbing that the PET data in patients with Parkinson disease seem to be quite similar to the data from Alzheimer patients. There may be some similarity clinically, although that in my experience is rather unusual even in the early stages of Alzheimer disease. But has that been followed up on, and how consistent has that parallelism been?

PAHL: I think that the appropriate use of radioligands (i.e., ^{18}F-fluorodopa vs. ^{18}F-fluorodeoxyglucose) would help in the differentiation of the two conditions. ^{18}F-fluorodopa scans typically demonstrate decreased radiotracer uptake in the striatum in Parkinson disease but not in patients suffering from typical Alzheimer disease. ^{18}F-fluorodeoxyglucose PET scans on the other hand have a normal appearance in Parkinson disease while showing areas of hypometabolism that are characteristically seen bilaterally in the posterior temporo-parietal regions in Alzheimer disease. Patients with "Parkinson's plus" may actually be suffering from both Alzheimer disease and Parkinson disease. You would therefore expect, Adam, that the PET scans would reflect the chemical alterations of both Parkinson disease and Alzheimer disease where the two conditions coexist in a single individual.

ARCHITECTURE AND CONNECTIONS OF CEREBRAL CORTEX: IMPLICATIONS FOR BRAIN EVOLUTION AND FUNCTION

DEEPAK N. PANDYA, MD

Edith Nourse Rogers Memorial Veterans Hospital,
Boston University School of Medicine, and Beth Israel Hospital

EDWARD H. YETERIAN, PhD

Edith Nourse Rogers Memorial Veterans Hospital and Colby College

INTRODUCTION

At the most fundamental stage, neuronal processing and communication occur at the level of the synapse. It is essential therefore to understand precise neuronal morphology at the micro- or ultrastructural level. Somal and axodendritic articulations provide the essential underpinnings for cognitive and behavioral processes. However, microstructural features are difficult to correlate with specific behavioral functions, at least at the present time. Hence, a detailed knowledge of the next level of neuroanatomic organization, that is, architecture and connections, would seem to be useful in understanding function. Realizing the need for such knowledge, neuroanatomists such as Reil (1809) and Burdach (1819–1826), almost two centuries ago, attempted to describe cortical organization in terms of axonal pathways. Subsequent investigators provided further information on cortical connectivity. For example, Déjerine's (1895) descriptions and outlines of major cortical pathways are still a mainstay for our understanding of many clinical disorders (Geschwind, 1965a, 1965b). In addition to cortical pathways, descriptions of neurons and their mode of laminar distribution within cerebral cortex (i.e., architectonics) fascinated several investigators in the early 1900s (Campbell, 1905; Brodmann, 1909; Vogt & Vogt, 1919; Economo & Koskinas, 1925; Bonin & Bailey, 1947). During the period from the 1920s through the

Acknowledgments: We are highly grateful to Dr. Clifford Barnes for his generous help in the preparation of this chapter. We are also thankful to Mr. Michael Schorr and Mr. Timothy Murphy for their excellent technical assistance. This study is supported by the Veterans Administration, Edith Nourse Rogers Memorial Veterans Hospital, Bedford, Massachusetts, by NIH grant 16841, and by Colby College Social Science grant 01-2274.

1950s, however, cortical architecture and connections received relatively little attention despite some efforts to further describe cortical connectivity (e.g., Mettler, 1935a, 1935b, 1935c, 1935d; Bonin & Bailey, 1947; Krieg, 1963). With the availability of selective silver impregnation methods (Nauta, 1957; Fink & Heimer, 1967) and tracer techniques (Cowan, Gottlieb, Hendrickson, Price, & Woolsey, 1972; LaVail & LaVail, 1972; Kuypers, Catsman-Berrevoets, & Padt, 1977; Mesulam, 1982), cortical connections have been explored extensively since 1960.

Anatomic investigations, in conjunction with physiological studies (Figure 1), have revealed several principles regarding cortical morphology (e.g., Jones & Powell, 1970; Pandya & Seltzer, 1982a; Van Essen & Maunsell, 1983; Mishkin, Ungerleider, & Macko, 1983; Pandya, Seltzer, & Barbas, 1988). Initially, based on connectional studies during the 1960s, it was suggested that the main mechanism for information processing in the cerebral cortex is sequential processing. Anatomic studies showed that the connections from a primary sensory area advance further in a sequential manner toward association areas (Pandya & Kuypers, 1969; Jones & Powell, 1970). However, further anatomic and physiological studies suggested another mode of information flow in the cerebral cortex, namely, "parallel processing." According to this concept, various cortical association areas receive simultaneous input from the thalamus rather than only by way of the

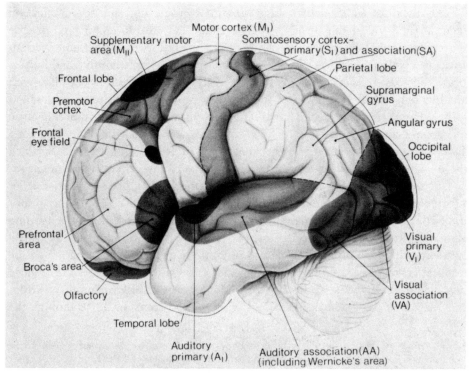

Figure 1. Diagram of the human cerebral cortex depicting various primary and association areas (Pandya & Yeterian, 1985).

primary sensory areas and thus are capable of carrying out analyses of incoming information in a parallel manner.

Yet another element of cortical organization became evident during the 1970s. It was found that in addition to the so-called primary and secondary sensory and motor areas, there are several adjacent regions that have physiological properties like the primary areas and are termed rerepresentations or multiple representations (Merzenich & Brugge, 1973; Paul, Merzenich, & Goodman, 1975; Zeki, 1978; Kaas, Nelson, Sur, Lin, & Merzenich, 1979; Muakkassa & Strick, 1979; Woolsey, 1981a, 1981b, 1981c; Van Essen & Maunsell, 1983). Finally, a number of studies have shown that in parallel with the forward flow of connections there are also sequential backgoing or reciprocal connections as well as side-to-side or lateral connections within the cerebral cortex (e.g., Kuypers, Szwarcbart, Mishkin, & Rosvold, 1965; Tigges, Spatz, & Tigges, 1973; Seltzer & Pandya, 1978; Vogt & Pandya, 1978; Rockland & Pandya, 1979; Galaburda & Pandya, 1983; Van Essen & Maunsell, 1983).

Although the revelation of these connectional principles has provided better understanding and appreciation of cortical connections, it has at the same time raised several additional issues. One major challenge that we now face is how to organize this new information on cortical morphology in a coherent manner, to begin to use it for understanding cortical functions and for generating hypotheses for further studies. Therefore, it seems that we are in need of a more comprehensive and systematic approach with regard to cortical morphology. We would like to propose an evolutionary approach in regard to cortical architecture and connections. It is reasonable to assume that the cerebral cortex has evolved in parallel with the development of increasingly complex functions. In other words, as organisms have experienced different environments and have undergone adaptations, such progressive changes must have been reflected in the central nervous system, in particular the cerebral cortex. We realize the term "evolutionary approach" may be controversial. In this regard, we must emphasize that the use of this term refers strictly neither to phylogeny nor to ontogeny. Rather, the intent is to describe cortical structural changes that are observed in a given primate species as one attempts to follow the patterns of progressive cortical elaboration between so-called older and newer regions.

Our aim is first to elaborate on the organizational principles underlying cortical architecture. Secondly, we attempt to correlate progressive architectural changes with patterns of cortical connectivity. Finally, we discuss cortical substrates of higher processes and focus on the morphology and possible functional roles of so-called multimodal areas.

ARCHITECTONICS AND CONNECTIONS

The notion of progressive changes in brain morphology was proposed a half century ago in the architectonic studies of Dart (1934) and Abbie (1940). Both investigators suggested a dual origin of cerebral cortex based on their studies in reptilian and marsupial brains, respectively. Their observations received little attention until the 1960s. Sanides (1969) came to similar conclusions based on his architectonic studies in several different mammals including primates. This concept regarding the dual origin of the primate cerebral cortex begins with the proposition that the cerebral cortex has evolved from two primordial moieties, namely, the archicortex (hippocampus) and the paleocortex (olfactory cortex) (Pandya & Yeterian, 1985). It is suggested that from each of these allocortices, a cortical architectonic trend can be traced characterized by progressive differentiation of cortical laminae. Each of these two trends first passes through steps designated as periallocortex (PAll) and proisocortex (Pro) before culminating in true six-layered isocortex (Figure 2). The isocortical areas that stem from archi- and paleocortical moieties show progressive laminar differentiation, which can be traced from proisocortex towards the primary sensory and motor regions as successive waves of elaboration of cortical laminae. This laminar differentiation occurs in each cortical layer. The overall pattern, however, seems to show progressive development of the supragranular layers as one moves from proiso-

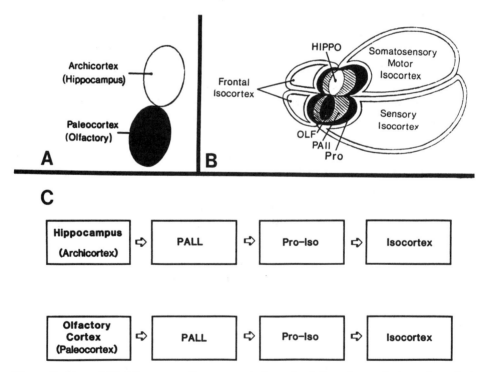

Figure 2. (A and B) Diagrammatic representations depicting the evolution of cortical areas from two moieties, archicortical (hippocampus) and paleocortical (olfactory). (C) Block diagram showing the successive steps in the two cortical architectonic trends. OLF, olfactory cortex; PAll and PALL, periallocortex; Pro, proisocortex.

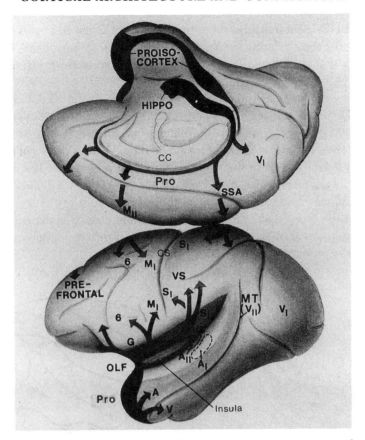

Figure 3. Diagrammatic representation of further architectonic progression from the two trends shown in Figure 2 on the lateral and medial surfaces. The Sylvian fissure is opened to expose both of its banks and the insula. A, auditory association area; A_I, primary auditory area; A_{II}, second auditory area; CC, corpus callosum; CS, central sulcus; G, gustatory area; M_I, primary motor cortex; M_{II}, supplementary motor cortex; S_I, primary somatosensory cortex; S_{II}, second somatosensory area; SSA, supplementary somatosensory area; V, visual association area; V_I, primary visual area; V_{II}, equivalent to area MT (middle temporal region) of the superior temporal sulcus; VS, vestibular area.

cortex towards the primary region. Thus, according to this concept, the temporal polar and insular proisocortices are derived from the paleocortical (olfactory) moiety. Further progression from these proisocortices would lead to the development of the auditory-related areas of the superior temporal region, the areas relating to the central visual field in the inferotemporal and occipital regions, the somatosensory and motor areas subserving the head, face, and neck in the ventral part of the post- and precentral cortices, and the gustatory and vestibular areas (Figure 3). From this paleocortical trend would also evolve the different regions of the ventral prefrontal cortex. From the proisocortices of the hippocampal or archicortical trend, which are located in the ventral temporal and cingulate regions, would revolve the ventromedial temporal and occipital areas (including their dorsomedial sectors) subserving the peripheral visual field and somatosensory and motor areas relating to the trunk and limb structures. From this medial proisocortex would also evolve the medial and dorsolateral prefrontal regions (Pandya & Yeterian, 1985).

Further architectonic studies (Pandya & Seltzer, 1982b; Galaburda & Pandya, 1983; D. L. Rosene & D. N. Pandya, unpublished observations) show that three different parallel sequences of architectonic differentiation can be identified among areas relating to each sensory modality. Thus, as shown in Figure 4, in the auditory-related areas in the superior temporal region, one line would progress from the temporal polar proisocortex in the supratemporal plane (STP) in a sequential manner leading ultimately to the primary auditory area (AI). In this line, termed the "core line," the main architectonic change is the acquisition of progressively more granule cells. The second line of differentiation occurs in the

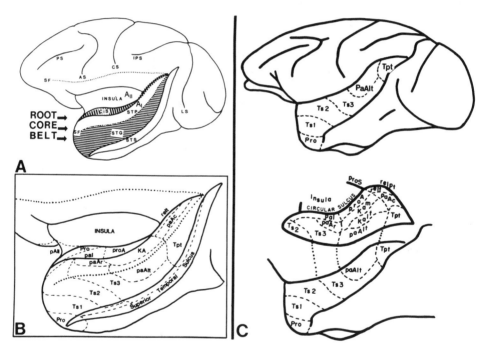

Figure 4. (A) Diagram of the lateral surface of the cerebral hemisphere showing three architectonic lines (root, core, and belt) in the superior temporal region (STR). (B) Architectonic areas in the three trends shown in A (Galaburda & Pandya, 1983). (C) Architectonic areas of the STR according to Pandya and Sanides (1973). KA, koniocortex; paAc, caudal parakoniocortex; paAlt, lateral parakoniocortex; paAr, rostral parakoniocortex; pal, parinsular cortex; pAll, periallocortex; Pro, proisocortex; proA, auditory prokoniocortex; proS, somatosensory prokoniocortex; reIpt, retroinsular parietotemporal cortex; reIt, retroinsular temporal cortex; Tpt, temporoparietal cortex; Ts₁, Ts₂, Ts₃, temporalis superior cortex 1, 2, 3; TPO, temporal–parietal–occipital cortex; AS, arcuate sulcus; CS, central sulcus; IOS, inferior occipital suclus; IPS, intraparietal sulcus; LS, lunate sulcus; PS, principal sulcus; SF(LF), Sylvian fissure; STS, superior temporal sulcus.

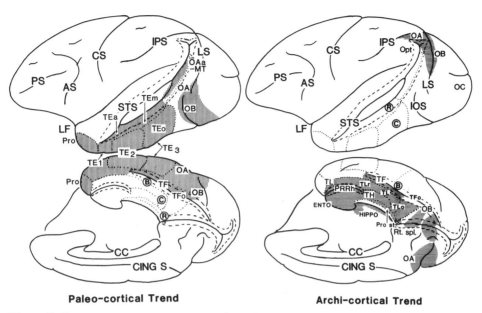

Figure 5. Diagrammatic representation of the distribution of different architectonic areas within the two trends in the visual system. Note the locations of the root (R), core (C), and belt (B) lines in each trend.

superior temporal gyrus (STG) and is thought to represent the auditory association areas. In this "belt line," the predominant architectonic changes involve the acquisition of more third-layer neurons along with increased numbers of granule cells. The third line, known as the "root line," is organized in the circular sulcus (CiS) of the Sylvian fissure and leads to the second auditory area (AII). In this line, differentiation between supra- and infragranular layers is somewhat less than that in the other two architectonic lines (core and belt).

The visual areas of the occipital and inferotemporal cortices also may be organized according to the concept of core, belt, and root lines (Figure 5). However, in the visual system the three lines are doubly represented: one set in the inferotemporal region originating from the paleocortical moiety and dealing with the central visual field and the other set in the ventral temporal or posterior parahippocampal region involved in peripheral vision, beginning from the hippocampal moiety. Likewise, in the somatosensory system, two sets of three architectonic lines can be identified (Figure 6). One set progresses from the paleocortical moiety towards the inferior parietal lobule, which subserves the head, neck, and face. The second set originates from the hippocampal moiety and leads to the medial and superior parietal cortices relating to the trunk and limb representations.

In summary, in each modality there are three different types of differentiation: the root line leads to so-called second sensory areas, the core line culminates in the primary sensory areas, and the belt line represents the association areas

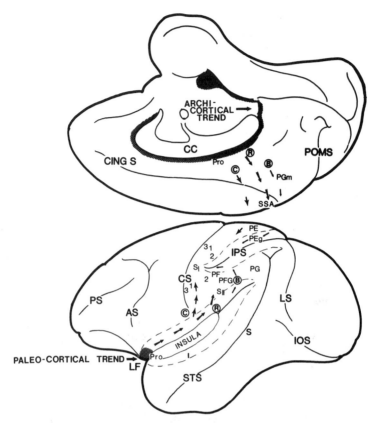

Figure 6. Diagrams of the medial and lateral surfaces of the cerebral hemisphere showing the architectonic progressions in the parietal lobe associated with the trends. The insular trend (paleocortical) leads toward the inferior parietal lobule, and the cingulate trend (archicortical) is toward the superior parietal lobule. These diagrams also indicate the three different architectonic lines within each trend—root (R), core (C), and belt (B).

(Figure 7). Further observations of the auditory system of the superior temporal region (STR) show that different areas in these three lines can be grouped into four rostrocaudal stages from temporal proisocortex towards the primary region (Figure 8). Each stage contains an area of the root line medially, the core line centrally, and the belt line laterally. The cortical connections within and between architectonic lines are consistent with the organization just described. Thus, in the auditory system, it has been shown that there are sequential forward and backward connections (Figure 9). The forward connections from a given area in these lines originate from the third-layer neurons and terminate in a columnar manner in the next rostral region in the supragranular layers including layer IV. These connections can be followed sequentially up to the proisocortex of the temporal pole. Parallel to these sequential forward connections, there are also backgoing or reciprocal connections. These reciprocal connections can be traced from the temporal polar cortex to the primary and association areas. Quite distinct from

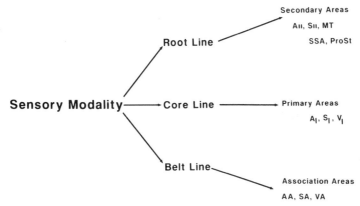

Figure 7. Diagram showing the root, core, and belt lines culminating, respectively, in second sensory areas, primary areas, and association areas. ProSt, prostriate area.

forward connections, these backgoing connections originate mainly from the infragranular layers and terminate in adjoining caudal areas in the subsequent stage in layer I (Figure 10A). These sequential forward and backward connections give support to the concept of progressive differentiation of cortical areas described above. Thus, it appears that forward connections would advance the information about the external environment in a sequential manner, whereas the backgong connections may modify or modulate the incoming information on

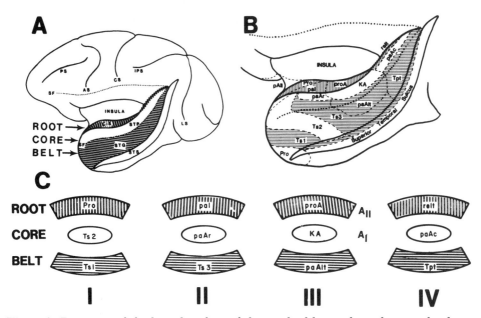

Figure 8. Diagrams of the lateral surface of the cerebral hemisphere showing the three architectonic lines (A) and architectonic areas (B) of the STR. (C) Arrangement of four rostral-to-caudal architectonic stages within the root, core, and belt lines of the STR.

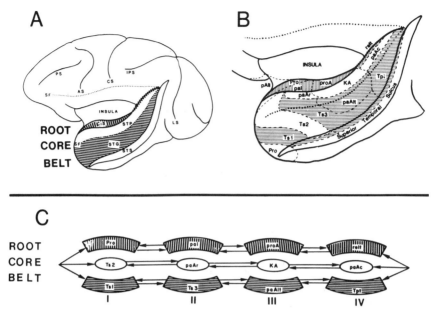

Figure 9. Diagrams of the lateral surface of the cerebral hemisphere showing the three architectonic lines (A) and architectonic areas (B) of the STR. (C) Four architectonic stages within the STR and intrinsic forward and reciprocal connections within the root, core, and belt lines.

the basis of internal states. A combination of the bidirectional information from within and from outside may play a role in the integration and interpretation of stimuli in relation to ongoing behavior. Although the data are not yet complete, preliminary investigations suggest that the forward and backgoing connections in cortical stages exist in the visual (Figure 10B) and somatosensory modalities as well.

Another key aspect of cortical connectivity involves the distant or long association connections. It has been known for quite some time that the primary sensory areas project preferentially to the parasensory association areas. The parasensory association areas in turn have sequential forward connections not only within the same system as described above but also to other more distal parts of the cortex such as the limbic and multimodal areas and the frontal lobe (Pandya & Kuypers, 1969; Jones & Powell, 1970; Chavis & Pandya, 1976; Barbas & Mesulam, 1981, 1985; Petrides & Pandya, 1984). As mentioned above, the prefrontal cortex also has evolved from two moieties, archi- and paleocortical, in a sequential manner (Figure 11). Accordingly, the orbital and medial proisocortices and immediately surrounding regions show more emphasis in the infragranular layers and have less prominent fourth layers. The laminar pattern changes as one moves toward the lateral surface of the prefrontal cortex. Initially, there is equal density of neurons in supra- and infragranular layers, and, as one approaches the caudal part of the prefrontal cortex, there seems to be more empha-

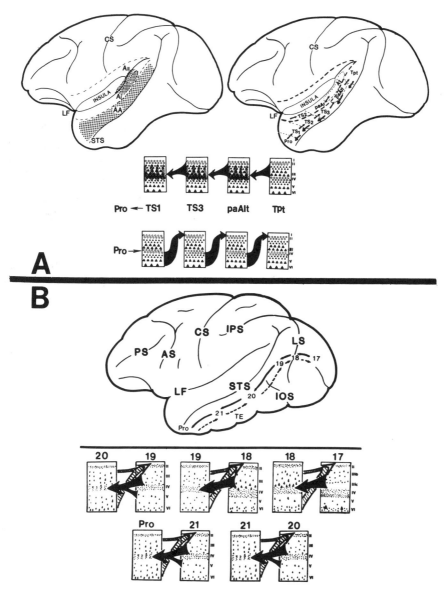

Figure 10. Diagrams showing the common patterns of laminar origins and terminations of intrinsic connections of the auditory (A) and visual (B) association areas.

sis on supragranular layers (III and IV). These progressive laminar changes beginning in the proisocortices take place in two directions, the dorsolateral and ventrolateral, respectively, from medial and ventral proisocortices (Figure 12).

In terms of long connections from the sensory association areas, the belt line regions, there are general patterns common to all modalities. Thus, in the auditory system, rostral sensory association areas with less differentiated cortical lamination project to medial and orbital regions having less differentiated architecture.

The sensory association areas with intermediate laminar architecture project preferentially to lateral prefrontal areas showing similar intermediate types of architectonic differentiation. Finally, the post-Rolandic parasensory association areas with well-developed supragranular layers send their connections mainly to the caudalmost part of prefrontal cortex, the so-called frontal eye-field, which also has well-developed supragranular layers (Figure 13).

The long association connections from visual association areas to the frontal lobe show dual patterns of organization. Sensory association areas related to central vision (inferotemporal areas) are connected preferentially with ventral and ventrolateral prefrontal areas. These visual association areas as well as their connected prefrontal regions have evolved from the paleocortical trend. In contrast, the sensory association areas relating to peripheral vision (ventral and dorsomedial occipitotemporal areas) seem to have their main frontal lobe connections with the dorsal, lateral, and medial prefrontal areas. These visual association areas and their related prefrontal regions have evolved from the archicortical trend (Figure 14). Thus, it seems that the frontal lobe connections of the belt areas

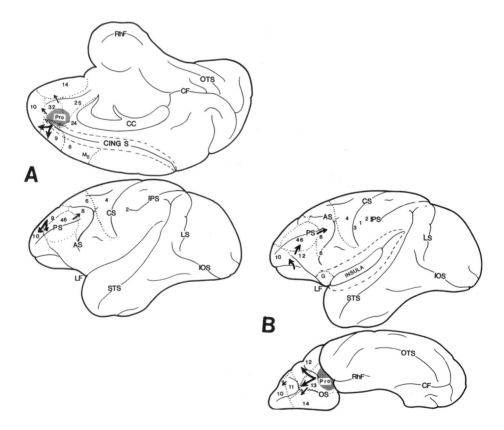

Figure 11. Diagrams showing the progressive architectonic steps from the medial proisocortex (A) and orbital proisocortex (B) of the frontal lobe.

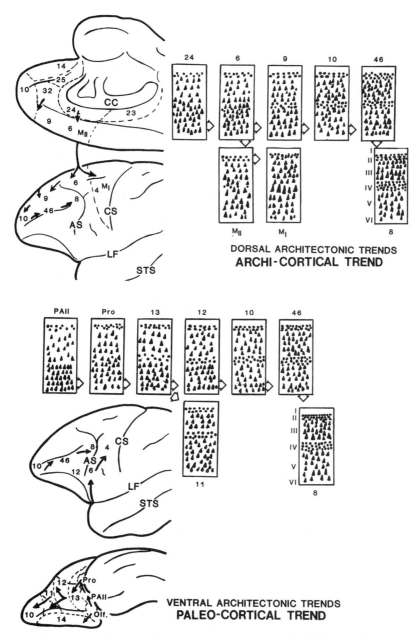

Figure 12. Depictions of camera lucida diagrams showing the differential laminar organization within the dorsal (archicortical) and ventral (paleocortical) architectonic trends of the frontal lobe.

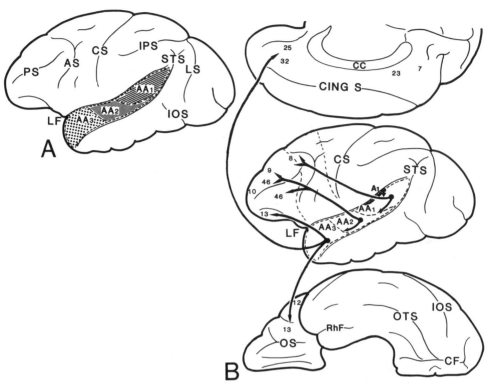

Figure 13. Diagrams showing the three divisions of the auditory association areas of the STR (A) and their long association connections to the frontal lobe (B).

are organized according to the principles of progressive architectonic development from two moieties. A similar pattern of long association connections is observed for somatosensory association regions. Thus, the somatosensory association areas of the IPL relating to face, neck, and head are connected preferentially with ventral and ventrolateral prefrontal areas. In contrast, the somatosensory areas of SPL relating to trunk and limbs appear to be most strongly connected with medial and dorsal prefrontal regions (Figure 15).

There is one more dimension that is related to cortical architecture and connections. In addition to the forward and backgoing and long connections, each sensory-related area has side-to-side or lateral connectivity (Figure 16). Thus, a core area is connected with a belt area laterally as well as a root area medially within a given stage (Galaburda & Pandya, 1983). Likewise, the root area and belt area within a given stage are interconnected. This circuitry may allow local integration of information prior to advancing it forward to other parts of the cortex. Recent studies have revealed two aspects of these side-to-side connections. For example, a core area such as the primary auditory cortex would receive connections not only from the root and belt areas of the same stage but also from the root, core, and belt areas of the rostrally and caudally adjacent

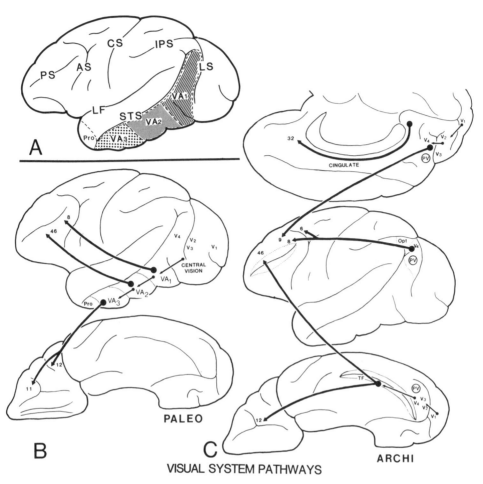

VISUAL SYSTEM PATHWAYS

Figure 14. Diagrammatic representations of the three visual association regions of the inferotemporal cortex (A) and their long association connections to the frontal lobe (B). (C) Long association connections to the frontal lobe of areas subserving peripheral vision (PV) on the medial, dorsal, and ventral surfaces of the cerebral hemisphere.

stages (Figure 17A). Thus, a core area that is highly differentiated architectonically and is located between a medial and a lateral line is connected preferentially with the cortical areas immediately surrounding it. Sanides (1969), while postulating the notion of progressive development of cortical areas, suggested that architectonic differentiation occurs in two ways: first, a gradual laminar differentiation from a proisocortex toward primary areas (linear differentiation), and second, differentiation from the peripheral areas toward a center or core region. He terms this latter concept "growth ring development." The selective connections between circumferentially situated belt and root areas and a central core region as outlined above support this notion of growth ring development (Figure 17B). Additional evidence for this growth ring concept comes from another

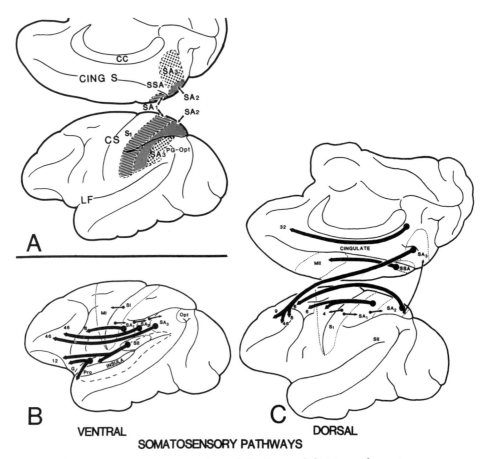

Figure 15. Diagrammatic representations of the three subdivisions of somatosensory association cortex of the inferior and superior parietal lobules (A). (B) Diagram of the frontal lobe connections of the inferior parietal lobule (ventral trend). (C) Diagram of the frontal lobe connections of the superior parietal lobule (dorsal trend).

observation. A belt area is connected with core and root areas of the same stage but additionally is connected with belt and root areas of adjacent rostral and caudal stages. Thus, a given cortical area is connected preferentially with other areas within the circumference of the growth ring (Figure 18).

The center or core, with more cellular differentiation compared to peripheral cortex, has another dimension related to multimodal areas. We focus on the multimodal areas of the parietotemporal region. Physiological and anatomic studies have shown that there are several multimodal regions in post-Rolandic cortex, especially at the junction of the sensory modalities (Figure 19). These regions receive input from unimodal parasensory association areas of the auditory, visual, and somatosensory systems (Jones & Powell, 1970; Seltzer & Pandya, 1978). Likewise, the neurons of these regions respond to more than one modality

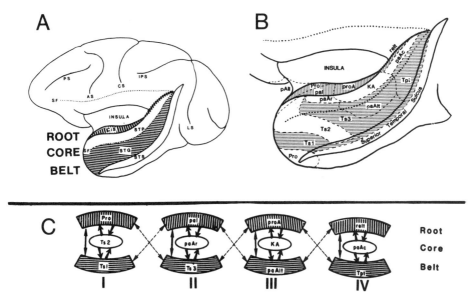

Figure 16. (A and B) Diagrams showing the root, core, and belt lines and architectonic areas of the STR. (C) Schematic representation showing the side-to-side connections between the subregions of the root, core, and belt lines in the STR.

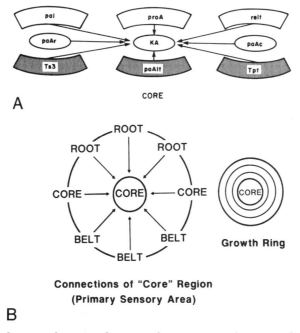

Figure 17. (A) Schematic diagrams depicting the connectional pattern of a core area (KA) of the superior temporal region. (B) Schematic diagrams showing the growth ring concept in the auditory system with regard to primary (core) regions.

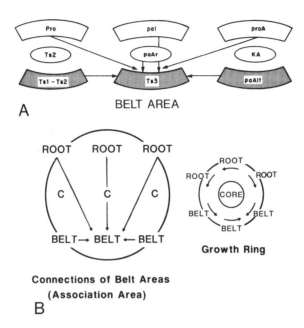

Figure 18. (A) Schematic diagrams showing the connectional pattern of a belt area (Ts_3) in the superior temporal region. (B) Diagrams illustrating the growth ring concept with regard to association area (root and belt) connections in the auditory system.

and have a role in complex functions such as the perception of faces or body movement (Benevento, Fallon, Davis, & Rezak, 1977; Desimone & Gross, 1979; Bruce, Desimone, & Gross, 1981; Baylis, Rolls, & Leonard, 1987; Perrett, Mistlin, & Chitty, 1987). Seven such regions have been described in the post-Rolandic cortex (Figure 20). They are in the insular cortex (Mesulam & Mufson, 1982b), the superior temporal sulcus (areas TPO and PGa) (Seltzer & Pandya, 1978), the inferior parietal lobule (area PG-Opt), the lower bank of the intraparietal sulcus (area POa) (Seltzer & Pandya, 1980), the caudal medial parietal lobe (area PGm), the cingulate retrosplenial region (Barnes & Pandya, 1987), and the parahippocampal gyrus (Seltzer & Pandya, 1978).

The precise way in which these multimodal regions fit into a cortical evolutionary architectonic framework is currently under investigation. We wish, however, to present preliminary data to elaborate on the organization of the multimodal areas. As shown previously, the superior temporal region relates to the auditory modality. This region comprises four stages, each containing root, core, and belt areas. These unimodal areas are flanked by the superior temporal sulcus (STS) on one side and the insula on the other (Figure 21). Both of these regions, insula and STS, contain multimodal areas. Likewise, the unimodal visual area of the inferotemporal region lies between the multimodal areas of the STS and the parahippocampal gyrus (Desimone & Gross, 1979). The somatosensory association areas of IPL are surrounded by multimodal areas of STS ventrally and areas

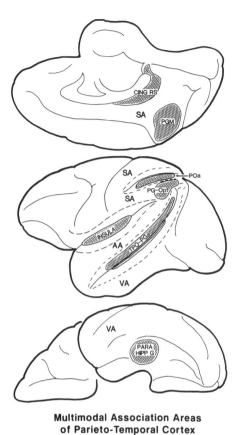

**Multimodal Association Areas
of Parieto-Temporal Cortex**

Figure 19. Diagrams showing the locations of post-Rolandic multimodal areas of the medial, lateral, and ventral regions of the cerebral hemisphere.

POa as well as PG-Opt dorsocaudally. Similarly, the somatosensory association areas of SPL are positioned between area PGm and the cingulate retrosplenial cortex (Figure 19).

The significance of the location of these multimodal areas at the borders of each of the major sensory modalities is not clear. However, it seems that these multimodal areas have selective connectivity with the parasensory association areas of the belt line. Thus, a belt line region of the superior temporal gyrus—the auditory association area—is connected with multimodal area TPO of STS on one hand and with the insula on the other (Figure 22). Architectonic studies have differentiated insular cortex into four regions: proisocortical, agranular, dysgranular, and granular insula (Roberts & Akert, 1963; Mesulam & Mufson, 1982a). Likewise, our recent observations (Seltzer & Pandya, 1986) seem to show that there are four rostrocaudal subdivisions having progressive laminar differentiation in the multimodal cortex of STS (Pro, TPO$_1$, TPO$_2$, TPO$_3$). These architectonic and connectional data suggest that the peripherally located multimodal areas, which are undifferentiated in regard to sensory functions, may comprise the outermost ring from which modality-specific areas may be developed (Figure

Multimodal Areas of Parieto-Temporal Cortex

①   INSULAR CORTEX
(SOMATOSENSORY, GUSTATORY, AUDITORY)

②   SUPERIOR TEMPORAL SULCUS (TPO, PGa)
(AUDITORY, SOMATOSENSORY, VISUAL)

③   CAUDAL INFERIOR PARIETAL LOBULE (PG, Opt)
(VISUAL, SOMATOSENSORY)

④   INTRAPARIETAL SULCUS (POa)
(SOMATOSENSORY, VISUAL)

⑤   MEDIAL PARIETAL (PGM)
(SOMATOSENSORY, VISUAL, AUDITORY) (PO)

⑥   CINGULATE RETROSPLENIAL
(SOMATOSENSORY, VISUAL, AUDITORY)

⑦   PARAHIPPOCAMPAL GYRUS
(AUDITORY, VISUAL, SOMATOSENSORY)

Figure 20. Summary of the nature of sensory convergence in the post-Rolandic multimodal areas shown in Figure 19.

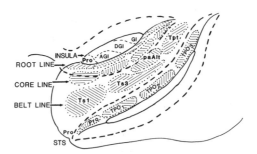

Multimodal Areas of INSULA and STS
and Modality Related Areas
of Superior Temporal Gyrus

Figure 21. Diagram showing the root, core, and belt line regions of the STR as well as the architectonic subregions of the adjoining multimodal areas of the insula and the superior temporal sulcus (STS). Note that the insular cortex contains four discrete rostrocaudal regions: Pro, proisocortex; AGI, agranular insula; DGI, dysgranular insula; and GI, granular insula. Note also that the multimodal area of the STS contains four rostrocaudal regions: Pro, TPO_1, TPO_2, and TPO_3.

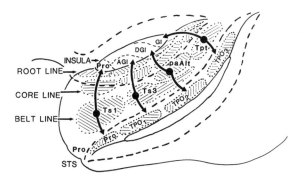

**Connections of Unimodal Association Areas
with Surrounding Association Area of INSULA and STS**

Figure 22. Diagram showing the connectional relationship between the auditory association area of the belt line and the adjoining multimodal regions of the insula and the superior temporal sulcus.

23). Like the unimodal areas, these multimodal regions may also have evolved from proisocortices, but they have remained undifferentiated in regard to specific modality. Going one step further, these multimodal areas located at the periphery of unimodal sensory areas can be thought of as the outermost parts of the developing growth rings. Multimodal areas have long been regarded as representing the highest development in the cerebral cortex, endowing us with the ability to carry out complex functions such as language and attention. It should be pointed out that these functions must have evolved from basic mechanisms as differentiation took place in both modality-specific and multimodal regions. This concept may be extended to the multimodal areas surrounding the somatosensory and visual regions as well.

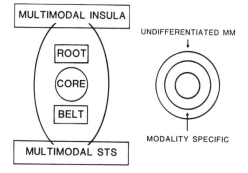

Figure 23. Schematic diagram (left) depicting the interrelationship between unimodal (root, core, and belt) and multimodal regions of the insula and superior temporal sulcus (STS). Diagrammatic representation (right) of the growth ring concept based on the relationship between modality-specific and undifferentiated multimodal (MM) regions (see text).

Discussion

In recent years, anatomic, physiological, and behavioral studies have emphasized a "sequential processing" model of cerebral organization (Mishkin, 1966; Hubel & Wiesel, 1968, 1972; Jones & Powell, 1970; Diamond, 1979; Pandya & Seltzer, 1982a, 1982b). According to this notion, peripheral sensory input, by way of the thalamus, first reaches the level of the cerebral cortex in the various primary sensory cortices. This input is then relayed through a series of adjoining parasensory regions, each step presumably involving the sequential analysis and elaboration of the incoming elementary sensory information. Furthermore, each parasensory area then sends distant projections to diverse regions of the hemisphere such as the frontal lobe and the post-Rolandic polymodal cortices.

According to the sequential processing model, each intrinsic or distant connection is related to some differential function, albeit within the confines of a given modality. For example, in the visual system, the more distant one is from primary visual regions, the more contingencies are evident in the response properties of visually related cortical areas (e.g., Wurtz, Goldberg, & Robinson, 1980). Although the sequential processing model has received experimental support as a valid approach to the analysis of cerebral function, recent anatomic and physiological observations raise certain questions. The first of these concerns the demonstration of reciprocal sequences leading to, rather than from, primary cortex. In addition, the traditional "association" areas of the cortex also receive relatively simple sensory input from the periphery by way of various subcortical structures without the mediation of their primary cortical areas (Diamond, 1979; Van Essen & Maunsell, 1983). Furthermore, many physiological studies have shown that it is possible to record responses to relatively simple, albeit subtly different, auditory, visual, and somatic sensory stimuli in many of the traditional association areas of the cerebral cortex. These so-called "multiple sensory and motor representations" have been attributed to a parallel processing of various types of sensory and motor information by way of subcortical projections to primary and association areas of the cortex (Trevarthen, 1968; Merzenich & Brugge, 1973; Zeki, 1978; Kaas et al., 1979; Muakkassa & Strick, 1979; Stone, Dreher, & Levinthal, 1979; Lennie, 1980; Woolsey, 1981a, 1981b, 1981c; Stone & Dreher, 1982; Ungerleider & Mishkin, 1982; Dykes, 1983; Maunsell & Van Essen, 1983; Van Essen & Maunsell, 1983).

Although there may appear to be a conflict between the sequential and parallel processing models, this need not be the case. The organization of the cerebral cortex proposed here views different areas of the cortex in the context of their stage of architectonic differentiation. This adds an entirely new dimension to our understanding of cortical function. According to this approach, the multiple sensory and motor representations that have been demonstrated in recent physiological and anatomic studies may correspond to the progressive architectonic stages. Thus, each successive architectonic step may be conceptualized as involving the addition of a new sensory or motor representation and the acquisition of an additional functional dimension. Since the most distal zones, corresponding to the primary and supplementary sensory and motor cortices, are the most differentiated in terms of cortical architectonics, they may also represent the most complex level of cortical functions. This situation is well illustrated by the auditory system, where Merzenich and Brugge (1973) have shown that multiple auditory representations recorded in the parakoniocortical regions of the superior temporal region correspond with the various cytoarchitectonic areas (Figure 24). Similarly, in the somatic sensory system, Kaas et al. (1979) have shown a correlation between physiologically defined representations and architectonic regions.

The existence of both forward and reciprocal flows of connectivity within each sensory modality is consistent with the evolutionary architectonic concept. Thus, as new areas evolved progressively within cortical sensory systems, specific patterns of connectivity between older and newer regions also developed. The bidirectional connectivity observed within cortical sensory systems allows for communication between proisocortical and more highly developed areas. Such connectivity may subserve the integration of peripheral input with the internal state of the organism. Just as afferent sensory information arrives via the thalamus at the primary cortical level and is subsequently elaborated on through sequential association connections, so also may internal or limbic information proceed from proisocortices towards primary regions via reciprocal connections. The forward and reciprocal flows of information may interact at some level within cortical sensory areas and thereby play a role in processes such as selective attention and memory formation and retrieval.

Studies of the long corticocortical projections of post-Rolandic sensory systems reveal common principles of organization. As pointed out above, on the basis of architecture as well as their connections to the frontal cortices, the association areas in each modality can be divided into three major sectors. The first-order association areas in each modality send projections predominantly to the periarcuate (premotor) regions, whereas second-order areas are most strongly connected with prearcuate (prefrontal) regions. Finally, the third-order visual and auditory association areas project preferentially to orbital and medial frontal regions, whereas the third-order somatosensory association areas project to the rostral prefrontal region. It is of great interest to note that each sector of the sensory association areas is connected with a frontal lobe region that has basically similar architectonic features and that the predominant laminar origins of the post-Rolandic projections are consistent with the predominant architectonic characteristics of the frontal areas to which they project. In other words, each post-Rolandic area tends to be connected with a portion of the frontal lobe that appears to occupy a similar stage of architectonic differentiation. This implies that each sensory association area, from first order through second order to third order, may have developed in parallel with a specific frontal lobe region and,

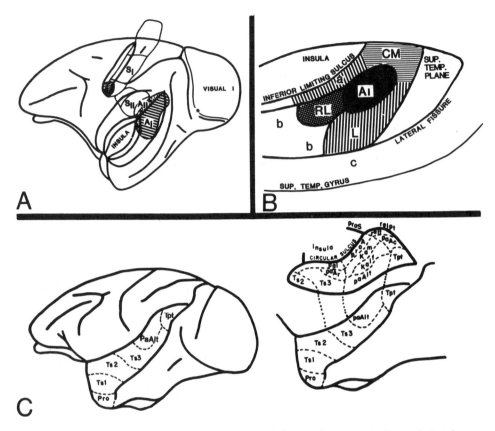

Figure 24. (A) Diagram of the lateral surface of the cerebral hemisphere of the rhesus monkey showing locations of primary and secondary auditory (A_I and A_{II}), somatosensory (S_I and S_{II}), and visual (V_I) areas as described by Woolsey and Fairman (1946). Note that the Sylvian fissure is opened to expose the depths. (B) Schematic drawing of the supratemporal plane and superior temporal gyrus showing major subdivisions of auditory areas based on the cytoarchitectonic and physiological observations of Merzenich and Brugge (1973). A_I, primary auditory field; RL, rostrolateral field; L, lateral field; CM, caudomedial field; a, field bordering AI medially and rostrally, buried in the circular sulcus; b, area of auditory cortex rostral and lateral to other fields; c, lateral surface of superior temporal gyrus with additional auditory fields. (C) Architectonic parcellation of the superior temporal gyrus and supratemporal plane as described by Pandya and Sanides (1973).

with that region, may constitute a functional subsystem within the cerebral cortex. Additional support for this concept is provided by the existence of recriprocal connections from frontal regions back to post-Rolandic sensory association areas (Pandya & Yeterian, 1985).

It is of interest to note that the existence of dual architectonic trends is reflected in the patterns of connectivity between post-Rolandic and frontal regions. Thus, in the somatosensory system, the inferior parietal association regions relating to the head, neck, and face project to the ventral frontal cortices—the paleocortical trend. In contrast, the superior and medial parietal association areas relating to the trunk and limbs project to the dorsal and medial regions—the archicortical trend of the frontal lobe (Figure 15). In the visual system, the association areas of the inferior temporal region relating to central vision project to the ventral portion of the frontal lobe—the paleocortical trend. In contrast, the dorsomedial and ventral visual association areas relating to peripheral vision project to the dorsal and medial portions of the frontal lobe—the archicortical trend (Figure 14).

This connectivity is consistent with the concept of a dual nature of cortical origin and implies that these connectional systems subserve differential functions. Thus, based on its connections from the face, head, and neck regions of the somatosensory association cortex, from the inferior temporal region relating to central vision, and from ventral temporal paralimbic regions, the ventral frontal areas appear to be closely tied to the synthesis of object–emotion relationships in a behavioral context. It is not unreasonable to view the information regarding object identity and significance conveyed from post-Rolandic areas to the frontal lobe as a key aspect of the emotional reactivity long ascribed to ventral frontal regions (Figure 25). Damage to the ventral frontal region has been associated with shallow mentation or emotion (e.g., Stuss & Benson, 1986).

The connectivity from the trunk and limb regions of the somatosensory association cortex, from visual association areas relating to peripheral vision, as well as from medial paralimbic cortices may be involved in the integration of visuospatial and motivational processes (Figure 26). In this regard, it is reasonable to consider the coming together of trunk and limb information and peripheral visual and midline limbic influences as essential for the energizing and guidance of behavior in three-dimensional space. This notion receives support from clinical observations that damage to the cingulate gyrus leads to an akinetic state and likewise that supplementary motor area damage leads to a hesitancy in speech and in initiating movement (Figure 26). Moreover, medial prefrontal damage leads to so-called apathetic states (e.g., Damasio, 1985; Stuss & Benson, 1986).

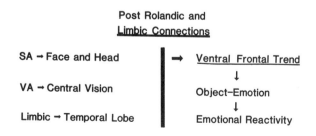

Figure 25. Summary of post-Rolandic and limbic connections of the ventral (paleocortical) trend with regard to functional significance.

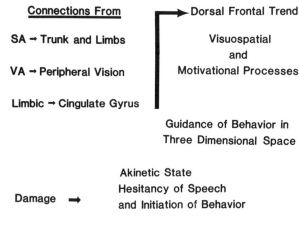

Figure 26. Summary of post-Rolandic and limbic connections of the dorsal (archicortical) trend with regard to functional significance.

The multimodal areas have long been regarded as representing the highest level of development in the cerebral cortex. These areas have been considered as substrates for complex functions such as language and attention. From the perspective of evolutionary architectonics and local cortical connectivity, it seems that the multimodal areas occupy a most peripheral position, from which modality-specific cortices may have evolved. It is thought that the primary sensory areas deal with the elementary analysis of sensory information. However, viewed in light of the growth ring concept, primary areas may have evolved from the undifferentiated multimodal areas to provide for more specific and complex functions, albeit within single sensory modalities. The multimodal areas, which are undifferentiated with regard to sensory modality, may deal with broadly integrative functions and appear to lack the potential for highly specialized analysis of sensory-specific information (Figure 27). In this regard, it is interesting to note that in lower animals, modality specificity is less clear-cut, and a greater proportion of the cerebral cortex is multimodal in nature. Although it may be true that multimodal areas collectively are less differentiated than the modality-specific regions, it should be emphasized that multimodal areas themselves show a progressive architectonic differentiation from the proisocortex just as the sensory-specific areas do. This suggests that within the progression of multimodal areas, differential levels of functional complexity may have evolved. Thus, for example, the angular gyrus, which represents a high level of multimodal differentiation, seems to be concerned with the most advanced processes of communication in humans, namely, linguistic function.

It has been traditional to consider the primary sensory and modality-specific association areas as subserving elementary functions, whereas the multimodal areas are thought to be involved in complex integrative processes. According to

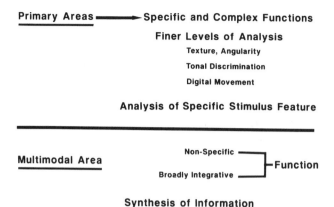

Figure 27. Summary of the relationship of primary and multimodal cortical regions to analytical and synthetic functions, respectively.

the concepts of evolutionary architectonics and growth rings described above, primary regions that are located at the central point of their respective growth rings may be viewed as cortical areas with the greatest architectonic differentiation. Thus, the primary sensory and motor areas, rather than being considered to subserve relatively simple functions, may be viewed as being involved in finer levels of analysis. For example, the perception of texture and angularity, tonal discrimination, as well as digital movements may be considered to be highly refined aspects of sensory and motor function that are subserved by the primary cortices. In contrast, multimodal areas that are at the periphery of modality-specific regions are relatively less differentiated and subserve nonspecific functions. That is, multimodal areas appear to play a role in the *synthesis* of information at the cortical level rather than in the *analysis* of specific stimulus features (Figure 27). The analytical aspect of cortical function that involves the fractionation of sensory and motor spheres into smaller units is perhaps related to the primary cortices. This is not to imply that analytic and synthetic functions are mutually exclusive. Rather, our intent is to provide an overall functional framework that may be helpful in understanding cortical architecture and evolutionary progression. Thus, within the cerebral cortex, it appears that the evolution of primary sensory and motor areas represents an elaboration of analytic processes, whereas the evolution of multimodal regions is in the direction of synthetic capabilities.

REFERENCES

Abbie, A. A. (1940). Cortical lamination in the monotremata. *Journal of Comparative Neurology, 72,* 429–467.

Barbas, H., & Mesulam, M.-M. (1981). Organization of afferent input to subdivisions of area 8 in the rhesus monkey. *Journal of Comparative Neurology, 200,* 407–432.

Barbas, H., & Mesulam, M.-M. (1985). Cortical afferent input to the principalis region of the rhesus monkey. *Neuroscience, 15,* 619–637.

Barnes, C. L., & Pandya, D. N. (1987). Multimodal efferent projections from the posterior cingulate cortex in the rhesus monkey. *Society for Neuroscience Abstracts, 12,* 1099.

Baylis, G. C., Rolls, E. T., & Leonard, C. M. (1987). Functional subdivisions of the temporal lobe neocortex. *Journal of Neuroscience, 7,* 330–342.

Benevento, L. A., Fallon, J., Davis, B. J., & Rezak, M. (1977). Auditory–visual interaction in single cells in the cortex of the superior temporal sulcus and orbital frontal cortex of the macaque monkey. *Experimental Neurology, 57,* 849–872.

Bonin, G. von, & Bailey, P. (1947). *The neocortex of Macaca mulatta.* Urbana: University of Illinois Press.

Brodmann, K. (1909). *Vergleichende Lokalisationlehre der Grosshirnrinde in ihren Prinzipien dargestellt auf Grund des Zellenbaues.* Leipzig: Barth.

Bruce, C., Desimone, R., & Gross, C. G. (1981). Visual properties of neurons in a polysensory area in superior temporal sulcus of the macaque. *Journal of Neurophysiology, 46,* 369–384.

Burdach, K. F. (1819–1826). *Vom Baue und Leben des Gehirns* (Vol. 2, 1822). Leipzig: Dyk'schen Buchhandlung.

Campbell, A. W. (1905). *Histological studies on the localisation of cerebral function.* London: Cambridge University Press.

Chavis, D. A., & Pandya, D. N. (1976). Further observations on corticofrontal connections in the rhesus monkey. *Brain Research, 117,* 369–386.

Cowan, W. M., Gottlieb, D. I., Hendrickson, A. E., Price, J. L., & Woolsey, T. A. (1972). The autoradiographic demonstration of axonal connections in the central nervous system. *Brain Research, 37,* 21–51.

Damasio, A. R. (1985). The frontal lobes. In K. M. Heilman & E. Valenstein (Eds.), *Clinical neuropsychology* (2nd ed., pp. 339–375). New York: Oxford University Press.

Dart, R. A. (1934). The dual structure of the neopallium: Its history and significance. *Journal of Anatomy, 69,* 3–19.

Déjerine, J. (1895). *Anatomie de centres nerveux.* Paris: Rueff.

Desimone, R., & Gross, C. G. (1979). Visual areas in the temporal cortex of the macaque. *Brain Research, 178,* 363–380.

Diamond, I. T. (1979). The subdivisions of neocortex: A proposal to revise the traditional view of sensory, motor and association areas. *Progress in Psychobiology, Physiology and Psychology, 8,* 1–43.

Dykes, R. W. (1983). Parallel processing of somatosensory information: A theory. *Brain Research Reviews, 6,* 47–115.

Economo, G. von, & Koskinas, G. N. (1925). *Die Cytoarchitektonik der Hirnrinde des erwachsenen Menschen.* Berlin: Springer.

Fink, R. P., & Heimer, L. (1967). Two methods for selective silver impregnation of degenerating axons and their synaptic endings in the central nervous system. *Brain Research, 4,* 369–374.

Galaburda, A. M., & Pandya, D. N. (1983). The intrinsic architectonic and connectional organization of the superior temporal region of the rhesus monkey. *Journal of Comparative Neurology, 221,* 169–184.

Geschwind, N. (1965a). Disconnexion syndromes in animals and man: Part I. *Brain, 88,* 237–294.

Geschwind, N. (1965b). Disconnexion syndromes in animals and man: Part II. *Brain, 88,* 585–644.

Hubel, D. H., & Wiesel, T. N. (1968). Receptive fields and functional architecture of monkey striate cortex. *Journal of Physiology (London), 195*, 215–243.

Hubel, D. H., & Wiesel, T. N. (1972). Laminar and columnar distribution of geniculo-cortical fibers in the macaque monkey. *Journal of Comparative Neurology, 146*, 421–450.

Jones, E. G., & Powell, T. P. S. (1970). An anatomical study of converging sensory pathways within the cerebral cortex of the monkey. *Brain, 93*, 793–820.

Kaas, J. H., Nelson, R. J., Sur, M., Lin, C.-S., & Merzenich, M. (1979). Multiple representations of the body within the primary somatosensory cortex of primates. *Science, 204*, 521–523.

Krieg, W. J. S. (1963). *Connections of the cerebral cortex.* Evanston, IL: Brain Books.

Kuypers, H. G. J. M., Catsman-Berrevoets, C. E., & Padt, R. E. (1977). Retrograde axonal transport of fluorescent substances in the rat's forebrain. *Neuroscience Letters, 6*, 127–135.

Kuypers, H. G. J. M., Szwarcbart, M. K., Mishkin, M., & Rosvold, H. E. (1965). Occipito-temporal corticocortical connections in the rhesus monkey. *Experimental Neurology, 11*, 245–262.

LaVail, J. H., & LaVail, M. M. (1972). Retrograde axonal transport in the central nervous system. *Science, 176*, 1416–1417.

Lennie, P. (1980). Parallel visual pathways: A review. *Vision Research, 20*, 561–594.

Maunsell, J. H. R., & Van Essen, D. C. (1983). The connections of the middle temporal visual area (MT) and their relationship to a cortical hierarchy in the macaque monkey. *Journal of Neuroscience, 3*, 2563–2586.

Merzenich, M. M., & Brugge, J. F. (1973). Representation of the cochlear partition on the superior temporal plane of the macaque monkey. *Brain Research, 50*, 275–296.

Mesulam, M.-M. (1982). Principles of horseradish peroxidase neurohistochemistry and their applications for tracing neural pathways—axonal transport, enzyme histochemistry and light microscopic analysis. In M.-M. Mesulam (Ed.), *Tracing neural connections with horseradish peroxidase* (pp. 1–151). Chichester: John Wiley & Sons.

Mesulam, M.-M., & Mufson, E. J. (1982a). Insula of the Old World monkey. I. Architectonics in the insulo-orbito-temporal component of the paralimbic brain. *Journal of Comparative Neurology, 212*, 1–22.

Mesulam, M.-M., & Mufson, E.J. (1982b). Insula of the Old World monkey: III. Efferent cortical output and comments on function. *Journal of Comparative Neurology, 212*, 38–52.

Mettler, F. A. (1935a). Corticofugal fiber connections of the cortex of *Macaca mulatta.* The occipital region. *Journal of Comparative Neurology, 61*, 221–256.

Mettler, F. A. (1935b). Corticofugal fiber connections of the cortex of *Macaca mulatta.* The frontal region. *Journal of Comparative Neurology, 61*, 509–542.

Mettler, F. A. (1935c). Corticofugal fiber connections of the cortex of *Macaca mulatta.* The parietal region. *Journal of Comparative Neurology, 62*, 263–291.

Mettler, F. A. (1935d). Corticofugal fiber connections of the cortex of *Macaca mulatta.* The temporal region. *Journal of Comparative Neurology, 63*, 25–47.

Mishkin, M. (1966). Visual mechanisms beyond the striate cortex. In R. W. Russell (Ed.), *Frontiers in physiological psychology* (pp. 93–119). New York: Academic Press.

Mishkin, M., Ungerleider, L. G., & Macko, K. A. (1983). Object vision and spatial vision: Two cortical pathways. *Trends in Neurosciences, 6*, 414–417.

Muakkassa, K. F., & Strick, P. L. (1979). Frontal lobe inputs to primate motor cortex: Evidence for four somatotopically organized (premotor) areas. *Brain Research, 17*, 176–182.

Nauta, W. J. H. (1957). Silver impregnation of degenerating axons. In W. F. Windle (Ed.), *New research techniques of neuroanatomy* (pp. 17–26). Springfield, IL: Charles C. Thomas.

Pandya, D. N., & Kuypers, H. G. J. M. (1969). Cortico-cortical connections in the rhesus monkey. *Brain Research, 13,* 13–36.

Pandya, D. N., & Sanides, F. (1973). Architectonic parcellation of the temporal operculum in the rhesus monkey and its projection pattern. *Zeitschrift für Anatomie und Entwicklungsgeschichte, 139,* 127–161.

Pandya, D. N., & Seltzer, B. (1982a). Association areas of the cerebral cortex. *Trends in Neurosciences, 5,* 386–390.

Pandya, D. N., & Seltzer, B. (1982b). Intrinsic connections and architectonics of posterior parietal cortex in the rhesus monkey. *Journal of Comparative Neurology, 204,* 196–210.

Pandya, D. N., Seltzer, B., & Barbas, H. (1988). Input–output organization of primate cerebral cortex. In H. D. Steklis & J. Erwin (Eds.), *Comparative primate biology: Vol. 4. Neurosciences* (pp. 39–80). New York: Alan R. Liss.

Pandya, D. N., & Yeterian, E. H. (1985). Architecture and connections of cortical association areas. In A. Peters & E. G. Jones (Eds.), *Cerebral cortex* (Vol. 4., pp. 3–61). New York: Plenum Press.

Paul, R. L., Merzenich, M. M., & Goodman, H. (1975). Mechanoreceptor representation and topography of Brodmann's areas 3 and 1 of *Macaca mulatta.* In H. H. Kornhuber (Ed.), *The somatosensory system* (pp. 262–269). Stuttgart: G. Theime.

Perrett, D. I., Mistlin, A. J., & Chitty, A. J. (1987). Visual neurones responsive to faces. *Trends in Neurosciences, 10,* 358–364.

Petrides, M., & Pandya, D. N. (1984). Projections to the frontal cortex from the posterior parietal region in the rhesus monkey. *Journal of Comparative Neurology, 228,* 105–116.

Reil, J. C. (1809). Die sylvische Grube. *Archiv der Physiologie (Halle), 9,* 195–208.

Roberts, T. S., & Akert, K. (1963). Insular and opercular cortex and its thalamic projections in *Macaca mulatta. Schweitzer Archiv der Neurologie Neurochirurgie und Psychiatrie, 92,* 1–43.

Rockland, K. S., & Pandya, D. N. (1979). Laminar origins and terminations of cortical connections of the occipital lobe in rhesus monkey. *Brain Research, 179,* 3–20.

Sanides, F. (1969). Comparative architectonics of the neocortex of mammals and their evolutionary interpretation. *Annals of the New York Academy of Sciences, 167,* 404–423.

Seltzer, B., & Pandya, D. N. (1978). Afferent cortical connections and architectonics of the superior temporal sulcus and surrounding cortex in the rhesus monkey. *Brain Research, 149,* 1–24.

Seltzer, B., & Pandya, D. N. (1980). Converging visual and somatic sensory cortical input to the intraparietal sulcus of the rhesus monkey. *Brain Research, 192,* 339–351.

Seltzer, B., & Pandya, D. N. (1986). Frontal lobe connections of the superior temporal sulcus in the rhesus monkey. *Journal of Comparative Neurology, 281,* 97–113.

Stone, J., & Dreher, B. (1982). Parallel processing of information in the visual pathways. A general principle of sensory coding? *Trends in Neurosciences, 5,* 441–446.

Stone, J., Dreher, B., & Leventhal, A. (1979). Hierarchical and parallel mechanisms in the organization of visual cortex. *Brain Research Reviews, 1,* 345–394.

Stuss, D. T., & Benson, F. D. (1986). *The frontal lobes.* New York: Raven Press.

Tigges, J., Spatz, W. B., & Tigges, M. (1973). Reciprocal point-to-point connections between parastriate and striate cortex in the squirrel monkey (*Saimiri*). *Journal of Comparative Neurology, 148,* 481–490.

Trevarthen, C. B. (1968). Two mechanisms of vision in primates. *Psychologische Forschung, 31*, 299–337.

Ungerleider, L. G., & Mishkin, M. (1982). Two cortical visual systems. In D. J. Ingle, M. A. Goodale, & R. J. W. Mansfield (Eds.), *Analysis of visual behavior* (pp. 549–586). Cambridge, MA: MIT Press.

Van Essen, D. C., & Maunsell, J. H. R. (1983). Hierarchical organization and functional streams in the visual cortex. *Trends in Neurosciences, 6*, 370–375.

Vogt, B. A., & Pandya, D. N. (1978). Corticocortical connections of somatic sensory cortex (areas 3, 1 and 2) in the rhesus monkey. *Journal of Comparative Neurology, 177*, 179–192.

Vogt, C., & Vogt, O. (1919). Allgemeine Ergebnisse unserer Hirnforschung. *Journal für Psychologie und Neurologie, 25*, 279–461.

Woolsey, C. N. (1981a). *Cortical sensory organization: Vol. 1. Multiple somatic areas.* Clifton, NJ: Humana Press.

Woolsey, C. N. (1981b). *Cortical sensory organization: Vol. 2. Multiple visual areas.* Clifton, NJ: Humana Press.

Woolsey, C. N. (1982). *Cortical sensory organization: Vol. 3. Multiple auditory areas.* Clifton, NJ: Humana Press.

Woolsey, C. N., & Fairman, D. (1946). Contralateral, ipsilateral and bilateral representation of cutaneous receptors in somatic areas I and II of the cerebral cortex of pig, sheep and other mammals. *Surgery, 19*, 684–702.

Wurtz, R. H., Goldberg, M. E., & Robinson, D. L. (1980). Behavioral modulation of visual responses in the monkey: Stimulus selection for attention and movement. *Progress in Psychobiology and Physiological Psychology, 9*, 43–83.

Zeki, S. M. (1978). Functional specialization in the visual cortex of the rhesus monkey. *Nature, 274*, 423–428.

DISCUSSION

ERAN ZAIDEL: I'm sorry, but I'm not quite sure I understand. With regard to the progression you are showing, is this something embryonic? Is it something that develops? When did all this happen? I have a comment too. It seems to me that what you're proposing is a very nice neural basis for what the cognitive psychologists call "top-down processes" in which you go from more general global features of the stimulus to more specific analyses. Usually we think about it the other way.

DEEPAK PANDYA: As I said before, this is neither ontogeny nor phylogeny. This is a sort of progression that we see by analyzing the cortex of a monkey brain, adult or young.

ZAIDEL: Where did the progression come from?

PANDYA: Architectonic progression described here is based on the hypothesis of dual origin of cerebral cortex as proposed by Dart, Abbie, and Sanides. But I have not studied all species, so I cannot say that the progression has come from lower vertebrates to the higher primate.

ARNOLD SCHEIBEL: I must admit I have a little trouble in the same area.

Ordinarily when we talk about the rise of the primate brain, we contrast the very large areas of what we call "committed," which essentially means specific, cortex with the very small amounts of what we then call "uncommitted" or association cortex in rodents, in carnivores, and in lower primates. And yet if I understood you, you're saying that in some way, association cortex or uncommitted cortex predates committed or specific sensory areas.

PANDYA: Yes. That is precisely what I'm saying. It is the undifferentiated periphery that represents the initial type of cortex. From there the modality specificity occurs, and it occurs with its limbic root line, which is called the primary line, and with its association lines. That's a totally different type of concept, but that's what we come out with.

JASON BROWN: I think it's fairly exciting and revolutionary, and I think there's a good deal of clinical neuropsychology supporting it. Eran and I have been talking about this, and I think the bottom line is whether processing in cognition retraces the phyloontogenetic progression that you described. One thing comes to my mind when you describe these changes or these gradual movements. I have the feeling of a kind of wave-like transition, but when you describe the beautiful connectivity in the system, the symmetry of connections across levels and the reciprocity between levels, one suspects a discontinuity in the processing. The possibility of either a wave-like or a saltatory progression comes to mind. I wonder whether you would address that.

PANDYA: There are two modes of progression. The best-known type is linear progression from the proisocortex toward the primary region. The other progression seems to occur from surrounding multimodal areas in circular fashion. Thus the linear and circular progressions lead to modality-specific regions.

JOHN SCHLAG: This is a continuation of Dr. Scheibel's question. It's surprising and interesting that we should start with the uncommitted and go to the committed, and I guess the cortex is becoming committed when it receives an input from a specific modality. Could you tell us at what stage the thalamic system is coming into the picture?

PANDYA: Very good. Unfortunately I haven't brought the slide because this time I was not going to talk about thalamus. But we have ongoing thalamic connectivity studies that concur with the model. In thalamic connectivity, let's say in the auditory region, the surrounding fields (i.e., root and belt areas) are connected with the pulvinar. The rootline areas are mainly connected with VPI and MGmc (magnocellular division of medial geniculate nucleus), whereas the beltline areas are preferentially connected with the medial pulvinar and supragreniculate nuclei. The primary region (i.e., core line area) is the one that connects with the medial geniculate. These progressions occur in parallel to the progression that we see in cortex.

SCHEIBEL: This is a very interesting concept.

NEURONAL DISCRIMINATION AND SHORT-TERM MEMORY IN ASSOCIATION CORTEX

JOAQUIN M. FUSTER, MD, PhD
University of California, Los Angeles

INTRODUCTION

The cognition and re-cognition of the world around us depend on the functional integrity of two large and interrelated groups of neural structures. One is made up of the so-called "sensory systems," that is, the subcortical and cortical regions and pathways that subserve the analysis of the physical attributes of sensory stimuli; we may assume that its infrastructure and functions are firmly determined by evolution and subject to relatively little modification by postnatal experience. The other group of structures is made up of limbic cortex and its ancient derivatives, notably the amygdala and hippocampus and, in addition, large expanses of temporal and parietal neocortex; we may assume that its infrastructure and functions are heavily dependent on individual experience.

Cognitive representations are presumably evoked and reevoked in associative cortex by the intervention of limbic structures in ways that are not well understood. It is clear, however, from the results of lesions in humans and monkeys that temporal and parietal regions of that cortex are critically implicated in neural representations of sensory percepts and memories. In any event, lesion studies cannot provide evidence of either the neural elements that participate in those representations or the mechanisms that mediate them. The recording of neuronal activity during the well-controlled exercise of cognitive functions is more revealing. This chapter summarizes some of the evidence gathered by my colleagues and me concerning the participation of neurons in certain areas of associative cortex in the representation of sensory percepts and memories.

INFEROTEMPORAL CORTEX AND VISUAL REPRESENTATION

It has long been known that, in the monkey, the inferior temporal (IT) cortex (area TE of Von Bonin & Bailey, 1947) is essential for visual discriminations.

Acknowledgments: The research reported in this chapter was supported in part by grants from the National Science Foundation (BNS 82-13806), the Office of Naval Research (N00014-86-K-0174), and the National Institute of Mental Health (Research Scientist Award, MH25082).

Animals that have sustained lesions of this cortex are notoriously deficient in the learning and performance of visual discrimination tasks (Chow, 1951; Cowey & Gross, 1970). Electrophysiological experiments have revealed that IT cells have exceptionally broad receptive fields, which almost invariably include the fovea, and are tuned to a wide range of visual properties, including color, form, contrast, and orientation (Gross, Rocha-Miranda, & Bender, 1972). Furthermore, some IT cells have been shown to be tuned to complex visual stimuli of presumptive ethological significance such as facial images (Perrett, Rolls, & Caan, 1982).

In monkeys (Delacour, 1977; Fuster, Bauer, & Jervey, 1981) and humans (Milner, 1968), reversible or irreversible lesions of IT cortex have been noted to result in visual memory deficits, which may be at least in part responsible for the discrimination deficits mentioned above. All of these deficits are supposedly attributable to the disruption of the neuronal substrate for visual representation. In order to gain insight into the functional organization of that substrate, we conducted a series of investigations of IT neuronal activity in monkeys performing visual short-term memory tasks. In such tasks the cognitive operations of perception, mnemonic retention, and recognition are discretely bracketed in time, and behavioral performance provides adequate external indices of these operations. Figure 1 shows an example of one such task: delayed matching to

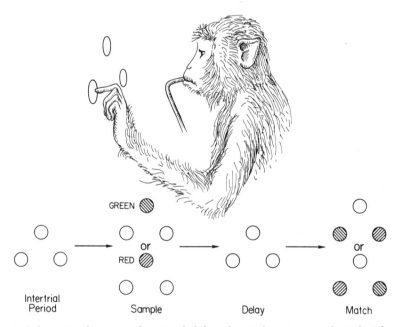

Figure 1. Schematic diagram of a visual delayed matching-to-sample task. The animal faces a panel with three stimulus/response buttons. A trial begins with the brief presentation of a red or green light on the top button (the sample). After a delay of a few seconds or minutes, the two lower buttons show two colors, one of them the sample. The animal is then supposed to press (match) the button with the sample color. If he does so, he is rewarded with juice. The sample and its position in the lower buttons are changed at random from one trial to the next.

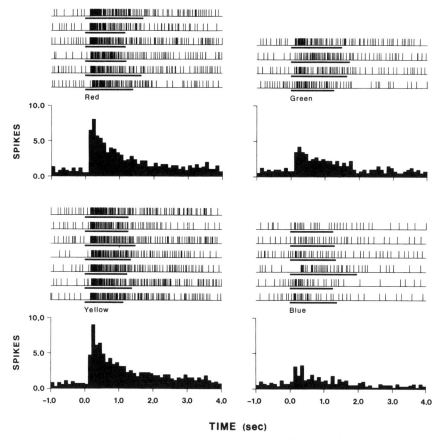

Figure 2. Responses of an IT cell to samples of four different colors in the DMS task. Spike records are grouped by color of the sample (turned off by the animal's pressing of the sample button and lasting as indicated by black horizontal bars). Under each raster of spikes, the average frequency histogram is displayed (bin duration 100 msec). Note that the cell is especially responsive to the two "warm" colors, red and yellow.

sample (DMS). Essentially, each trial of that task requires successively the discrimination, short-term retention, and recognition of a sensory stimulus (the sample).

Inferior Temporal Cells and Visual Discrimination

Using a DMS task with four sample colors (red, green, blue, and yellow), we found (Fuster & Jervey, 1981, 1982) a substantial proportion of IT cells that reacted to those colors with different firing rates (Figure 2). Thus, they were attuned to color and, in that sense, had chromatic properties and preferences similar to those exhibited by cells in certain parts of the geniculostriate system. In the IT cortex, however, fewer cells than in the striate cortex were found that could be characterized as color-opponent, that is, excited by one color and inhibited by another. Most color-differential IT cells simply showed a different level of excitation depending on the sample color, as the cell in Figure 2 did.

A highly pertinent question is whether the differential color reactivity of IT cells we observed in the fully trained animal had already been present—"wired in"—in the untrained animal or, instead, was a product of training, reflecting not so much the physical attributes of the sample stimuli as their acquired relevance for performance of the task. Because of the impossibility of recording from the same units through the training process and the difficulty in comparing unit data obtained before and after training, we are obliged to approach this question with an *ad hoc* strategy. One such strategy is to manipulate the behavioral relevance of one stimulus attribute, color in our case, in the course of recording from a given unit. This can be accomplished if the animal has been trained to attend to or to ignore that attribute depending on discrete changes of the context in which it appears. Such a procedure allows the study of the effects of attention on the reactions of IT cells to a given visual attribute without changing its physical properties.

In order to examine these questions, I (Fuster, 1988) recorded the activity of IT units during performance of a DMS task with compound stimuli (Figure 3). The brief (0.5 to 1.0 sec) sample stimulus for each trial was a symbol (=, X, or O) on a circular colored disk (red or green) subtending about 8° of visual angle. For the fully trained and performing animal, the symbol was always relevant: it signified whether the symbol itself or the background color had to be retained in memory for ulterior action. The symbol = indicated that the color had to be retained, whereas X or O indicated that the symbol had to be retained and the color ignored. In other words, color was relevant if accompanied by = and irrelevant if accompanied by X or O. In either case, the location, brightness, and extent of the colored sample area remained invariant. It seemed reasonable to assume that the animal's attention to the color was attracted by = and not by the other two symbols.

A large proportion of IT cells responded to the six symbol/color samples in a nondifferential manner. They showed a similar activation of firing on presentation of any of the sample stimuli. A second group of cells either did not respond to any of the samples or was inhibited by one or more of them.

Another category of IT units showed selective or preferential activation by one of the symbols regardless of the background color. Conversely, yet another group of cells showed selective or preferential activation by one of the two colors (red or green). Apparently, those two groups of cells were attuned to one of the two components of the sample: either the symbol or the color. They seemed to extract that feature from the compound stimulus.

Among cells that discriminated color, there was a subcategory of them (about 6% of the IT data base) that were significantly more activated by their preferred color if it was relevant (i.e., accompanied by =) than if it was not (i.e.,

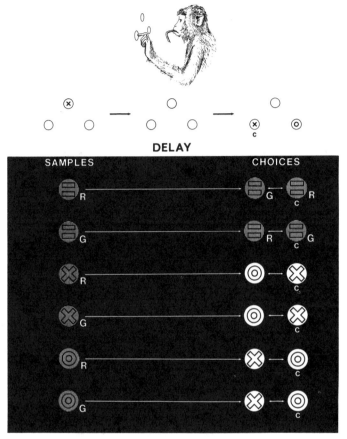

Figure 3. Samples and choices in a DMS task with compound stimuli. R, red (vertical lines); G, green (horizontal lines). In the first two samples (with = sign), color is relevant; color is irrelevant in all the others. Correct choices indicated by C.

accompanied by X or O) (Figure 4); I called these "color-attentive" cells. No cells were found showing the reverse (i.e., greater color activation if color was irrelevant). Furthermore, no "color-attentive" units were found either in striate cortex (V_1) or in the upper bank of the superior temporal sulcus.

On closer analysis, it was noted that whereas the phenomenon of attentive enhancement of reactions to color was only statistically significant in approximately 6% of all IT cells examined, it was present, albeit to a lesser degree, in practically all color-discriminant IT cells (nearly one-quarter of the total IT sample). Thus, we may speak of a gradient of attentive modulation of color-discriminant cells and conclude that any such cell falls somewhere within that gradient.

In order to quantify the degree of attentive modulation of color-discriminant cells, I devised an attention index (AI): the quotient of the reaction of a given cell to its preferred color in the color-relevant condition over its reaction to the same

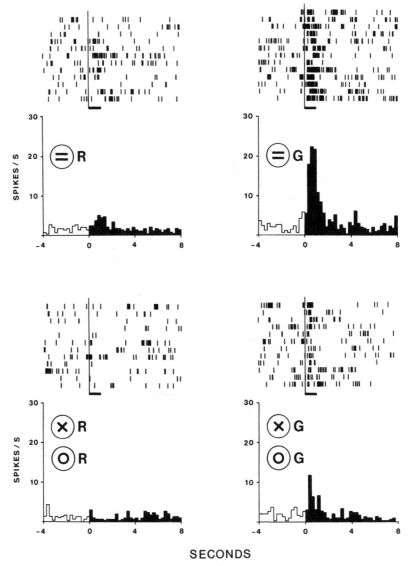

Figure 4. Records of response to the sample from a cell that preferred green over red (histogram bin duration 250 msec). Onset of sample indicated by vertical lines, its average duration by horizontal bars. Note that the response to green was greater when color was relevant (=) than when it was not (X or O).

color in the color-irrelevant condition. Accordingly, a cell not modulated by attention would have an AI of 1.00; any degree of attentive facilitation would result in AIs greater than unity.

The median AI for color-discriminant IT neurons was found to be 1.23. In contrast, the median AI of color-discriminant striate cortex neurons was 0.97. The two medians differed significantly from one another ($\chi^2 = 7.68$; $p < .01$). We can conclude that IT cells, unlike striate cells, are susceptible to attentive facilitation of their response to the visual attribute to which they are attuned.

The analysis of cell-response latencies revealed that "color-attentive" cells tended to respond to their preferred color with a relatively long latency. By plotting AI as a function of latency in all color-discriminant cells, a degree of correlation was observed between those two variables, although that relationship appeared to be nonlinear (Figure 5). In any event, the finding that "color-attentive" cells have long latency indicates that such cells are placed deeply—that is, far away from receptor stages—in the neural organization devoted to the analysis of visual information. That finding is also in accord with the presumption that selective visual attention is largely a serial process, unlike preattentive vision, which seems to involve a parallel process (Koch & Ullman, 1985).

Inferior Temporal Cells and Visual Memory

Every trial of a DMS task requires an act of memory: the retention of the just-presented sample for the prospective match after the delay, a few seconds or minutes hence. It is a form of short-term memory called by some investigators "operant" or "working" memory. Its content (the sample) is discrete, and its behavioral usefulness is sharply defined in the temporal domain by the duration of the delay. On the presumption that IT cells might be involved in visual short-

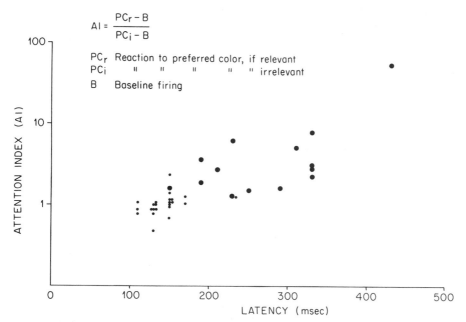

Figure 5. Relationship between the "attention index" (AI) of 37 color-discriminant IT cells and their response latency. Large dots denote AIs significantly higher than 1.0 ($p < .05$).

term memory, we scrutinized the discharge of such cells during the delay periods of a visual DMS task with colors (Fuster & Jervey, 1981, 1982). Our objective was to uncover evidence of sample-related activity that reflected the participation of the cells in the mnemonic retention of the critical information that the animal was to use in the subsequent match and response.

Confirming our supposition, we found that some of the cells differentiating the color of the sample at the time of its presentation continued to do so during the ensuing delay, when the sample was no longer physically present. In other words, during the delay, those cells showed a different level of discharge depending on the color of the sample most recently presented. Surprising, however, was the evidence of neurons that differentiated the sample during the delay without having done it in the sample period itself. Thus, a cell's discrimination of the sample in its presence was not a precondition for its discrimination after it was gone from the visual environment. In other words, a cell might not respond to the sample or be inhibited by it, yet show a differential activation during the delay depending on the sample color. The cell in Figure 6, for example, showed no alteration of firing in the presence of the sample yet was significantly activated during the delay of red-sample trials but not green-sample trials. Note that in this unit, as in most delay-differential units, the differentiation of the two colors is no longer present after the choice, even though at this time, as at the time of the sample, the animal is forced to look at the sample color.

Delay-differential cells constituted about 10% of the IT data base. They appear to be part of the neural substrate for the retention of color. Since such units did not coincide with those showing color differentiation at the time of sample presentation, it seems that we are dealing with two separate but probably interrelated populations of IT cells: one reacting differentially to the sample stimuli and the other taking part in the mnemonic, short-term, representation of such stimuli. The former type of cells are especially common in the cortex of the inferior temporal convexity, the latter in the cortex of the lower bank of the superior temporal sulcus. It is tempting to speculate that the sensory information contained in the sample is first represented primarily in the inferotemporal cortex and then, for its temporary retention, in the cortex of the superior temporal sulcus.

POSTERIOR PARIETAL CORTEX AND HAPTIC REPRESENTATION

Clinical evidence and experimental lesion studies in monkeys indicate that the associative cortex of the parietal lobe is involved in somesthetic discriminations and memory. In the monkey, areas 2 and 5 (Brodmann) have been implicated by electrophysiological studies in the discrimination of cutaneous and proprioceptive stimuli (see Hyvarinen, 1982, for review). These studies, together with the anatomic evidence thus far obtained (Pandya & Yeterian, 1985), suggest a parietal hierarchy of interconnected cortical areas for somatic processing that

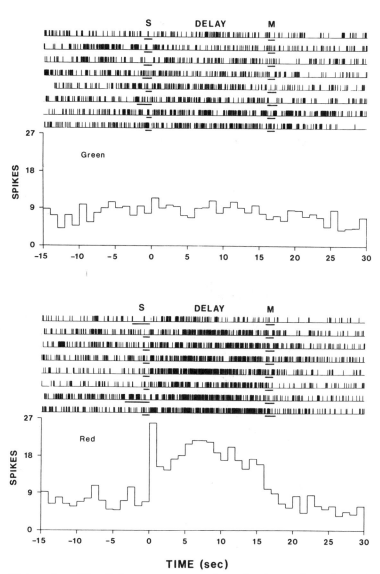

Figure 6. Firing of an IT cell during green-sample and red-sample trials in a DMS task with simple colors. Note that the cell is only activated during the delay (18 seconds) of red-sample trials, after the color is no longer present but needs to be retained in short-term memory.

would in some respects be similar to the occipitotemporal hierarchy for visual processing (Hubel & Wiesel, 1968; Duffy & Burchfiel, 1971). Area 5 and its subdivisions in posterior parietal (PP) cortex seem to be placed at the top of that hierarchy and therefore to form the substrate for the integration of somatic information from various sources that is required for the recognition of objects by touch, that is, for stereognosis.

In order to investigate the electrophysiological correlates of stereognosis, Kevin Koch and I (Koch & Fuster, 1989) recorded unit activity from the PP cortex of monkeys trained to perform a haptic DMS task (Figure 7).

Posterior Parietal Cells and Haptic Discrimination

One of the most significant findings of our study was the existence of cells that were not only activated by the touch and manipulation of the sample object but also, with a surprisingly short latency, by the auditory click that signaled the presence of the object within the reach of the hand. Such cells seemed to react to the auditory stimulus by virtue of its role as an associated precursor of movement

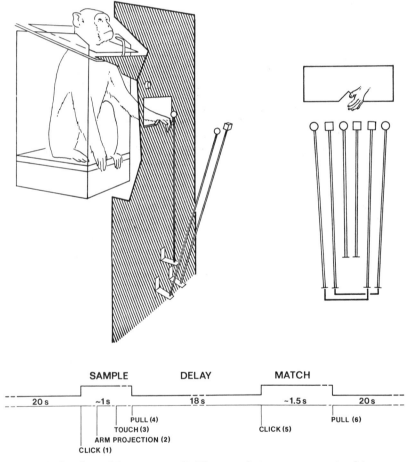

Figure 7. A DMS task with haptic stimuli. The sample is a stereometric object perceived by touch. After the delay, two objects are presented for choice (match), one of them the sample. Choice of the sample is then automatically rewarded. Sample and sample position at the choice are changed in random order from trial to trial. Below, the sequence of events of a trial is depicted.

and object manipulation. This inference is strengthened by the evidence that the same cells were usually also activated by the subsequent arm projection and sample manipulation.

The activity of some PP units was clearly related to the projection or withdrawal movements of the arm as the animal either approached or released the sample object. These units seemed to be exclusively involved in the motor aspects of the task and perhaps activated by some kind of central or peripheral *efferent copy* of the movement.

A substantial number of PP units responded to manipulation of the sample objects, although the majority of them did so in a nondifferential manner: they were equally excited or inhibited by manipulation of a cube and a sphere, the two objects utilized by the animal in performance of the task. However, among those cells that responded to manipulation of the sample objects, there was a subgroup (approximately 15% of all cells in area 5) that responded differentially to the cube and the sphere (Figure 8).

In more general terms, there was in PP cortex a rostral-to-caudal gradient of diminishing responsiveness—differential as well as nondifferential—to sample object manipulation: fewer responsive cells in area 5a than in area 2, and still fewer in area 5b.

Posterior Parietal Cells and Haptic Memory

Just as IT neurons are apparently involved in visual memory, PP neurons seem involved in haptic memory. We infer this from our finding that, like some IT units, some PP units showed sustained activation during the delay of a DMS task, although here the stimuli were tactile instead of visual. Such units were particularly common in area 5a. Also in this area we encountered a substantial number of cells that discriminated between the two objects during the delay, that is, *after* they had been palpated by the animal (Figure 9).

In all PP areas, however, delay-inhibited cells predominated over delay-activated cells. It seemed that whereas the latter might code more or less specific aspects of the object in temporary memory, the former constituted a large population of neurons that at the same time underwent inhibition, inasmuch as they were in charge of representing other kinds of information that in the context of the task was treated as "noise" and, therefore, suppressed.

It is worth noting that in PP cortex we reencountered another phenomenon already observed in IT cortex: cells immediately activated (differentially or not) on sample presentation were not necessarily the same cells that were activated during the ensuing delay. Thus, in the haptic task, cells responding to object manipulation were distinct from those subsequently activated during retention. The two cell populations might support two different but complementary processes: haptic perception and haptic short-term memory. The two processes are intimately interrelated, and, therefore, it is reasonable to assume a close functional cooperation between those two neuronal populations.

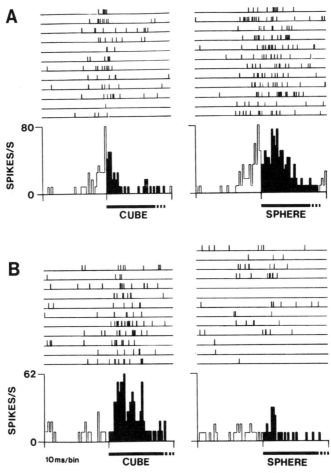

Figure 8. Reactions of two PP cells to manipulation of two sample objects (manipulation period indicated by horizontal bars). The unit on top (A) prefers the sphere, the unit below (B) the cube.

SUMMARY AND CONCLUSIONS

Essentially, the studies recently conducted in my laboratory and briefly presented in this chapter provide evidence for the participation of neurons of association cortex in the representation of sensory percepts and working memories. The cells in question may be the constituent elements of cortical representational networks that are activated by behaviorally significant stimuli. Both the perception and the temporary retention of those stimuli in the context of a behavioral task may be direct consequences of those activations. In more concrete terms, our data lead to the following conclusions:

1. Cellular populations of IT and PP cortex discriminate, respectively, visual and tactile attributes of objects in the external world.

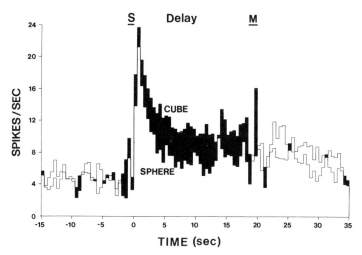

Figure 9. Activity of a PP cell in haptic DMS trials. During the delay, the unit is more active after the cube sample than the sphere sample. S̲, sample; M̲, match.

2. Neurons in IT cortex that are attuned to one particular attribute (color) are subject to modulation as a function of the degree of behavioral relevance of that attribute at any given time and, therefore, the attention that the animal pays to it.

3. Among the cells that discriminate color, those that are most susceptible to attention modulation exhibit the longest latency of response to their preferred color. This finding indicates that such cells lie in higher levels of a cortical hierarchy of areas for visual processing.

4. Neurons in PP cortex seem to represent not only haptic attributes but attributes of another modality (auditory) that, by training and experience, have become associated with them.

5. In both IT and PP cortex, certain neurons appear involved in the temporary memory of, respectively, visual and tactile information. In the two regions, cells engaging in memory seem different from cells engaging in sensory discrimination. The two populations show a degree of overlap, and it is reasonable to suppose that transactions between them subserve the transactions between perception and memory.

REFERENCES

Chow, K. L. (1951). Effects of partial extirpations of posterior association cortex on visually mediated behavior in monkeys. *Comparative Psychology Monographs, 20,* 187–217.

Cowey, A., & Gross, C. G. (1970). Effects of foveal prestriate and inferotemporal lesions on visual discriminations by rhesus monkeys. *Experimental Brain Research, 11,* 128–144.

Delacour, J. (1977). Cortex inférotemporal et mémoire visuelle à court terme chez le singe. Nouvelles données. *Experimental Brain Research, 28*, 301–310.

Duffy, F. H., & Burchfiel, J. L. (1971). Somatosensory system: Organizational hierarchy from single units in monkey area 5. *Science, 172*, 273–275.

Fuster, J. M. (1988). Attentional modulation of inferotemporal neuron responses to visual features. *Society for Neuroscience Abstracts, 14(1)*, 10.

Fuster, J. M., Bauer, R. H., & Jervey, J. P. (1981). Effects of cooling inferotemporal cortex on performance of visual memory tasks. *Experimental Neurology, 71*, 398–409.

Fuster, J. M., & Jervey, J. P. (1981). Inferotemporal neurons distinguish and retain behaviorally relevant features of visual stimuli. *Science, 212*, 952–955.

Fuster, J. M., & Jervey, J. P. (1982). Neuronal firing in the inferotemporal cortex of the monkey in a visual memory task. *Journal of Neuroscience, 2*, 361–375.

Gross, C. G., Rocha-Miranda, C. E., & Bender, D. B. (1972). Visual properties of neurons in inferotemporal cortex of the macaque. *Journal of Neurophysiology, 35*, 96–111.

Hubel, D. H., & Wiesel, T. N. (1968). Receptive fields and functional architecture of monkey striate cortex. *Journal of Physiology (London), 195*, 215–243.

Hyvarinen, J. (1982). Posterior parietal lobe of the primate brain. *Physiological Reviews, 62*, 1060–1129.

Koch, C., & Ullman, S. (1985). Shifts in selective visual attention: Towards the underlying neural circuitry. *Human Neurobiology, 4*, 219–227.

Koch, K., & Fuster, J.M. (1989). Unit activity in monkey parietal cortex related to haptic perception and temporary memory. *Experimental Brain Research, 76*, 292–306.

Milner, B. (1968). Visual recognition and recall after right temporal-lobe excision in man. *Neuropsychologia, 6*, 191–209.

Pandya, D. N., & Yeterian, E. H. (1985). Architecture and connections of cortical association areas. In E. G. Jones & A. Peters (Eds.), *Cerebral cortex* (Vol. 4, pp. 3–61). New York: Plenum Press.

Perrett, D. I., Rolls, E. T., & Caan, W. (1982). Visual neurones responsive to faces in the monkey temporal cortex. *Experimental Brain Research, 47*, 329–342.

Von Bonin, G., & Bailey, P. (1947). *The neocortex of Macaca mulatta.* Urbana: University of Illinois Press.

DISCUSSION

MARIAN DIAMOND: Have you ever tried to have one monkey teach another one?

JOAQUIN FUSTER: I have not tried that, but it's curious to see how the later monkeys pick up so much knowledge on day 1, when the earlier ones took months to learn the task. . . . Perhaps we're getting better at training them. Or else they are getting better because they talk to each other!

GEORGE OJEMANN: I have two questions. The first is whether you've done these studies introducing any kind of activity in the delay period. As you know, in man there's some evidence that memory that has an interpolated delay that has the same general quality as the items to be remembered may have a somewhat different anaotmic substrate than memory that doesn't have such a delay—the immediate memory versus the postdistractional quality. That's the first question.

FUSTER: We have not studied this systematically. We have done some such examinations in the frontal cortex, where you find some of those sustained activities. In my paper in 1973 in the *Journal of Neurophysiology*, I described a series of tests that I did with introduction of monkey sounds—voices—during the period of delay. I did see that there was an interruption of elevated unit activity during the delay, but because of the limited sample of units investigated, I cannot make any categorical statement about it.

OJEMANN: My second question is a preliminary to our own chapter. In man, as you probably know, there has been found a moderate number of lateral cortical neurons that show prolonged activity at what would be your initial and delayed sampling times but not during the time that the memory is stored. I was wondering if you'd seen anything like that in your monkeys. These are basically cells that show activity lasting periods of 5 to 6 seconds at the time the information entered memory, which in your case is the initial sample, and then for a similar period at the time that the information has to be retrieved, which in your case is the delayed match. We have not seen the activity during what you call your delay.

FUSTER: Yes, we have seen those cells too.

ISAK PROHOVNIK: With regard to those "intelligence" cells, which are presumably at the end of a long chain of other events, what else characterizes them? I know one thing is the dimension of their position in the anterior temporal lobe. What about the cortical layers? Are they located in one particular layer more than another? Is there anything else that you can tell us about them that will help us understand how they're organized?

FUSTER: That's a very good question, of course, and one that we've asked ourselves many times. It is very difficult to obtain precise localization of cells in terms of layers. It is very difficult to drive microelectrodes into cortex with the control that we would like. The only thing I can tell you is that those cells appear to be concentrated in the depths of the superior temporal sulcus, in areas in front of stereotactic plane 10.0 on the stereotactic map, and probably near the pole of the amygdala. I cannot tell yet whether they are more common in infragranular or supragranular layers. I can tell you one thing though. Among the cells that seem to retain information, those that are in supragranular layers are more susceptible to influences from frontal lobe. We know that from cooling experiments in which we cool the frontal cortex and record infratemporally.

ARNOLD SCHEIBEL: In terms of what Joaquin says, it's rather interesting that cortex that is located in the depth of a sulcus is quite different from that located on the crown of a gyrus. Sulcal cortex is thinner, the cells tend to have shorter apical dendrites, and there are very dense horizontal plexuses of basal dendrites, which form thick bundles. You just don't see those horizontal dendrite masses when you're at the crown of a gyrus.

JÖRG PAHL: The cells that you were talking about seem to be very committed. We all know about plasticity in the brain. How do you explain plasticity? Is it a difference in connections that occurs?

FUSTER: Well, not all cells that are shown are completely committed. There is a wide range of patterns that seem to vary depending on levels of feature relevance or nonrelevance to the context of the moment. Presumably what's happening is that, in the course of learning, the accretion of experience develops with the facilitation of those synaptic connections that tie the representational network together. It's very important to remember that feature detection *per se* is not the only factor involved. We're dealing with context, and context is essential to how the network works. What defines the network is not just the stimulus and the response but rather the context in which the stimulus and the response occur. In other words, it is probably the backdrop, formed by experience through epigenetic connectivity, and covering wide portions of the cortex, that represents the accretion of all the associated features of the stimulus–response scheme. Let me give you a personal experience. I drive my car, and I listen to music from my Walkman through its headset earphones. I almost never do that—it's against the law—but, in the absence of any traffic, I reckon the danger is zero. The volume has to be adjusted several times. Every time, for at least five times, I find myself trying to adjust the dial of my car-panel radio. That, of course, is not the dial that controls the sound in the headset. Five times I realize I am doing something silly, but I keep doing it. So much is built into the context of changing volume.

ERIC HALGREN: I think it's an appropriate inference that the cells that are differentially respondent to the two stimuli and have sustained response during the delay might be subserving primary memory. And I think it's very important. The other sort of function that has been brought up during the delay period has to do with sets, inhibiting competing responses, and so forth. Do you have a way of detecting unit responses that might be related to that type of function? What proportion of the cells in the posterior association cortex versus the frontal association cortex seemed to be related to primary memory as opposed to set?

FUSTER: I guess the best way to start my answer is to recall our work on the frontal cortex where we have most data on this question. There you find two broad categories of cells that are activated during that delay. Some go down in firing as the delay progresses. They seem to trail off the stimulus. Others seem to be looking forward. They increase their activity as the motor-response time approaches. If you test the animals with repeated equal-time delays within a short period, they accelerate their activity as the response approaches. In the frontal cortex, where we find much more differentiation related to motor response than we find here, you can tell more clearly that there are some cells that indeed are anticipating the response and presumably are involved in motor sets. This is not too unusual in that we know that the prefrontal cortex has a lot to do with the organization of behavioral action.

ERAN ZAIDEL: I still have a question about this very interesting cell that you showed before, one of a population of cells that respond with different frequencies to different colors. Remember, you tended to interpret it as a yellow cell because its response level was highest for yellow, but the point I'm trying to make is this. Here's a cell that responds differentially to different colors, so in a sense it codes for all colors at once. Now I'm asking myself, "How would we represent information about color (forget about context for a minute) during the delay period?" One way would be to have a set of cells that fire off for yellow, another set for green, another red, and so forth. Then we sample all of them, and we see which one is most active. Another way is actually to look at one cell—especially these cells, the kind that you mention here—and see which way they fire. Now what would be the advantage of one or the other? The advantage of this cell is that it's coded very efficiently. One cell tells me immediately which one of four colors it is. I don't have to sample four different kinds of cells. But the other system is much more distributed. It even provides some advantages because I can code more easily for conjunctions of features. For example, I would need a very specialized cell for the conjunction.

FUSTER: In answer to this question I'll say that, indeed, we're dealing with a distributed system, and the categorization within it is by virtue of association. So it is that the network codes certain features, be it color or whatever. And what we see with our microelectrode is not necessarily a "yellow cell," but rather a cell that participates in a distributed network that codes the color yellow in the context of the task the animal is performing. Otherwise, we run into a methodological problem, namely, the problem of induction. After you have developed extensive color tuning curves for a cell, the possibility still exists that you have not yet tested the hue best driven and coded (?) by the cell. It is a kind of reductionism that has no logical basis either in psychophysics or in behavior.

INSIGHTS FROM EVOKED POTENTIALS INTO THE NEUROPSYCHOLOGICAL MECHANISMS OF READING

ERIC HALGREN, PhD

University of California, Los Angeles, Wadsworth Veterans
Administration Hospital, and INSERM U.97, Paris

INTRODUCTION: EVOKED POTENTIALS
AS COGNITIVE STAGES IN READING

Evoked potentials (EPs) allow the real-time monitoring of normal human brain activity as it assimilates events (Halgren, in press). EPs are generated by the net extracellular current flows that result when the synapses terminating in a given layer of a laminated structure are activated more or less synchronously. Under favorable conditions, the EP produced by simple averaging of the EEG evoked by 50 to 100 events can reveal the activation of about 1% of the synapses in a 2-cm² area of cortex (Nunez, 1981). As the extracellular current flows propagate to the scalp, they superimpose, resulting in partial smearing of activity generated by adjacent neurons. Consequently, EPs are not capable of distinguishing the distinct patterns of activation within a neural population that encode individual events. Conversely, however, EPs *can* detect the population postsynaptic potentials that result in information-specific neuronal firing patterns.

Because EPs are simple, inexpensive, and noninvasive on-line measures of brain activity, many hundreds of studies of EPs during cognitive tasks have been conducted in normal human subjects (Harmony, 1984; Karrer, Cohen, & Tueting, 1984; Rosler et al., 1986; Desmedt, 1981; Donchin & Coles, 1988; Halgren, in press; Hillyard & Picton, 1988). For the most part, these studies were conducted without any knowledge of the underlying brain generators of the EPs. Consequently, latency, scalp topography, polarity, and waveform have been used to divide the EP into successive components that can consistently be identified across tasks, subjects, and even species. Changes in these components can then be correlated with the component cognitive processes evoked by the task or with

Acknowledgments: Supported by the U.S. Public Health Service (NS18741), by the Veterans Administration, and by the French Institute National de la Santé et de la Recherche Médicale. Michael Smith, Gary Heit, and June Stapleton conducted many of the studies from my laboratory reported here. I am grateful to Marta Kutas and Michael Rugg for sharing their unpublished manuscripts with me, and to Sarah Copeland and Ksenija Marinkovic for valuable discussions.

neural damage the subject may have sustained. In this way, cognitive EPs can be used to link cognitive stages with neural systems.

This chapter is concerned with the temporal stages in reading at both the psychological and neural levels. Reading is perhaps the most versatile and effective means of transmitting complex information yet invented, and thus, by studying reading, one can observe human information processing operating at peak efficiency. The reader passes through the embedded hierarchical levels of edges, letters, words, clauses, sentences, paragraphs, and stories, eventually arriving at understanding. Understanding text requires that successive words be integrated with many additional sources of information, across time (remote, recent, and primary memories), and forms of knowledge (syntactic, semantic, episodic, and pragmatic). These multiple contextual constraints must operate via the interactions of large and widespread cortical ensembles. Information processing in these various cortical regions needs to be synchronized so that they may interact, or be sequenced if the input of one structure depends upon the output of another. Furthermore, the parameters used by the neural network to process the information may need to be optimized for different words and contexts. The most straightforward way to synchronize, sequence, and optimize processing would be to impose an active modulation on widespread cortical sites.

The cholinergic and monoaminergic systems, directly and via the nucleus reticularis thalami, possess the anatomical projections and physiological effects to exert this modulation. Recent evidence suggests that the late cognitive EP components evoked during reading may result from activation of these brainstem neuromodulatory systems. Furthermore, cognitive EPs are being reliably correlated with the final information-processing stages in reading, and are generated by synaptic current flows in widespread cortical regions. Thus, cognitive EPs may be interpreted as embodying these modulatory processes, which aid the integration of a word with its semantic context.

In the first part of this chapter, the cognitive correlates and neural generators of the EP components in reading are reviewed, leading to the model summarized in Figure 1. Although the internal mechanisms of the stages in this model are still largely unknown, a consideration of their characteristics, together with data from behavioral experiments, provides new insights into some as yet outstanding questions in the psychology of reading: Is the early perceptual analysis of the word influenced by the semantics of the sentence context (for example, is the feature detector for a curved line just left of fixation preactivated by "He jump-started his _____")? When a word is read, does its sound have to be found first, before its meaning can be accessed? Does the process of identifying the word and accessing its meaning involve scanning down a mental list sequentially, or is the word somehow encoded so as to access its meaning directly? Is the meaning of the word integrated with the preceding words of the sentence as soon as the word's meaning is accessed, or is integration delayed until the sentence's end?

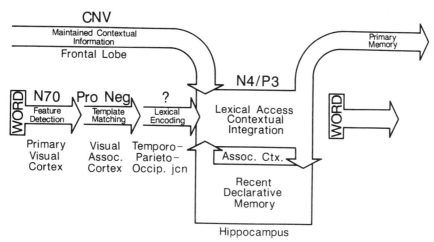

Figure 1. Psychological, physiological, and anatomic stages in reading, according to the model proposed here. The first EP component evoked by an individual word is a negativity peaking at 70 msec generated in the primary visual cortex and reflecting simple feature detection. In the next 200 msec various poorly described processing negativities in the visual association cortex match the visual stimulus against letters and letter groups, culminating in lexical encoding. Lexical encoding triggers the widespread N4/P3 (or N400/P300) EP components. During the N4/P3, the lexically encoded word stimulus is integrated with (1) the contents of recent declarative memory (for example, an earlier part of the story) stored in the hippocampus, (2) maintained contextual information providing the gist of the preceding text and stored primarily in the firing of frontal lobe neurons (generating the CNV EP component), and (3) remote semantic memory, embedded in the structure of the association cortex. The result of this contextual integration is a neuronal ensemble that encodes the correct meaning of the word (termed lexical access) within its text. This result is stored in recent declarative memory and in primary memory for integration with the next word.

When the word, sentence, or story is understood within a larger semantic system, is this system the same as is used for understanding nonverbal information?

VISUAL PROCESSING POTENTIALS

The earliest EP component in reading is a scalp negativity at 70 to 75 msec latency. Studies in monkeys suggest that this component is generated by presynaptic depolarization of primary visual afferents as well as by stellate cell postsynaptic potentials in layer IV of striate cortex (Arezzo, Vaughan, Kraut, Steinshneider, & Legatt, 1986; Kraut, Arezzo, & Vaughan, 1985). This N70 is followed by a scalp positivity at 100 msec, possibly reflecting GABAergic inhibition, mainly localized to primary visual cortex (Zemon, Kaplan, & Ratliff, 1986). An occipital origin for these potentials is confirmed by their large amplitude in direct recordings from human occipital cortex (Darcey, Wieser, Meles, Skrandies, & Lehmann, 1980) and their abolition at the scalp after human occipital lobe lesions

(Streletz, Bae, Roeshman, Schatz, & Savino, 1981). However, it should be noted that information passes very rapidly to visual association cortex in the inferior temporal lobe (only about 8 msec later than striate cortex in the monkey according to Ashford & Fuster, 1985).

In the 160 to 310 msec range, a number of visual "processing" or "match-detection" negativities appear (Naatanen & Picton, 1986). These processing negativities are topographically distinct, but their division into separate components is as yet unclear (Pritchard, Shappell, & Brandt, 1988). However, the earlier (around 185 msec) and possibly more posterior potentials appear to be related to relatively simple stimulus features, such as size, spatial location, or orientation (Harter & Guido, 1980; Hillyard, Woldorff, Mangun, & Hansen, 1987; Harter & Previc, 1978). The later processing negativities (up to 310 msec) are more prominent over the posterior temporal cortex and are associated with the extraction of features and matching them to an internal template (Ritter et al., 1984). These potentials require complex stimuli such as letters or words and are observed when these stimuli change unpredictably from trial to trial and when stimulus identification is important for task performance (Ritter, Simson, Vaughan, & Macht, 1982). For example, Lovrich, Simson, Vaughan, and Ritter (1986) found a component evoked by simple grapheme-to-phoneme conversion in this range that was maximal over the left posterior temporal region.

Single words also evoke a broad negativity (onset about 180 msec, peak about 310 msec) that is maximal over the same region (Smith & Halgren, 1988). An inferotemporal generator for this component was suggested by its decrease after left or right anterior temporal lobectomy (ATL). Left ATL reduced the N310 only over the left temporal lobe, whereas right ATL decreased the N310 bilaterally (especially over the right). The greater effect of right ATL is consistent with Kimura's (1963) observation of visuoperceptual deficits after right but not left ATL.

More generally, these EPs suggest a progression of activation from primary visual (area 18) to visual association areas devoted to progressively more complex feature extraction (area 19) and then matching of these features in anterior inferotemporal cortex with templates stored in long-term memory in order to identify objects (Desimone, Schein, Moran, & Ungerleider, 1985; Kaas, 1989). This is consistent with the cortical pathways described by Pandya and Yeterian in this volume. It is also consistent with single-unit studies in primates demonstrating progressively more complex feature detectors in posterior visual assocation areas (Van Essen & Maunsell, 1983; Marrocco, 1986), culminating in units firing to hands, eyes, mouths, and ultimately faces in the middle temporal sulcus at a latency of about 80–160 msec (Gross, 1973; Perrett, Rolls, & Caan, 1982; Rolls, Baylis, & Hasselmo, 1987). The apparent anatomic and functional progression of visual processing EPs also corresponds to progressively more complex pattern recognition deficits after progressively more anterior lesions in primates (Mishkin, 1982) and humans (Luria, 1966; Hecaen & Albert, 1978).

Contextual Integration Potentials N4 and P3

Cognitive Correlates

N4

Because of artifacts from eye movements (Picton, 1987), EPs have not been recorded during natural reading. However, Kutas, Hillyard, and colleagues have systematically explored the EPs evoked by reading sentences when words are presented one at a time at a constant rate in the center of the visual field (Kutas & Van Petten, 1987). This task is termed here "stationary reading." They find that following the early potentials related to visual processing, each word evokes a negativity sensitive to semantic variables peaking at 400 or more milliseconds after stimulus onset. This component is termed the "N400" or "N4." In the initial studies of Kutas and Hillyard (1980a), a large N4 was observed to the terminal word of sentences when that word was not expected given the preceding words in the sentence (Table 1). A large N4 was also evoked by words that formed a meaningful ending, as long as they were unusual (Kutas & Hillyard, 1984). In contrast, small N4s were evoked if the terminal word was only syntactically or orthographically incongruent with those preceding it (Kutas & Hillyard, 1980b, 1983). These findings gave rise to the hypothesis that the N4 is evoked by semantic incongruity, a special case of the hypothesized cognitive correlate of the EP components N2–P3 with incongruity in general.

However, subsequent studies have found that the N4 is evoked in many situations that do not involve incongruity with the established context (Halgren & Smith, 1987; Rugg, Kok, Barrett, & Fischler, 1986; Kutas & Van Petten, 1987; see also Table 1). The evoking stimulus can be individually presented words, printed, spoken, or signed (McCallum, Farmer, & Pocock, 1984; Kutas, Neville, & Holcomb, 1987). The N4 can also be evoked by photographs of faces or drawings of familiar objects (Smith & Halgren, 1987a; Smith, Stapleton, & Halgren, 1986; Stuss, Sarazin, Leech, & Picton, 1983; Barrett, Rugg, & Perrett, 1988). Effective tasks include reading, recognizing, naming, categorizing, and rhyming. In some cases, the N4 is not evoked by words if the discrimination required by the task depends solely upon the physical features of the stimulus (Rugg, Furda, & Lorist, 1988; Rugg & Nagy, 1987). Finally, complex abstract sounds and pictures have not been found to evoke an N4. Thus, it is apparently necessary and sufficient for N4 generation that the stimulus be potentially meaningful within a complex associative cognitive system. At the neural level, it appears that the N4 is evoked by any stimulus capable of activating a widespread cerebral associative network, within any task that requires or permits such activation.

Once the N4 is evoked by a word, its amplitude and duration are inversely related to the *ease* with which the word is integrated into the current cognitive context. According to this interpretation, the larger N4s evoked by incongruous as compared to congruous sentence-terminal words do not result from an enhancing

TABLE 1
TASK CORRELATES OF THE N4

Recognition memory: Words; repeats are targets[a]
  dog, cat, friend, . . . , cat, world, . . .

Recognition memory: Nonrepeats are targets[b]
  dog, cat, friend, . . . , cat, world, . . .

Lexical decision[c]
  dog, dag, cgt, cat, rhombus, . . . ,
    . . . , cat, world, dag, rhombus, fiend, cgt, . . .

Recognition memory: Faces[d]
  face 1, face 2, face 3, . . . , face 2, face 33, . . .

Recognition memory: Auditory > auditory > visual[e]
  "dog", "cat", "friend", . . . , "cat", "world", . . . , wish, cat, . . .

Recognition memory: Patterns (black/white or color); Sounds (complex)[f]
  no N4

Sentence learning[g]
  The dog howled at the full
    moon. / MOON. / moonlike. / house. / peace.

Categorization; Words[h]
  dog, cat, cow, sheep, goat

  square, circle, triangle, oval, monkey

Naming[i]
  "cat"

Note. Double underscore, large N4; single underscore, small N4; no underscore, no N4.
  [a]Smith & Halgren (1989); [b]Smith (1986); [c]Smith & Halgren (1987b); [d]Smith & Halgren (1987a); [e]Domalski et al. (1989); [f]E. Halgren (unpublished data); [g]Desmedt (1981), Kutas & Hillyard (1980b, 1983); [h]Stuss et al. (1988); [i]Stuss et al. (1983).

effect of incongruity but rather from a diminishing effect of congruity. That is, it is supposed that all words evoke an N4, but that congruous words are easier to integrate and thus evoke a smaller N4. This interpretation permits a common explanation for all N4s regardless of whether the evoking word is presented in a sentence or in isolation. In contrast, the existence of N4s to isolated words is difficult to explain as a result of contextual incongruity, inasmuch as isolated words usually have no context to be incongruous with.

The ease-of-integration explanation also encompasses many other influences on the N4, most of which can be thought of as reflecting a preexisting memory trace for that word. This memory trace can be remote, recent, or primary and is especially effective if it relates the word to the current context. For example, the influence of remote lexical memory is apparent in the smaller N4 evoked by commonly used (i.e., high-frequency) English words as compared to uncommon words (Smith & Halgren, 1987b; Van Petten & Kutas, in press). Remote semantic memory also influences the N4: if the terminal word of a sentence is in accord with a known fact, then a smaller N4 will be evoked than if the sentence were false (Fischler, Bloom, Childers, Roucos, & Perry, 1983; Fischler, Bloom, Childers, Arroyo, & Perry, 1984). The N4 decrease to semantically congruous words within sentences can also be thought of as due to a preexisting semantic memory. Similarly, a decreased N4 is evoked by an isolated word that follows a sentence, if the word is semantically related to that sentence (Neville, Kutas, Chesney, & Schmidt, 1986). Finally, the N4 to a target word is smaller if it is preceded by words of the same category (Stuss, Picton, & Cerri, 1988) or by a synonym (Bentin, McCarthy, & Wood, 1985; Holcomb, 1986; Paller, Kutas, & Mayes, 1987; Sanquist, Rohrbaugh, Syndulko, & Lindsey, 1980). All of the above influences on the N4, with the exception of word frequency, require both remote semantic memory (determining which knowledge structure is activated by the preceding words) and primary memory (maintaining that knowledge structure in an active state until the target word arrives).

Very strong modulatory effects on the N4 are also induced by contextual repetition in recent memory. Repetition of a word or face induces a large decrease of the N4, even if the repetition is not task relevant (Smith & Halgren, 1987b). The imposition of a delay or of distracting stimuli between initial and subsequent presentation of the target word does not appreciably reduce the effect up to about a minute (Rugg & Nagy, 1987). Similarly, sentences that are consistent with information learned the preceding day evoke a smaller N4 than do false sentences (Fischler, Childers, Achariyapaopan, & Perry, 1985). The memory trace underlying these effects is not modality specific: the repetition-induced N4 decrease persists when words are learned in one modality and tested in another (Domalski, Smith, & Halgren, 1989). However, the stimulus must be meaningful; delayed repetition of a pronounceable nonword has no effect on the size of the N4 it evokes (Smith & Halgren, 1987b) (Figure 2).

P3

The N4 after the final word of a sentence is usually followed by a late positivity at 600 msec. This is equivalent to the well-known "P3" or "P300" EP component but has a long latency due to the complexity of the preceding cognitive processing (Kutas, McCarthy, & Donchin, 1977). More generally, the tasks described above evoke an N4/P3 sequence with the amplitude of the P3 changing across task conditions in the opposite direction from the N4. For example, a large P3 follows the small N4 evoked by a repeated word or face (Halgren & Smith, 1987).

As the scalp N4 becomes smaller, it becomes more positive. As the P3 becomes larger, it also becomes more positive. Furthermore, the scalp topographies of the N4 and the P3 are similar. Thus, the possibility is raised that it is not the N4 and P3 themselves that change with ease of contextual integration, but rather that this ease superimposes a prolonged positivity onto both the N4 and P3

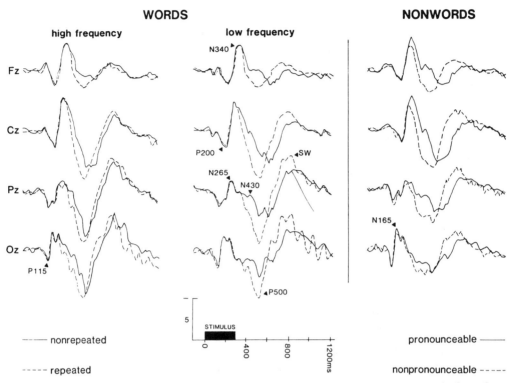

Figure 2. Effects of repetition, frequency, and pronounceability on EPs to words and nonwords. The grand average EP waveforms across subjects are displayed with negativity up. Left and middle columns illustrate the effects of repetition on high- and low-frequency words. The N4 (N430) decreases in amplitude with word repetition, whereas the P3 (P500) increases. The EPs evoked by repeated words are approximately equal regardless of whether the word occurs with high or low frequency in general usage (dotted lines, left and center columns). However, the N430 to nonrepeated words is larger if the word is low frequency (compare solid lines at Pz in center and left columns). The right column illustrates the effect of pronounceability on nonwords. Repeated and nonrepeated nonwords have been averaged together because no effect of repetition was found for nonwords. Note that the EPs evoked by pronounceable nonwords closely resemble those evoked by low-frequency nonrepeated words. Vertical scale is 5 µV. From M. E. Smith & E. Halgren, 1987b. Event-related potentials during lexical decision: Effects of repetition, word frequency, pronounceability, and concreteness. *Electroencephalography and Clinical Neurophysiology, Supplement, 40,* 417–421. Copyright 1987 by Elsevier Science Publishers. Reprinted by permission.

(Rugg, 1987; Rugg et al., 1988; Rugg & Nagy, 1987). However, with depth recordings (see below), it is possible to record from sites where only the N4 or only the P3 is visible or where they have the same polarity (Smith, Stapleton, & Halgren, 1986). At these sites, it is clear that the N4 decreases as words are repeated *and* that the P3 increases.

Previous reviews of the cognitive process represented by the P3 have concentrated on experiments using simple stimuli, and have developed a concept of the P3 as representing the brain's reaction of "surprise" to "rare" stimuli (Donchin, 1981; Pritchard, 1981). In the clinical standard "auditory oddball" task, the subject listens to brief high- or low-pitched tones presented once every second. The high-pitched tones comprise 20% of the total and occur in random order with the low tones. The high tones are silently counted; the low tones are ignored. The high tones evoke a P3 in this task; the low do not. "Rare" stimuli in the other sensory modalities also evoke P3s with the same scalp topography and presumed brain generators (Simson, Vaughan, & Ritter, 1977).

In contrast to these experiments with simple stimuli, experiments using words or other complex stimuli have not found a positive correlation between the amplitude of the P3 and the rarity of the stimulus that evokes it. Rather, an inverse relationship is often found. For example, in lexical decision, words that are *rarely* used in general usage evoke a *smaller* P3 than do more common words (Smith & Halgren, 1987b). Furthermore, words that occur only once in a particular task and thus are *rare* within the task context evoke a *smaller* P3 than do words that occur many times (Smith & Halgren, 1989). The inverse relationship between rarity and the P3 in these tasks can be explained by the fact that for words, rarity implies a lack of familiarity in recent or remote memory, and such words are relatively more difficult to integrate with the cognitive context than are familiar words. Thus, in these tasks, the P3 is correlated not with rarity but with ease of integration.

A confounding factor in comparing the influence on the P3 of rarity in tasks comprised of words versus the influence of rarity in tasks using simple stimuli is that each word is identifiably unique and has an *a priori* intrinsic meaning within a semantic structure, whereas simple stimuli do not. Consequently, the types of rarity possessed by words in the tasks discussed above (by uncommon words or by words only occurring once in a task) may have no direct parallel to the rarity of high as compared to low tones in the auditory oddball task. The rarity of high tones in this task derives from their membership in a relatively less frequent task-relevant category. It is therefore important to note that the P3 correlation with easily integrated words obtains even when the words belong to a task-relevant category that is not rare. For example, repeated words evoke a large P3 even if they constitute 50% of the stimuli (Smith & Halgren, 1989) and regardless of whether the repeating words are the behavioral targets or nontargets (Smith, 1986). Similarly, in a lexical decision task where all words are behavioral targets, only those words that repeat evoke a large P3 (Smith & Halgren, 1987b). Finally, Kutas and colleagues (reviewed in Kutas & Van Petten, 1987) have systematically varied the proportion of sentences ending incongruously without affecting the increased positivity evoked by congruous sentences. Thus, even if the "rarity" of a word is determined by the rarity of the task-relevant category to which it belongs, rarity of words is not associated with a large P3.

Although it is therefore not possible to interpret the P3 evoked by words as a response to rarity, it *is* possible to interpret the P3 evoked by simple tones as a response to ease of integration. This analysis begins by recognizing the similarities between the P3s evoked by words and those evoked by simple tones. First, as the P3 to words is preceded by the N4, the P3 to simple tones is also preceded by a widespread negative cognitive EP component termed the N2 (Pritchard et al., 1988). Furthermore, like the N4/P3, the N2/P3 is only evoked if the stimulus satisfies some minimal criteria during processing *antecedent* to the N2/P3. The minimal antecedent criterion for the N4/P3 is that the stimulus be potentially meaningful (i.e., is word-like or face-like). The minimal criterion for the N2/P3 is less restrictive, requiring only that the stimulus be potentially significant in the task context. That is, an N2/P3 is triggered by every attended stimulus unless antecedent processing (completed by 150 msec after stimulus onset) establishes that the stimulus could not be a target. Finally, this model assumes, as for the P3 following words, that once evoked, the amplitude of the P3 to simple stimuli is also proportional to the ease of processing the stimulus to completion.

Thus, complex attended stimuli generally all evoke P3s, with the size proportional to the ease of contextual integration. Similarly, for simple stimuli, large P3s are evoked by rare target stimuli (e.g., high tones in the auditory oddball task) because they cannot be ignored and they are very easy to process. Conversely, frequent nontarget stimuli evoke no P3 because they *can* be ignored. As predicted by this model, simple tones evoke P3s even if all stimuli are identical, provided that they are difficult to ignore because they are occurring at a low rate and are all targets (Stapleton, O'Reilly, & Halgren, 1987).

Across many tasks, the latency to the peak of the P3 is approximately equal to the latency of the behavioral response (Kutas et al., 1977). Since the time from P3 onset to peak is about equal to the time from decision to movement, this implies that the P3 begins when stimulus categorization is complete (Desmedt, 1981). This in turn has suggested that the P3 reflects "context updating" (Donchin & Coles, 1988) or "contextual closure" (Verleger, 1988). The additional correlation of the P3 with stimuli that are too easy (given the processing resources assigned to them) suggests that the P3 may represent an active termination of processing.

Neural Generators

MEDIAL TEMPORAL LOBE RECORDINGS IN HUMANS

Most of our knowledge regarding the neural basis of the N4/P3 arises from direct recordings from the medial temporal lobe (MTL; hippocampus, parahippocampal gyrus, and amygdala) in behaving humans. Complex partial seizures are often not possible to control with anticonvulsant medications and often begin in the MTL. In order to localize the seizure focus prior to its surgical removal, it is sometimes necessary to implant electrodes into the MTL. While awaiting a spontaneous seizure, the patient may consent to perform time-locked cognitive tasks as his or her MTL EEG and units are recorded. Perhaps fortuitously

(Halgren et al., in press), the MTL is also an area of great intrinsic neuropsychological interest because of the severe but very selective amnesia that results from bilateral MTL lesions (Corkin, 1984; Squire, 1987). Due to its well-organized anatomy and phylogenetic conservation across all mammals, the hippocampus is especially well studied (O'Keefe & Nadel, 1978). In particular, the dense bidirectional connections between the MTL and the highest levels of association cortex (Van Hoesen, 1982; Insausti, Amaral, & Cowan, 1987) make the MTL an ideal vantage point from which to view integrated association cortex activity. Connections within the MTL are highly plastic, as exhibited by the phenomena of kindling and long-term potentiation (LTP) (McNaughton, 1983; Racine, Milgram, & Hafner, 1983). Hippocampal LTP has several properties (pre- and postsynaptic specificity, long time constant, associativity) consistent with models suggesting that the recent memory trace lies within the hippocampus (Gardner-Medwin, 1976; Halgren, 1984; Marr, 1971; Lynch, 1986).

Hippocampal amnesia is restricted to the loss of memory for recent cognitive events (Squire, 1987). Remote semantic memory (e.g., the vocabulary) is intact, as is primary memory (e.g., the conceptual structure constructed as a paragraph is read). Priming, the facilitated reactivation of recently activated but preexisting cognitive elements (e.g., reading a particular word faster the second time it appears in a paragraph), is also preserved (Schacter, 1987). Noncognitive sensorimotor learning (e.g., conditioning or learning to read or draw in a mirror) is normal (Corkin, 1984).

Consequently, it seems that MTL involvement would be restricted to stages of information processing that invoke input and/or output from recent cognitive memory. In practice, this does not result in much of a limitation: all major cognitive EP components are prominent in the MTL, with evidence for local generation; only sensorimotor components have not yet been observed (Stapleton & Halgren, 1987; Halgren, in press). In the neurocognitive model outlined here, this corresponds to the introspection that recent cognitive memories are constantly being formed out of current experience (we remember now what we had for dinner last night without having consciously tried to enter it into memory) and that current experience is constantly being compared with recent cognitive memory (we may notice that our spouse is serving the same meal as he did last night, without having made any conscious effort to recall it).

MEDIAL TEMPORAL LOBE GENERATORS

The synaptic pathways active within the brain during the N4/P3 to words have only partially been identified (Halgren, Squires, Wilson, & Crandall, 1982; Halgren, Stapleton, Smith, & Altafullah, 1986; Knight, in press). Thus far, the largest depth potentials in the latency range of the N4/P3, and with similar cognitive correlates, have been recorded in the MTL. Such EPs, recorded within the MTL, are termed the MTL-N4 and MTL-P3 (Halgren, Squires, Wilson,

Rohrbaugh, & Babb, 1980; Stapleton & Halgren, 1987; Wood, McCarthy, Squires, Vaughan, & Woods, 1984; McCarthy, Wood, Williamson, & Spencer, in press). The MTL-N4 has been recorded (larger in the left or dominant hemisphere) primarily in a task requiring the detection of repetition of particular words within context, but it has also been observed in lexical decision (word/nonword discrimination) and naming (McCarthy & Wood, 1985; Smith, Stapleton, & Halgren, 1986) and to incongruent words at the end of sentences (McCarthy & Wood, 1984). The MTL-N4 to repeated words at 460 msec is followed by an MTL-P3 with latency to peak of 620 msec.

Like the scalp P3, an MTL-P3 with the same voltage topography is also evoked by visual or auditory stimuli or even by the omission of an expected stimulus (Squires, Halgren, Wilson, & Crandall, 1983; Simson et al., 1977; McCarthy & Wood, 1987; Halgren et al., 1983; Stapleton & Halgren, 1987). The large amplitude of the MTL-N4 and -P3 relative to simultaneously recorded EPs in adjacent structures, the steep voltage gradients and polarity inversions of these components within the MTL, together with the correlated unit activity, all establish that the MTL-N4 and -P3 are locally generated (Halgren et al., 1980). The MTL-P3 appears to be generated in the hippocampus (HC) proper, whereas the MTL-N4, with a slightly different voltage topography, may also receive contributions from the parahippocampal and/or fusiform gyri (Smith, Stapleton, & Halgren, 1986). Neurons in the latter structures have been found to respond to novel complex stimuli in primates (Wilson, Brown, & Richies, 1988).

EFFECTS OF LESIONS

Analyses of the propagation of electrically or spontaneously induced potentials from the MTL to the scalp have suggested that such propagation may result in some but not all of the scalp-recorded N4 and P3 (Altafullah, Halgren, Stapleton, & Crandall, 1986; Smith et al., 1983). Extratemporal generators have also been implicated by scalp recordings after unilateral anterior temporal lobotomy (ATL) for seizure relief. Neither left nor right ATL significantly affects the topography or amplitude of the N4 to words (Smith & Halgren, 1989) or of the P3 to rare tones (Stapleton, Halgren, & Moreno, 1987; Johnson, 1988; Wood et al., 1982). However, left ATL abolishes the P3 to repeated words, frontal lesions greatly decrease the P3 to complex nontarget stimuli, and temporal–parietal junction lesions abolish the P3 to rare tones (Smith & Halgren, 1989; Knight, 1984, in press). These effects are all specific for the P3 evoked in a particular task but not other tasks. Furthermore, the P3 decreases are all bilateral and symmetrical even though the lesions are unilateral. Thus, these effects appear to reveal structures that are necessary to release the P3 in some situations, rather than structures that exclusively generate the P3. That is, the frontal, temporal–parietal, and anteromedial temporal cortices can all function as antecedent structures to the P3, depending upon the task.

A similar interpretation may be applied to a recent study by Kutas, Hillyard, and Gazzaniga (1988). They presented sentences to patients who had previously received complete sections of the corpus callosum and anterior commissure. All except the last word of the sentence was presented binaurally. The last word was presented to either the left or right visual field and was either semantically congruous or incongruous with the rest of the sentence. In normal subjects, incongruous words in either hemifield evoked an N4 over both hemispheres, and this N4 was greatly attenuated to congruous words. However, in commissurotomized patients with left hemisphere speech, only right hemifield (i.e., left hemisphere) words evoked an N4. This suggests that a critical antecedent structure for the N4 to sentence terminal words lies in the left hemisphere.

EXTRATEMPORAL GENERATORS AND BRAINSTEM TRIGGERS

The extratemporal N4/P3 generators are not precisely known, but their general locations are suspected. Local maxima and inversions of the P3 have been observed in the frontal lobe (Smith et al., in press; McCarthy & Wood, 1987; Wood & McCarthy, 1985). P3 polarity inversions have not been observed in the parietal lobe, but relatively large-amplitude P3s with local voltage gradients are present in the inferior parietal lobule (Smith et al., in press). Since the absence of local polarity inversion may result from a diffuse local generator and/or a local generator that overlaps with far-field potentials from another structure, these data are consistent with an additional P3 generator in the inferoparietal cortex.

Although a systematic survey of intracranial sites for N4 generators is not yet complete, our initial observations suggest that it also may have multiple cortical generators in addition to the bilateral MTL generators described above (Smith et al., 1986). In normal subjects, relative glucose metabolism in the left angular gyrus is significantly increased during the performance of a lexical decision task with nonrepeated words but not during the same task with repeated words (Nenov, Halgren, Mandelkern, Ropchan, & Blahd, 1989). As expected, the nonrepeated words evoke a large N4, whereas the repeated words do not. Furthermore, across subjects the size of the N4 to nonrepeated words has a significant positive correlation with the size of the left angular gyrus metabolic increase in the same task. The implied left temporal–parietal N4 generator is further supported by unit changes in superior temporal cortex in response to word stimuli (Ojemann & Creutzfeldt, 1989).

Both frontal and posterior association cortex generators are consistent with the P3's scalp topography and the N4's as well (Kutas, Van Petten, & Besson, 1988; Stapleton et al., 1987; Simson et al., 1977; Smith & Halgren, 1987b). Unlike the P3, the topography of the N4 is modality specific, suggesting that higher-order sensory association as well as polymodal association cortices may participate in its generation (Domalski et al., 1989). The N4 evoked by words presented to the left hemisphere in commissurotomized patients is nearly symmetrical at the scalp (Kutas, Hillyard, et al., 1988). Since the interhemispheric connections have been severed in these patients, this implies that left-hemisphere processing activates a brainstem N4 *trigger*, which in turn induces the N4 in multiple generators in *both* hemispheres. Similarly, the existence of a brainstem P3 trigger is implied by the apparent existence of multiple P3 generators in both hemispheres.

Neither the N4 nor the P3 trigger needs to possess powerful intrinsic information-processing capabilities, inasmuch as there appears to be little selectivity as to which generating structures are activated across the various tasks where the N4 or P3 is evoked. Rather, the selectivity seems to lie in the cortical antecedent structures that decide the timing and extent of trigger activation. The triggers, although not complex, do need to have widespread bilateral cortical and limbic projections, possibly implicating, as have recent animal studies, the cholinergic (Harrison, Buchwald, Kaga, Woolf, & Butcher, 1988) or noradrenergic (Pineda, Foote, & Neville, 1987) systems (Halgren, in press).

Simultaneous Action Potentials

MODULATORY

Although the effects of rarity in MTL unit firing are not universal or large, some MTL neurons do change their firing rate to rare tones (Halgren et al., 1980, 1983). In general, these effects are a decrease in firing during the P3, suggesting that the P3 may represent neuronal inhibition (Heit, Smith, & Halgren, in press). A similar conclusion may be drawn from comparison of the MTL-P3 with the typical slow wave that follows interictal epileptiform spikes in the hippocampus (Altafullah et al., 1986). Interictal spikes reflect the nearly simultaneous activation of a large proportion of the neuronal pool. This activation leads, via both intracellular and local circuit mechanisms, to a profound inhibition of cell firing and to a simultaneous large field potential. The relative amplitude and polarity of this potential across MTL sites and across patients are very similar to (but larger than) the amplitude and polarity of the P3 recorded from the same MTL sites and from the same patients. This similar topography suggests that the MTL-P3 and the postspike slow wave have similar synaptic generators and, thus, that the MTL-P3 may also represent synaptic inhibition.

Neuronal inhibition during the P3 is consistent with the psychological correlates of the P3 (reviewed above), which suggest that the P3 represents active closure of processing in the second phase of contextual integration (Halgren & Smith, 1987). In contrast, the psychological correlates of the N4 suggest that it represents the first phase of associative activation. Relative excitation during this phase would encourage connections to be formed linking the disparate semantic elements activated by the stimulus with those contextual elements already active in primary memory. However, runaway excitation could result if this initial N4 period of divergent associations continued indefinitely. Relative inhibition during the following P3 phase of cognitive closure would result in convergent excitation from several sources being required for an element to remain activated. Thus, the N4/P3 is conceived as representing excitation/inhibition encouraging divergent/convergent associations during the evolution of a cognitive gestalt (Figure 3). Similar mechanisms have been found to be useful in neural network models in which the optimal representation of an event as a distributed pattern of activity needs to be constructed from an incomplete initial input (Ackley, Hinton, & Seijnowski, 1985; Gardner-Medwin, 1976; Nenov, Read, Halgren, & Dyer, 1990).

INFORMATION SPECIFIC

If this model is correct, and the N4/P3 functions to assist contextual integration of disparate information, then signs of specific information encoding should be found in widespread cortical and subcortical areas during the N4/P3, paralleling the widespread generators of the N4/P3. In neural network models, neuronal encoding of an event is manifested as a pattern of cell firing across a neuronal ensemble. Distinct events are encoded with distinct patterns. Thus, it is to be expected that distinct events encoded by the same neuronal ensemble will evoke identical EPs, inasmuch as EPs spatially average synaptic current flows from the entire ensemble. On the other hand, individual neurons should reveal different levels of activation to different events. Simulation experiments with neural networks have found that many individual units fire specifically to particular events, even though information representation is distributed across the network (Anderson & Mozer, 1981).

This indeed is what was found when MTL units were recorded during the contextual word recognition task described above to evoke an N4/P3 (Heit, Smith, & Halgren, 1988). In this task, each of the 10 repeated words occurs a total of nine times during the task, in random order with other repeated and nonrepeated words. About three-quarters of the units tested, located throughout the MTL, had visually and statistically significant evidence for specific activation to one of the 10 repeating words (Figure 4). Of the 14 units tested during an analogous recognition memory for repeated faces, two responded to an individual face. Units with word- or face-specific responses were distinguished from those with simple sensory responses by their longer latency, more anterior location, and lack of response to a reversing checkerboard. These units were distinguished from the response-related units (Halgren, Babb, & Crandall, 1978; Heit et al., in press) by their earlier latency and occurrence in the absence of a key-press response.

The specific firing is too common, given our limited sampling and the large number of words in the average vocabulary, to avoid the conclusion that these cells would fire to other words in other circumstances. In fact, of the 13 units tested with two sets of words, eight responded specifically to a different word in each set. This may imply that the cells are encoding the stimulus within a particular context (i.e., the event) rather than the stimulus itself.

The cells fired at a high enough rate that, if the basic synaptic parameters of the human hippocampus are similar to those of the rat's, then long-term potentia-

ERP Component:	N4	P3
Associative Activation:	Divergent	Convergent
Firing Threshold:	Low	High

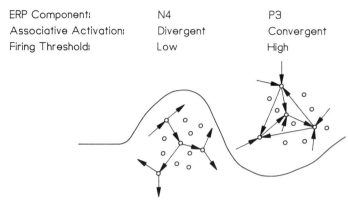

Figure 3. The cycle of neurally encoding a word within its context. At the beginning of the first stage, a small number of elements are active, representing the lexically encoded word and contextual constraints. During this stage (embodied by the N4), excitation easily spreads outward from these elements, causing divergent associations because of the low firing threshold of cortical elements. In the second stage (embodied by the P3), the higher firing threshold results in elements only being activated if they receive convergent inputs. By allowing distant associations, the first stage tests many possible solutions to the problem of encoding the word within its context. The second stage ensures that the solution chosen will be a good one (i.e., that it will satisfy multiple constraints).

tion of the specific synapses activated by the event should have occurred. However, these units showed no overall change in firing rate to repeated versus nonrepeated stimuli, nor did they increase their rate to a given stimulus as it was repeated. Thus, these data suggest that if long-term potentiation is involved in recent memory, its role might be to stabilize the MTL encoding of a particular event rather than to augment the MTL response to repeated events (Heit et al., 1988). If, as suggested above, the P3 represents neuronal inhibition in the hippocampus, then the lack of change in word-specific cell firing to repeated words may reflect the canceling influences of increased synaptic drive (due to long-term potentiation) counteracted by increased inhibition (reflected by the P3). The increased P3 may reflect activation of homeostatic intrinsic hippocampal circuitry, where powerful feedforward and feedback inhibition functions to maintain a relatively constant level of overall excitation (Buzsaki, 1984). This homeostatic circuitry focalizes excitation in those neurons that have received convergent input against a background of diffuse inhibition.

The word- and face-specific responses occur during the N4, beginning at about the time that the MTL-N4s to repeated versus nonrepeated words begin to diverge (Figure 4). This suggests that the word- and face-specific MTL firing may project to the neocortex and contribute to the repetition-induced decrease of the N4. This is also consistent with the fact that removal of the region containing these word-context-specific cells eliminates the repetition-induced decrease of the N4 (Smith & Halgren, 1989).

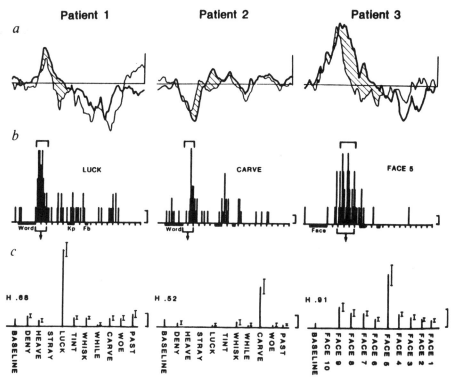

Figure 4. Responses of hippocampal neurons to a particular word or face. Displayed are simultaneous averaged field potentials (*a*), sum histograms of neuronal firing in response to preferred stimuli (*b*), and total number of action potentials in response to all repeated stimuli during a selected time period (*c*) for three left anterior hippocampal units in three patients. (*a*) Stimulus repetition produces a smaller, earlier N4 (nonrepeated versus repeated N4/P3 difference is shaded). The EPs are averages of all repeated (thin lines) and nonrepeated (thick lines) stimuli. Each EP was recorded from the same electrode as the accompanying unit data. The N4 in column 2 is positive, presumably because it was recorded across the N4 reversal plane, near the N4-generating synapses. Vertical calibration, 50 μV. Negative is up. (*b*) Time course of the stimulus-specific responses to the nine presentations of the preferred word (patient 1, 2) or face (patient 3). Vertical calibration, 10 spikes per second; horizontal scale, 100 msec per division. (*c*) The unit response to the specific stimulus ($p < .0001$) is compared to that of the other nine repeated stimuli ($p > .1$). Displayed is the total activity ($\pm$S.E.) for the time window bracketed in *b*. Vertical calibration, 5 spikes per second. Abbreviations: Kp, averaged key press; Fb, feedback tone; H, breadth of tuning index. From G. Heit, M. E. Smith, & E. Halgren, 1988. Neural encoding of individual words and faces by the human hippocampus and amygdala. *Nature, 333,* 773–775. Copyright 1988 by Macmillan Publishers Ltd. Reprinted by permission.

More generally, these results are consistent with specific events being encoded by unique patterns of cell firing distributed across widespread cortical and subcortical structures. The segment of the pattern in each structure makes a distinct contribution to contextual integration by virtue of that structure's distinct intrinsic physiology and extrinsic connections. The nature of that structure's contribution determines, in turn, the neuropsychological deficit observed after its removal.

PRIMARY MEMORY POTENTIALS: THE CNV

The EPs to successive individual words in a sentence are superimposed on a slow negative potential that resolves when the sentence is completed (Kutas, Van Petten, et al., 1988). The identity of this slow potential is not known, but it is probably similar to the central part of the contingent negative variation ("CNV") (Halgren, in press). The CNV is observed between two stimuli (S1 and S2) when the response to the second (S2) depends upon its relationship to the first (S1) (Walter, 1964). The implication that the CNV may represent, in part, neural activity supporting the maintenance of S1 in an active state in primary or working memory has been supported by studies in animals demonstrating information-specific firing during the CNV. Units may exhibit sustained firing during the S1–S2 interval that differentiates among the different S1s present in the task (see Fuster, this volume).

Although the CNV has primarily been associated with frontal cortex, intracranial recordings in humans have also found large CNVs in central and parietal cortex (Papakostopoulos, Cooper, & Crow, 1976; Groll-Knapp, Ganglberger, Haider, & Schmid, 1980) as well as in numerous subcortical nuclei (McCallum & Papakostopoulos, 1976; McCallum et al., 1973; Tsubokawa & Moriyasu, 1978; Tsubokawa, Katayama, Nishimoto, Kotani, & Moriyasu, 1976). A similar CNV distribution has been recorded in monkeys (Donchin, Otto, Gerbrandt, & Pribram, 1971; Rebert, 1973; Stamm & Raven, 1972; McSherry & Borda, 1973). Furthermore, cell firing correlated with the CNV has been found in the primate dorsolateral and orbital frontal lobe, the MTL, the supplementary motor cortex, and the frontal eye fields (see Halgren, in press; Fuster, this volume, for review).

Sustained firing by local neurons may evoke the CNV by causing extracellular potassium accumulation (Caspers, Speckmann, & Lehmenkuhler, 1980). The potassium is shunted through a radially oriented glial syncytium, resulting in the generating dipole (Somjen, 1973, 1979). Sustained cellular activation appears to rely on a pathway from the mesencephalic reticular formation (Skinner & Yingling, 1977; Desmedt, 1981) with a relay in the cholinergic cells of the nucleus basalis (Pirch, Corbus, Rigdon, & Lynes, 1986; Rebert, Tecce, Marczynski, Pirch, & Thompson, 1986). This mechanism is consistent with the effects of lesions upon the CNV in humans: localized cortical lesions produce a decrease of the CNV at the overlying scalp but not elsewhere (McCallum & Cummins, 1973; Cohen,

1975; Zappoli, Papini, Briani, Benvenuti, & Pasquinelli, 1976), whereas widespread decreases in the CNV may result from small diencephalic lesions (Low, 1979).

The sustained information-specific firing patterns represented by the CNV are hypothesized to maintain contextual information between successive words in a sentence. This contextual information is integrated with each word during the N4/P3 (Figure 1). Anatomically, the contextual information can be maintained in the frontal lobe while the posterior sensory association cortex lexically encodes the word. Subsequent integration involves posterior, frontal, and limbic supramodal association cortices. Consistent with this model, frontal lobe lesions impair the retrieval of contextual aspects of recent memory (Squire, 1987). For example, although patients with frontal lobe dysfunction may recall recent events, they may be mistaken in recalling when or where they occurred. Some preliminary evidence suggests that frontal lobe lesions may also reduce the complexity of the context constructed internally as a sentence is read (Tyler, 1987).

PSYCHOLOGICAL IMPLICATIONS OF NEURAL STAGES

The utility of the neural model of reading proposed here lies in the novel insights it may provide into the mechanisms of reading. These mechanisms have been intensively studied in normal subjects using the latency of behavioral response when reading individual words or complete sentences. Separate processing stages are deduced when variables have independent effects on reaction time (Sternberg, 1969; Posner, 1978). The durations of these stages are inferred from the influence of a primary stimulus on the behavioral reaction to a subsequent target stimulus as the prime–target delay is varied (Welford, 1980; Van Petten & Kutas, 1987). These studies are inevitably ambiguous, because only the end product of reading is observed. Earlier stages can be directly observed using EPs. Thus, consideration of EPs together with the psychological evidence can help resolve outstanding questions regarding the nature and timing of the successive information-processing stages during reading.

Immediate Contextual Integration

ON-LINE CONTROL OF EYE MOVEMENTS IN READING

The most salient observable behavior during reading is eye movement (Just & Carpenter, 1987). When reading for comprehension a text appropriate to his or her level, a reader will fixate nearly every content word at least once. Fixations are short on the average (about 240 msec) and are separated by saccades lasting 10–20 msec. A given word may receive multiple fixations, which in aggregate is termed a gaze (Just & Carpenter, 1980). Gaze duration is extremely variable (standard deviation about 170 msec). This variation is systematically related to the physical, lexical, semantic, syntactic, and contextual characteristics of the current word (Carpenter & Just, 1983; Just & Carpenter, 1980; Frazier & Rayner, 1982). Thus, the currently fixated word must be processed to the level of these characteristics before the gaze is terminated with a saccade. Such on-line control of fixation duration is also implied by the effects of masking the word as soon as it is fixated. Fixation then persists until after the word is unmasked (Rayner, Inhoff, Morrison, Slowiaczek, & Bertera, 1981).

A similar conclusion can be drawn from "garden path"-type sentences, for example, *Keshiva contemplated his navel orange*. When first read, "navel" is interpreted as a noun; then when "orange" is encountered, "navel" is reinterpreted as an adjective. The fact that "navel" had to be reinterpreted implies that it was interpreted when first encountered beyond simple identification as a word, but with a part of speech and place in the sentence (direct object). Tentatively assigning case roles to words as soon as possible may result in misinterpretations, which could in most cases be avoided if this assignment were delayed until the end of the sentence. However, delaying assignment would entail a more severe cost—keeping in working memory a combinational explosion of meanings, case roles, and referents for all the preceding words. Garden path sentences are rare—words are seldom misinterpreted—precisely because so much information is brought to bear on interpretation of each word as it is fixated (Just & Carpenter, 1980). This information includes the history of the word (Has it been read recently? Is it a common word?) and the various meanings of the word in view of the current semantic, syntactic, and pragmatic context (Who has written the passage and for what audience? What are the preceding words in the sentence? What's the topic?).

N4s TO INTERMEDIATE WORDS IN SENTENCES

Van Petten and Kutas (1987) have found that an N4 is evoked by every word of a sentence (see also Van Petten & Kutas, in press; Kutas, Van Petten, et al., 1988). The N4 to "closed-class" words such as "the" or "a" is much smaller than the N4s to content words. N4s are largest to the initial words in a sentence and decline in size as contextual constraints develop, provided that the evoking word is in harmony with those constraints. This occurrence of an N4 to each word in stationary reading is most consistent with models of reading that propose that each word is interpreted as soon as it is encountered (Just & Carpenter, 1980).

Alternative "wait-and-see" models (Kimball, 1973; Marcus, 1980) are not strictly ruled out for natural reading, inasmuch as stationary reading is considerably slower than natural reading and thus may encourage on-line contextual integration. However, Marton and Szirtes (1988) studied the EPs evoked by the last word in a normal reading paradigm. They found an N4/P3 sequence following the final saccade of approximately the same size as had previously been found at the end of a sentence read in the stationary mode. In contrast, a "wait-and-see" model would predict a larger N4 to the final word in normal reading because contextual integration would be delayed until that time. Marton and Szirtes further found that the N4 was quite small to the last word if it was contextually highly constrained. This would also not be expected in a "wait-and-see" model, because the contextual constraints would not develop until after the final word.

Contextual Influences in Lexical Access

MODULARITY IN READING

A fundamental characteristic distinguishing psychological models of reading is whether word recognition is influenced by the semantic context and, if so, at what level? For example, does reading the sentence fragment "I like my coffee with cream and" make it easier to access the word "sugar"? If so, is this influence limited to the level of the word itself, or does it extend further to letter identification (e.g., by priming feature detectors for S-U-G-A-R) or even to lower-level perceptual processes (e.g., by priming a feature detector for a curved line in the left visual field). Some models posit that lexical processing is modular. For example, Seidenberg (1985) divided reading into (1) *prelexical* processes that analyze the visual input to the point where it is identified as a particular word, (2) *lexical access*, the activation of semantic, phonological, and other information associated with that word, and (3) *postlexical* processes that select, elaborate, and integrate lexical information for comprehension. He proposes that contextual information influences only postlexical, not prelexical, processes and thus that the speed that information is made available by lexical access as well as the content of that information will be constant across sentence contexts. He does, however, allow for simple activation to spread between semantically related words (intra-lexical priming). In contrast, other authors (Rumelhart, 1977; Marslen-Wilson & Tyler, 1980) have proposed models in which information from different levels interacts in a relatively unconstrained manner.

Evoked potential waveforms are not influenced by contextual constraints until about 260 msec after word onset, the beginning of the N4. Thus, EPs clearly support the distinction between later processes subject to contextual influences and earlier processes that are not. The critical question then becomes the relationship of the N4 to lexical access. If N4 onset is the point where lexical access occurs, then contextual influences would evidently be confined to postlexical processes. On the other hand, if the N4 reflects processes leading to lexical access, then it would have to be concluded that prelexical processes are also subject to contextual influences.

In deciding this question, it is necessary to distinguish between processes that are antecedent to and trigger the N4 (see above) and those processes that are actually embodied in the brain activity generating the N4 (Figure 5). Variables that affect an antecedent process will determine if the N4 occurs or not and, if it does, its onset latency. In contrast, variables that act on an embodied process will modulate the amplitude and duration of the N4. Consequently, the antecedent process can be inferred to be the minimum necessary to distinguish the categories

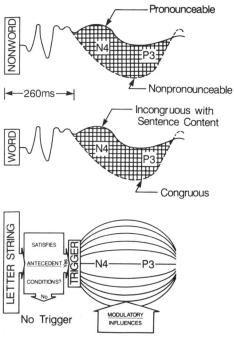

Figure 5. Logic of inferring the psychological process embodied by the N4 from its cognitive task correlates. The *antecedent* process is deduced as the *minimum* that is *necessary* and *sufficient* to distinguish the situations in which the N4 is triggered from those in which it is not. There is no difference in the N4s evoked by words as compared with pronounceable nonwords; thus, access to meaning is not a necessary antecedent process. Conversely, the lack of an N4 to nonpronounceable nonwords implies that antecedent processing must include a test of the stimulus for legality as a symbolic entry to the semantic system. This test is sufficient to distinguish other situations that trigger the N4 (e.g., recognizable drawings, and known or unknown faces) from those that do not (e.g., abstract drawings). In contrast, *modulatory* influences are those that, once the N4 has already been triggered, affect its duration and amplitude. Modulatory influences are differentiated from the antecedent process in that modulatory influences are graded rather than all or none and are either not necessary or not sufficient to distinguish situations that evoke an N4 from those that do not. For example, the incongruity of a word with the preceding sentence context has a strong correlation with N4 amplitude (Kutas & Van Petten, 1987). However, this influence is graded according to how incongruous the word is. Furthermore, both pronounceable and nonpronounceable nonwords are equally incongruous, but only pronounceable nonwords trigger an N4; thus, incongruity is not sufficient to distinguish those situations that evoke an N4. Similarly, N4s are evoked by words or nonwords outside sentence contexts where there is nothing to be incongruous with; thus, incongruity is not necessary for triggering the N4. Consequently, despite the similar EP differences associated with pronounceability (of nonwords) and incongruity (of sentence terminal words), they are interpreted as reflecting antecedent conditions or modulatory influences on the N4, respectively. Furthermore, since the onset latencies of these EP differences are approximately equal (at 260 msec), and the ease with which a word is integrated into the sentence context is dependent on that word's meaning, it is apparent that meaning must begin to be accessed at the beginning of the N4. The implication, then, is that the N4 embodies a process that is triggered by lexical encoding of a potentially meaningful stimulus, and is modulated by the ease of integrating the meaning of that stimulus within the cognitive context. These characteristics provide an operational definition for a single process of lexical access and contextual integration.

of stimuli that evoke the N4 from those that do not. The experimental data clearly indicate that a necessary and sufficient antecedent process for the N4 is the evaluation of the stimulus for potential meaningfulness. That is, words evoke an N4, but so do nonword letter strings provided that they are pronounceable (Smith & Halgren, 1987b). Similarly, known faces evoke an N4, but so do strangers' faces, whereas equally complex visual stimuli that cannot be encoded in these ways evoke no N4 (Smith & Halgren, 1987a; Barrett et al., 1988). Furthermore, the onset latency of the N4 is the same for high- and low-frequency words (as defined by their point of divergence from nonpronounceable nonwords), indicating that the ease of lexical access does not influence N4 onset (Smith & Halgren, 1987b; Van Petten & Kutas, in press). In short, the fact that nonwords can evoke an N4 is inconsistent with lexical access being completed by N4 onset.

Rather than lexical access, it appears that N4 onset reflects the point of lexical encoding: the point at which the visual stimulus can begin to gain access to its meaning. Preceding lexical encoding is a separable, modular, and necessary process for detecting letters and combinations of letters and recasting the visual stimulus into a form that can access the lexicon. The completion of this process may be identified as the point where the EPs to words (or pronounceable nonwords) diverges from those to nonpronounceable letter strings. This does not occur before the beginning of the N4, as identified by the point at which semantic contextual constraints influence the EP. Therefore, EP evidence indicates that processing prior to lexical encoding is not influenced by contextual information. However, lexical access itself must occur later, during the N4, under contextual influence.

Although lexical access cannot be completed before the N4, lexical access must start as soon as the N4 starts because the influence of context is dependent on the meaning of the word, and this influence is apparent from N4 onset. For example, in the sentence "The dog howled at the full <word>," the N4 to the word "peace" cannot diverge from the N4 to "moon" until the meaning of peace and/or moon begins to be accessed. This raises the question of whether the N4 embodies only lexical access or whether it embodies contextual integration as well. The fact that the N4 is modulated by the relationship of the word to information in primary, episodic, and semantic memories is consistent with either position, inasmuch as these variables could influence lexical access as well as contextual integration. However, the relative influence of these variables on the N4 follows more closely their putative importance for contextual integration than for lexical access. For example, word frequency (commonness of usage) is thought to be important for lexical decision but has a weaker effect on the N4 than does sentence context (Van Petten & Kutas, in press), delayed repetition in episodic memory (Smith & Halgren, 1987b), or semantic relatedness to a category prime (Stuss et al., 1988). Furthermore, the latency of the word-frequency effect on the N4 is no earlier (and may be later) than the contextual effects, so there is no evidence for successive phases of the N4 devoted first to lexical access and then to contextual integration.

Finally, the behavioral response in tasks that require contextual integration, not just lexical access, usually occurs shortly after the N4 terminates. For example, recognition of the delayed repetition of words within a context requires 600 to 700 msec, and the N4 terminates at about 550 msec (Smith & Halgren, 1989). During the intervening period, MTL units fire to targets but not to nontargets (Halgren et al., 1978; Heit et al., in press). This decision-related firing requires an antecedent process of contextual integration during the N4 period.

TIMING CONSIDERATIONS IN THE GENERALIZATION
FROM STATIONARY TO NATURAL READING

Rugg et al. (1988) noted that the average duration of eye fixations in natural reading is about the same as the N4's onset latency. Since, as reviewed above, eye-fixation duration is sensitive to semantic influences, it must be sufficient to complete lexical access. Thus, they concluded that the N4 follows lexical access. Actually, the duration of eye fixations must be adequate both to acquire the lexical information and to issue a command to move the eyes. That is, the existence of semantic influences on eye-fixation duration implies that an eye fixation must be long enough to include lexical access, the eye-movement decision process, and the time from decision to movement. Therefore, the maximum time necessary for lexical access must be less than eye-fixation duration minus the time from decision to eye movement (Figure 6).

The latency from motor command to saccade onset is uknown. An upper limit is provided by the observation that subjects instructed to move their eyes as rapidly as possible between targets spaced like words fixate for about 210 msec on each target (Rayner, 1983). A lower limit is provided by the observation that moving visual targets can influence a saccade until 70 msec before saccade onset, but this may be due to a brainstem mechanism (Becker & Jurgens, 1979). However, it is consistent with the 25-msec latency for evoking saccades by frontal eye field stimulation in monkeys (Robinson, Petersen, & Keys, 1986). This scales up to about 80 msec in humans. Furthermore, whereas the cognitive influence of the current word on gaze duration is large, its influence on the first fixation onto the current word is much smaller. This is because a difficult-to-understand word will be read with two or more sequential fixations, each of normal duration, separated by microsaccades (McConkie, 1983). Consequently, the cognitive signal controlling gaze duration does not need to precede the motor command for eye movement, provided that it can influence the saccade's destination. Assuming a fixation duration of 240 msec, this implies that saccade destination can be influenced until 160 msec after fixation onset—much shorter than the 260-msec N4 onset latency in stationary reading.

In fact, a closer examination suggests that this apparent contradiction probably results from accelerated information processing during natural reading through parafoveal information and postsaccadic facilitation. Reading is impossible in the absence of foveal vision (Rayner et al., 1981; Teuber, Battersby, &

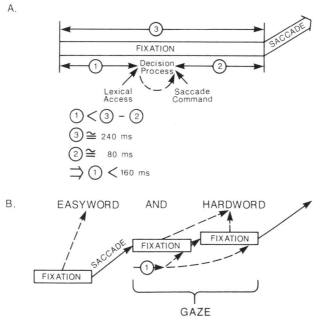

Figure 6. Implications of eye movements for the duration of lexical access. (A) Semantic influences on the timing and/or destination of a saccade imply that lexical access is complete before the final saccade command. Thus, the duration of lexical access (1) is less than the total duration of a saccade (3) minus the time from the saccade command to the eye movements (2). (B) Words that are particularly difficult to integrate (HARDWORD) may require multiple fixations. In this case, the timing of the second saccade may be influenced by the results of lexical access begun during the first fixation.

Bender, 1960), and vision is suppressed during the saccade preceding the fixation that foveates the word (Wolverton & Zola, 1983). Nonetheless, parafoveal vision is capable of detecting the length, shape, and initial letter of the word or two to the right of the currently fixated word (Pollatsek & Rayner, 1982; Rayner, 1981). The importance of this information is apparent in the increased fixation duration (to about 360 msec per word) that results when all except the currently fixated word is masked during reading (Rayner, 1983). Although much of the contribution of parafoveal vision to reading is in defining the optimal position to which to move the eyes on the next saccade, this information could also help prime possible candidates for the identity of next word, based on its length, shape, and initial letter. Combined with contextual constraints, this information may accelerate the next word's processing once it is encountered.

Visual information processing is also accelerated during natural reading because of postsaccadic facilitation: the more rapid processing of visual stimuli encountered immediately at the conclusion of a saccade. Allowing the word to be visible for only 50 msec after fixation onset has no effect on reading speed, suggesting that postsaccadic facilitation occurs during the crucial time for word encoding (Rayner et al., 1981). Marton et al. (Marton, Szirtes, & Breuer, 1985;

Marton, Szirtes, Donauer, & Breuer, 1985) compared the speed of word categorization when the word was presented to the subject at the point of visual fixation with that when the subject made a saccade to the word. The saccade was of sufficient distance (24°) to rule out any contribution of parafoveal vision. They found a postsaccadic facilitation of 75 msec in reaction time and 80–100 msec in N4 latency and speculated that this may be caused by an activating corollary discharge (Singer, 1977; Lal & Friedlander, 1989).

Thus, because of parafoveal vision and postsaccadic facilitation, word encoding is considerably faster during normal reading than during stationary reading. The above considerations suggest that if N4 onset were to be measured in natural reading, it might be found to be about 120 msec (260 msec in stationary reading, minus the 60-msec advantage from parafoveal information, minus the 80-msec advantage from postsaccadic facilitation). Clearly, these rough calculations would benefit from systematic studies of postsaccade EPs during completely natural reading. Nonetheless, they indicate that the eye-fixation data do not conflict with an onset of the N4 prior to lexical access.

Phonemic Encoding in Reading

DUAL-ROUTE MODELS OF READING

A classical problem in neuropsychology is whether the visually encoded word accesses its meaning(s) directly or whether it first is recoded phonemically. If phonemic recoding is necessary, then brain lesions that prevent understanding of spoken words should also prevent reading. This is generally true (Hecaen & Albert, 1978). The exception, pure word deafness, is a very rare syndrome and is thought to result from white matter lesions preventing auditory information from reaching Wernicke's area (Benson, 1979; Hecaen & Albert, 1978). On the other hand, three different types of reading disorders (dyslexias) have been described that seem to selectively impair either the direct or the phonemic route, implying that both exist (Coltheart, 1987). Patients with deep dyslexia typically misread the presented word as a word that is semantically related but phonemically unrelated (Coltheart, 1980). For example, "lizard" may be misread as "snake." The implication that the phonemic route is selectively impaired in these patients is supported by their inability to read nonwords aloud. An impairment of the phonemic route has also been inferred in patients with phonological dyslexia (Beauvois & Derouesne, 1979) from their inability to read nonwords. In contrast, the direct route seems to be selectively impaired in patients with surface dyslexia (Patterson, Marshall, & Coltheart, 1985). These patients can read nonwords but regularize words with irregular pronunciations. For example, they might mispronounce "throw" to rhyme with "cow."

The existence of dual routes to meaning in reading is also supported by more commonplace observations. The simple fact that normal subjects can read nonwords aloud implies that they are capable of inferring sounds from letters (termed grapheme-to-phoneme conversion); that is, the phonemic route exists. Conversely, the phonemic route cannot be necessary, because congenitally deaf individuals can learn to read, albeit in most cases only laboriously (Conrad, 1977). Furthermore, for skilled readers, normal reading proceeds without any sense of "internal speech."

In psychological studies of normal subjects, simple speech tasks (e.g., counting out loud) interfere with the comprehension of complicated passages (Slowaiczek & Clifton, 1980), suggesting that reading and speaking compete for the same cognitive resources. In visual lexical decision tasks (deciding if a letter string is a real word), pronounceable nonwords take longer to detect than do nonpronounceable nonwords (e.g., Rubenstein, Lewis, & Rubenstein, 1971), and real words are detected faster if they sound similar but not if they look similar to the preceding word (Meyer, Schvaneveldt, & Ruddy, 1974). This provides evidence that words are phonemically encoded in visual lexical decision tasks. However, this does not necessarily imply that phonemic encoding precedes lexical encoding in reading, because the reaction time in lexical decision (about 700 msec) is long enough to be influenced by both pre- and postlexical encoding processes. Furthermore, these effects are not always observed. For example, if phonemic encoding is important, then words with irregular pronunciations should take longer to be read aloud or to be recognized than words with regular pronunciations. This effect is indeed observed, but only for uncommon words (Seidenberg, 1985).

These findings have been accommodated in a variety of cognitive models (Just & Carpenter, 1987). In the original model of Morton (1969), each word is associated with an internal node termed a logogen, to which various information (semantic, phonemic, etc.) associated with the word is attached. The visually presented word is phonemically encoded before activation of the word's logogen, providing lexical access. Succeeding models have incorporated the direct route as an independent route that races with the phonemic route to activate the logogen (Morton & Patterson, 1980). However, much evidence (e.g., semantic priming influences on nonword pronunciation) suggests that these routes are not independent (Humphreys & Evett, 1985). Furthermore, the neuropsychological evidence for dissociable impairments of the two routes is based on very few patients. In any case, this evidence at most implies only that the routes are dependent on different structures and does not rule out the possibility that activity in these structures interacts during reading. These considerations have led to models in which the dual routes interact (Seidenberg, 1985; Patterson & Morton, 1985). Of course, with sufficient interaction it is a moot point whether there are still two routes. For example, some models reject the use of discrete rules explicitly mapping letters (or short letter strings) to sounds. Rather, they propose that nonwords are pronounced via an approximate matching of the nonword (or fragments thereof) to real words (or fragments thereof) and then basing pronunciation on that of the best-fitting real words and fragments (Glushko, 1979; Henderson, 1982; Shallice & McCarthy, 1985).

N4/P3 AND VISUOPHONEMIC ENCODING

Properties of the N4/P3 evoked in verbal tasks suggest that phonemic infor-mation plays a critical role in lexical encoding and that lexical access involves both the direct and phonemic routes, simultaneously and interactively. I argued above that the onset of the N4 is the point of lexical encoding, and the N4 itself embodies lexical access and the integration of the meanings activated by lexical access with the current semantic context. Nonwords in lexical decision tasks also evoke a large N4, but only if they are pronounceable (Smith & Halgren, 1987b; Rugg & Nagy, 1987). Nonpronounceable nonwords evoke no N4, even though they resemble the real words visually as much as do the pronounceable nonwords (Figure 2). Furthermore, pronounceable nonwords that rhyme with the imme-diately preceding nonword evoke a smaller N4 (Rugg, 1984). Thus, at least for nonwords, lexical encoding is essentially phonemic.

Phonemic encoding of visually presented words does not imply or require internal speech. Internal speech is almost certainly postlexical and may assist the formation of verbatim primary verbal memories (Just & Carpenter, 1987; Badde-ley, 1979). Perhaps it is more accurate to refer to the lexical encoding process as visuophonemic. The integrated influence of visual and phonemic codes in lexical encoding is suggested by their simultaneous and interacting effects on the N4 from its onset. For example, word pairs were presented successively, and subjects were required to judge if they rhymed (Kramer & Donchin, 1987; Polich, McCarthy, Wang, & Donchin, 1983). Both orthographic and phonemic similarity of the words reduced the N4 evoked by the second word. Both effects were visible from the onset of the N4 at 260 msec.*

*A somewhat different pattern of results has been obtained in purely orthographic tasks (for example, detecting words that are written in lower case). The N4 in these tasks to a given word was decreased if the preceding letter string was orthographically similar (i.e., had a similar spelling) but not if it was phonemically similar to the preceding word (Rugg, 1984; Kramer & Donchin, 1987). This suggests that phonemic encoding can be suppressed if it is not useful for task performance. The stimulus sets used in these tasks included many word pairs that rhymed but were spelled differently (e.g., weight–fate) or didn't rhyme but were spelled similarly (e.g., tough–although). With these word pairs, identification of the word not only was irrelevant to the orthographic task but actually could interfere with performance if it resulted in phonemic activation. This is in contrast to rhyming tasks, which require that the word be identified in order to determine its pronunciation, precisely because English spelling-to-sound rules are not regular. Thus, it is possible that lexical encoding is not consistently evoked by orthographic tasks and that the negativity evoked by words in this task is not an N4 but a late processing negativity. This is consistent with the observation that this negativity is substantially smaller than the N4 evoked in phonemic or lexical tasks (Rugg et al., 1988).

An alternative interpretation is possible wherein words in these orthographic tasks are visuopho-nemically encoded, leading to lexical access/contextual integration and a true N4. Under this interpre-tation, the lack of effect of phonemic similarity within word pairs on the N4 evoked by the second word would be caused by a suppression of phonemic information during the delay between the word pairs. Resolution of this issue will require better definition of the neural substrates of the negativities observed in different tasks. In any case, these interpretive difficulties are confined to tasks in which lexical access is unnecessary and perhaps unlikely, which thus do not critically affect the ideas advanced in this chapter.

The neural mechanism of lexical encoding is unknown, but addressing schemes with similar properties have been developed in parallel distributed network models of information processing (Rumelhart & McClelland, 1982; Hinton & Anderson, 1981). In these models, the input layer is often a relatively small collection of feature detector units. The units activated by a given stimulus feed into a larger pool of "hidden" units, activating those previously associated with it through various learning algorithms. This activation of the hidden units would correspond to the onset of direct lexical access. The feature-detection phase in these models is typically of constant duration, corresponding to the constant N4 onset latency for high- and low-frequency words. Note that in these models the word does not need first to be encoded and then its address be found. Rather, these processes are simultaneous: the encoded form of the word constitutes its address. Initial N4 amplitude is also nearly equivalent to high- versus low-frequency words and even to pronounceable nonwords. This may correspond to the property of parallel distributed models insofar as they work best when they include a feedback mechanism to ensure that a fairly constant proportion of hidden units is activated by a given encoded stimulus, regardless of how much previous learning has occurred with it.

Thus far, no separate EP component correlated with lexical encoding has been identified between the encoding negativities and the N4. However, an increased positivity to repeated words (Rugg & Nagy, 1987) and faces (Barrett et al., 1988) has occasionally been found between 160 and 220 msec after stimulus onset. The existence of such a component, restricted to Wernicke's area, is predicted by the model proposed here, especially if visuophonemic encoding is via the best-fit word fragment method (described in the preceding section) rather than by a rule-based method. The best-fit method is well adapted for implementation in a small parallel network situated between rule-based letter-detecting circuits and the much larger associative network.

Whereas speech is at least as old as *Homo sapiens* and is associated with clear cerebral specialization (see chapter by Rosen, Galaburda, & Sherman, this volume), reading is very recent and by no means universal. It therefore seems reasonable that the written word may profit from the brain's language specializations by being recast into a phonemic code. Clearly, this happens when one first learns to read, long after one understands speech. By the time the average reader graduates from high school, he or she has read about 50 million words, giving ample opportunity for the visual and phonemic codes to become well integrated.

VOCABULARY ACQUISITION

Although at first it might seem strange that pronounceable nonwords are lexically encoded and thus provoke an effort toward lexical access, in fact this is appropriate given that in real life (i.e., outside of the bizarre realm of psychological tests), pronounceable letter strings are seldom *non*words but rather are words that we just don't happen to know yet. The average college freshman knows about 40,000 to 50,000 words (Just & Carpenter, 1987). Vocabulary is acquired at a fairly constant rate of about seven new words per day by integrating the visuophonemic code with a meaning inferred from the cognitive context. This integration was identified above with the N4/P3 sequence. The anterior temporal lobe (Meyer, 1959) and especially the hippocampal formation (Gabrieli, Cohen, & Corkin, 1988) have been shown to be necessary for new word learning in adults. Words (and pronounceable nonwords) evoke a large N4/P3 in the MTL. Words also evoke hippocampal unit activity specific to particular words in context. Norepinephrine has been implicated in generation of the P3 (Pineda et al., 1987) and has been shown to promote long-term potentiation (Hopkins & Johnston, 1984; Bliss, Goddard, & Riives, 1983). Taken as a whole, these neural and psychological data suggest that the recent memory traces essential to new word learning may be formed in the hippocampus as a result of a norepinephrine-mediated modulation at the conclusion of contextual integration. Although very speculative in its details, this line of reasoning demonstrates the utility of cognitive neurophysiological models for linking psychological phenomena to biological processes.

From Lexical Encoding to Contextual Integration

SERIAL VERSUS DIRECT LEXICAL ACCESS

Evoked potentials also provide evidence relevant to whether lexical access occurs via a serial search (Glanzer & Ehrenreich, 1979) or through direct access (Just & Carpenter, 1987; Henderson, 1982). In a serial model, the encoded word is compared sequentially against a list or lists of words until a match is found, releasing the word meanings. In a direct-access model, the encoded word somehow directly provides the location of the desired word. These models diverge in their explanation of how word frequency affects behavioral performance. The frequency of a word is the number of times it occurs in ordinary written or spoken discourse. For example, "table" is a moderately high-frequency word, and "awl" is moderately low. High-frequency words are recognized as words more quickly in lexical decision tasks (Gordon, 1985) and are fixated for a shorter duration during reading (Carpenter & Just, 1983). Many serial models of lexical access suppose that high-frequency words are processed faster because they come at the beginning of the look-up list. Some direct-access models explain the frequency effect by postulating that high-frequency words have a lower threshold for "firing" their meanings. Other direct-access models suppose that all lexical entries are activated with about the same latency but that postaccess contextual integration occurs more rapidly for high-frequency words. Experimental psychological evidence for a postlexical locus of word-frequency effects has been obtained using the additive factors strategy (Sternberg, 1969). These studies have shown that the increased time necessary to recognize words by degrading their visual presentation is additive to the increase produced by de-creasing their frequency (Becker & Killion, 1977; Stanners, Jastrzembski, & Westbrook, 1975).

In the model proposed here, N4 onset corresponds to the completion of lexical encoding and the beginning of lexical access, and N4 termination corre-sponds to the completion of lexical access and contextual integration. In both lexical decision (Smith & Halgren, 1987b) and stationary reading (Van Petten & Kutas, in press), the N4 begins at about the same time for common as compared to uncommon words. Specifically, the latency of sentence context influences on the EP is the same for common as compared to uncommon words. Since sentence context cannot influence the EP evoked by a word until that word's meaning is at least partially accessed, this implies that lexical access begins at the same time regardless of word frequency and thus supports direct access rather than serial search models of lexical access. However, this access cannot be completed immediately at N4 onset, or pronounceable nonwords would not evoke large N4s. Rather, the observation that the N4 terminates earlier for common than for uncommon words is consistent with the direct-access models of lexical access that postulate a gradual accumulation of activation and suggest that the locus of word-frequency effects is during the phase of lexical access that occurs after lexical encoding.

MULTIPLE SEMANTIC SYSTEMS

Another fundamental issue in neuropsychology is the number of semantic stores in the brain. On the basis of neuropsychological evidence for selective loss of different types of knowledge, Shallice (1987) proposes that the meaning of pictures is contained in a separate system from the meaning of words. Similarly, selective aphasias for auditory, visual, or somesthetic stimuli have been inter-preted as reflecting modality-specific semantic stores (McCarthy & Warrington, 1988). Even concrete versus abstract words have been postulated to access anatomically separate stores, again on the basis of aphasias relatively selective for one of these word classes (Warrington, 1981). Alternatively, these selective im-pairments may be interpreted as reflecting impaired access of pictures or words to a common general knowledge base (Riddoch, Humphreys, Coltheart, & Fun-nell, 1988).

If the N4 embodies contextual integration of the stimulus, then its evoking conditions should indicate how the semantic system is accessed, and its topogra-phy to different types of stimuli should indicate the degree of overlap between their respective semantic systems. Faces constitute a stimulus type that is very different from words but can nonetheless be considered semantic in that each known face is a symbolic entry point into a network of organized semantic and episodic memories. Furthermore, faces pass through a series of processing stages that are closely analogous to those utilized by words (Bruce, 1988; Smith, 1986): (1) sensory analysis/feature detection (analogous to letter discrimination); (2)

acceptance as a possible face or word, not just a complex visual stimulus (analogous to lexical encoding); (3) individual identification (analogous to lexical access); and (4) integration of the individual face into the current social context (analogous to integration of the word into the sentence). Thus, it is not surprising that photographs of familiar or unfamiliar faces also evoke an N4 at about the same latency as the N4 to words (Barrett et al., 1988). Like the word N4, the face N4 is attenuated by familiarity in recent episodic memory (Smith & Halgren, 1987a) or in primary memory (Potter, Parker, & Ellis, 1987). The face N4 even shows semantic priming effects as an attenuation of the N4 evoked by a famous person's face when preceded by that of another person whose fame is related in the public's mind (B. Renault, personal communication). These results support interpretation of the face N4 as also embodying contextual integration.

It is thus of interest that the N4s evoked by words versus faces are very similar, although no study has specifically compared the N4s to words versus faces in the same subjects. The fact that the CNV between two contingent stimuli is relatively lateralized to the right when those stimuli are faces as compared to when they are words suggests that such a difference may also exist for the N4 (Potter et al., 1987). Furthermore a larger (and statistically significant) difference is observed in the scalp topography of the N4 evoked by words presented in the auditory as compared to the visual modalities (Domalski et al., 1989). Similarly, the N4 decrease when a word is synonymous to the preceding word tends to be more frontally distributed than the N4 difference when it is identical (Rugg & Nagy, 1987), and the N4 decrease when it is a rhyme is larger over the right hemisphere (Rugg, 1984). The N4 to isolated words is generally more frontal than that to words in sentences, possibly due to overlap with a parietal P3 (Kutas & Hillyard, 1989). Finally, the N4 decrease to a word that is congruous with the preceding words of a sentence is also slightly larger over the right hemisphere (Kutas, Van Petten, et al., 1988). On the other hand, concrete and abstract words evoke N4s with topographies that appear indistinguishable (Smith & Halgren, 1987b). The N4 evoked by line drawing of common objects also has a similar topography to that evoked by words, although this conclusion is based on fewer recording sites (Stuss et al., 1983).

In summary, N4s are evoked by words that are heard or seen (either printed or signed in American Sign Language), by faces, and by drawings of common objects. In all of these situations, the N4 can be recorded over the frontal, parietal, and temporal lobes of both hemispheres. Although differences in N4 topography have been noted, they tend to be small variations on this underlying theme. Because of ambiguities in inferring the intracerebral generator from scalp topography (Halgren, in press), it is not possible to exclude the possibility that different N4s have different generators (Kutas & Van Petten, 1987). However, in limited sampling, we have not yet observed differences in the intracranial voltage topography of the N4s evoked in various tasks (Smith, Stapleton, & Halgren, 1986;

unpublished observations). The electrophysiological data are thus most consistent with models that posit a single semantic store, with additional smaller specialized modules for different modalities of presentation (auditory versus visual) and for different symbolic systems (words versus faces).

It is possible to reconcile the neurophysiological evidence for a widespread semantic system with the neuropsychological evidence for separate semantic stores by supposing that the semantic system is divided into interacting modules with relative specialization in the information they store but that are all activated by meaningful stimuli. Stimuli would then be encoded in a distributed fashion with an information-specific contribution integrated from each of the modules. This model for different aspects of semantic memory is similar to recent neural models for the relationship between remote semantic memory and recent episodic memory (Halgren, 1984).

The lesion evidence can best be interpreted as indicating that recent episodic memories are stored in the hippocampal formation, whereas remote semantic memories reside in the neocortex (Halgren, in press). More specifically, if a word is presented, then patients with left MTL damage will not be able to access recent episodic memories associated with that word (Jones-Gotman, 1987; Smith & Halgren, 1989), whereas patients with Wernicke's area damage will not be able to access the word's meaning. Yet, depth and scalp recordings indicate that N4 differences related to either remote semantic or recent episodic memories are present in both neocortex and the MTL (Smith, Halgren, & Heit, 1986; McCarthy & Wood, 1985). Furthermore, although the N4 change caused by repetition of a word in recent episodic memory is somewhat larger in the left MTL, it is clearly present bilaterally (Smith, Stapleton, & Halgren, 1986). Evidence that the N4 represents the integrated contributions of several modules is found in N4 recordings after a module has been removed: surgical removal of the left MTL and overlying cortex eliminates the change in the cortical N4/P3 induced by repetition of words in recent episodic memory (Smith & Halgren, 1989). Finally, the presence of word-specific firing by MTL neurons is consistent with distributed encoding during the N4/P3 (see above).

CONCLUSION: LEXICAL ENCODING FOR ASSOCIATIVE FANOUT

There is a fundamental incompatibility between feature-extraction and associative-activation strategies of neural information processing. In feature extraction, neural pools are relatively small and hierarchically organized, with features at a given level of abstraction encoded as the firing of small numbers of neurons specifically assigned to those features regardless of the other features present. Progressively more abstract features are extracted by the convergence of cells in a lower level onto cells of the next higher level. Information representation is discrete, and information flow is mainly between levels and is polarized from lower to higher levels. In contrast, associative activation relies upon masses of nonpolarized connections within one large neuronal pool, and information representation is diffuse and situational.

This transition in information-processing strategies implies a corresponding transition in the functional processes embodied by EP components. The early feature-extraction stages involve few variables interacting in a deterministic fashion over a small area and thus do not need modulation. The corresponding EP components reflect the envelope of specific interactions in these stages. In contrast, psychological studies demonstrate an enormous number of influences on the subsequent stage of lexical access and contextual integration.

Computational models of contextual integration require active modulation in order to efficiently evolve an activity pattern that optimally satisfies these multiple constraints. The psychological and neural properties of the N4/P3 are those that would be expected if they embodied this active modulation. First, the N4/P3 are subject to many influences derived from the current context, recent events, general knowledge, as well as the lexicon. At the neural level, this probably corresponds to the generation of the N4/P3 in multiple cortical association areas in both hemispheres and in all lobes and in associated limbic structures. Second, the cognitive correlates of the N4/P3 with difficulty or ease of contextual integration, and their possible synaptic bases of excitation or inhibition, correspond to the divergent or convergent phases of modulation in model neural networks. Finally, the fundamental concept of active modulation implies that it does not passively reflect the envelope of information processing in the generating structure but rather reflects a bias actively imposed upon that information processing. This bias logically requires a source, termed here a trigger. The effects of lesions on the N4/P3 and CNV suggest that their triggers lie in the brainstem and diencephalon. Psychologically, the fact that antecedent task and stimulus preconditions must be met before an N4/P3 is evoked again implies the existence of a trigger that must be activated before entry to contextual integration.

In summary, the neural and psychological properties of successive EP components are consistent with the contrasting information-processing requirements of feature extraction and contextual integration. These properties imply a model in which stimuli that are potentially meaningful within a semantic structure trigger a widespread modulation of multiple information structures. It seems that both the antecedent preconditions of the trigger and the particular regions that are modulated during the integration of particular classes of stimuli possess minimal specificity. That is, the regions modulated during the integration of various types of words, or even of faces, are very similar. This lack of specificity may be understood as a consequence of the fact that modulation cannot be more precise in its application than the results of the information processing up to the point when the modulation is invoked. When one initially encounters a word in context, one doesn't know what type of word it will be or what type of knowledge will be required for its integration. Activation of a diffuse semantic system gives all types of knowledge an opportunity to contribute to the neural network encoding the event during the N4/P3 cycle. Similarly, activation of a diffuse semantic network, if initial analysis indicates that the stimulus is potentially meaningful, allows meaningfulness itself to be judged by the entire semantic system.

The above considerations imply that lexical encoding is the crucial gateway from the sequential hierarchical feature detection and template matching that visuophonemically encode the word to the simultaneous activation of semantic associates and contextual integration that determine the word's correct meaning and consequences within the evolving cognitive schema (Figure 7). At the neural level, lexical encoding seems to mark a crucial and corresponding transition from the relatively restricted sequential and well-defined firing patterns representing the stimulus as extracted features to the distributed network of activation that seems to characterize the stimulus integrated with its context. Finally, whereas the preceding feature detection and, to a lesser degree, the following contextual integration seem to be well developed in lower primates, the ability of the phonemic or visuophonemic codes to activate meanings would seem to be both crucial to language and uniquely human, suggesting that lexical encoding itself may constitute a key evolutionary adaptation in the development of language.

SUMMARY

Behavioral measures are of limited utility for inferring the intermediate information-processing stages contributing to reading because behavioral techniques measure directly only the outcome of the final stage. In contrast, evoked

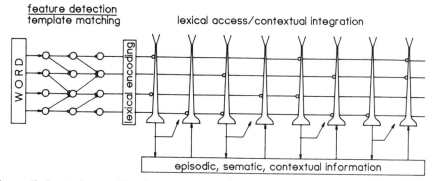

Figure 7. Lexical encoding for associative fanout. The initial stages of processing a visually presented word are conceived of as being relatively fixed, focal, and hierarchical. These feature detection and template matching operations culminate in the lexical encoding of the word into a neural format that permits it to enter into a widespread diffuse associative system. Within this system, the lexically encoded word is combined with episodic, semantic, and contextual information, thus resulting in simultaneous lexical access and contextual integration.

potentials can reveal the sequential brain processing stages evoked by a word as they occur. Initial potentials embody localized feature detection and template matching, from primary to secondary visual cortex and then inferotemporal cortex.

From about 260 to 800 msec after word onset, an N4 (or N400)/P3 (or P300) sequence is evoked by words and word-like stimuli. The N4/P3 is generated bilaterally in the hippocampal formation and probably also in association cortices of all lobes. The N4/P3 is hypothesized to represent a cycle of associative activation that integrates a word's meaning with the sentence context. Relative excitation during the N4 phase would encourage divergent associations. During the P3 phase, background inhibition would cause only those elements receiving convergent excitation to remain activated. The resulting evolution of a distributed pattern of neuronal activity that encodes the event may be embodied by the specific firing of individual hippocampal neurons to particular words in context during the N4/P3. The similar topography of the N4/P3 evoked by words, faces, and diagrams suggests that the semantic store is unitary.

The CNV is interposed between N4/P3 cycles evoked by successive words of a sentence. The CNV may be generated by sustained information-specific firing that maintains the developing sentence context in primary memory. The generation of an N4/P3 to intermediate words in sentences supports reading models in which words are immediately integrated with the sentence context. The fact that the N4 is also evoked by meaningless letter strings implies that the antecedent process triggering the N4 does not access the meaning of the letter string but only encodes the letter string so that its meaning (if any) can then be accessed. Since meaningless letter strings only evoke an N4 if they are pronounceable, this lexical encoding process is at least partly phonemic. Whereas earlier potentials are insensitive to sentence context, the N4/P3 is very sensitive to context and in addition is modulated by recent episodic and remote semantic memory as well as lexical information. Thus, evoked-potential data suggest that sentence context does not influence the processes leading up to lexical encoding but plays a pronounced role (during the N4/P3) in lexical access and contextual integration.

REFERENCES

Ackley, D. H., Hinton, G. E., & Seijnowski, T. J. (1985). A learning algorithm for Boltzmann machines. *Cognitive Science, 9*, 147–169.

Altafullah, I., Halgren, E., Stapleton, J. M., & Crandall, P. H. (1986). Interictal spike–wave complexes in the human medial temporal lobe: Typical topography and comparisons with cognitive potentials. *Electroencephalography and Clinical Neurophysiology, 63*, 503–516.

Anderson, J. A., & Mozer, M. C. (1981). Categorization and selective neurons. In G. E. Hinton & J. A. Anderson (Eds.), *Parallel models of associative memory* (pp. 213–236). Hillsdale, NJ: Lawrence Erlbaum.

Arezzo, J. C., Vaughan, H. G., Kraut, M. A., Steinshneider, M., & Legatt, A. D. (1986). Intracranial generators of event-related potentials in the monkey. In R. Cracco & I. Bodis-Wollner (Eds.), *Evoked potentials* (pp. 141–154). New York: Alan R. Liss.

Ashford, J. W., & Fuster, J. M. (1985). Occipital and inferotemporal responses to visual signals in the monkey. *Experimental Neurology, 90*, 444–466.

Baddeley, A. D. (1979). Working memory and reading. In P. A. Kolers, M. Wrolstad, & H. Bouma (Eds.), *Processing of visible language* (Vol. 1, pp. 355–370). New York: Academic Press.

Barrett, S. E., Rugg, M. D., & Perrett, D. I. (1988). Event-related potentials and the matching of familiar and unfamiliar faces. *Neuropsychologia, 26*, 105–117.

Beauvois, M. F., & Derouesne, J. (1979). Phonological alexia: Three dissociations. *Journal of Neurology, Neurosurgery and Psychiatry, 42*, 1115–1124.

Becker, C. A., & Killion, T. H. (1977). Interaction of visual and cognitive effects in word recognition. *Journal of Experimental Psychology: Human Perception and Performance, 3*, 389–401.

Becker, W., & Jurgens, R. (1979). An analysis of the saccadic system by means of double step stimuli. *Vision Research, 19*, 967–983.

Benson, D. F. (1979). *Aphasia, alexia, and agraphia.* New York: Churchill Livingstone.

Bentin, S., McCarthy, G., & Wood, C. C. (1985). Event-related potentials, lexical decision and semantic priming. *Electroencephalography and Clinical Neurophysiology, 60*, 343–355.

Bliss, T. V. P., Goddard, G. V., & Riives, M. (1983). Reduction of longterm potentiation in the dentate gyrus of the rat following selective depletion of monoamines. *Journal of Physiology (London), 334*, 475–491.

Bruce, V. (1988). *Recognizing faces.* Hillsdale, NJ: Lawrence Erlbaum.

Buzsaki, G. (1984). Feed-forward inhibition in the hippocampal formation. *Progress in Neurobiology, 22*, 131–153.

Carpenter, P. A., & Just, M. A. (1983). What your eyes do while your mind is reading. In K. Rayner (Ed.), *Eye movements in reading: Perceptual and language processes* (pp. 275–307). New York: Academic Press.

Caspers, H., Speckmann, E., & Lehmenkuhler, A. (1980). Electrogenesis of cortical DC potentials. *Progress in Brain Research, 54*, 3–15.

Cohen, N. J. (1975). The CNV in cases of hemispheric vascular lesions. *Electroencephalography and Clinical Neurophysiology, 38*, 542.

Coltheart, M. (1980). Deep dyslexia: A review of the syndrome. In M. Coltheart, K. Patterson, & J. C. Marshall (Eds.), *Deep dyslexia* (pp. 22–47). London: Routledge and Keagan Paul, 1980.

Coltheart, M. (1987). Functional architecture of the language-processing system. In M. Coltheart, G. Sartori, & R. Job (Eds.), *The cognitive neuropsychology of language* (pp. 1–25). Hillsdale, NJ: Lawrence Erlbaum.

Conrad, R. (1977). The reading ability of deaf school-leavers. *British Journal of Educational Psychology, 47*, 138–148.

Corkin. S. (1984). Lasting consequences of bilateral medial temporal lobectomy: Clinical course and experimental findings in H.M. *Seminars in Neurology, 4*, 249–259.

Darcey, T. M., Wieser, H. G., Meles, H. P., Skrandies, W., & Lehmann, D. (1980). Intracerebral and scalp fields evoked by visual stimulation. *Electroencephalography and Clinical Neurophysiology, 49*, 111.

Desimone, R., Schein, S. J., Moran, J., & Ungerleider, L. G. (1985). Contour, color and shape analysis beyond the striate cortex. *Vision Research, 25*, 441–452.

Desmedt, J. E. (1981). Scalp-recorded cerebral event-related potentials in man as point of entry into the analysis of cognitive processing. In F. O. Schmitt, F. G. Worden,

G. Edelmann, & S. D. Dennis (Eds.), *The organization of the cerebral cortex* (pp. 441–473). Cambridge: MIT.

Domalski, P., Smith, M. E., & Halgren, E. (1989). *Cross-modal repetition effects on the N4*. Manuscript submitted for publication.

Donchin, E. (1981). Surprise! . . . Surprise. *Psychophysiology, 18,* 493–513.

Donchin, E., & Coles, M. G. H. (1988). Is the P300 component a manifestation of context updating? *Behavioral and Brain Sciences, 11,* 357–575.

Donchin, E., Otto, D., Gerbrandt, L. K., & Pribram, K. H. (1971). While a monkey waits: Electrical events recorded during the foreperiod of a reaction time study. *Electroencephalography and Clinical Neurophysiology, 31,* 115–127.

Fischler, I., Bloom, P. A., Childers, D. G., Arroyo, A. A., & Perry, N. W. (1984). Brain potentials during sentence verification: late negativity and long-term memory strength. *Neuropsychologia, 22,* 559–568.

Fischler, I., Bloom, P. A., Childers, D. G., Roucos, S. E., & Perry, N. W. (1983). Brain potentials related to stages of sentence verification. *Psychophysiology, 20,* 400–409.

Fischler, I., Childers, D. G., Achariyapaopan, T., & Perry, N. W., Jr. (1985). Brain potentials during sentence verification: Automatic aspects of comprehension. *Biological Psychology, 21,* 83–105.

Frazier, L., & Rayner, K. (1982). Making and correcting errors during sentence comprehension: Eye movements in the analysis of structurally ambiguous sentences. *Cognitive Psychology, 14,* 178–210.

Gabrieli, J. D., Cohen, N. J., & Corkin. S. (1988). The impaired learning of semantic knowledge following bilateral medial temporal-lobe resection. *Brain and Cognition, 7,* 157–177.

Gardner-Medwin, A. R. (1976). The recall of events through the learning of associations between their parts. *Philosophical Transactions of the Royal Society of London. Series B: Biological Sciences, 194,* 375–402.

Glanzer, M., & Ehrenreich, S. L. (1979). Structure and search of the internal lexicon. *Journal of Verbal Learning and Verbal Behavior, 18,* 381–398.

Glushko, R. J. (1979). The organisation and activation of orthographic knowledge in reading aloud. *Journal of Experimental Psychology: Human Perception and Performance, 5,* 674–691.

Gordon, B. (1985). Subjective frequency and the lexical decision latency function: Implication for mechanisms of lexical access. *Journal of Memory and Language, 24,* 631–645.

Groll-Knapp, E., Ganglberger, J., Haider, M., & Schmid, H. (1980). Stereoelectroencephalographic studies on event-related slow potentials in the human brain. In H. Lechner & A. Aranibar (Eds.), *Electroencephalography and clinical neurophysiology* (pp. 746–760). Amsterdam: Excerpta Medica.

Gross, C. G. (1973). Visual functions of the inferotemporal cortex. In R. Jung (Ed.), *Handbook of sensory physiology* (Vol. 7, Part 3B, pp. 451–482). Springer: Berlin.

Halgren, E. (1984). Human hippocampal and amygdala recording and stimulation: Evidence for a neural model of recent memory. In L. R. Squire & N. Butters (Eds.), *Neuropsychology of memory* (pp. 165–181). New York: Guilford Press.

Halgren, E. (in press). Evoked potentials. In C. Vanderwolf (Ed.), *Neuromethods* (Vol. 14). Clifton, NJ: Humana Press.

Halgren, E., Babb, T. L., & Crandall, P. H. (1978). Activity of human hippocampal formation and amygdala neurons during memory testing. *Electroencephalography and Clinical Neurophysiology, 45,* 585–601.

Halgren, E., & Smith, M. E. (1987). Cognitive evoked potentials as modulatory processes in human memory formation and retrieval. *Human Neurobiology, 6,* 129–139.

Halgren, E., Squires, N. K., Wilson, C. L., & Crandall, P. H. (1982). Brain generators of evoked potentials: The late (endogenous) components. *Bulletin of the Los Angeles Neurological Societies, 47*, 108–123.

Halgren, E., Squires, N. K., Wilson, C. L., Rohrbaugh, J. W., & Babb, T. L. (1980). Endogenous potentials generated in the human hippocampal formation and amygdala by infrequent events. *Science, 210*, 803–805.

Halgren, E., Stapleton, J., Domalski, P., Swartz, B. E., Delgado-Escueta, A., Treiman, D., Walsh, G. O., Mandelkern, M., Blahd, W., & Ropchan, J. (in press). Memory dysfunction in epileptics as a derangement of normal physiology. In D. Smith & D. M. Treiman (Eds.), *Advances in neurology: Neurobehavioral problems in epilepsy*. New York: Plenum Press.

Halgren, E., Stapleton, J. M., Smith, M. E., & Altafullah, I. (1986). Generators of the human scalp P3s. In R. Q. Cracco & I. Bodis-Wollner (Eds.), *Evoked potentials* (pp. 269–289). New York: Alan R. Liss.

Halgren, E., Wilson, C. L., Squires, N. K., Engel, J., Walter, R. D., & Crandall, P. H. (1983). Dynamics of the human hippocampal contribution to memory. In W. Seifert (Ed.), *Neurobiology of the hippocampus* (pp. 529–572). London: Academic Press.

Harmony, T. (1984). *Neurometric assessment of brain dysfunction in neurological patients*. Hillsdale, NJ: Lawrence Erlbaum.

Harrison, J. B., Buchwald, J. S., Kaga, K., Woolf, N. J., & Butcher, L. L. (1988). 'Cat P300' disappears after septal lesions. *Electroencephalography and Clinical Neurophysiology, 69*, 55–64.

Harter, M. R., & Guido, W. (1980). Attention to pattern orientation: Negative cortical potentials, reaction time, and the selection process. *Electroencephalography and Clinical Neurophysiology, 49*, 461–475.

Harter, M. R., & Previc, F. H. (1978). Size-specific information channels and selective attention: Visual evoked potential and behavioral measures. *Electroencephalography and Clinical Neurophysiology, Supplement, 45*, 628–640.

Hecaen, H., & Albert, M. L. (1978). *Human neuropsychology*. New York: John Wiley & Sons.

Heit, G., Smith, M. E., & Halgren, E. (1988). Neural encoding of individual words and faces by the human hippocampus and amygdala. *Nature, 333*, 773–775.

Heit, G., Smith, M. E., & Halgren, E. (in press). Neuronal activity in the human medial temporal lobe during recognition memory. *Brain*.

Henderson, L. (1982). *Orthography and word recognition in reading*. New York: Academic Press.

Hillyard, S. A., & Picton, T. W. (1988). Electrophysiology of cognition. In F. Plum (Ed.), *Handbook of physiology: The nervous system V* (pp. 519–584). Bethesda: American Physiological Society.

Hillyard, S. A., Woldorff, M., Mangun, G. R., & Hansen, J. C. (1987). Mechanisms of early selective attention in auditory and visual modalities. *Electroencephalography and Clinical Neurophysiology, Supplement, 39*, 317–324.

Hinton, G. E., & Anderson, J. A. (1981). *Parallel models of associative memory*. Hillsdale, NJ: Lawrence Erlbaum.

Holcomb, P. J. (1986). ERP correlates of semantic facilitation. In W. C. McCallum, R. Zappoli, & F. Denoth (Eds.), *Cerebral psychophysiology: Studies in event-related potentials (Electroencephalography and Clinical Neurophysiology, Supplement 38)* (pp. 318–322). Amsterdam: Elsevier.

Hopkins, W. F., & Johnston, D. (1984). Frequency-dependent noradrenergic modulation of long-term potentiation in the hippocampus. *Science, 226*, 350–352.

Humphreys, G. W., & Evett, L. J. (1985). Are there independent lexical and nonlexical routes in word processing? An evaluation of the dual-route theory of reading. *Behavioral and Brain Sciences, 8,* 689–740.

Insausti, R., Amaral, D. G., & Cowan, W. M. (1987). The entorhinal cortex of the monkey: II. Cortical afferents. *Journal of Comparative Neurology, 264,* 356–395.

Johnson, R., Jr. (1988). Scalp-recorded P300 activity in patients following unilateral temporal lobectomy. *Brain, 111,* 1517–1529.

Jones-Gotman, M. (1987). Commentary: Psychological evaluation: Testing hippocampal function. In J. Engel (Ed.), *Surgical therapy of epilepsy* (pp. 203–211). New York: Raven Press.

Just, M. A., & Carpenter, P. A. (1980). A theory of reading: From eye fixations to comprehension. *Psychological Review, 4,* 329–354.

Just, M. A., & Carpenter, P. A. (1987). *The psychology of reading and language comprehension.* Newton, MA: Allyn & Bacon.

Kaas, J. H. (1989). Why does the brain have so many visual areas? *Journal of Cognitive Neuroscience, 1,* 121–135.

Karrer, R. Cohen, J., & Tueting, P. (Eds.). (1984). *Brain and information: Event-related potentials (Annals of the New York Academy of Sciences,* Vol. 425). New York: New York Academy of Sciences.

Kimball, J. P. (1973). Seven principles of surface structure parsing in natural language. *Cognition, 2,* 14–47.

Kimura, D. (1963). Right temporal-lobe damage. *Archives of Neurology, 8,* 264–271.

Knight, R. T. (1984). Decreased response to novel stimuli after prefrontal lesions in man. *Electroencephalography and Clincal Neurophysiology, 59,* 9–20.

Knight, R. T. (in press). Neural mechanisms of event related potentials: Evidence from lesion studies. In J. Rohrbaugh, R. Johnson, & R. Parasuraman (Eds.), *Eighth international conference of event related potentials of the brain.* Oxford: Oxford University Press.

Kramer, A. F., & Donchin, E. (1987). Brain potentials as indices of orthographic and phonological interaction during word matching. *Journal of Experimental Psychology: Learning, Memory and Cognition, 13,* 76–86.

Kraut, M. A., Arezzo, J. C., & Vaughan, H. G. (1985). Intracortical generators of the flash VEP in monkeys. *Electroencephalography and Clinical Neurophysiology, 62,* 300–312.

Kutas, M., & Hillyard, S. A. (1980a). Reading senseless sentences: Brain potentials reflect semantic incongruity. *Science, 207,* 203–205.

Kutas, M., & Hillyard, S. A. (1980b). Event-related brain potentials to semantically inappropriate and surprisingly large words. *Biological Psychology, 11,* 99–116.

Kutas, M., & Hillyard, S. A. (1983). Event-related brain potentials to grammatical errors and semantic anomalies. *Memory and Cognition, 11,* 539–550.

Kutas, M., & Hillyard, S. A. (1984). Brain potentials during reading reflect word expectancy and semantic association. *Nature, 307,* 161–163.

Kutas, M., & Hillyard, S. (1989). An electrophysiological probe of incidental word association. *Journal of Cognitive Neuroscience, 1,* 38–49.

Kutas, M., Hillyard, S. A., & Gazzaniga, M. S. (1988). Processing of semantic anomaly by right and left hemispheres of commissurotomy patients. Evidence from event-related brain potentials. *Brain, 11,* 553–576.

Kutas, M., McCarthy, G., & Donchin, E. (1977). Augmenting mental chronometry: The P300 as a measure of stimulus evaluation time. *Science, 197,* 792–795.

Kutas, M., Neville, H. J., & Holcomb, P. J. (1987). A preliminary comparison of the N400 response to semantic anomalies during reading, listening and signing. *Electroencephalography and Clinical Neurophysiology, Supplement, 39,* 325–330.

Kutas, M., & Van Petten, C. (1987). Event-related brain potential studies of language. In P. K. Ackles, J. R. Jennings, & M. G. H. Coles (Eds.), *Advances in psychophysiology* (Vol. 3). Greenwich, CT: JAI Press.

Kutas, M., Van Petten, C., & Besson, M. (1988). Event-related potential asymmetries during the reading of sentences. *Electroencephalography and Clinical Neurophysiology, 69,* 218–233.

Lal, R., & Friedlander, M. J. (1989). Gating of retinal transmission by afferent eye position and movement signals. *Science, 243,* 93–96.

Lovrich, D., Simson, R., Vaughan, H. G., Jr., & Ritter, W. (1986). Topography of visual event-related potentials during geometric and phonetic discriminations. *Electroencephalography and Clinical Neurophysiology, 65,* 1–12.

Low, M. D. (1979). Event-related potentials and the electroencephalogram in patients with proven brain lesions. In J. E. Desmedt (Ed.), *Cognitive components in cerebral event-related-potentials and selective attention* (pp. 258–264). Basel: S. Karger.

Luria, A. R. (1966). *Higher cortical functions in man.* New York: Basic Books.

Lynch, G. (1986). *Synapses, circuits, and the beginnings of memory.* Cambridge: MIT Press.

Marcus, M. P. (1980). *A theory of syntactic recognition for natural language.* Cambridge: MIT Press.

Marr, D. (1971). A theory of archicortex. *Philosophical Transactions of the Royal Society of London. Series B: Biological Sciences, 1971, 262,* 23–81.

Marrocco, R. T. (1986). The neurobiology of perception. In J. E. LeDoux & W. Hirst (Eds.), *Mind and brain, Dialogues in cognitive neuroscience* (pp. 33–79). Cambridge: Cambridge University Press.

Marslen-Wilson, W. D., & Tyler, L. K. (1980). The temporal structure of spoken language comprehension. *Cognition, 8,* 1–71.

Marton, M., & Szirtes, J. (1988). Context effects on saccade-related brain potentials to words during reading. *Neuropsychologia, 26,* 453–463.

Marton, M., Szirtes, J., & Breuer, P. (1985). Electrocortical signs of word categorization in saccade-related brain potentials and visual evoked potentials. *Psychophysiology, 3,* 131–144.

Marton, M., Szirtes, J., Donauer, N., & Breuer, P. (1985). Saccade-related brain potentials in semantic categorization tasks. *Biological Psychology, 20,* 163–184.

McCallum, W. C., & Cummins, B. (1973). The effects of brain lesions on the contingent negative variation in neurosurgical patients. *Electroencephalography and Clinical Neurophysiology, 35,* 449–456.

McCallum, W. C., Farmer, S. F., & Pocock, P. V. (1984). The effects of physical and semantic incongruities on auditory event-related potentials. *Electroencephalography and Clinical Neurophysiology, 59,* 477–488.

McCallum, W. C., & Papakostopoulos, D. (1976). Distribution of CNV and other slow potential changes in human brainstem structures. In W. C. McCallum & J. R. Knott (Eds.), *The responsive brain* (pp. 205–210). Bristol: Wright.

McCallum, W. C., Papakostopoulos, D., Gombi, R., Winter, A. L., Cooper, R., & Griffith, H. B. (1973). Event related slow potential changes in human brain stem. *Nature, 252,* 465–467.

McCarthy, G., & Wood, C. C. (1984). Intracranially recorded event-related potentials during sentence processing. *Society for Neuroscience Abstracts, 10,* 847.

McCarthy, G., & Wood, C. C. (1985). Human intracranial ERPs during lexical decision. *Society for Neuroscience Abstracts, 11,* 880.

McCarthy, G., & Wood, C. C. (1987). Intracranial recordings of endogenous ERPs in humans. *Electroencephalography and Clinical Neurophysiology, Supplement, 39,* 331–337.

McCarthy, G., Wood, C. C., Williamson, P. D., & Spencer, D. D. (in press). Task-dependent field potentials in human hippocampal formation. *Journal of Neuroscience.*

McCarthy, R. A., & Warrington, E. K. (1988). Evidence for modality-specific meaning systems in the brain. *Nature, 334,* 428–430.

McConkie, G. W. (1983). Eye movements and perception during reading. In K. Rayner (Ed.), *Eye movements in reading: Perceptual and language processes* (pp. 65–96). New York: Academic Press.

McNaughton, B. L. (1983). Activity dependent modulation of hippocampal synaptic efficacy: Some implications for memory processes. In W. Seifert (Ed.), *Neurobiology of the hippocampus* (pp. 233–252). New York: Academic Press.

McSherry, J. W., & Borda, R. P. (1973). The intracortical distribution of the CNV in rhesus monkey. In W. C. McCallum & J. R. Knott (Eds.), *Event-related slow potentials of the brain: Their relations to behavior (Electroencephalography and Clinical Neurophysiology, Supplement 33)* (pp. 69–74). Amsterdam: Elsevier.

Meyer, D. E., Schvaneveldt, R. W., & Ruddy, M. G. (1974). Functions of graphemic and phonemic codes in visual word-recognition. *Memory and Cognition, 2,* 309–321.

Meyer, V. (1959). Cognitive changes following temporal lobectomy for relief of temporal lobe epilepsy. *Archives of Neurology and Psychiatry, 81,* 299–309.

Mishkin, M. (1982). A memory system in the monkey. *Philosophical Transactions of the Royal Society of London. Series B: Biological Sciences, 298,* 83–95.

Morton, J. (1969). Interaction of information in word recognition. *Psychological Review, 765,* 165–178.

Morton, J., & Patterson, K. E. (1980). A new attempt at an interpretation, or, an attempt at a new interpretation. In M. Coltheart, K. E. Patterson, & J. C. Marshall (Eds.), *Deep dyslexia* (pp. 91–118). London: Routledge and Keagan Paul.

Naatanen, R., & Picton, T. W. (1986). N2 and automatic versus controlled processes. In W. C. McCallum, R. Zappoli, & F. Denoth (Eds.), *Cerebral psychophysiology studies in event-related potentials (Electroencephalography and Clinical Neurophysiology, Supplement 38)* (pp. 169–186). Amsterdam: Elsevier.

Nenov, V. I., Halgren, E., Mandelkern, M., Ropchan, J., & Blahd, W. (1989). *Metabolic and electrophysiologic manifestations of recognition memory in humans.* Manuscript submitted for publication.

Nenov, V. I., Read, W., Halgren, E., & Dyer, M. G. (1990). The effects of threshold modulation on recall and recognition in a sparse auto-associative memory: Implications for hippocampal physiology. In *Proceedings of the International Joint Conference on Neural Networks* Washington, DC: IEEE.

Neville, H. J., Kutas, M., Chesney, G., & Schmidt, A. C. (1986). Event-related brain potentials during initial encoding and recognition memory of congruous and incongruous words. *Journal of Memory and Language, 25,* 75–92.

Nunez, P. L. (1981). *Electric fields of the brain.* New York: Oxford University Press.

Ojemann, G. A., & Creutzfeldt, O. D. (1989). Language in humans and animals: Contribution of brain stimulation and recording. In F. Plum (Ed.), *Handbook of physiology: The nervous system V* (pp. 675–699). Bethesda: American Physiological Society.

O'Keefe, J., & Nadel, L. (1978). *The hippocampus as a cognitive map.* Oxford: Clarendon Press.

Paller, K. A., Kutas, M., & Mayes, A. R. (1987). Neural correlates of encoding in an incidental learning paradigm. *Electroencephalography and Clinical Neurophysiology, 67,* 360–371.

Papakostopoulos, D., Cooper, R., & Crow, H. J. (1976). Electrocorticographic studies of the contingent negative variation and 'P300' in man. In W. C. McCallum & J. R. Knott (Eds.), *The responsive brain* (pp. 201–204). Bristol: Wright.

Patterson, K. E., Marshall, J. C., & Coltheart, M. (1985). *Surface dyslexia*. Hillsdale, NJ: Lawrence Erlbaum.

Patterson, K. E., & Morton, J. (1985). From orthography to phonology: An attempt at an old interpretation. In K. E. Patterson, J. C. Marshall, & M. Coltheart (Eds.), *Surface dyslexia: Neuropsychological and cognitive studies of phonological reading* (pp. 335–359). Hillsdale, NJ: Lawrence Erlbaum.

Perrett, D. I., Rolls, E. T., & Caan, W. (1982). Visual neurones responsive to faces in the monkey temporal cortex. *Experimental Brain Research, 47,* 329–342.

Picton, T. W. (1987). The recording and measurement of evoked potentials. In A. M. Halliday, S. R. Butler, & R. Paul (Eds.), *Textbook of clincal neurophysiology* (pp. 23–40). New York: John Wiley & Sons.

Pineda, J. A., Foote, S. L., & Neville, H. J. (1987). The effects of locus coeruleus lesions on a squirrel monkey late positive component: A preliminary study. In R. Johnson, R. Purasuraman, & J. W. Rohrbaugh (Eds.), *Current trends in event-related potential research (Electroencephalography and Clinical Neurophysiology, Supplement 40)* (pp. 481–486). Amsterdam: Elsevier.

Pirch, J. H., Corbus, M. J., Rigdon, G. C., & Lynes, W. H. (1986). Generation of cortical event-related slow potentials in the rat involves nucleus basalis cholinergic innervation. *Electroencephalography and Clinical Neurophysiology, 63,* 464–465.

Polich, J. (1985). Semantic categorization and event-related potentials. *Brain and Language, 26,* 304–321.

Polich, J., McCarthy, G., Wang, W. S., & Donchin, E. (1983). When words collide: Orthographic and phonological interference during word processing. *Biological Psychology, 16,* 155–180.

Pollatsek, A , & Rayner, K. (1982). Eye movement control in reading: The role of word boundaries. *Journal of Experimental Psychology: Human Perception and Performance, 8,* 817–833.

Posner, M. R. (1978). *Chronometric explorations of mind*. Hillsdale, NJ: Lawrence Erlbaum.

Potter, D. D., Parker, D. M., & Ellis, H. D. (1987). Processing negativites in a complex pattern recognition task: An event related potential study. *Neuroscience Letters Supplement, 29,* S126.

Pritchard, W. S. (1981). Psychophysiology of P300. *Psychological Bulletin, 89,* 506–540.

Pritchard, W. S., Shappell, S. A., & Brandt, M. E. (1988). Psychophysiology of N200/N400: A review and classification scheme. In P. K. Ackles, J. R. Jennings, & M. G. H. Coles (Eds.), *Advances in psychophysiology* (Vol. 4). Greenwich, CT: JAI Press.

Racine, R. J., Milgram, N. W., & Hafner, S. (1983). Long-term potentiation phenomena in the rat limbic forebrain. *Brain Research, 260,* 217–231.

Rayner, K. (1981). Eye movements and the perceptual span in reading. In J. Pirozzolo & M. C. Wittrock (Eds.), *Neuropsychological and cognitive processes in reading* (pp. 145–165). New York: Academic Press.

Rayner, K. (1983). The perceptual span and eye movement control during reading. In K. Rayner (Ed.), *Eye movements in reading, perceptual and language processes* (pp. 97–120). New York: Academic Press.

Rayner, K. (1981). Inhoff, A. W., Morrison, R. E., Slowiaczed, M. L., & Bertera, J. H. (1981). Masking of foveal and parafoveal vision during eye fixations in reading. *Journal of Experimental Psychology: Human Perception and Performance, 7,* 167–179.

Rebert, C. S. (1973). Elements of a general cerebral system related to CNV genesis. In

W. C. McCallum & J. R. Knott (Eds.), *Event-related slow potentials of the brain: Their relations to behavior (Electroencephalography and Clinical Neurophysiology, Supplement 33)* (pp. 63–67). Amsterdam: Elsevier.

Rebert, C. S., Tecce, J. J., Marczynski, T. J., Pirch, J. H., & Thompson, J. W. (1986). Neural anatomy, chemistry and event-related brain potentials: An approach to understanding the substrates of mind. In W. C. McCallum, R. Zappoli, & F. Denoth (Eds.), *Cerebral psychophysiology: Studies in event-related potentials (Electroencephalography and Clinical Neurophysiology, Supplement 38)* (pp. 343–392). Amsterdam: Elsevier.

Riddoch, M. J., Humphreys, G. W., Coltheart, J., & Funnell, E. (1988). Semantic systems or system? Neuropsychological evidence reevaluated. *Cognitive Neuropsychology, 5,* 3–25.

Ritter, W., Ford, J. M., Gaillard, A. W., Harter, M. R., Kutas, M., Naatanen, R., Polich, J., Renault, B., & Rohrbaugh, J. (1984). Cognition and event-related potentials. I. The relation of negative potentials and cognitive processes. *Annals of the New York Academy of Sciences, 425,* 24–38.

Ritter, W., Simson, R., Vaughan, H. G., Jr., & Macht, M. (1982). Manipulation of event-related potential manifestations of information processing stages. *Science, 218,* 909–911.

Robinson, D. L., Petersen, S. E., & Keys, W. (1986). Saccade-related and visual activities in the pulvinar nuclei of the behaving rhesus monkey. *Experimental Brain Research, 62,* 625–634.

Rolls, E. T., Baylis, G. C., & Hasselmo, M. E. (1987). The responses of neurons in the cortex in the superior temporal sulcus of the monkey to band-pass spatial frequency filtered faces. *Vision Research, 27,* 311–326.

Rosler, F., Sutton, S., Johnson, R., Jr., Mulder, G., Fabiani, M., Plooij-Van Gorser, E., & Roth, W. T. (1986). Endogenous ERP components and cognitive components: A review. In W. C. McCallum, R. Zappoli, & F. Denoth (Eds.), *Cerebral psychophysiology studies in event-related potentials (Electroencephalography and Clinical Neurophysiology, Supplement 38)* (pp. 51–92). Amsterdam: Elsevier.

Rubenstein, H., Lewis, S. S., & Rubenstein, M. A. (1971). Homographic entries in the internal lexicon: Effects of systematicity and relative frequency of meanings. *Journal of Verbal Learning and Verbal Behavior, 10,* 57–62.

Rugg, M. D. (1984). Event-related potentials and the phonological processing of words and non-words. *Neuropsychologia, 22,* 435–443.

Rugg, M. D. (1987). Dissociation of semantic priming, word and non-word repetition effects by event-related potentials. *Quarterly Journal of Experimental Psychology, 39,* 123–148.

Rugg, M. D., Furda, J., & Lorist, M. (1988). The effects of task on the modulation of event-related potentials by word repetition. *Psychophysiology, 25,* 55–63.

Rugg, M. D., Kok, A., Barrett, G., & Fischler, I. (1986). ERPs associated with language and hemispheric specialization. A review. *Electroencephalography and Clinical Neurophysiology, Supplement, 38,* 273–300.

Rugg, M. D., & Nagy, M. E. (1987). Lexical contribution to nonword-repetition effects: Evidence from event-related potentials. *Memory and Cognition, 15,* 473–481.

Rumelhart, D. E. (1977). Toward an interactive model of reading. In S. Dornic (Ed.), *Attention and performance VI.* Hillsdale, NJ: Lawrence Erlbaum.

Rumelhart, D. E., & McClelland, J. L. (1982). An interactive activation model of context effect in letter perception: Part 2. The contextual enhancement effect and some tests and extensions of the model. *Psychological Review, 89,* 60–94.

Sanquist, T. G., Rohrbaugh, J. W., Syndulko, K., & Lindsey, D. B. (1980). Electrocortical signs of levels of processing: Perceptual analysis and recognition memory. *Psychophysiology, 17,* 569–576.

Schacter, D. L. (1987). Implicit expressions of memory in organic amnesia: Learning of new facts and associations. *Human Neurobiology, 6,* 107–118.

Seidenberg, M. S. (1985). The time course of information activation and utilization in visual word recognition. In D. Besner, T. Waller, & G. MacKinnon (Eds.), *Reading research: Advances in theory and practice* (pp. 200–252). New York: Academic Press.

Shallice, T. (1987). Impairments of semantic processing: Multiple dissociations. In M. Coltheart, G. Sartori, & R. Job (Eds.), *The cognitive neuropsychology of language* (pp. 111–127). Hillsdale, NJ: Lawrence Erlbaum.

Shallice, T., & McCarthy, R. (1985). Phonological reading: From patterns of impairment to possible procedures. In K. Patterson, J. C. Marshall, & M. Coltheart (Eds.), *Surface dyslexia: Neuropsychological and cognitive studies of phonological reading* (pp. 361–397). Hillsdale, NJ: Lawrence Erlbaum.

Simson, R., Vaughan, H. G., Jr., & Ritter, W. (1977). The scalp topography of potentials in auditory and visual discrimination tasks. *Electroencephalography and Clinical Neurophysiology, 42,* 528–535.

Singer, W. (1977). Control of thalamic transmission by corticofugal and ascending reticular pathways in the visual system. *Physiological Reviews, 57,* 386–420.

Skinner, J. E., & Yingling, C. D. (1977). Central gating mechanisms that regulate event-related potentials and behavior. A neural model for attention. In J. E. Desmedt (Ed.), *Attention, voluntary contraction and event-related cerebral potentials. Progress in clincal neurophysiology* (Vol. 1, pp. 28–68). Basel: S. Karger.

Slowaiczek, M. L., & Clifton, C. (1980). Subvocalization and reading for meaning. *Journal of Verbal Learning and Verbal Behavior, 19,* 573–582.

Smith, D. B., Sidman, R. D., Henke, J. S., Flanigan, H., Labiner, D., & Evans, L. N. (1983). Scalp and depth recordings of induced deep cerebral potentials. *Electroencephalography and Clinical Neurophysiology, 55,* 145–150.

Smith, M. E. (1986). *Electrophysiology of human memory.* Doctoral dissertation, Los Angeles. University Microfilms DA8702646.

Smith, M. E., & Halgren, E. (1987a). Event-related potentials elicited by familiar and unfamiliar faces. In R. Johnson, R. Purasuraman, & J. W. Rohrbaugh (Eds.), *Current trends in event-related potential research (Electroencephalography and Clinical Neurophysiology, Supplement 40)* (pp. 422–426). Amsterdam: Elsevier.

Smith, M. E., & Halgren, E. (1987b). Event-related potentials during lexical decision: Effects of repetition, word frequency, pronounceability, and concreteness. *Electroencephalography and Clinical Neurophysiology, Supplement, 40,* 417–421.

Smith, M. E., & Halgren, E. (1988). Attenuation of a sustained visual processing negativity after lesions that include the inferotemporal cortex. *Electroencephalography and Clinical Neurophysiology, 70,* 366–370.

Smith, M. E., & Halgren, E. (1989). Dissociation of recognition memory components following temporal lobe lesions. *Journal of Experimental Psychology: Learning, Memory and Cognition, 15,* 50–60.

Smith, M. E., Halgren, E., & Heit, G. (1986). Repetition-sensitive components of neural activation: Evidence from intracranial recordings from the human medial temporal lobe. In *Proceedings of the eighth annual meeting of the Cognitive Science Society* (pp. 239–240). Amherst, MA: Lawrence Erlbaum.

Smith, M. E., Halgren, E., Sokolik, M., Baudena, P., Mussolino, A., Liegeois-Chauvel, C., & Chavel, P. (in press). Initial survey of the intracranial voltage distribution of endogenous potentials elicited during auditory discrimination. *Electroencephalography and Clinical Neurophysiology.*

Smith, M. E., Stapleton, J. M., & Halgren, E. (1986). Human medial temporal lobe potentials evoked in memory and language tasks. *Electroencephalography and Clinical Neurophysiology, 63,* 145–159.

Somjen, G. G. (1973). Electrogenesis of sustained potentials. *Progress in Neurobiology, 1,* 199–237.

Somjen, G. G. (1979). Extracellular potassium in the mammalian central nervous system. *Annual Review of Physiology, 41,* 159–177.

Squire, L. R. (1987). *Memory and brain.* Oxford: Oxford University Press.

Squires, N. K., Halgren, E., Wilson, C. L., & Crandall, P. H. (1983). Human endogenous limbic potentials: Cross-modality and depth/surface comparisons in epileptic subjects. In A. W. K. Gaillard & W. Ritter (Eds.), *Tutorials in ERP research: Endogenous components* (pp. 217–232). Amsterdam: North Holland.

Stamm, J. S., & Raven, S. C. (1972). Cortical steady potential shifts and anodal polarization during delayed response performance. *Acta Neurobiologiae Experimentalis, 32,* 193–209.

Stanners, R. F., Jastrzembski, J. E., & Westbrook, A. (1975). Frequency and visual quality in a word–nonword classification task. *Journal of Verbal Learning and Verbal Behavior, 14,* 259–264.

Stapleton, J. M., & Halgren, E. (1987). Endogenous potentials evoked in simple cognitive tasks: Depth components and task correlates. *Electroencephalography and Clinical Neurophysiology, 67,* 44–52.

Stapleton, J. M., Halgren, E., & Moreno, K. A. (1987). Endogenous potentials after anterior temporal lobectomy. *Neuropsychologia, 25,* 549–557.

Stapleton, J. M., O'Reilly, T., & Halgren, E. (1987). Endogenous potentials in simple cognitive tasks: Scalp topography. *International Journal of Neuroscience, 36,* 75–88.

Sternberg, S. (1969). The discovery of processing stages: Extension of Donders method. *Acta Psychologica, 30,* 276–315.

Streletz, L. J., Bae, S. H., Roeshman, R. M., Schatz, N. J., & Savino, P. J. (1981). Visual evoked potentials in occipital lobe lesions. *Archives of Neurology, 38,* 80–85.

Stuss, D. T., Picton, T. W., & Cerri, A. M. (1988). Electrophysiological manifestations of typicality judgment. *Brain and Language, 33,* 260–272.

Stuss, D. T., Sarazin, F. F., Leech, E. E., & Picton, T. W. (1983). Event-related potentials during naming and mental rotation. *Electroencephalography and Clinical Neurophysiology, 56,* 133–146.

Teuber, H., Battersby, W., & Bender, M. (1960). *Visual field defects after penetrating missile wounds of the brain.* Cambridge: Harvard University Press.

Tsubokawa, T., Katayama, T., Nishimoto, H., Kotani, A., & Moriyasu, N. (1976). Emotional slow negative potential shift (CNV) in the thalamus. *Applied Neurophysiology, 39,* 261–267.

Tusobokawa, T., & Moriyasu, N. (1978). Motivational slow negative potential shift (CNV) related to thalamotomy. *Applied Neurophysiology, 41,* 202–208.

Tyler, L.K. (1987). Spoken language comprehension in aphasia: A real-time processing perspective. In M. Coltheart, G. Sartori, & R. Job (Eds.), *The cognitive neuropsychology of language* (pp. 145–162). Hillsdale, NJ: Lawrence Erlbaum.

Van Essen, D. C., & Maunsell, J. H. R. (1983). Hierarchical organization and functional systems in the visual cortex. *Trends in Neuroscience, 6,* 370–375.

Van Hoesen, G. W. (1982). The parahippocampal gyrus: New observations regarding its cortical connections in the monkey. *Trends in Neuroscience, 5,* 345–350.

Van Petten, C., & Kutas, M. (1987). Ambiguous words in context: An event-related potential analysis of the time course of meaning activation. *Journal of Memory and Language, 26,* 188–208.

Van Petten, C., & Kutas, M. (in press). Interactions between sentence context and word frequency. *Biological Psychology.*

Verleger, R. (1988). Event-related potentials and cognition: A critique of the context updating hypothesis and an alternative interpretation of P3. *Behavioral and Brain Sciences, 11,* 343–427.

Walter, W. G. (1964). The convergence and interaction of visual, auditory and tactile responses in human nonspecific cortex. *Annals of the New York Academy of Sciences, 112,* 320–361.

Warrington, E. K. (1981). Concrete word dyslexia. *British Journal of Psychology, 72,* 175–196.

Welford, A. T. (1980). The single-channel hypothesis. In A. T. Welford (Ed.), *Reaction times* (p. 215). London: Academic Press.

Wilson, F. A. W., Brown, M. W., & Richies, I. P. (1988). Neuronal activity in the inferomedial temporal cortex compared with that in the hippocampal formation. In C. D. Woody, D. L. Alkon, & J. L. McGaugh (Eds.), *Cellular mechanisms of conditioning and behavioral plasticity* (pp. 313–328). New York: Plenum Press.

Wolverton, G. S., & Zola, D. (1983). The characteristics of visual information extraction during reading. In K. Rayner (Ed.), *Eye movements in reading* (pp. 41–51). New York: Academic Press.

Wood, C. C., & McCarthy, G. (1985). A possible frontal lobe contribution to scalp P300. *Society for Neuroscience Abstracts, 11,* 879.

Wood, C. C., McCarthy, G., Allison, T., Goff, W. R., Williamson, P. D., & Spencer, D. D. (1982). Endogenous event-related potentials following temporal lobe excisions in humans. *Society for Neuroscience Abstracts, 8,* 976.

Wood, C. C., McCarthy, G., Squires, N. K., Vaughan, H. G., & Woods, D. L. (1984). Anatomical and physiological substrates of event-related potentials. Two case studies. *Annals of the New York Academy of Sciences, 425,* 681–721.

Zappoli, R., Papini, M., Briani, S., Benvenuti, P., & Pasquinelli, A. (1976). CNV in patients with frontal lobe lesions and mental disturbances. In W. C. McCallum & J. R. Knott (Eds.), *The responsive brain* (pp. 158–163). Bristol: Wright.

Zemon, V., Kaplan, E., & Ratliff, F. (1986). The role of GABA-mediated intracortical inhibition in the generation of visual evoked potentials. In R. Cracco & I. Bodis-Wollner (Eds.), *Evoked potentials* (pp. 287–295). New York: Alan R. Liss.

DISCUSSION

JACKSON BEATTY: The units that seem to be specific for the specific words are in the hippocampus. Is that right?

ERIC HALGREN: We found that of the 39 cells we looked at, 30 had stimulus specificity that was statistically significant at the .01 level, and those were located throughout the medial temporal lobe. But the most highly significant ones were all in the anterior hippocampus.

ARNOLD SCHEIBEL: This is interesting. Having worked in the reticular formation many years ago, one gets used to the idea of seeing the largest responses and most intense unit activity accompanying the exotic, the unusual, and the unexpected. Yet rather early in your presentation you were showing us some responses that were larger to repeated presentations and much smaller to others. It seems to be the other side of the coin.

HALGREN: Right. I suspect that the earliest-latency waves might be larger because they are more passively reflecting the amount of associates that a particular stimulus has—and so the more it has the more familiar it is. The more potential you have, especially with the P3, the larger a P3 you find to repeated words because you already have strong connections. And so you need to inhibit associative activation rather than promote it. But in any case this is different from the orienting reflex and similar responses. This is cognitive. The person is not dozing off or doing something else. In such cases one can evoke an orienting response with a loud, rousing stimulus. Such stimuli are attended to and processed.

ISAK PROHOVNIK: Does left anterior temporal lobectomy abolish the N4 response unilaterally, and the right bilaterally?

HALGREN: In fact that was not what I said. That was for the processing negativity proceeding the N4. Let's back up a bit. The CNV is what is tying everything together. It's what's going on between words. It corresponds to primary memory or working memory. Then for each word you have to process the abstract features and encode the word into a neural temporal pattern. That's what the processing negativity could be. Then you have the N400, and that is not affected by right anterior temporal lobectomy. After left temporal lobectomy, you still have a large bump where the N4 is supposed to be. And I think it's still there, and the brain still generates it. What's happening is that you lose, all over the head, the difference in N4 with repetition. In contrast, behavioral performance is preserved. The evoked potential is not differentiating between repeated and nonrepeated words, but the behavior is. So, the evoked potential must be reflecting a particular aspect of the recognition process, one that Michael Smith and I proposed corresponds to the retrieval of the previous context of the word.

With regard to the problem of which response was abolished on the left side following right-sided lobectomy, I believe what is lost is the processing negativity. One might suspect that in cases such as these, you have a complex pattern of recognition and processing, perhaps more lateralized to the right, as in Kimura's studies, and you also have the lobectomy extending 1 cm further back on the right. That might be a critical factor, but in any case there's some critical processing going on in the right hemisphere that perhaps is transferred over the callosum and results in the left hemisphere showing the potential.

MAGNETOENCEPHALOGRAPHIC ANALYSIS
OF HUMAN COGNITIVE PROCESSES

JACKSON BEATTY, PhD
University of California, Los Angeles

INTRODUCTION

Over a century ago, William James—the great American psychologist and brother of novelist Henry James—recognized the importance of biological concepts in any attempt to comprehend cognitive processes. "Our first conclusion," he wrote in opening his classic textbook, "is that a certain amount of brain-physiology must be presupposed or included in Psychology" (James, 1890). Unfortunately that most sensible dictum was ignored by psychologists for many decades.

Recently, however, the situation has begun to change. Witness the recent resurgence of interest in classical neuropsychology, of which James would have assuredly approved. Detailed cognitive theories—some generated in the context of artificial intelligence research—are now being tested in individuals with specific and definable brain lesions (Posner, 1987). This is one promising approach to understanding the anatomy of cognitive processing.

It has also become possible to measure the activity of the human brain as it performs its cognitive functions. The event-related potentials provided the first indications of brain events underlying cognitive processing. Positron emission tomography and measures of regional cerebral blood flow opened the possibility of relating regional cortical activation to the theories of the modular mind (Fodor, 1983). Most recently, the analysis of magnetoencephalographic (MEG) measurements opened the possibility of localizing the intracranial current flows evoked by cognitive processes within the human brain (Beatty, Barth, Richer, & Johnson, 1986).

MODULAR ORGANIZATION OF CEREBRAL CORTEX

The basic anatomic principles of cortical organization were established over a century ago. It was realized that this great rind of gray matter covering the

Acknowledgments: Research supported in part by grants from the National Institute of Mental Health (MH 37430-07) and from the National Science Foundation (BBS-871057).

cerebral hemispheres was composed of six distinct layers. Further, it was known that the relative depths of these laminae varied systematically from region to region. The pioneering microscopic neuroanatomists such as Korbinian Brodmann and Constantin von Economo had constructed detailed maps parceling the cortex into distinct regions based on similarities and differences of microanatomic structure (Figure 1).

For a time, the functional significance of the cortical subdivisions was a matter of heated debate; today, however, there is little doubt as to their importance. It is now believed that each of the three score or more known areas is characterized by a unique cellular architecture, a distinctive pattern of inputs and outputs, and—most important—similar functional characteristics. Within each area, there is uniformity of both structure and function (Van Essen & Maunsell, 1983; DeYoe & Van Essen, 1988). Thus, it is useful to view the human cerebral cortex as a set of specialized mental engines. Each area contains the neural machinery to perform its own unique transformations between its inputs and its outputs.

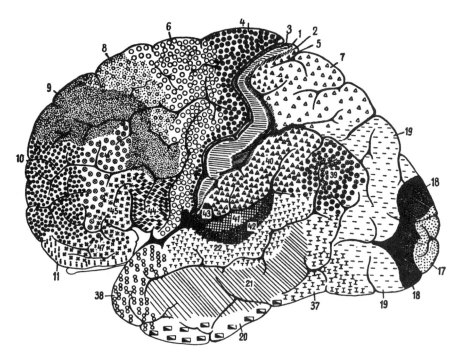

Figure 1. Brodmann's cytoarchitectonic map of the human cerebral cortex. Although somewhat modified over the past 80 years, Brodmann's original parcelation of the cerebral cortex based on variations in cellular pattern has stood the test of time. Each area is now believed to have its own unique pattern of connections and functional properties in addition to cytoarchitectural structure. After Brodmann (1909).

This modular conception of cortical organization fits nicely with contemporary models of cognitive processing. Ideas such as modularity of mind (Fodor, 1983) and distributed processing models (McClelland, Rumelhart, & the PDP Research Group, 1986a, 1986b) seem to make neuroanatomic sense. If it were possible to measure the activity of individual cortical areas, progress could be made in comprehending both the neurophysiology and neuroanatomy of cognitive function.

Brain Electrical and Magnetic Activity

One approach to measuring cortical activity is to record the electrical activity of cortical tissue from electrodes placed on the scalp, a procedure termed electroencephalography (EEG). When EEG activity is averaged with respect to a stimulus or behavioral event, the event-related potentials (ERPs) obtained offer an indication of the time course of cognitively related brain electrical activity. There is little question that ERPs provide a unique and powerful indication of ongoing cognitive processing on a millisecond-by-millisecond basis. Strong ERP correlates have been demonstrated for signal detection (Squires, Hillyard, & Lindsay, 1973) and recognition (Parasuraman & Beatty, 1980), short-term memory (Squires, Wickens, Squires, & Donchin, 1976), selective attention (Hillyard, Hink, Schwent, & Picton, 1973), and semantic anomaly (Kutas & Hillyard, 1980), among other aspects of cognition. Sometimes such results can be striking. However, despite these impressive relationships between ERPs and cognitive processing, ERPs have not contributed as much as they might toward a neural theory of cognition. This is because—with few exceptions—the neuroanatomic generators of the cognitively sensitive ERP components remain unknown (Allison, 1984).

By recording the magnetic, rather than electrical, signature of cortical activation, the three-dimensional location of the sources of EEG and ERP responses may be determined in many cases. Magnetic rather than electrical localization of intracranial current sources is possible for a number of reasons. Perhaps most important is the fact that, although the skull is electrically resistive, it is magnetically transparent (see Williamson & Kaufman, 1981; Beatty et al., 1986). Thus, the skull only minimally distorts the magnetic fields generated by intracranial currents and thereby preserves the localizing information that these fields may contain.

Neurogenesis of Extracranial Magnetic Fields

The extracranial neuromagnetic field consists of the summated magnetic fields produced by electrical currents within populations of active neurons. The details of neurogenesis of the measured field are only now being experimentally clarified on the basis of animal experimentation. However, it is now apparent that the extracranial neuromagnetic field results from the relatively high-density intra-cellular currents rather than the lower-density volume currents that constitute the EEG (Barth, Sutherling, & Beatty, 1984).

Theoretical analyses of the physical properties of possible neuronal sources of such fields are also instructive (see Williamson & Kaufman, 1981). For example, action potentials, although characterized by very strong intracellular currents, probably contribute insignificantly to the extracranial field. This is a necessary consequence of the fact that the intracellular currents underlying this propagated potential are symmetrical and opposite, extending at approximately equal strength both before and after the point of propagation. Thus, the magnetic fields produced by these opposing intracellular currents are nearly perfectly self-canceling when measured at any distance from the cellular source. For this reason, action potentials of the axons play virtually no role in determining the form of the extracranial neuromagnetic field. Thus, the intracellular currents of the dendrites and soma are more likely to be net neuromagnetic generators.

Further, large cells with asymmetrical dendrites are likely to produce larger net magnetic fields than will small cells with relatively symmetrical radically oriented dendrites. This conclusion rests on the facts that larger cells can generate larger dipole moments and that radially oriented dendrites are more likely to produce self-canceling magnetic fields. For the cerebral cortex, the large pyramidal and pyramidal-like cells should contribute much more to the extracranial fields than the smaller, radially symmetrical stellate cells. This conclusion is strengthened by the fact that the apical dendrites of the pyramidal cells are aligned in parallel so that the individual fields produced by a simultaneously activated population of such neurons may summate in a manner not possible for the intrinsic cortical neurons.

Finally, the importance of cortical rather than subcortical contributions to the measured extracranial magnetic field follows from the fact that magnetic fields decrease in magnitude with the square of the distance between the generator and the point of measurement. Thus, the contribution of cortical sources in the human magnetoencephalogram (MEG) is greatly magnified with respect to fields produced by deeper—and therefore more distant—structures such as the hippocampus.

Measuring Brain Magnetic Fields

The magnetic fields produced by coherent intracellular currents within the large pyramidal cells of the cerebral cortex are the strongest of the brain magnetic fields but are nonetheless extraordinarily small when compared with other, more familiar magnetic phenomena. Brain magnetic fields average a few hundred femtotesla (10^{-15} T) in strength. By comparison, the magnetic field produced by a moving automobile is on the order of a microtesla (10^{-6} T), and the magnetic field of the earth is several hundred times larger still. Accordingly, the magnetic signals of the brain are about a million times smaller than the magnetic fields commonly encountered in an urban environment. For this reason, very specialized techniques are required to measure brain magnetic events accurately.

The only sensor capable of resolving such small magnetic fields is a superconducting quantum interference device, or SQUID, which, in today's technology, must operate at the temperature of liquid helium ($-453°F$). The SQUID sensor itself is contained within a superinsulated container or dewar holding the liquid helium. Because of the physical constraints imposed by the dewar, the design of flexible MEG systems that can conform to the actual irregular geometry of the human head has been impossible. However, recent advances in warm-temperature superconductivity hold forth the promise of much less expensive and more adaptable MEG systems in the future.

The problem of intense environmental magnetic noise is treated in two ways. First, the SQUID magnetometer is linked to coils that are configured as a gradiometer of first or second order. By sensing the spatial gradient of the magnetic field, this gradiometer attenuates the effects of distant sources such as moving vehicles or the earth's magnetic field, whereas signals from nearby biological sources are relatively preserved. Second, a magnetically shielded chamber may also be employed to further reduce environmental magnetic contaminants.

To determine the location of the intracranial currents that give rise to an extracranial brain magnetic field, a substantial portion of the field must be measured. This is because it is the shape of the measured magnetic field that provides the localizing information (see below). However, today's helium-filled MEG systems are capable of measuring only a small portion of that field at any one time. As a consequence, the experiment must of necessity be repeated a number of times, each time with the sensor in a different position over the head. The entire field that one would wish to measure simultaneously may be sequentially reconstructed in this manner.

ACCURACY OF MEG SOURCE LOCALIZATION

Neuromagnetic source localization is accomplished by analysis of measured evoked magnetic field patterns. For spatially limited sources, the measured field approximates that generated by an equivalent current dipole (Williamson & Kaufman, 1981). Figure 2 shows such a theoretical distribution produced by a small current source beneath a surface such as that of the head. The measured magnetic field passes through the surface twice, once emerging from the head and again reentering it. The source itself is located between the entering and exiting fields; its depth is indicated by the separation of the two field maxima.

In practice, significant geometric simplifications have been employed in

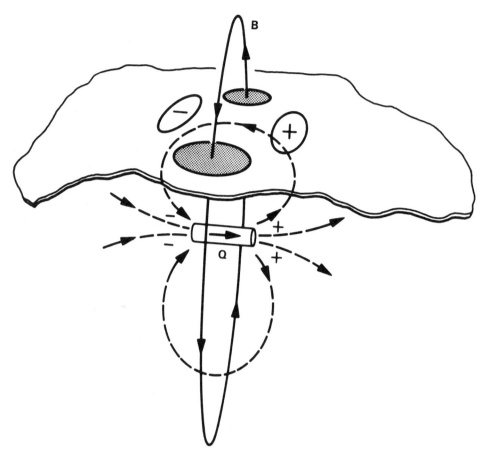

Figure 2. Theoretical distribution of electrical and magnetic fields produced by a current dipole beneath the scalp. Dotted lines represent the electrical volume currents that constitute the EEG. The solid line represents the magnetic field produced by the current dipole. From J. Beatty, D. S. Barth, F. Richer, & R. A. Johnson, 1986. Neuromagnetometry. In M. G. H. Coles, E. Donchin, & S. W. Porges (Eds.), *Psychophysiology: Systems, processes, and applications* (pp. 26–40). New York: Guilford Press. Copyright 1986 by The Guilford Press. Reprinted by permission.

estimating actual three-dimensional source locations from measured MEG data (Williamson & Kaufman, 1981). For posterior regions of the skull, the head is often modeled as a sphere; in the temporal region, a half-space model is often used. Such geometric assumptions greatly reduce the computations required to locate an intracranial current source. These assumptions, however, severely compromise the accuracy with which the source may be located. Barth, Sutherling, Broffman, and Beatty (1986) provided an empirical test of the adequacy of such geometric simplifications. A dipole-like current source was implanted at various positions and orientations within the head of a human cadaver. In this preparation it is possible to compute the putative source position using conventional simplifying assumptions and to compare those results with the actual probe position as determined from skull x-rays.

Using the spherical model to predict source position resulted in significant errors. In the sagittal plane, the mean localization error was approximately 5 mm under the best of circumstances; mean errors of approximately 10 mm were obtained for deeper estimates. Although impressive by some standards, this level of precision is insufficient for a detailed examination and identification of specific cortical fields (Figure 3).

Much of this error can be attributed to simplifications introduced by the spherical model. A more detailed model taking into consideration both actual head geometry and position of the sensing coil achieved significantly better results, at least for more superficial sources. With a measured geometry, sagittal localization errors were reduced to 2 mm. For all but the deepest source position, the computed and actual depths deviated by approximately 1.6 mm. However, problems still remain for localizing very deep sources. Even allowing for measured geometry, a significant error of about 10 mm remained. However, millimeter neuromagnetic localization accuracy can be routinely obtained for sources located within the superficial cerebral cortex.

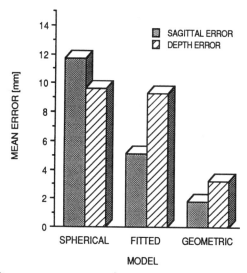

Figure 3. MEG localization accuracy as a function of the measurement model employed. Errors in both the sagittal or surface plane and the depth averaged about 10 mm for the commonly employed spherical model. By permitting the sphere to be statistically fitted, some improvement was obtained for the sagittal plane but not for the depth. By using measured head geometry instead of a spherical model, substantial improvements in localization accuracy were obtained. The remaining error for the depth could be attributed primarily to the deepest source (9.5 mm); the average error for the four most superficial sources was only 1.6 mm.

Topographic Organization of
the Primary Sensory Cortices

The first clear demonstration that evoked brain magnetic fields contain localizing information was provided by Brenner, Lipton, Kaufman, and Williamson (1978). Brenner et al. measured the neuromagnetic fields evoked by electrical stimulation of either the thumb or little finger. For each stimulation site, the entering and exiting fields were tightly constrained in the approximate region of the contralateral somatosensory cortex. However, when the thumb was stimulated, the entire field pattern shifted downward by approximately 2 cm. This displacement is in rough correspondence to the somatotopic organization of area S1 in subhuman primates. A somewhat more detailed mapping of the human somatosensory region was provided later by Okada, Tanenbaum, Williamson, and Kaufman (1984), who expanded the range of the map explored to include two fingers, the thumb, and ankle.

Although such maps are far from complete, they do suggest that the cortical magnetic fields elicited by electrical stimulation of the skin are generated in restricted regions of the cortex. The approximate locus of the generators is congruent with established principles of somatotopic organization. However, it is now known that there are four separate somatosensory areas on the postcentral gyrus: areas 1, 2, 3a, and 3b (Kaas, Nelson, Sur, & Merzenich, 1981). Because of the nature of electrical stimulation, cells in more than one of these areas may be contributing to the observed neuromagnetic responses.

Kaukoranta, Hämäläinen, Sarvas, and Hari (1986) have addressed precisely this question. They compared the neuromagnetic fields evoked by stimulation of the mixed median nerve of the wrist and its cutaneous branches at the surface of the fingers. The fields elicited by mixed-nerve stimulation were stronger and appeared to originate from a deeper source. This pattern of results suggests that stimulation of the cutaneous surface activates primarily area 3b, which receives input from cutaneous receptors. In contrast, median nerve stimulation would activate both 3b and 3a, which receive input from depth receptors. This would account for the increased strength and the spatial displacement of the median nerve response.

Topographic cortical organization also marks the primary auditory and visual cortices. The primary auditory cortex in many species maintains a tonotopic organization, with high frequencies represented at the anterior and low frequencies at the posterior portion of the field. Romani, Williamson, and Kaufman (1982) were able to obtain neuromagnetic fields consistent with a tonotopic organization using sinusoidally modulated pure tones of four different frequencies. The relative positions of the putative current generators obtained using a spherical model were ordered systematically in accordance with tonotopic principles discovered in lower primates.

Nonetheless, Pelizzone, Williamson, and Kaufman (1985) were unable to confirm a tonotopic organization for components of the transient event-related field (ERF) elicited by tones of different pitch. But, in a more extensive study of the transient auditory evoked potential and the ERF, evidence for a frequency-dependent source of at least the magnetic counterpart of the electrical N100 component was provided by Pantev et al. (1988). This finding is in accord with the known functional anatomy of the primary auditory cortex in subhuman primates (Merzenich & Brugge, 1973).

In primates and most other species, the primary visual cortex (Brodmann's area 17) maintains a detailed retinotopic organization. Neuromagnetic evidence of this organization in humans has also been presented. Maclin, Okada, Kaufman, and Williamson (1983) have provided indications of the polar aspect of the retinotopic mapping using sinusoidally modulated visual stimuli. Richer, Barth, and Beatty (1983) have reported similar findings for the transient ERF. In a subsequent and ongoing project, we have found evidence of a meridional organization in the cortical generators of a strong neuromagnetic field component occurring at a latency of approximately 120 msec.

Thus, for the three sensory systems—vision, audition, and somatosensation—neuromagnetic data are at least congruent with established concepts of topographic organization of cortical tissue. Such evidence provides a basis for more detailed investigations in which new knowledge concerning the functional organization of these areas in the human, not subhuman, brain may be obtained.

Magnetic Signals from Secondary Sensory Areas

Attempts have also been made to record neuromagnetic signals originating from nonprimary sensory areas. For example, Hari, Hämäläinen, Kaukoranta, Reinikainen, and Teszner (1983) measured neuromagnetic fields evoked by electrical stimulation of the median nerve. In addition to the contralateral field in the vicinity of primary somatosensory cortex, they reported an ipsilateral field in the vicinity of the Sylvian fissure. They interpret this response as an indication of neuronal activity in the secondary somatosensory cortex (SII) on the upper bank of the fissure.

Memory-Related Magnetic Fields

It is customary in ERP research to distinguish between exogenous and endogenous potentials, the former being obligatory brain responses to sensory stimuli and the latter being dependent on the processing of that sensory information. The mismatch negativity is one example of an endogenous potential. It is elicited by an infrequently presented tone that differs in pitch from the standard tones in an ignored stimulus sequence (Näätänen, Gaillard, & Mäntysalo, 1978; Näätänen, Simpson, & Loveless, 1982). The mismatch negativity reaches its peak at a latency of 150 to 200 msec. Because it is the rarity of the deviant stimulus that elicits the mismatch negativity, that potential is said to be memory dependent.

Sams and colleagues (1985) at Helsinki measured the magnetic fields elicited by both standard and deviant stimuli in an attempt to discern the locus of the mismatch negativity. Both stimuli elicited a clear electrical N100 wave, following which the responses to standards and deviants began to differ; the deviants showed the mismatch negativity, which peaked at a latency of about 220 msec. A similar pattern was also observed magnetically. The evoked magnetic field to both stimuli acquired a dipolar pattern by about 110 msec. This magnetic component appears to correspond to the electrical N100. For standard stimuli, the organized field then dissipates. For the deviants, the field is prolonged, maintaining a clear dipolar form that peaks at 240 msec. This field is rotated with respect to the 110-msec field. Nonetheless, calculations of location of the putative current dipoles indicated that both fields originate in primary auditory cortex. Such results, if corroborated, suggest that even the earliest cortical fields involved in sensory processing have memory-sensitive properties.

LANGUAGE-RELATED MAGNETIC FIELDS

The study of language represents a particular challenge for cognitive neuroscience. Although the language regions of the left hemisphere were the first cortical areas to be anatomically identified, relatively little is known concerning their functional activity. R. A. Johnson, M. Collaer, and J. Beatty (unpublished data) have approached the problem of understanding the cortical physiology of speech perception using magnetoencephalographic methods. Using digitally generated speech segments (consonant–vowel pairs) and pure tone bursts, they have mapped the magnetic fields evoked by linguistic and nonlinguistic auditory stimuli.

The magnetic field at 100 msec following the pure-tone stimulus is well behaved and dipolar in its structure. Similarly, the M100 field for the syllable /da/ is highly organized and has a form congruent with a dipolar source located in superficial cerebral cortex. Although both fields are similar in appearance, there are interesting differences between them.

The ERF elicited by the pure tone is of a size and position that have been interpreted traditionally as originating within the primary auditory cortex. Thus, this field may be taken as an approximate model of activating the nonlinguistic auditory system. In particular, the position of the phonemically evoked field is shifted both posteriorly and dorsally with respect to the pure-tone field. It is reasonable to conjecture that the phonemic field includes the contribution of a linguistic processor, possibly located within Wernicke's area, to the total complex field evoked by the presented phoneme. What is required is a quantitative procedure capable of decomposing complex magnetic fields into their multiple component fields.

The Late Positive Complex

Perhaps none of the classical ERP components seems more cognitive or endogenous than that known as P300. This positive component of the ERP, occurring at latencies varying from under 300 msec to two or three times that figure, has been given a variety of psychological interpretations (Donchin, Karis, Bashore, Coles, & Gratton, 1986). In a long series of experiments, this and related waveforms have been shown to covary with a variety of higher-order task parameters. However, what originally was conceptualized as a unitary waveform now appears to constitute a family of potentials. Thus, the term late positive complex (LPC) appears preferable when referring to these waveforms in general. Since the origin or origins of the LPC are not well understood, it seemed a natural candidate for magnetoencephalographic localization.

At least two groups of investigators, one at NYU and the other at UCLA, pursued this problem at some length. In 1983, Okada, Kaufman, and Williamson published a report suggesting that the late positive complex had its origin in or near the hippocampal formation. But two aspects of this report present cause for concern. First is the small sample size employed: extensive data were obtained from two subjects with additional data from one hemisphere of a third individual. Second is the fact that the localization depended on the geometric simplification of the spherical model. Although it was not known in 1983, the cadaver simulation studies have now shown that the spherical model produces substantial errors in localization, particularly for sources as deep as the hippocampus. Thus, any conclusions suggesting deep origins based on that model must now be treated with caution.

During the same period in my own laboratories at UCLA, we obtained data suggesting a superficial cortical source for the LPC that was modality specific (Richer, Johnson, & Beatty, 1983). The measured fields appeared to be related to neural processes associated with the LPC in that their amplitude varied inversely with stimulus probability. However, such data were difficult to replicate in a larger series of individuals. It was not that the data gave other indications but simply that they became unruly. Thus, our early evidence for a superficial source of the late positive complex was also equivocal.

What should one conclude about the neural origin of the late positive complex? First, one should be aware that the late positive complex probably is a complex of neuronal responses, and the idea that it has multiple generators not only should be kept in mind but almost certainly must be correct. Second, all available magnetoencephalographic data bearing on the issue are inconclusive at best. Third, and perhaps most important, is the realization that the types of cognitive processes related to the LPC are fragile and labile. An identical LPC cannot be evoked and reevoked by even relatively simple tasks over and over again during the hours of testing required to obtain a satisfactory field map. For more complex cognitive processes, the problem is even worse. This, I believe, is the principal methodological reason why the origins of this most evident of cognitive ERP waveforms have remained hidden.

MULTIPLE CURRENT SOURCES

The problem of localizing several simultaneously active intracranial current sources is a matter of some seriousness. The magnetic fields of such sources linearly summate to produce a single measured extracranial magnetic field. This field must be decomposed in some manner if the origins of its several sources are to be determined. To do so, additional information is required.

If there is reason to believe that the several active generators may operate over differing time periods, then sequential information may be used to disentangle the contributing sources. Barth, Sutherling, Engel, and Beatty (1984) were able to identify four separate components of interictal spike complexes by analyzing the time-varying properties of the magnetic field data.

A second source of information that may be of use in resolving complex field patterns employs a strategy similar to the subtractive procedure recently employed by Petersen, Fox, Posner, Mintun, and Raichle (1988) for the analysis of positron emission images evoked in word processing. They utilized a series of graded experimental conditions, each of which included the processes evoked by the previous condition while adding putative cognitive processes of interest. By differencing the complex images obtained in successive conditions, cortical processes presumably evoked by each processing stage might be selectively portrayed. Such an approach seems useful for analyzing complex MEG fields.

It seems clear that the problem of complex field sources must be resolved if MEG is to make a significant contribution to the study of higher mental problems. This difficult question deserves much more attention than it has received in the past.

CONCLUSION

Measuring brain magnetic fields is a tedious and time-consuming process; only the strongest and most repetitive brain signals are well suited to neuromagnetic analysis. Thus, it is not surprising that progress has been made in mapping recurring interictal spikes in epileptic patients and in charting the obligatory exogenous sensory evoked fields. But the really interesting questions concerning higher mental functions remain unanswered. Which fields are related to language, attention, and thought? Where do they originate? What can they tell us about the functional anatomy of the vast human cerebral cortex? These and similar questions challenge the limits of MEG analysis.

Nonetheless, there has been progress. By combining MEG measures with carefully designed cognitive tasks and by using MEG data in conjunction with data obtained using other imaging methods, some of the riddles of cognitive processing are beginning to be unraveled. In doing so, we approach—albeit slowly—a biological understanding of human thought.

REFERENCES

Allison, T. (1984). Recording and interpreting event-related potentials. In E. Donchin (Ed.), *Cognitive psychophysiology: Event-related potentials and the study of cognition* (pp. 1–36). Hillsdale, NJ: Lawrence Erlbaum Associates.

Barth, D. S., Sutherling, W., & Beatty, J. (1984). Fast and slow magnetic phenomena in focal epileptic seizures. *Science, 226,* 855–857.

Barth, D. S., Sutherling, W., Broffman, J., & Beatty, J. (1986). Magnetic localization of a dipolar current source implanted in a sphere and a human cranium. *Electroencephalography and Clinical Neurophysiology, 63,* 260–273.

Barth, D. S., Sutherling, W., Engel, J., Jr., & Beatty, J. (1984). Neuromagnetic evidence of spatially distributed sources underlying epileptiform spikes in the human brain. *Science, 223,* 293–296.

Beatty, J., Barth, D. S., Richer, F., & Johnson, R. A. (1986). Neuromagnetometry. In M. G. H. Coles, E. Donchin, & S. W. Porges (Eds.), *Psychophysiology: Systems, processes, and applications* (pp. 26–40). New York: Guilford Press.

Brenner, D., Lipton, J., Kaufman, L., & Williamson, S. J. (1978). Somatically evoked magnetic fields of the human brain. *Science, 199,* 81–83.

Brodmann, K. (1909). *Vergleichende Lokalisationslehre der Großhirnrinde in ihren Prinzipien dargestellt auf Grund des Zellenbaues.* Leipzig: Barth.

DeYoe, E. A., & Van Essen, D. C. (1988). Concurrent processing streams in monkey visual cortex. *Trends in Neurosciences, 11*(5), 219–226.

Donchin, E., Karis, D., Bashore, T. R., Coles, M. G. H., & Gratton, G. (1986). Cognitive psychophysiology and human information processing. In M. G. H. Coles, E. Donchin, & S. W. Porges (Eds.), *Psychophysiology: Systems, processes, and applications* (pp. 244–267). New York: Guilford Press.

Fodor, J. A. (1983). *The modularity of mind: An essay on faculty psychology.* Cambridge, MA: MIT Press.

Hari, R., Hämäläinen, M., Kaukoranta, E., Reinikainen, K., & Teszner, D. (1983). Neuromagnetic responses from the second somatosensory cortex in man. *Acta Neurologica Scandinavica, 68,* 207–212.

Hillyard, S. A., Hink, R. F., Schwent, V. L., & Picton, T. W. (1973). Electrical signs of selective attention in the human brain. *Science, 182,* 177–180.

James, W. (1890). *The principles of psychology.* New York: Henry Holt & Co.

Kaas, J. H., Nelson, R. J., Sur, M., & Merzenich, M. M. (1981). Organization of somatosensory cortex in primates. In F. O. Schmitt, F. G. Worden, G. Adelman, & S. G. Dennis (Eds.), *The organization of the cerebral cortex* (pp. 237–261). Cambridge, MA: MIT Press.

Kaufman, L., Okada, Y., Brenner, D., & Williamson, S. J. (1981). On the relation between somatic evoked potentials and fields. *International Journal of Neuroscience, 15,* 223–239.

Kaukoranta, E., Hämäläinen, M., Sarvas, J., & Hari, R. (1986). Mixed and sensory nerve stimulations activate different cytoarchitectonic areas in the human primary somatosensory cortex SI: Neuromagnetic recordings and statistical considerations. *Experimental Brain Research, 63,* 60–66.

Kutas, M., & Hillyard, S. A. (1980). Reading senseless sentences: Brain potentials reflect semantic incongruity. *Science, 207,* 203–205.

Maclin, E. Y., Okada, Y. C., Kaufman, L., & Williamson, S. J. (1983). Retinotopic map on the visual cortex for eccentrically placed patterns: First noninvasive measurement. *Il Nuovo Cimento, 2*(2), 410–419.

McClelland, J. L., Rumelhart, D. E., & the PDP Research Group. (1986a). *Parallel distributed processing: Explorations in the microstructure of cognition: Vol. I. Foundations.* Cambridge, MA: MIT Press.

McClelland, J. L., Rumelhart, D. E., & the PDP Research Group. (1986b). *Parallel distributed processing: Explorations in the microstructure of cognition: Vol. II. Psychological and biological models.* Cambridge, MA: MIT Press.

Merzenich, M. M., & Brugge, J. F. (1973). Representation of the cochlear partition on the superior temporal plane of the macaque monkey. *Brain Research, 50,* 275–296.

Näätänen, R., Gaillard, A. W. K., & Mäntysalo, S. (1978). Early selective-attention effect on evoked potential reinterpreted. *Acta Psychologica, 42,* 313–329.

Näätänen, R., Simpson, M., & Loveless, N. E. (1982). Stimulus deviance and evoked potentials. *Biological Psychology, 14,* 53–98.

Okada, Y. C., Kaufman, L., & Williamson, S. J. (1983). The hippocampal formation as a source of the slow endogenous potentials. *Electroencephalography and Clinical Neurophysiology, 55,* 417–426.

Okada, Y. C., Tanenbaum, R., Williamson, S. J., & Kaufman, L. (1984). Somatotopic organization of the human somatosensory cortex revealed by neuromagnetic measurements. *Experimental Brain Research, 56,* 197–205.

Pantev, C., Hoke, M., Lehnertz, K., Lütkenhöner, B., Anogianakis, G., & Wittkowski, W. (1988). Tonotopic organization of the human auditory cortex revealed by transient auditory evoked magnetic fields. *Electroencephalography and Clinical Neurophysiology, 69,* 160–170.

Parasuraman, R., & Beatty, J. (1980). Brain events underlying detection and recognition of weak sensory signals. *Science, 210,* 80–83.

Pelizzone, M., Williamson, S. J., & Kaufman, L. (1985). Evidence for multiple areas in the human auditory cortex. In H. Weinberg, G. Stroink, & T. Katila (Eds.), *Biomagnetism: Theory and applications* (pp. 326–330). New York: Pergamon Press.

Petersen, S. E., Fox, P. T., Posner, M. I., Mintun, M., & Raichle, M. E. (1988). Positron emission tomographic studies of the cortical anatomy of single-word processing. *Nature, 331,* 585–589.

Posner, M. I. (1987). *Structures and functions of selective attention.* Master lecture. New York: American Psychological Association.

Richer, F., Barth, D. S., & Beatty, J. (1983). Neuromagnetic localization of two components of the transient visual evoked response to patterned stimulation. *Il Nuovo Cimento, 2*(2), 420–423.

Richer, F., Johnson, R. A., & Beatty, J. (1983). Sources of late components of the brain magnetic response. *Society for Neuroscience Abstracts, 9,* 656.

Romani, G. L., Williamson, S. J., & Kaufman, L. (1982). Tonotopic organization of the human auditory cortex. *Science, 216,* 1339–1340.

Sams, M., Hari, R., Kaukoranta, E., Reinikainen, K., Alho, K., Hämäläinen, M. S., Ilmoniemi, R. J., Näätänen, R., & Salminen, J. (1985). Magnetic responses to pitch changes in a sequence of short auditory stimuli. In H. Weinberg, G. Stroink, & T. Katila (Eds.), *Biomagnetism: Applications and theory* (pp. 331–335). New York: Pergamon Press.

Squires, K. C., Hillyard, S. A., & Lindsay, P. H. (1973). Vertex potentials evoked during auditory signal detection: Relation to decision criteria. *Perception and Psychophysics, 14*, 265–272.

Squires, K. C., Wickens, C., Squires, N. K., & Donchin, E. (1976). The effect of stimulus sequence on the waveform of cortical event-related potentials. *Science, 193*, 1142–1146.

Van Essen, D. C., & Maunsell, J. H. R. (1983). Hierarchical organization and functional streams in the visual cortex. *Trends in Neurosciences, 6*, 370–375.

Williamson, S. J., & Kaufman, L. (1981). Biomagnetism: Topical review. *Journal of Magnetism and Magnetic Materials, 22*, 129–201.

DISCUSSION

ISAK PROHOVNIK: With regard to localization of sources, you could do your experiment, use the MRI, and see a source in the ventricle because of the basic assumption of a single dipole. And you might as well have a complicated source with a weighted average someplace in the ventricle.

JACKSON BEATTY: That's absolutely correct. One of the fundamental limitations at present is the assumption of single current sources generating a field map. Under some circumstances that's probably appropriate. Under other circumstances, it isn't, and what is required are some very clever techniques for decomposing both spatially and temporally those sources that are coming from a handful of powerful simultaneous generators. That is the fundamental difficulty. That is the blindness of MEG in looking at the human brain.

JÖRG PAHL: I just wanted to clear up one thing. You showed that you measured these magnetic dipoles on an individual when he was exposed to some sort of auditory clicking.

BEATTY: Correct.

PAHL: Then exposed to language.

BEATTY: Yes, tones and "dahs."

PAHL: O.K. Then what was the second?

BEATTY: It was either a 1,000-Hz tone or a /da/ or a /ba/.

PAHL: And then what were you showing by subtracting the first from the second?

BEATTY: The plain, brute, empirical result is that there were two different dipole-like fields resulting in different locations. The question is, should a possible contribution of the nonlinguistic auditory system be taken into account in interpreting the linguistic response? We used linear least-square fitting to remove the effects of the nonlinguistic auditory response from the linguistic evoked field. This is one method of decomposing a complex field.

ERIC HALGREN: In localizing a complex potential, I'm sure it may represent several sources. I'm sure also that any given source could be a plane instead of just one dipole. And I'm wondering if you had a whole bunch of dipoles lined up against each other, whether the magnetic flux from one could cancel another?

BEATTY: That could be modeled very explicitly. What you get is the centroid of the contributing field elements, so that if you've got a large area, like one of Brodmann's areas, which has some length, it will localize to a point that is in the geometric center of that area.

HALGREN: It won't be below the field?

BEATTY: No, that has been simulated by Okada. An extended field must be very, very, broad to change the appearance of its depth.

JASON BROWN: How do you handle the problem of the radial currents? You tell me they don't make any difference, but in fact you don't know, since you don't pick them up.

BEATTY: It is only in a perfect sphere that that is true. But most heads are so far from being perfectly spherical that the radial component can be calculated to be attenuated by as much as 60, 70, or 80%. But not 100%.

BROWN: How do you know how much is being attenuated by that amount? In other words, you don't know whether there is normally a very large or very small radial component that you need to deal with.

BEATTY: There are a couple of answers to that question. One has to do with the percentage of the human cortex that is radial, perfectly radial, which is rather little. A second one again . . .

PAHL: Is everything going down in the sulci, for example?

BEATTY: No, those are tangential. Those are the sources you can see. It's just a generator right at the top of a gyrus that is theoretically invisible in a spherical head.

PAHL: Which current do you think you are picking up?

BEATTY: Dendritic currents. That's one answer. The real answer is that's the least of our worries right now, and if we've got something that will pick up many signals from cortex and localize them, that's just fine.

STRUCTURAL CORRELATES OF COGNITION
IN THE HUMAN BRAIN

SANDRA F. WITELSON, PhD
McMaster University

INTRODUCTION

The concept of cerebral dominance, now more precisely referred to as functional asymmetry of the hemispheres, brain lateralization, or hemispheric specialization, was born as an inference by Dax and again later by Broca in the mid-19th century from the observed clinical deficits shown by a small series of neurological patients with unilateral brain damage (see Benton, 1964). This inference has now gained the status of a well-documented feature in the organization of the human brain.

Many cognitive tasks involving verbal or sequential components are particularly dependent on the functioning of left hemisphere regions; other tasks involving aspects of the perception of form or three-dimensional space are more dependent on right hemisphere regions. The different roles that the two hemispheres have in mental functioning have been demonstrated by several corroborating lines of evidence: from neurological patients with focal lesions, from patients with commissurotomy, and from studies of the performance of neurologically intact people on various perceptual and electrophysiological measures (see reviews, e.g., Bryden, 1982; Heilman & Valenstein, 1985). Functional asymmetry has been clearly demonstrated in children, even in infancy, for verbal (Witelson, 1987a) and spatial skills (Witelson & Swallow, 1988). Such results indicate that although environmental factors may influence the development and manifestation of functional asymmetry, early neurobiological factors play a role in determining the existence and pattern of lateralization.

But many issues are not resolved. It has not been clarified what is the essential nature of the different types of information processing that differentiate the hemispheres and result in each hemisphere being specifically suited for mediating a specific group of tasks. It has not been resolved whether the differences between hemispheres are absolute or relative (relative meaning that each hemisphere can or does process each type of task, but one does so less efficiently than the other). It is not known whether a structural (anatomical or chemical) basis underlies functional asymmetry or what the developmental mechanisms may be. These issues are elaborated elsewhere (Witelson, 1987b). In this chapter I focus on the status of the evidence supporting an anatomical basis of functional asymmetry, including some of my recent research findings.

TEMPORAL LOBE ASYMMETRY

Anatomical asymmetry between the hemispheres in the human brain has been well documented. The morphology of the Sylvian fissure and adjacent cortical regions was noted to be asymmetrical by numerous investigators starting in the previous century (see reviews, e.g., in Geschwind, 1974; Witelson, 1977; Witelson & Kigar, 1988). Within the Sylvian fissure, the planum temporale—the posterior region of the superior surface of the temporal lobe—was noted by several early workers to be larger more frequently on the left than on the right (see Figure 1).

The prevalence and size of asymmetry in the planum temporale was first quantified by Geschwind and Levitsky (1968), who reported that 65% of a sample of 100 brain specimens showed greater expansion on the left side and that on average the left planum temporale was approximately one-third greater than the right planum. This anatomical asymmetry has been documented subsequently in numerous studies from different laboratories. In a recent review of 13 studies to date measuring right–left asymmetry in the planum temporale in adults, each one reported that the planum was larger on the left than right side in the majority of cases (reviewed in detail in Witelson & Kigar, 1988, Table 3). The same situation holds for the five studies of planum asymmetry in children and infants (also reviewed in Witelson & Kigar, 1988).

The planum temporale is a gyrus well within the cortical region described as Wernicke's region, the area important for the perception of language. Accordingly, it is tempting to hypothesize that the larger left-sided planum reflects or underlies in some way an anatomical substrate for the greater role of the left temporal region in the perception of language and to plan studies to address this issue. However, many authors have not waited for empirical evidence and have assumed that anatomical asymmetry is a substrate of functional asymmetry. In addition to a lack of empirical evidence of an association between the two asymmetries, there are reasons to question such an association. Most people have left hemisphere speech representation, and most people have greater expansion of left temporal regions. Any observed association between these two asymmetries may be just a reflection of two independent asymmetries. Moreover, the distribution of the prevalence of right- and left-sided temporal lobe asymmetry is not congruent with that for right- and left-sided representation of speech. Additionally, the apparently paradoxical issue that the right posterior temporal lobe has a greater role in some nonverbal functions, yet has a smaller right temporal planum, has been ignored (for detailed discussion, see Witelson, 1977).

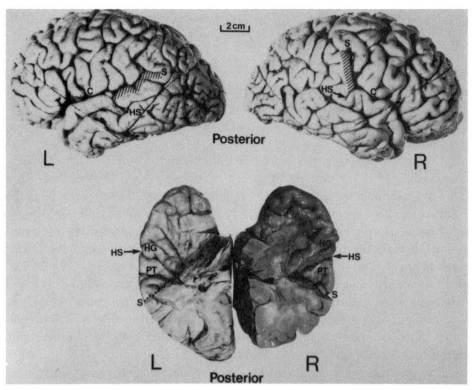

Figure 1. Lateral views of the two hemispheres and the exposed superior surface of each temporal lobe of a human adult showing the typical asymmetries of a sharper upswing of the Sylvian fissure on the right side, a larger posterior parietal operculum on the left side, and a larger planum temporale on the left side. The superior surface of each planum was exposed by dissection that followed the curve of the Sylvian fissure to its end. Note that the anterior end of the right temporal block is tilted upward so that the planum is photographed in a horizontal plane. S, posterior end of the Sylvian fissure; C, inferior tip of the central sulcus; HS, Heschl sulcus; HG, Heschl gyrus; PT, planum temporale. Dotted lines indicate the posterior boundary of the planum; hatched lines indicate the lateral edge of the planum. Adapted from Witelson (1987b).

To date the evidence regarding functional correlates of asymmetry in size of the planum temporale is still preliminary. The anatomical studies of planum asymmetry have involved direct measurement of dissected postmortem specimens. This has been essential, as the location, boundaries, and therefore size of the planum are not readily ascertained by study of the lateral aspect of the hemispheres (see Figure 1). The position and orientation of the posterior segment of the Sylvian fissure, which forms the roof of the planum, is often markedly different in the right and left hemispheres (Witelson, 1987b). *In vivo* brain images obtained from the usual two-dimensional representations from computerized tomography (CT) or from magnetic resonance (MR) imaging do not readily portray the planum. The right and left plana would usually be most prominent in scans taken at different levels. Reliable measures of any specific dimension of the planum (whether maximal length, breadth, area, or volume) would require definition of boundaries that are visible in scans and three-dimensional (3-D) reconstruction of the images.

Accordingly, investigations of the association between measures of functional asymmetry and anatomical asymmetry of the planum are still few in number. To date, there are no reports on the association of hand preference or speech lateralization by amobarbital testing in relation to postmortem studies of the planum.

One preliminary report measured ear asymmetry in a verbal dichotic listening task, considered to be an index of speech lateralization (see Bryden, 1982). In a series of seven brain specimens, greater right-ear accuracy (REA) was found in the four cases having a greater left planum. A lack of REA was found in the three brains not showing a larger left planum (Witelson, 1983). The one other study of planum asymmetry in relation to functional asymmetry involved arteriograms of the middle cerebral artery in which planum breadth was inferred by a measure in a coronal plane. Asymmetry in ear accuracy on a dichotic verbal stimulation task was found to have a low but statistically significant correlation with this anatomical measure of temporal lobe asymmetry. In contrast, however, in the same study, speech lateralization based on amobarbital testing was not correlated with the temporal lobe asymmetry (Strauss, LaPointe, Wada, Gaddes, & Kosaka, 1985).

The remaining relevant literature also is at most suggestive of a correlation between functional and anatomical asymmetry. Briefly, in brain arteriograms, the arch formed by the middle cerebral artery in the posterior part of the Sylvian fossa has been found to be asymmetrical in several reports (e.g., Hochberg & LeMay, 1975). Studies of this anatomical measure in relation to functional lateralization found in one case that this anatomical asymmetry was associated with speech lateralization based on amobarbital testing (Ratcliff, Dila, Taylor, & Milner, 1980), but in another case, it was not associated with either amobarbital testing or dichotic ear asymmetry (Strauss et al., 1985).

Hand preference as an index of functional asymmetry has been studied frequently as a correlate of asymmetry in the breadth of the occipital lobes in CT and MR scans. Several studies found greater asymmetry in right handers than left handers—left handedness defined in various ways in the different studies—but other studies found no difference between hand groups (for detailed reviews on handedness, see Witelson, 1980; for functional asymmetry in general, see Witelson & Kigar, 1988, Table 5).

In summary, the evidence to date suggests at most a modest correlation between functional asymmetry and anatomical asymmetry in gross features such as gyral size or Sylvian fissure morphology. Such research is just beginning, and it remains to be determined whether future studies may uncover more robust structure–function correlations. It is also possible that the gross anatomical asymmetries represent variation in histological features, which may be the structural aspects more closely associated with functional asymmetry.

FRONTAL LOBE ASYMMETRY

The comprehension of language skills is represented in left temporoparietal regions in most individuals. It appears that some aspects of language comprehension may be processed by the right hemisphere, the hemisphere typically nondominant for language. For example, simple auditory and visual word recognition tasks or semantic aspects of language may be processed by the minor hemisphere for language (Zaidel, 1978). Whether the minor hemisphere may truly process linguistic stimuli as does the language-dominant hemisphere or whether different cognitive strategies are involved in right and left hemisphere processing of language tasks is not established. In contrast, the functional lateralization of language expression or speech to one hemisphere appears more marked than for language comprehension. Moreover, the production of language or propositional speech seems less confounded by possibly different strategies. One might thus expect that the frontal opercular region, which is essential for speech, might show anatomical asymmetry at least as marked as in temporal regions. Fewer studies are available concerning anatomical asymmetry of frontal opercular regions. The results to date provide little evidence of asymmetry. There has been almost no study of structure–function relationships for frontal regions.

In a recent literature review, Kigar and I have been able to find five studies of asymmetry in gross morphology in the frontal operculum, particularly in the pars opercularis and pars triangularis, two gyri on the lateral aspect of the brain typically included in "Broca's region" (see Figure 2). There were almost as many different anatomical definitions of "Broca's region" as there were studies (see legend in Figure 2). In four of the five studies, a trend toward greater left-sided regions was observed, but the difference was always statistically nonsignificant. The fifth study (Wada, Clarke, & Hamm, 1975) found the opposite result, a significantly larger region on the right side. The authors commented on this unexpected result by noting that in this region the gyri appeared more tightly packed on the left than right side. This, in fact, may be the case. The clearest picture of asymmetry in Broca's region may be that reported by Falzi, Perrone, and Vignolo (1982). They developed one measure that included the cortical surface within sulci as well as on the lateral surface of the cortex defined as Broca's region (the only study to do this). For this measure, Broca's region tended to be larger on the left than right side. Sample size was small ($n = 12$), and the lack of significance may reflect low statistical power.

All cases in the Falzi et al. sample were right handed, suggesting that hand preference may be a factor in frontal opercular asymmetry. None of the other studies investigated the possible association of anatomical asymmetry to functional asymmetry. A few *in vivo* brain-imaging studies investigated asymmetry in breadth of the frontal lobe with hand preference. Frontal lobe asymmetry itself has not been a reliable finding (Witelson & Kigar, 1988). Study of structure–function association has been minimal, and the results have been very inconsis-

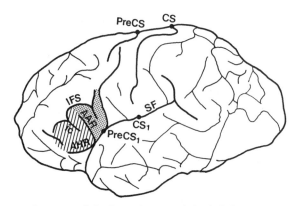

Figure 2. Schematic drawing of the lateral view of the left hemisphere of a human adult brain showing the anatomy of the frontal operculum, including Broca's region. AAR, anterior ascending ramus of the Sylvian fissure (SF); AHR, anterior horizontal ramus of SF; CS, CS_1, PreCS, $PreCS_1$, superior and inferior ends of the central and precentral sulci, respectively; ic, incisura capitis, a ramus of the IFS; IFS, inferior frontal sulcus; the stippled area indicates the pars opercularis (approximately Brodmann's area 44), the hatched lines indicate the pars triangularis (approximately Brodmann's area 45), both regions typically included as Broca's region. However, different studies used various definitions of Broca's region for measurement purposes. Kononova (1935, cited in Adrianov, 1979) defined Broca's region on the basis of cytoarchitectonic regions, once as Brodmann's areas 44 and 45, and in another measure as areas 44, 45, and 47. Galaburda (1980) measured only area 44. Wada et al. (1975) and Nikkuni et al. (1981) defined Broca's region as the gyral area extending from the precentral sulcus to the ic, bounded dorsally by the IFS. Falzi et al. (1982) measured the entire pars opercularis and pars triangularis, bounded dorsally by the IFS, with one measure involving only lateral cortex and another involving cortical area within the sulci as well.

tent. For example, LeMay and Kido (1978) and Bear, Schiff, Saver, Greenberg, and Freeman (1986) found an association, but Chui and Damasio (1980) and Kertesz, Black, Polk, and Howell (1986) did not.

Three studies of size of right versus left frontal operculum in children are available and revealed no asymmetry. The frontal operculum studies are presented in detail in Witelson and Kigar (1988, Table 4).

The story of anatomical asymmetry in the frontal operculum may still be incomplete, but the lack of asymmetry in gross morphology compared to the asymmetry observed for the posterior language regions in the temporal lobes may be noteworthy. On the basis of such results, I suggest that the initial biological basis of functional lateralization may occur in the temporal lobes and that this anatomical asymmetry may drive the functional asymmetry of the frontal lobes. In other words, functional lateralization of speech may result in part from connectivity patterns set up between the frontal language regions and the asymmetrical posterior language regions. If this proves to be the case, it has major implications for the origins and mechanisms leading to the neurobiological basis of lateralization.

Overall, the results of asymmetry in gross measures of cortical regions are only suggestive of an association between functional and anatomical asymmetry. Histological differences between right and left homologous regions may be a key factor. Research in this area is just beginning. One report has revealed right–left differences in the pattern of dendritic branching of neurons in frontal operculum tissue, with a suggestion that opposite patterns may occur in right and left handers (Scheibel et al., 1985). Histological studies have the advantage of more readily indicating developmental mechanisms. For example, the measure of patterns of dendritic branching is one that may reveal the relative timing of such arborization between right and left sides.

CORPUS CALLOSUM

The selection of precise boundaries of a gyrus for purposes of measurement is a longstanding problem. Sulcal pattern varies markedly from brain to brain and hemisphere to hemisphere. The issue is further complicated by the observation that the anatomical localization of cognitive functions varies among individuals (Whitaker & Selnes, 1976). Moreover, it is difficult to know what constitutes a specific functional region, since brain damage in neurological patients is not usually localized to specific gyri. Additionally, linear and areal measures may not best reflect a functional region, which is a three-dimensional structure. In this context, studies of the size of the corpus callosum may have some advantages: the anatomical boundaries of the callosum are relatively clear.

Several studies of areal measurement of the midsagittal section of the corpus callosum have been reported in the last several years. All attest to the large variation in size of the callosum. The correlates of variation in callosal size still remain to be delineated. Some of the earliest studies (e.g., Bean, 1906) indicated that overall callosal size correlated positively with brain size and also was different between the sexes, with men having a larger callosum than women. Most of the recent studies, some using direct measurement from brain specimens and others obtained from MR scans, have observed similar callosal variation in regard to brain size and sex. The sex difference was often not significant, but males tended to have the larger callosum (reviewed in Witelson, 1989). In contrast, a sex difference in the opposite direction was found for one subregion of the callosum, the splenium, which is the posterior bulbous segment of the callosum. This was found, however, only in one laboratory (de Lacoste-Utamsing & Holloway, 1982; Holloway & de Lacoste, 1986) but not in any of the dozen other available studies (Witelson, 1989).

The corpus callosum is the main interhemispheric fiber tract, and accordingly, it may be part of any anatomical substrate of functional lateralization. Variation in its anatomy may vary with different patterns of functional asymmetry. In a series of studies investigating the possible association of anatomical asymmetry with functional asymmetry, the anatomical variation of the callosum was studied in relation to measures of functional lateralization, such as handedness. The anatomical measures were obtained directly from postmortem brain specimens of cognitively normal people who had taken a series of neuropsychological tests before their death.

In a first study of 42 brains, midsagittal area of the callosum was found to vary with hand preference based on performance on a 12-item questionnaire of Annett (1967). People were divided into two categories following Annett's (1972) theory of the genetics of hand preference: consistent-right-handers (CRH) and non consistent-right-handers (nonCRH). By definition, the latter group could include right- or left-handed writers as long as they preferred their left hand on at least one of the 12 items. For nonCRH, overall callosal area and both anterior and posterior halves of the callosum, but *not* the posterior one-fifth (the splenium), were larger compared to CRH (Witelson, 1985). Interestingly, even two cases of forced right-handers (in the nonCRH group) showed larger callosa than did CRH. A subsequent study using MR scans and the same classification of hand preference observed very similar results (Habib, 1989).

Differences in gross area of the callosum must reflect some histological difference: either the number of fibers per unit area is the same, making the total number of fibers greater in the larger callosum, or the total number of fibers in the callosum are the same, making their packing density different. It is also possible that differences occur in the proportion of myelinated to unmyelinated fibers or in the extent of myelination. It was hypothesized that *if* a larger callosum reflects greater total fiber number, then the larger callosum of nonCRH might allow for greater interhemispheric communication in left handers. Such a situation would be consistent with the neurological and experimental neuropsychological results that, as a group, left handers have a higher prevalence of bihemispheric or right-sided speech lateralization (e.g., Bryden, 1982; Hécaen, De Agostini, & Monzon-Montes, 1981).

One subdivision of the callosum, the splenium, was found not to differ between CRH and nonCRH. The splenium contains fibers connecting the right and left occipital lobes and right and left inferior regions of the temporal lobe, based on findings in monkeys and people. These cortical regions may be less involved in the representation of lateralized cognitive functions. it was hypothesized that some regions of the callosum might be more associated with behavioral indices of lateralization than other regions. In particular, it was hypothesized that the callosal areas connecting the right and left parietotemporal cortical regions and the right and left frontal opercular regions might show the greatest association with behavioral indices or hemispheric functional asymmetry. These callosal regions would be (1) the posterior region of the body of the callosum, the isthmus, which is just anterior to the splenium, and (2) the rostrum, the inferior caudal tip of the genu. Extensive experimental work with monkeys (e.g., Pandya & Seltzer, 1986) and some corroborative evidence in humans (de Lacoste,

Kirkpatrick, & Ross, 1985) provide such a pattern of topography for the callosum in its relationship to cortical regions.

In a second study, the callosum was subdivided into seven regions (Figure 3). The area of each was measured in a sample of 50 cases (which included the 42 cases of the previous study). The results were close to prediction. Overall callosal area was greater in nonCRH than CRH, but the difference varied for different callosal segments. The area of the isthmus was greater in nonCRH than CRH by 18%. A marked sex difference was observed in the anatomy of the isthmus. For a group of 19 men, isthmal area and hand preference score reflecting degree and direction (+12 to −12) were significantly correlated ($r = -.57$, $p = .01$). The correlation was even higher with age and brain size controlled. The region of the callosal body just anterior to the isthmus was also greater (by 10%) in nonCRH. The difference between hand groups for the rostrum was close to 10% but not statistically significant because of high variation (Witelson, 1989). It

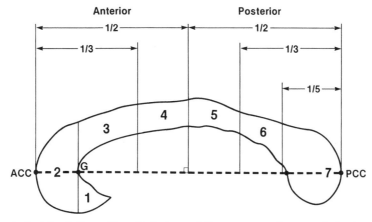

Figure 3. A sketch of the midsagittal view of the corpus callosum of the human adult showing seven subdivisions measured, numbered 1 to 7. ACC–PCC, the line joining the anteriormost and posteriormost points of the callosum, was used as the linear axis to subdivide the callosum. The line perpendicular to the axis at point G was used to define the anteriormost division of the callosum, roughly congruent with the genu (region 2) and the rostrum (region 1). Region 3 was defined as the anterior one-third minus regions 1 and 2. Region 4 was defined as the anterior one-half minus the anterior one-third. Region 5 was defined as the posterior one-half minus the posterior one-third. Region 6, the isthmus, was defined as the posterior one-third minus the posterior one-fifth. Regions 3, 4, 5, and 6 constitute the body of the callosum. The posterior one-fifth region (region 7) is roughly congruent with the splenium. Adapted from Witelson (1989). A rough topography of callosal fibers in relation to cortical regions of origin and termination is also given, based mainly on experimental work with monkeys and on some clinical work with humans. Callosal region 1 relates to caudal/orbital prefrontal and inferior premotor cortex; region 2 to prefrontal cortex; region 3 to premotor and supplementary motor cortex; region 4 to motor cortex; region 5 to somesthetic and posterior parietal cortex; region 6 to superior temporal and posterior parietal cortex; and region 7 to occipital and inferior temporal cortex.

remains to be determined in a larger sample whether the association of rostral area and hand preference becomes significant. The relationship of callosal size with handedness was different for the sexes and is described further in a later section.

The finding that only specific callosal regions, those related to cortical regions particularly relevant for functional asymmetry, were associated with hand preference supports the hypothesis that callosal anatomy is part of a substrate of functional asymmetry. A further test of this hypothesis would be to study whether these callosal regions are associated with other behavioral measures of functional asymmetry.

Hand preference is a motoric behavior. One might expect indices of functional asymmetry based on auditory or visual perception that are more directly dependent on temporoparietal regions of the cortex to show even more marked association with size of the isthmus. Another study focused on the correlation of isthmal size and asymmetry in right–left ear accuracy on a free-recall consonant–vowel (CV) dichotic listening task. It was predicted that greater right-ear accuracy (reflecting greater left-sided speech lateralization) would be associated with a smaller isthmal area. The results revealed such negative correlations, as indicated in a preliminary report (Witelson, 1987c). In a group of 13 men and another of 21 women who received the dichotic test, the correlation of ear asymmetry with isthmal area was significant ($r = -.55$, $p = .05$, and $r = -.42$, $p = .06$, respectively).

The relatively clearer correlations to date for callosal size than for specific gyri with behavioral measures of lateralization may occur because the callosum is an index of large cortical regions, which may be more valid functional units. In this respect, the callosum may prove to be a window to the study of the cortex and a guide for specific further investigations. The study of the genetics of functional asymmetry may be approached by using anatomical measures rather than behavioral measures to describe phenotype. This could have several methodological advantages. At a clinical level, *in vivo* imaging of brain structure might serve as an index of functional lateralization in patients for whom information on speech lateralization is important but for whom more traditional methods such as amobarbital testing are not possible.

AXON ELIMINATION AS A MECHANISM IN LATERALIZATION

What mechanism might underlie the variation in callosal size that is associated with behavioral measures of functional asymmetry? Functional asymmetry appears present from birth, and therefore any neuroanatomical substrate might be expected to be present, at least in part, early on. The naturally occurring regressive phenomena of cell death and of axon elimination without cell death (Cowan, Fawcett, O'Leary, & Stanfield, 1984) provide one possible mechanism for variation in anatomic structure, including callosal size and shape. It is suggested that the difference between CRH and nonCRH arises not because nonCRH develop more fibers during postnatal development but rather because CRH lose more fibers, resulting in the smaller callosum, particularly in some regions. The process of axon elimination is thus suggested to be regionally selective. This may be one neurobiological factor determining lateralization, possibly for both direction and degree. Greater axonal elimination may lead to stronger right-hand preference and more marked hemisphere specialization.

Axon elimination of callosal fibers early in development has been demonstrated experimentally in cat (Koppel & Innocenti, 1983) and monkey (LaMantia & Rakic, 1984). The time frame of callosal axon elimination has also been studied in experimental animals. Its onset appears to be coincident with the rapid increase in cortical synaptogenesis *in utero*; its completion is coincident with the start of myelination of that fiber tract. For the human brain, it has been estimated that axon elimination starts at approximately 26 weeks of gestation and ends at about the fourth to seventh postnatal month (Innocenti, 1986). Such a maturational process would indicate that these aspects of development of the brain at this time are determining factors of functional asymmetry in humans. Such a biological base does not preclude possible effects of experience on fiber number, fiber size, and gross size of the callosum (e.g., Juraska & Kopcik, 1988).

SEX DIFFERENCES IN STRUCTURE–FUNCTION RELATIONSHIPS

Two differences between the sexes in callosal anatomy have emerged. One involved a difference in size of one subregion and a different relative morphology of the callosum between men and women. Overall callosal size was larger in men. Similarly, all subregions were larger in men, proportionate to their larger overall brain size. In contrast, the area of the isthmus was larger in women. The difference was accentuated when the isthmus was considered relative to overall callosal area (Witelson, 1989).

Whether this difference has any functional significance remains to be determined. It is noted again that the isthmus is part of an anatomical network with cortical regions relevant to language and visuospatial skills, represented predominantly in the left and right hemispheres, respectively, in most people. Group differences between the sexes have frequently been reported for some specific tasks in these two sets of cognitive skills (e.g., Linn & Petersen, 1985; Hyde & Linn, 1988). It is possible that the anatomical difference in the isthmus between the sexes is related to these psychological differences. Any association, however, would have to be relatively complex, since, for example, the smaller isthmus in men would have to be related to a greater ability in one cognitive area (visuospatial) and lesser ability in another (verbal). It may be that the right and left sides are histologically different and that cortex with different histological structure is better suited for one kind of processing than another.

A second difference between the sexes was as marked but of a more subtle nature. It involved a sex difference in the relationship of callosal size to handedness. In males, handedness was associated with callosal anatomy. The isthmus was 60% larger in nonCRH than CRH and showed a significant negative correlation with a measure of hand preference. Among females, there was no association: the two hand groups did not differ, nor was there any correlation. In other words, isthmus size predicts handedness in men. Callosal size does not predict handedness in females (Witelson, 1989). Whatever the neuroanatomical substrate of handedness is in females, it is different than for men. This is the first observation to my knowledge of a difference in structure–function relationships between men and women.

Functional asymmetry has been reported to be less marked in females than males. For example, in one of the first reports, Lansdell (1964) reported sex differences in the lateralization of verbal and spatial skills to each hemisphere in brain-damaged people. Witelson (1976), using perceptual tasks in neurologically intact children, reported greater lateralization of spatial skills to the right than left hemisphere in boys than in girls. Numerous subsequent studies with normal and brain-damaged patients have consistently observed such sex differences (reviewed in, e.g., McGlone, 1980; Beaton, 1985). The sex difference in the association of callosal size with hand preference is not inconsistent with such neuropsychological findings. For example, the findings of more focused representation of speech and language functions in the left frontal regions in women than men, and of greater bihemispheric representation of some language skills in posterior cortical regions in women than men (Kimura, 1987), are compatible with the sex differences in callosal anatomy.

Such sex differences in brain morphology and brain–behavior relationships have implications for the structure of other anatomical regions and for other brain–behavior relationships. A sex difference in the size of the isthmus could indicate a difference in the relative proportion of contralateral versus ipsilateral connections in cortical regions interconnected with the callosal neurons in parietotemporal regions. The sex difference in the association of callosal size and hand preference suggests that the neuroanatomical basis of lateralized cognitive processes, the mechanism of lateralization, and possibly the basis of other cognitive skills may be different in the sexes.

The sex difference in callosal anatomy and its relationship to handedness raises the possibility that early sex hormonal levels influence the proposed mechanism of axon elimination. Future studies of the correspondence between anatomical and functional measures may be more readily done with MR scans. With this technique, studies of callosal anatomy in clinical groups having atypical early levels of sex hormones, such as people with congenital adrenal hyperplasia or testicular feminization, may help test the role of sex hormones on callosal anatomy.

In summary, investigation of a possible neuroanatomical substrate of hemispheric functional asymmetry has led to results indicating that anatomical variation may underlie variation in behavior. If future research upholds this finding, this would yield a general principle of correspondence between variation in brain anatomy and behavior within a species, a principle generally only considered to be the case between species.

REFERENCES

Adrianov, O. S. (1979). Structural basis for functional interhemispheric brain asymmetry. *Human Physiology, 5,* 359-363.

Annett, M. (1967). The binomial distribution of right, mixed and left handedness. *Quarterly Journal of Experimental Psychology, 19,* 327-333.

Annett, M. (1972). The distribution of manual asymmetry. *British Journal of Psychology, 63,* 343-358.

Bean, R. B. (1906). Some racial peculiarities of the Negro brain. *American Journal of Anatomy, 5,* 353-432.

Bear, D., Schiff, D., Saver, J., Greenberg, M., & Freeman, R. (1986). Quantitative analysis of cerebral asymmetries. Fronto-occipital correlation, sexual dimorphism and association with handedness. *Archives of Neurology, 43,* 598-603.

Beaton, S. (1985). *Left side, right side.* New Haven: Yale University Press.

Benton, A. L. (1964). Contributions to aphasia before Broca. *Cortex, 1,* 314-327.

Bryden, M. P. (1982). *Laterality, functional asymmetry in the intact brain.* New York: Academic Press.

Chui, H. S., & Damasio, A. R. (1980). Human cerebral asymmetries evaluated by computed tomography. *Journal of Neurology, Neurosurgery and Psychiatry, 43,* 873-878.

Cowan, W. M., Fawcett, J. W., O'Leary, D. D. M., & Stanfield, B. B. (1984). Regressive events in neurogenesis. *Science, 225,* 1258-1265.

de Lacoste, C., Kirkpatrick, J. B., & Ross, E. D. (1985). Topography of the human corpus callosum. *Journal of Neuropathology and Experimental Neurology, 44,* 578-591.

de Lacoste-Utamsing, C., & Holloway, R. L. (1982). Sexual dimorphism in the human corpus callosum. *Science, 216,* 1431-1432.

Falzi, G., Perrone, P., & Vignolo, L. A. (1982). Right-left asymmetry in anterior speech region. *Archives of Neurology, 39,* 239-240.

Galaburda, A. M. (1980). La région de Broca: Observations anatomiques faites un siècle après la mort de son découvreur. *Revue Neurologique (Paris), 136,* 609-616.

Geschwind, N. (1974). The anatomical basis of hemispheric differentiation. In S. J. Diamond & J. G. Beaumont (Eds.), *Hemisphere function in the human brain* (pp. 7-24). London: Paul Elek.

Geschwind, N., & Levitsky, W. (1968). Human brain: Left-right asymmetries in temporal speech region. *Science, 161,* 186-187.

Habib, M. (1989). Anatomical asymmetries of the human cerebral cortex. *International Journal of Neuroscience, 45,* 170-171.

Hécaen, H., De Agostini, M., & Monzon-Montes, A. (1981). Cerebral organization in left-handers. *Brain and Language, 12,* 261-284.

Heilman, K. M., & Valenstein, E. (Eds.). (1985). *Clinical neuropsychology* (2nd ed.). New York: Oxford University Press.

Hochberg, F. H., & LeMay, M. (1975). Arteriographic correlates of handedness. *Neurology, 25,* 218-222.

Holloway, R. L., & de Lacoste, M. C. (1986). Sexual dimorphism in the human corpus callosum: An extension and replication study. *Human Neurobiology, 5,* 87-91.

Hyde, J. S., & Linn, M. C. (1988). Gender differences in verbal ability: A meta-analysis. *Psychological Bulletin, 104,* 53–69.

Innocenti, G. M. (1986). General organization of callosal connections in the cerebral cortex. In E. G. Jones & A. A. Peters (Eds.), *Cerebral cortex* (Vol. 5, pp. 291–353). New York: Plenum Press.

Juraska, J. M., & Kopcik, J. R. (1988). Sex and environmental influences on the size and ultrastructure of the rat corpus callosum. *Brain Research, 450,* 1–8.

Kertesz, A., Black, S. E., Polk, M., & Howell, J. (1986). Cerebral asymmetries on magnetic resonance imaging. *Cortex, 22,* 117–127.

Kimura, D. (1987). Are men's and women's brains really different? *Canadian Journal of Psychology, 28,* 133–147.

Koppel, H., & Innocenti, G. M. (1983). Is there a genuine exuberancy of callosal projections in development? A quantitative electron microscopic study in the cat. *Neuroscience Letters, 41,* 33–40.

LaMantia, A.-S., & Rakic, P. (1984). The number, size, myelination, and regional variation of axons in the corpus callosum and anterior commissure of the developing Rhesus monkey. *Society for Neuroscience Abstracts, 10,* 315.6.

Lansdell, H. (1964). Sex differences in hemispheric asymmetries of the human brain. *Nature, 203,* 550.

LeMay, M., & Kido, D. K. (1978). Asymmetries of the cerebral hemispheres on computed tomograms. *Journal of Computer Assisted Tomography, 2,* 471–476.

Linn, M. C., & Petersen, A. C. (1985). Emergence and characterization of sex differences in spatial ability: A meta-analysis. *Child Development, 56,* 1479–1498.

McGlone, J. (1980). Sex differences in human brain asymmetry: A critical survey. *The Behavioral and Brain Sciences, 3,* 215–263.

Nikkuni, S., Yashima, Y., Ishige, K., Suzuki, S., Ohno, E., Kumashiro, H., Kobayashi, E., Awa, H., Mihara, T., & Asakura, T. (1981). Left–right hemispheric asymmetry of critical speech zones in Japanese brains. *Brain Nerve, 33,* 77–84.

Pandya, D. N., & Seltzer, B. (1986). The topography of commissural fibers. *Neurology and Neurobiology, 17,* 47–73.

Ratcliff, G., Dila, C., Taylor, L., & Milner, B. (1980). The morphological asymmetry of the hemispheres and cerebral dominance for speech: A possible relationship. *Brain and Language, 11,* 87–98.

Scheibel, A. B., Paul, L. A., Fried, I., Forsythe, A. B., Tomiyasu, U., Wechsler, A., Kao, A., & Slotnick, J. (1985). Dendritic organization of the anterior speech area. *Experimental Neurology, 87,* 109–117.

Strauss, E., LaPointe, J. S., Wada, J. A., Gaddes, W., & Kosaka, B. (1985). Language dominance: Correlation of radiological and functional data. *Neuropsychologia, 23,* 415–420.

Wada, J. A., Clarke, R., & Hamm, A. (1975). Cerebral hemispheric asymmetry in humans. Cortical speech zones in 100 adult and 100 infant brains. *Archives of Neurology, 32,* 239–246.

Whitaker, H. A., & Selnes, O. A. (1976). Anatomic variations in the cortex: Individual differences and the problem of the localization of language functions. *Annals of the New York Academy of Sciences, 280,* 844–854.

Witelson, S. F. (1976). Sex and the single hemisphere: Right hemisphere specialization for spatial processing. *Science, 193,* 425–427.

Witelson, S. F. (1977). Anatomic asymmetry in the temporal lobes: Its documentation, phylogenesis and relationship to functional asymmetry. *Annals of the New York Academy of Sciences, 299,* 328–354.

Witelson, S. F. (1980). Neuroanatomical asymmetry in left handers: A review and implications for functional asymmetry. In J. Herron (Ed.), *The neuropsychology of left-handers* (pp. 79-113). New York: Academic Press.

Witelson, S. F. (1983). Bumps on the brain: Right–left anatomic asymmetry as a key to functional asymmetry. In S. Segalowitz (Ed.), *Language functions and brain organization* (pp. 117-143). New York: Academic Press.

Witelson, S. F. (1985). The brain connection: The corpus callosum is larger in left handers. *Science, 229,* 665-668.

Witelson, S. F. (1987a). Neurobiological aspects of language in children. *Child Development, 58,* 653-668.

Witelson, S. F. (1987b). Brain asymmetry, functional aspects. In G. Adelman (Ed.), *Encyclopedia of neuroscience* (pp. 152-156). Cambridge: Birkhauser Boston.

Witelson, S. F. (1987c). Hand preference and sex differences in the isthmus of the corpus callosum. *Society for Neuroscience Abstracts, 13,* 48.

Witelson, S. F. (1989). Hand and sex differences in the isthmus and genu of the human corpus callosum: A postmortem morphological study. *Brain, 112,* 799-835.

Witelson, S. F., & Kigar, D. L. (1988). Asymmetry in brain function follows asymmetry in anatomical form: Gross, microscopic, postmortem and imaging studies. In F. Boller & J. Grafman (Eds.), *Handbook of neuropsychology* (Vol. 1, pp. 111-142). Amsterdam: Elsevier.

Witelson, S. F., & Swallow, J. (1988). Neuropsychological study of the development of spatial cognition. In J. Stiles-Davis, M. Kritchevsky, & U. Bellugi (Eds.), *Spatial cognition: Brain bases and development* (pp. 373-409). Hillsdale, NJ: Lawrence Erlbaum.

Zaidel, E. (1978). Lexical organization in the right hemisphere. In P. A. Buser & A. Rougeul-Buser (Eds.), *Cerebral correlates of conscious experience* (pp. 177-197). Amsterdam: Elsevier/North-Holland.

DISCUSSION

GLENN ROSEN: I'm interested in the fact that your functional data point to a greater functional asymmetry for the anterior than the posterior language areas, and yet the anatomical work suggests just the reverse. Do you have any thoughts about that?

SANDRA WITELSON: That perplexes us too. We looked hard for asymmetry in Broca's region. It is interesting that Arnold Scheibel's work has shown histological differences in the frontal operculum. One possible scenario is that everything is driven from the posterior parietal region and that although at a behavioral level we see marked asymmetry in the frontal regions, the essence of the frontal phenomenon may be dictated by posterior asymmetry. That's one hypothesis. Another possibility is that the functional asymmetry may be as marked in the posterior region as in the frontal region. It is just that it is not as clear for psychologists to document it. So, for example, there are some tasks of phonetic discrimination that can only be mediated by left-sided regions. What happens is that the comprehension of language involves many components. It gets back to the kind of thing we were talking about yesterday, so that in the case of comprehension by the right hemisphere, it may not be done in the same way as by the left hemisphere. It may be handled in terms of the overall association to an auditory gestalt, the way a dog may respond to auditory perception. At the receptive end one can use more than one cognitive strategy to perform many of the receptive aspects of language, but in terms of the productive aspects of language, there aren't many different strategies, and the sequential aspect of delivering speech can only be performed in one way. It's really dependent on the left hemisphere. In this way it may be less puzzling.

MARIAN DIAMOND: I'm wondering, Sandra, whether you are also collecting brains from individuals who do not have cancer, so that one could study normal, healthy brains such as those from accident victims.

It's fairly premature to be talking in this direction, but since we're all friends it's fair to mention the role of the cerebral cortex in the immune system. We worked with nude mice, which are thymic deficient, and we found deficient frontal lobes. I just wonder, as we're trying to understand the true picture in the callosum, whether it might not be wise to get as many healthy patients as possible.

WITELSON: We do have a couple of healthy people from whom I have psychological data, and there's no question that we must continue to try to get such cases to study anatomically.

DIAMOND: In de Lacoste's work in which she dealt with the prenatal brains and measured the callosum and found sex differences, with the splenium larger in the female than the male, were those healthy individuals?

WITELSON: Those were obtained from Yakovlev's collection. De Lacoste does not report the cause of death. Actually, she doesn't specify the source, but I think that these cases were probably a subset from the same collection that Rakic and his colleagues used for an earlier large study of the development of the callosum. Getting back to your previous comment, it would be better if our cases had acute rather than agonal death. On the other hand, the size of the callosum, for example, in our work is very similar in absolute value to those of previous studies that have reported magnitude. At the histological level one would be more concerned, and it will be interesting to see, for example, if the number of neurons that we find through the depth of the cortex will be comparable to Powell's work, which reported 110 neurons within a particular column. We'll soon know if we're getting similar results. With regard to the possible use of MRI scans for taking cortical measurements, the asymmetry in the planum is such that you wouldn't be able to get measures of the left and right planum from the same scan, but if one had a series, one could eventually take the left measure from one scan and the right from another. There have been a couple of papers that have reported callosal size based on MRI scans. The size of the callosum has been very close to the actual values that one gets on postmortem examination.

ERAN ZAIDEL: I was going to ask a couple of brief questions. First, did you look at familial sinistrality at all? Second, were you able to look at consistent left handers—at least in females? Finally, in the context of the dichotic listening test,

$R - L$ may not be a very good laterality measure as you know. It interacts with performance levels and so on. $(R - L)/(R + L)$ may be better.

WITELSON: We tried to look at familial sinistrality. The problem is that most of our patients are in the 40 to 60 age range. They don't really have enough information, so we can't get their family histories. We have only sporadic information. With regard to the second question, we do not have even one person who is a consistent-left-hander. As you know, a consistent-left-hander is only found in 2% to 4% at most in the population. In relation to dichotic listening, there is very little variation in overall accuracy from one patient to another. So whether we examine right minus left or right minus left as a proportion of total accuracy, we get similar results.

LOCALIZATION AND PHYSIOLOGICAL CORRELATES OF LANGUAGE AND VERBAL MEMORY IN HUMAN LATERAL TEMPOROPARIETAL CORTEX

GEORGE A. OJEMANN, MD, DAVID F. CAWTHON, MD,
and ETTORE LETTICH, REEGT
University of Washington

INTRODUCTION

This chapter discusses the neurobiology of language and verbal memory in human lateral temporoparietal cortex from the perspective of observations made by Ojemann and his associates during craniotomies under local anesthesia. Those observations include the identification of areas essential for several language functions and verbal memory using electrical stimulation mapping techniques and the changes in activity of neurons and the surface electrocorticogram (ECoG) during measures of the same functions. Although the majority of these observations were made in patients with medically intractable epilepsy beginning in early life, generally similar findings have been obtained in patients with adult acquired lesions, suggesting that these findings may be generalized to populations without conditions leading to neurosurgery. The observations obtained during these operations are organized by the function examined, beginning with object naming.

The interpretation of these data will be facilitated by considering the different information derived from the electrical stimulation mapping studies compared to the physiological (neuron and ECoG) studies. Stimulation mapping localizes a function by a failure in performance when a current just below the threshold for afterdischarge is applied to a cortical site. That current probably temporarily disrupts local neuronal function, most likely through depolarization blockade. Thus, stimulation mapping identifies cortex that is *essential* for the behavior. Localization with stimulation mapping, then, is analogous to localization with lesions, where an area is also related to a behavior when the behavior fails with inactivation of the area. In both cases, determining the role of the area

Acknowledgments: Supported by National Institutes of Health Grants NS21724, NS17111, and NS20482. Professor Otto Creutzfeldt provided invaluable advice in the recording and analysis of neuronal activity.

of cortex where inactivation was associated with a failure of the behavior is a matter of the design of the behavioral measures to allow separation of effects on perception, arousal, or motor output systems and the more cognitive components of the behavior such as different language functions or types of memory. Stimulation mapping has major advantages in this respect, since the block of local cortical function can be selectively applied during one phase of the behavioral measure, for example, only when an object is named and not during its subsequent recall.

By contrast, the presence of statistically significant changes in activity of neurons or the ECoG during measures of a behavior indicates nothing about how essential the site of the recording is for that behavior. Indeed, as indicated below, wide areas that are clearly not essential for language, based on stimulation and lesion effects, show such changes. These areas then participate in a function but are not essential for it. Similar identification of participatory but not necessarily essential areas is provided by techniques (such as positron emission tomography) that indicate where blood flow or metabolism changes during a behavior. As with identification of essential areas, appropriate design of the behavioral measures can begin to separate the roles of changes in activity in these participatory areas. The neurobiology of language and memory includes processes in both participatory and essential areas.

NAMING

Essential Areas

Object naming has been the language behavior most extensively studied intraoperatively. Deficits in object naming characterize all types of aphasias; thus, it is particularly valuable as a screening procedure to indicate if a cortical site in the language-dominant hemisphere is essential for any language function. In addition, Ojemann and Dodrill found that when a dominant hemisphere resection encroached on a temporoparietal site identified as essential for naming by stimulation mapping, there was an increase in errors on an aphasia test battery that measured all aspects of language, an effect that was absent when the resection did not encroach on such essential sites and that could not be related to size of the resection, preoperative level of language performance, or degree of postoperative seizure control (Ojemann, 1983).

Stimulation mapping indicates that essential areas for naming in temporoparietal cortex of the dominant hemisphere are often localized to one or more surface areas of 1 to 1.5 cm² each. Figure 1 is one such example; others are illustrated in Figure 1 of Ojemann (1983) with two separate discrete areas in temporal lobe and Figure 1 of Ojemann (1988). These areas often have sharp boundaries separating them from cortex where stimulation has no effect on naming. Thus, the essential areas for naming in temporoparietal cortex are often

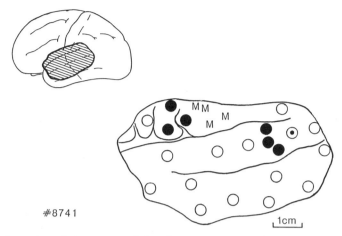

Figure 1. Location of sites essential for object naming in left lateral cortex of 24-year-old female. Stimulation mapping with 4-second trains of 60-Hz biphasic square-wave pulses, 1 msec/phase, at current of 2mA measured between pulse peaks, delivered through bipolar electrodes separated by 5 mm, to each cortical site identified by circle. Three samples of stimulation effect on naming obtained at each site: filled circle, errors on all samples; open circles, no errors; circle with dot, single error in three samples. Error rate in absence of stimulation, 1.2%. From G. A. Ojemann, J. G. Ojemann, E. Lettich, & M. Berger, 1989. Cortical language localization in left, dominant hemisphere. *Journal of Neurosurgery, 71,* 316–326. Copyright 1989 by *Journal of Neurosurgery.* Reprinted by permission.

localized in one or more mosaics. This type of discrete localization of sites with evoked naming errors has been identified in children as young as 4, suggesting that it reflects some aspect of the innate structure of language cortex.

The location of these mosaics is quite variable between subjects, even when only patients with left hemisphere dominance are considered (Ojemann, 1979, 1983; Ojemann, Ojemann, Lettich, & Berger, 1989). In 117 such patients, naming errors were evoked from some temporoparietal site in 90% but from sites anywhere in superior temporal gyrus in only two-thirds and anywhere in inferior parietal lobe or middle temporal gyrus in only slightly over one-third each. Indeed, there were left-dominant patients in this series with no evidence of naming sites in left inferior frontal cortex, patients with naming sites only in frontal cortex despite extensive temporoparietal mapping, and cases with naming sites only in anterior inferior parietal cortex with no changes on extensive frontal or temporal mapping (Ojemann, Ojemann, et al., 1989).

Some of this variability represented differences in localization between males and females. Males with poorer preoperative verbal abilities, as measured by the verbal IQ (VIQ), were more likely to have sites that evoked naming errors in parietal cortex than were females with similar verbal abilities. In addition, some of the variability represented differences between males (but not females) with high or low preoperative verbal abilities. Males with low VIQs were more likely to have naming errors evoked from parietal or superior temporal cortex, whereas males with high VIQs were more likely to have such errors evoked from middle temporal gyrus sites. Thus, there seem to be differences in organization of language in temporoparietal cortex that are reflected in verbal ability.

Over one-half of temporoparietal cortex is buried in sulci. Thus, if 1-cm² sites essential for naming were randomly distributed between the surface and buried cortex, they should not have been identified in over 90% of patients. Moreover, stimulation effects at surface sites predict whether resections that include the buried cortex will or will not interfere with language, indicating that any buried essential areas for language must not extend far from surface sites. There is thus a special predilection for sites essential for naming to develop on the gyral surface. Often, but not invariably, these sites were oriented transversely to the long axis of the gyrus, as illustrated in Figure 1. In the cases where mapping of a sulcus could be accomplished, the area essential for naming extended only slightly into the buried cortex if at all, but not to its depths (Ojemann, Ojemann, et al., 1989). Neither the pattern of orientation nor the size of the areas essential for naming correspond to presently described cytoarchitectonic divisions of temporoparietal cortex. It seems more likely that this pattern reflects location of some specific cortical afferents.

Investigation of the effects of stimulation on naming of the same objects in two different languages in bilingual patients illustrates another principle of cortical organization for essential language areas. Some degree of separation in sites with evoked changes in naming in one or the other language has been observed in nearly all cases where this has been assessed (Ojemann & Whitaker, 1978; Ojemann, 1983; Cawthon, Lettich, & Ojemann, 1987). Thus, somewhat different cortical areas seem to be essential for the same linguistic process, naming, in different languages. A similar separation was observed in temporoparietal sites, where stimulation disturbed oral and manual communication systems (Mateer, Polen, Ojemann, & Wyler, 1982).

Neuronal Correlates

The pattern of organization of temporoparietal cortex for naming that emerges from investigation of changes in neuron activity during that function is quite different. Extracellular microelectrode recording is sufficiently invasive that it is restricted to cortex that is subsequently resected. Thus, no recordings have been obtained from areas essential for language. However, in areas of left-dominant temporal lobe that are not essential for language in that no errors were evoked by stimulation and no deficit followed subsequent resection, substantial changes in activity of populations of one to several neurons during naming have been recorded (Cawthon et al., 1987; Ojemann, Creutzfeldt, Lettich, & Haglund, 1988). The specificity of these changes to naming was determined by comparison to activity during several control measures. One control measure allowed separation of changes related to naming from those associated with perception or arousal *per se*. This was a spatial line-matching task to the same visual cues used for naming, a task that has been related to function of the nondominant hemisphere (Benton, Hanney, & Varney, 1975). Activity was also compared between overt and silent naming to allow separation of changes related to motor aspects of language. In addition, in the case illustrated in Figure 2, comparison was made between naming the same visual cues in two languages (Cawthon et al., 1987). The inhibition during naming in only English evident in that case was recorded at an anterior middle temporal gyrus site over 4 cm removed from the nearest site that evoked errors in naming in the same language. These findings indicate that the area of dominant temporoparietal cortex with neuronal populations participating in naming is much larger than the localized essential areas. In addition, the finding in the case illustrated in Figure 2, that the change in activity occurred only during naming in English and not Spanish, is additional independent evidence of the separation of neuronal populations involved in the same linguistic process in different languages.

The change in activity illustrated in Figure 2 was a tonic depression of activity throughout the time naming in English was performed, with an abrupt increase in activity as soon as the patient was instructed to begin another task (naming the same objects in Spanish). This tonic shift in activity was the common pattern of change related to naming. In most cases, however, it represented excitation, as illustrated in Figure 3, recorded from the superior part of the

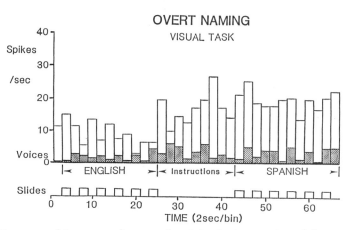

Figure 2. Frequency histogram of neuronal activity during naming of the same objects in English and Spanish recorded from anterior middle temporal gyrus of left hemisphere in 27-year-old female. Each column represents activity in 2-second epochs. Note abrupt increase in activity with instruction to name in Spanish. Activity also remained at higher level during subsequent word reading in English and Spanish but then abruptly decreased when the patient was instructed to generate animal names in English, remained at lower level while those names were produced, and then returned abruptly to higher level when that task ended. (That change in activity with animal naming is illustrated in Figure 1 of Cawthon et al., 1987.)

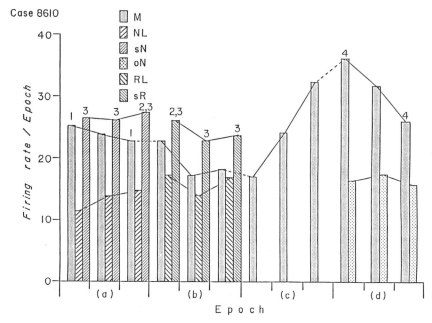

Figure 3. The frequency of neuronal activity recorded from left middle temporal gyrus of a 31-year-old female during measures of language and memory. Each trial of memory measure (M) consisted of four visual cues. The first visual cue (a) was a picture of an object to be silently named. This was the information to be entered into memory. The second and third visual cues (b, c) were a memory-distracting task. The second visual cue required silent reading of words; the third visual cue silent and overt reading of a sentence. The fourth visual cue (d) acted as an indication to retrieve the name of the object aloud from memory, a name that had been retained over the distractors provided by the reading tasks. The activity recorded during each of these visual cues was divided into three equal epochs of 1.2 seconds' duration. The bars represent the average activity during six trials of the memory measure for each of those epochs. Activity during the first visual cue of the memory task, the one requiring silent naming, was compared to the same visual cues presented in a line-matching task (NL) and in a silent naming task without a memory component (SN). The differences in activity between those tasks were compared statistically for each epoch of a: 1 indicates a significant difference ($p < .05$, two-tailed) between the memory and line-matching tasks, 2 between the language and line-matching tasks, and 3 between the memory and language tasks. The second visual cues of the memory task were also utilized in a line-matching task (RL) and in silent word reading without a memory component (SR). Similar statistical comparisons between activity recorded under the different conditions were made for each epoch of b. The activity recorded during retrieval from memory was compared to overt naming (ON), a task that involves generating exactly the same words as are involved in memory retrieval, thus providing control for any effects related to motor speech. A 4 indicates a statistically significant difference in activity between these conditions for that epoch of d. The significant increase in activity throughout the entire period of silent naming and silent word reading is evident, as is the apparent reduction in activity when a recent verbal memory is stored. In addition, the increased activity at the time of recent memory retrieval is evident. For the details of the tasks and data see Ojemann et al. (1988).

middle temporal gyrus of another patient (Ojemann et al., 1988). This site and several others showing tonic excitation during naming were closer to essential areas for naming than was the site showing tonic inhibition; in the case illustrated in Figure 3 the recording site was within 2 cm of an area identified as essential for naming by stimulation mapping. A tentative model for some changes in temporal lobe neuronal activity during naming, then, includes an area of tonically increased activity extending for at least several centimeters around the essential areas, and a more peripheral tonic inhibition. The abruptness with which this tonic activity shifts with changes in tasks is illustrated in Figure 2.

Electrocorticogram

Electrocorticogram surface recording is sufficiently noninvasive that it can be safely accomplished from cortical sites that are essential for language. Thus, this technique can be used to address the question: What, if any, physiological changes recorded during language behaviors distinguish those essential sites from surrounding cortex? It is, of course, apparent from the preceding section that changes in neuronal activity *per se* do not provide this distinction. Fried, Ojemann, and Fetz (1981) compared average ECoG patterns recorded during silent object naming and a spatial line-matching task to the same visual cues at sites essential for naming (based on stimulation mapping) and surrounding cortex not essential for naming. Desynchronization, a loss of activity in the 7- to 12-Hz range, was the ECoG change during naming that seemed to distinguish temporoparietal naming sites from surrounding cortex. Subsequently, the specificity of this change to naming sites during naming has been shown quantitatively, using spectral density measures on individual ECoG segments (Ojemann, Fried, & Lettich, 1989). The desynchronization at temporal naming sites appeared shortly after the appearance of the visual cue for naming and lasted nearly a second, approximately the time required for naming.

One source for such a localized desynchronization is the thalamocortical activating system. In animals, activation of that system evokes desynchronization in local cortical sites (Jasper, 1960; Skinner & Yingling, 1977). The source for that system is the interlaminar and reticular nuclei of the thalamus. Although stimulation of these structures did not seem to alter naming, stimulation of the ventrolateral thalamic nucleus and adjacent anterior superior pulvinar evoked naming changes (Ojemann, Fedio, & Van Buren, 1968; Ojemann & Ward, 1971; Ojemann, 1975). The pattern of stimulation-evoked changes in ventrolateral thalamus was interpreted as evidence that this effect involved highly behaviorally specific attentional mechanisms mediated through the thalamocortical activating system (Ojemann, 1975). There is some evidence of functional interactions between the ventrolateral nucleus and the interlaminar and reticular thalamic nuclei. Moreover, anterior superior pulvinar has direct connections with temporal association cortex.

Thus, an attractive hypothesis for at least one physiological event occurring during naming is activation of the thalamocortical activating system, desynchronizing the cortical mosaics essential for naming. That desynchronization may be the surface reflection of an intense increase in tonic neuronal activity, with lesser levels of tonic activity evoked by the same mechanism occurring in the several centimeters of surrounding participatory temporal cortex. This, in turn, is delineated by a tonic inhibitory surround. Superimposed on these tonic changes are briefer changes in neuronal activity with more temporal specificity to the actual act of naming. Such briefer changes with silent word reading, overt speech, word listening, and verbal memory are discussed later in this chapter; brief changes in activity lasting less than the 1 or 2 seconds required for silent naming were identified in one patient (Ojemann et al., 1988). The essential sites may reflect a node of convergence of activity from the surrounding participatory cortex.

In a recent study conducted by Ojemann, Fried, and Lettich, 2 of 16 temporoparietal sites identified as essential for naming by stimulation mapping did not show desynchronization. This occurred only in patients with other temporoparietal sites that evoked naming errors and desynchronization. Neither the type of naming error nor any other feature of stimulation effect at these sites seemed to differentiate naming sites with or without desynchronization. The reason for the difference remains obscure.

Essential Areas and Neuronal Correlates of Other Language Functions

Reading

The areas of dominant temporoparietal cortex that were likely to contain sites identified as essential for reading of simple sentences in a series of 14 patients are illustrated in Figure 4. These areas extended over a considerably larger part of temporoparietal cortex than the areas where sites essential for naming were likely to be found in the same patients. Midportions of superior and middle temporal gyrus were particularly likely to have sites essential for sentence reading but not naming. The more posterior part of middle temporal gyrus contained sites where stimulation altered only the syntactic aspects of sentence reading: errors occurred only in conjunctions, pronouns, and verb endings and not in nouns and verb stems (Ojemann, 1983).

Recording of neuronal activity also suggested that a wider area of left-dominant temporal cortex was active during reading than in naming. These recordings were made at sites that were not essential for reading, based on stimulation mapping. Activity was recorded during single-word reading, with changes in activity compared to a spatial matching task analogous to that used in the studies of changes in neuronal activity with naming (Ojemann et al., 1988). Thirty-five percent of 17 neuronal populations recorded from lateral temporal cortex in 13 patients showed changes with word reading, compared to 12% with

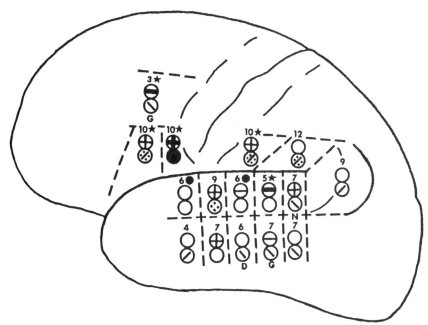

Figure 4. Organization of language and verbal memory in the perisylvian cortex of the dominant hemisphere, derived from mapping of naming, reading, verbal memory, phoneme identification, and orofacial mimicry at 118 sites in 14 patients. Maps from individual patients were aligned in relation to motor cortex and the end of the Sylvian fissure and then grouped into 16 zones, bordered by dashed lines. Within each zone: numbers, number of patients with at least one site sampled (most showed only one site/zone); star, change in some language function evoked at all sites; small filled circle, zones where stimulation of ≧50% of sites produced no changes in any language function. Upper circle contains symbols defining whether naming and/or reading changes occurred at ≧50% of sites in that zone; horizontal line, reading changes; vertical line, naming changes; heavier lines, zones with naming changes at ≧70% of sites or reading changes at ≧80% of sites. Lower circle contains symbols indicating zones where changes in speech production, memory, or single language functions were frequently encountered; filled circle, 50% of sites had features of final motor mechanism for speech production; stippling, ≧25% of sites had changes in mimicry of sequences of orofacial speech gestures; slash to left, ≧33% of sites were related to memory; slash to right, ≧50% of sites produced changes in only one of the other language functions. In zones with two symbols, stimulation at one set of sites produced changes in naming, reading, mimicry of sequences of orofacial speech gestures, and phoneme identification but not in memory, whereas stimulation at another set from different patients showed only memory changes. N, zone where majority of evoked changes in naming occurred in the absence of changes in the other measured functions. D, zone where changes in phoneme identification and orofacial movement occurred at separate sites; in other zones where mimicry of orofacial sequences were altered, phoneme changes occurred at most of same sites. G, zones where ≧67% of sites showed reading errors of syntactic type. A site was related to a language function only when change during stimulation differed from nonstimulation performance at 5% level. Mean age, 28.4 years (range 17 to 49 years); 5 males, 9 females; mean preoperative verbal IQ, 99.4 (range 81 to 120). Mean stimulating current, 5.3 mA (range 3 to 8 mA). All stimulations employed biphasic square-wave, constant-current pulses of 60 Hz, 2.5 msec total duration, delivered t̲ rough bipolar electrodes placed 5 mm apart. Mean number of stimulated sites per patient, 8.4 (range 4 to 16). All tasks measured at 80% of sites; naming, reading, and memory only at the remainder. Control error rates (mean values followed by range in parentheses): naming, 2.4 (0 to 6.25); reading, 17.2 (0 to 41.7); verbal memory, 12.7 (0 to 35.7); phoneme identification, 13.66 (0 to 47.6); single orofacial movements, 2.2 (0 to 11.1); sequential orofacial movements, 4.1 (0 to 20). From G. A. Ojemann, 1983. Brain organization for language from the perspective of electrical stimulation mapping. *Behavioral and Brain Sciences, 6,* 189–230. Copyright 1983 by Cambridge University Press. Reprinted by permission.

naming in the same patients. Although often in a different location, the nature of at least one physiological change with reading, a tonic change in activity in participating cortex, seems to be the same as that with naming. Figure 3 illustrates one such population. That population showed tonic changes in activity with both naming and reading; other populations showed such changes only with reading. Thus, both participatory and essential areas for reading in temporoparietal cortex are larger than those for naming, perhaps explaining the observation that reading deficits are particularly prominent in specific language disability ("dyslexic") patients. Brief increases in activity lasting only the second or two required for silent word reading have also been identified in a few patients (Ojemann et al., 1988).

Speech Gestures and Speech Sound Identification

In the study illustrated in Figure 4, the effects of stimulation on measures of the production of single and sequential orofacial speech gestures and on perception of speech sounds (stop consonants) was also assessed (Ojemann & Mateer, 1979; Ojemann, 1983, 1984). As indicated in Figure 4, areas of temporal and parietal cortex were identified where stimulation was likely to disrupt production of sequences of orofacial speech gestures, although single gestures were intact. At many of these same sites stimulation also disturbed perception of speech sounds, and these sites accounted for a large proportion of the temporoparietal sites with evoked changes in speech sound perception. These findings suggested that (1) the area of cortex involved in motor aspects of language included not only frontal sites but also superior temporal and inferior parietal areas, and (2) common cortical areas were involved in motor and perceptual aspects of language, identifying an area of cortex that could represent the anatomic substrate for the "motor theory of speech perception" (Liberman, Cooper, Shankweiler, & Studdert-Kennedy, 1967).

Recording of neuronal activity provides independent support for both of these suggestions. Changes in activity related to overt speech have been recorded from superior temporal gyrus and adjacent superior bank of middle temporal gyrus but not elsewhere in middle or inferior gyri (Ojemann et al., 1988). These changes included both excitation and inhibition and were not present during silent language tasks. The onset of the change in activity was occasionally before but usually just at or slightly after the onset of overt speech, with the change in activity outlasting overt speech. Most of these neuronal populations did not show changes in activity with speech perception. However, a few populations, such as the one illustrated in Figure 5, demonstrated increased activity with onset of both speech perception and overt production (Creutzfeldt, Ojemann, & Lettich, 1987). These populations, then, provide a cellular substrate for common motor and perceptual speech mechanisms. This would seem to resolve one of the controversies that surrounded the stimulation mapping findings, controverting the proposal

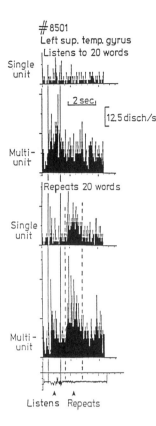

Figure 5. Neuronal activity in the left superior temporal gyrus of a 28-year-old female with verbal IQ of 88 during listening and speaking. Responses of a single neuron (top histogram) and a neuronal population (bottom record) recorded with the same microelectrode. Upper two records: Patient listens to 20 words (words appear between the two vertical lines; see also phonogram at the bottom). Lower two records: Patient repeats each word (between the two broken vertical lines). Note the activation of both the single unit and the unit cluster during both word perception and repetition. Modified from Creutzfeldt et al. (1987).

that neuronal populations involved in motor and perceptual speech mechanisms were adjacent to each other rather than the same population involved with both (Studdert-Kennedy, 1983).

An unexpected and presently poorly explained finding from the recording of neuronal activity during language tasks was the identification of several neuronal populations in anterior temporal lobe of several patients that changed activity only with silent and not overt speech tasks (Ojemann et al., 1988). This finding raises the possibility that anterior temporal lobe activity may be involved in suppressing overt speech production.

RECENT VERBAL MEMORY

Essential Areas

Several studies have demonstrated disruption of verbal memory performance with lateral temporoparietal cortical stimulation (Fedio & Van Buren, 1974; Ojemann, 1978; Ojemann & Dodrill, 1985). The tasks used in these investigations measured a postdistractional recent verbal memory, not an immediate (digit span) or long-term memory. Sites essential for recent verbal memory frequently surrounded but rarely overlapped with sites where stimulation altered naming or reading, as illustrated for one series of patients in Figure 4 (Ojemann, 1983). When a memory measure was designed to separate effects of stimulation during entry of information into memory from those during the time the memory was stored or when it was retrieved, temporoparietal stimulation was found to alter memory most often when the current was applied during information entry, and especially when the memory was stored, but less often when it was retrieved (Ojemann, 1978, 1983; Ojemann & Dodrill, 1985). This suggested that the neuronal events related to memory storage might be located in lateral temporal cortex. Moreover, Ojemann and Dodrill (1985, 1987) found that the severity of verbal memory deficits after anterior temporal lobectomy was related to the extent of the resection of lateral cortex and the degree to which that resection encroached on lateral cortical sites identified as essential to memory entry or storage by stimulation mapping. The memory deficit did not correlate with the size of the medial resection. These findings indicate that dominant hemisphere lateral temporal cortex contains sites essential for recent verbal memory, and these are to some extent separate from the better-known role of medial temporal structures in that type of memory.

Neuronal Correlates

Ojemann et al. (1988) recorded activity of dominant lateral temporal neuronal populations during a recent verbal memory measure in which silent naming represented the information entering memory, information that was stored during distracting tasks involving silent and overt reading and was retrieved overtly at a visual cue. Changes in activity during the entry and storage phases of that measure were contrasted to these during the silent language tasks alone as well as spatial matching tasks using the same visual cues. Changes in activity with memory retrieval were contrasted to overt naming. Changes with only the memory task were identified in 41% of 17 neuronal populations from 13 patients. One such population is illustrated in Figure 6. An additional 29% demonstrated changes with both language and memory. Figure 3 is an example. Thus, a large proportion of lateral temporal neuronal populations seems to participate in recent verbal memory processes, providing further independent evidence that this cortex is involved in that function. However, in this participatory area, some populations were related to both language and memory functions rather than showing the separation between these functions frequently evident with stimulation mapping of essential areas.

The pattern of activity in all neuronal populations related in some way to memory was remarkably similar. Activity was increased during memory entry and again at retrieval (Figure 6). The increased activity lasted considerably longer than the time required for the language task associated with memory entry, silent naming, or with overt retrieval. Occasionally, as in the neuronal

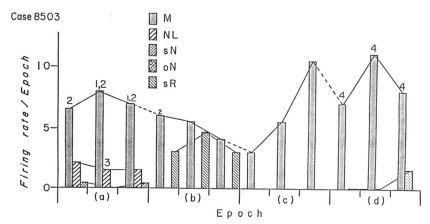

Figure 6. Frequency of neuronal activity recorded from the left middle temporal gyrus of a 30-year-old female with verbal IQ 75 during the same language, memory, and spatial tasks as in Figure 3 and presented in the same manner except that each epoch lasts 2 seconds. The only significant changes were during the memory task, where there were significant increases in activity during memory entry and retrieval compared to the analogous language and spatial tasks.

population illustrated in Figure 3, activity during the time the memory was stored was significantly less than during the analogous language tasks without the recent memory storage. Sustained increases in activity during memory storage were not observed. A common pattern of lateral temporal neuronal activity with recent verbal memory, then, is an increase when information enters memory and when it is retrieved. Perhaps a recent verbal memory is maintained by this period of activity each time it is retrieved. The finding that temporal cortical stimulation during entry and storage disrupts memory indicates that this activity at entry is needed to retain the memory (the increased activity extends into the beginning of the storage period and thus is disturbed by stimulation in both phases). The stimulation paradigms have not been designed to investigate whether sustained activity after retrieval is necessary to the later retention of the memory.

Further evidence of a difference in activity during memory entry and retrieval, compared to memory storage, was provided by investigation of the intervals between neuronal discharges (interspike interval, ISI). Although the neuron illustrated in Figure 7 showed a significant increase in activity only with memory retrieval, there is an obvious difference in the ISIs for memory entry and retrieval compared to that during the several distracting tasks during which the memory was stored. The memory measure used in this study included silent naming of one object picture as the information to be retained in memory and silent naming of another picture as part of the distracting tasks. Moreover, another of the distracting tasks and retrieval both required overt production of the object names. Thus, the ISI difference occurs between tasks that involve

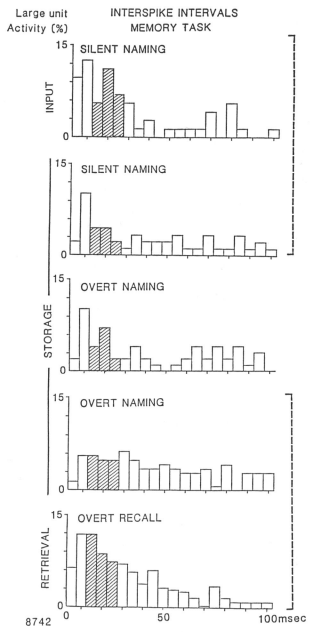

Figure 7. Interspike interval histograms of single neuronal activity recorded during a verbal memory measure from superior temporal gyrus in a 31-year-old male. In this memory measure, silent naming was used as the input to memory and as the first distracting task, with overt naming as the remaining two distracting tasks prior to cued retrieval. Each histogram represents the percentage of total interspike intervals in each 5-msec increment for one phase of the memory measure. Each histogram covers the entire 4 seconds of that phase of the memory task and is the sum of the intervals from all six trials of the memory task. Separate histograms are shown for memory entry, each of the three distracting tasks, and retrieval. Both the visual cues and the required language tasks are

identical perceptual, language, and motor functions and that differ only in the role in recent memory. The ISI difference is a greater percentage of intervals in the 10.1- to 25-msec range with memory entry and retrieval than during storage. The possibility that ISIs within this interval contain a sequence coding these memories of this neuronal population is suggested and is the subject of ongoing investigation.

Conclusions

In this chapter, findings on the neurobiology of language and memory in lateral temporoparietal cortex of the dominant hemisphere derived from stimulation mapping have been compared to those independently derived with physiological techniques, ECoG, and neuronal recording. Many parallels have been identified: evidence from both that different neuronal populations are used in the same linguistic process, naming, in two different languages; evidence from both that some of the same neuronal populations are involved in speech production and perception; evidence from both for a lateral temporal role in recent verbal memory.

However, the different techniques provide major contrasts also. Stimulation mapping indicates that lateral temporoparietal cortex includes quite localized essential areas, with neuronal recordings indicating much wider surrounding areas where neuronal activity changes with these behaviors but is apparently not essential for them. Essential areas seem to be rather specific to specific functions, whereas activity in the participating areas sometimes changes with several functions. What makes the localized areas essential is not evident. They do not correspond to described anatomic features and seem to vary considerably in location between patients. However, they are distinguished from surrounding cortex by more intense desynchronization during the behavior for which they are essential. A tentative hypothesis is that they represent a convergence of connections from the surrounding participatory areas.

Sustained changes in activity during a specific behavior characterized some of the neurobiological events in participating cortex. This included tonic shifts in activity with specific behaviors, shifts that sometimes lasted tens of seconds (cf. Figure 1, Cawthon et al., 1987) but then abruptly changed with instruction to alter the behavior (cf. Figure 2). These tonic changes in activity seemed to be excitatory at sites closer to essential areas and inhibitory at more distant sites. The thalamocortical activating system has been suggested as a source for this change and for the desynchronization at essential sites.

---

identical for memory entry and the first distracting slide, and the overt language task is identical for the last distracting slide and memory retrieval. The percentage of interspike intervals in the 10.1- to 25-msec epochs (indicated by hatched bars) was greater for memory entry (22%) and retrieval (29%) compared to the distracting tasks (average 12%). The difference between distracting tasks and memory entry and retrieval was significant at $p < .05$ (two-tailed).

Sustained changes in activity also characterized the pattern of lateral temporal neuronal activity related to memory, but this sustained activity lasted only some seconds at the time of entry of information into memory and with its retrieval (but not throughout the time it was stored). Within this sustained activity, there may be an increase of particular intervals between action potentials, perhaps representing a code for the particular memory for that neuronal population, that is repeated each time the memory is retrieved. In this way a memory may be maintained.

The studies reviewed here are ongoing. They indicate some approaches to elucidating the neurobiology of language and verbal memory, approaches that have provided glimpses into some of these events. Undoubtedly, future studies will identify many other events related to those uniquely human functions.

REFERENCES

Benton, A., Hannay, H. J., & Varney, N. R. (1975). Visual perception of line direction in patients with unilateral brain disease. *Neurology, 25,* 907–910.

Cawthon, D., Lettich, E., & Ojemann, G. (1987). Human temporal lobe neuronal activity: Inhibition during naming in only one of two languages. *Society for Neuroscience Abstracts, 13,* 839.

Creutzfeldt, O., Ojemann, G., & Lettich, E. (1987). Single neuron activity in the right and left human temporal lobe during listening and speaking. In J. Engel, Jr., H. Luders, G. Ojemann, & P. Williamson (Eds.), *Fundamental mechanisms of human brain function* (pp. 69–82). New York: Raven Press.

Fedio, P., & Van Buren, J. M. (1974). Memory deficits during electrical stimulation of speech cortex in conscious man. *Brain and Language, 1,* 29–42.

Fried, I., Ojemann, G. A., & Fetz, E. E. (1981). Language-related potentials specific to human language cortex. *Science, 212,* 353–356.

Jasper, H. H. (1960). Unspecific thalamocortical relations. In J. Field & H. W. Magoun (Eds.), *Handbook of physiology. Neurophysiology* (pp. 1307–1321). Washington, DC: American Physiological Society.

Liberman, A. M., Cooper, F. S., Shankweiler, D. P., & Studdert-Kennedy, M. (1967). Perception of the speech code. *Psychological Reviews, 74,* 431–461.

Mateer, C. A., Polen, S. B., Ojemann, G. A., & Wyler, A. R. (1982). Cortical localization of finger spelling and oral language: A case study. *Brain and Language, 17,* 46–57.

Ojemann, G. A. (1975). Language and the thalamus: Object naming and recall during and after thalamic stimulation. *Brain and Language, 2,* 101–120.

Ojemann, G. A. (1978). Organization of short-term verbal memory in language areas of human cortex: Evidence from electrical stimulation. *Brain and Language, 5,* 331–348.

Ojemann, G. A. (1979). Individual variability in cortical localization of language. *Journal of Neurosurgery, 50,* 164–169.

Ojemann, G. A. (1983). Brain organization for language from the perspective of electrical stimulation mapping. *Behavioral and Brain Sciences, 6,* 189–230.

Ojemann, G. A. (1984). Common cortical and thalamic mechanisms for language and motor functions. *American Journal of Physiology, 246,* R901–R903.

Ojemann, G. A. (1988). Effect of cortical and subcortical stimulation on human language and verbal memory. In F. Plum (Ed.), *Language communication and the brain* (pp. 101–116). New York: Raven Press.

Ojemann, G. A., Creutzfeldt, O., Lettich, E., & Haglund, M. (1988). Neuronal activity in human lateral temporal cortex related to short-term verbal memory, naming and reading. *Brain, 111*, 1383–1403.

Ojemann G. A., & Dodrill, C. B. (1985). Verbal memory deficits after left temporal lobectomy for epilepsy. *Journal of Neurosurgery, 62*, 101–107.

Ojemann, G. A., & Dodrill, C. (1987). Intraoperative techniques for reducing language and memory deficits with left temporal lobectomy. *Advances in Epileptology, 16*, 327–330.

Ojemann, G. A., Fedio, P., & Van Buren, J. M. (1968). Anomia from pulvinar and subcortical parietal stimulation. *Brain, 91*, 99–116.

Ojemann, G. A., Fried, I., & Lettich, E. (1989). Electrocorticographic (ECoG) correlates of language: I. Desynchronization in the temporal language cortex during object naming. *Electroencephalography and Clinical Neurophysiology, 73*, 453–463.

Ojemann, G., & Mateer, C. (1979). Human language cortex: Localization of memory, syntax and sequential motor–phoneme identification systems. *Science, 205*, 1401–1403.

Ojemann, G. A., Ojemann, J. G., Lettich, E., & Berger, M. (1989). Cortical language localization in left, dominant hemisphere. *Journal of Neurosurgery, 71*, 316–326.

Ojemann, G. A., & Ward, A. A., Jr. (1971). Speech representation in ventrolateral thalamus. *Brain, 94*, 669–680.

Ojemann, G. A., & Whitaker, H. A. (1978). The bilingual brain. *Archives of Neurology, 35*, 409–412.

Skinner, J., & Yingling, C. (1977). Central gating mechanisms that regulate event-related potentials and behavior: A neural model for attention. *Progress in Clinical Neurophysiology, 1*, 30–69.

Studdert-Kennedy, M. (1983). Mapping speech: More analysis, less synthesis, please. *Behavioral Brain Science, 6*, 218–219.

DISCUSSION

JOAQUIN FUSTER: When you test for naming errors with stimulation, do you use a number of target stimuli on each location?

GEORGE OJEMANN: Yes.

FUSTER: Did you find any naming errors differentially distributed depending on either the phonetics or the category of the stimulus?

OJEMANN: We have looked at that a number of times, and it's been mildly disappointing. Naming is very easy. It's deliberately picked so that the baseline error rates are quite low. These patients make anywhere from zero to 2% errors in the nonstimulation trials. The result is that the mistakes they make tend not to be very exciting. It's generally either an omission of the object name—the patient producing a carrier phrase, such as "This is a," and we turn the current off and they then name. Or the patient doesn't say anything at all. Once in a while they'll say, "I know what that is; its a ah, ah." And that's all. We don't very often evoke jargon. Only once in a while, and we don't very often evoke paraphasias.

Occasionally but not very often. The classification of naming errors has not been particularly helpful in terms of figuring out what's going on. We get multiples of each run through, a second time and a third time, and three samples per site is our minimum level of stimulation.

FUSTER: So when you find a naming error area, are the errors for all the stimuli that you test?

OJEMANN: The black dots that I showed you on the various pictures are all sites of repeated errors on different targets that are significantly different from control performance.

FUSTER: Thank you.

MARIAN DIAMOND: Can you comment at all on the relationship between aging and naming tasks?

OJEMANN: Only to the extent of the data that I showed you. Four-year-olds show highly localized sites with naming disruption, and 70-year-olds do. I haven't looked at the relationship between age and localization yet. That's on the docket to do in these 115 cases. I just haven't gotten to them.

ARNOLD SCHEIBEL: In terms of your earlier question about cortical organization in the depth of a sulcus as opposed to a gyrus, I remember now that there are a couple of classic papers that indicate that in general the inputs to sulcal cortex are different from the inputs to gyral cortex, and I'm really reaching now, but it seems to me that one of them is very much richer in U fibers from adjacent cortex, whereas the other (I believe it's the sulcus) shows a lot more nonspecific fibers.

OJEMANN: I guess my question then is: Whichever way it is—why is that important to language? Because it surely looks as though the crown and the crown just into the sulcal depths have something special about them.

DEEPAK PANDYA: Using the newer anatomic techniques like autoradiography, we find the sulcal connections from local as well as distant sites represented in both gyral and sulcal areas.

ADAM WECHSLER: I said I would allow one more question, and to show George that I'm not biased against neurosurgeons I'll let him have the last word.

OJEMANN: I guess the question I really need some kind of help on is the anatomic one. What is it that produces localized sites that have distributions that are so very different from person to person? Such isolated and unpredictable sites seem characteristic, although you know that neurons involved in the function are spread over a much wider area. That's what troubles me! If we were wise enough, this might provide us with an important clue as to what is going on.

WECHSLER: I suspect you're right. As a matter of fact, what I'd like to ask the participants to do is think about that question, and perhaps we can come back to it.

SPACE AND TIME IN CEREBRAL MAPPING
OF THE VISUAL WORLD

JOHN SCHLAG, MD, and MADELEINE SCHLAG-REY, PhD
University of California, Los Angeles

Introduction

Our brain recreates the visual world from images taken at a rate far exceeding 1,000 frames a day. From this continuous flow derives a coherent model of what surrounds us, a model that we can use to locate trees, recognize an old trail, and give directions to find the Arrowhead Conference Center.

A model of the visual environment specifies the spatial relations between objects or other landmarks. Relations can be read and described verbally, but their primary importance lies in the possibility to direct our behavior, whether it is approaching, avoiding, reaching, grasping, or exploring.

For planning any action, one's own position relative to the environment should also be known. Usually, the initial interface with the environment is a visual image. But images shift whenever the eyes move. How do we decide that what we see is in front of us or to the left or to the right? The gaze axis is the first link anchoring the observer to the observed world. The orientation of head and body toward an object is deduced by using extraretinal signals, either afferent (proprioceptive) or efferent (corollary discharge). These signals indicate first the position of eye in orbit, second that of head relative to body, and so on. If any action has to be taken relative to a visual target, such as pointing to it, target coordinates have to be recalculated in a frame of reference that each part of the motor system can use. The coordinate translation may be very complex. For instance, to point with a finger, the following spatial relations enter into the neural computation to determine the relative position of fingertip to target goal: target/eye, eye/head, head/body, body/arm, arm/forearm, forearm/wrist, and wrist/finger.

Does this mean that we carry in our brain a series of maps with these many frames of reference? The evidence is for a single spatial reconstructor in which the transformation from retinotopic to spatial coordinates is accomplished (Jeannerod, 1983). The term spatial in this context is still ambiguous. Whether the actual reference is head or body is undecided (Paillard, 1986). It only seems clear that retinotopic coordinates are not used as such to program movements.

The single case in which retinotopic coordinates might be used directly is programming ocular saccades. Intuitively, the easiest way to construct the saccade vector to a target seems to be to copy it from the signal of retinal error, that is, target eccentricity with respect to the fovea (Schiller & Koerner, 1971). However, it has never been possible to prove that the oculomotor system proceeds in this simple manner. In a crucial experiment, Hallett and Lightstone (1976) required human subjects to look successively at the sites where two targets were flashed before saccades could be performed. (Locating things tachistoscopically is not an unusual situation. We can imagine our ancestors having to figure out their surroundings at the glimpse of a lightning flash in a pitch-dark night.) Humans and monkeys have no difficulty in performing Hallett and Lightstone's task. Yet, the second saccade, from one to the other target, cannot be executed on the basis of a retinal signal alone. In this experiment, the first saccade has the role of diverting the eyes from the fixation point from which target coordinates were computed. Without reference, the retinal error signal to the second target becomes meaningless.

In a study on monkeys, Sparks and Mays (1983) modified this paradigm slightly, replacing the first target by an electrical stimulation of the superior colliculus evoking an eye movement. Target acquisition was not impaired. Since, in this situation, only one photic stimulus is presented in complete darkness, no other visual cue is available. The only way to explain correct targeting in that case is to assume that the brain estimates target spatial location by summing two signals: retinal error and eye position.

SPACE: NEUROPHYSIOLOGICAL CORRELATES OF INTERNAL MAPS

We are thus led to a concrete hypothesis amenable to neurophysiological testing. From the early time when experiments were performed on anesthetized, immobilized preparations, it has been learned that neurons of the visual system have receptive fields that are retinotopic (referred to the retina). In alert animals, they move with the eyes. We are postulating the existence of something different: a particular type of "receptive field" referred to the head (or body) and, consequently, indifferent to changes in ocular orientation.

Over two decades ago, Wiersma (1966) described neurons in crayfish having this property, which he related to space constancy. Space constancy is the ability to recognize the stability of objects in space despite one's own movements. Figure 1 shows the extent of the receptive field (in black) when the eye rotates transversely. The size of the receptive field varies with the orientation of the animal's eye. The cell is "blind" when the eye looks at the floor. The presence of a response not ony signals the appearance of a photic stimulus but also indicates its source above the horizon.

Are there anywhere in the mammalian brain cells that "see" visual stimuli in an other than retinocentric frame of reference? The question can be answered

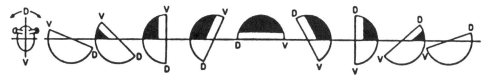

Figure 1. Response of a "space-constant" cell (identified as sustaining fiber 23) in crayfish with variations in eye position. The animal is rotated around its length axis. D and V indicate dorsal and ventral poles of eye. Receptive field is darkened area. Cell responds solely to stimuli located above the horizon. Adapted from Wiersma (1966).

only if the experimental paradigm provides for independent manipulation of both angle of gaze and retinotopic location of stimuli. Only the latter has been experimentally varied in most of the classical studies, more concerned with feature detection than with the behavioral use of vision.

In cats, a small number of visual units similar to those described by Wiersma were found in a thalamic region centered on the internal medullary lamina (IML). The complex (IMLc), which includes intra- and paralaminar cell populations, is the part of the thalamus concerned with oculomotor function. It contains cells discharging before saccades. Electrical stimulation at their site induces eye movements at lower threshold than at any other place in the thalamus. Three types of cells sensitive to the position of a target in space have been distinguished (Schlag, Schlag-Rey, Peck, & Joseph, 1980). Their firing patterns are schematically illustrated in Figure 2. The rectangles represent a tangent screen onto which a single visual target (black circle) is successively projected at three different locations (three trials are condensed in B and C). The cat's head is fixed, and the experiment is run in complete darkness. The dashed line indicates the eye position that, combined with the target location, elicits the intensity of response shown at the top. Some thalamic cells come close to providing the neural substrate of space constancy, modeled in Figure 2A, because their firing rate remains invariant with changes of eye position but it is linearly correlated with target position in space, not on the retina. These cells fire only when a discrete visual stimulus is presented in their receptive fields, but these fields are extremely large.

Whereas eye-position-independent space-coding cells appear to be most directly involved in signaling location in space, such information may be indirectly derived from eye-position-dependent cell types, which seem more frequently encountered. Among those found in the cat thalamus, one group is characterized by relatively small central receptive fields (Figure 2B). These cells are activated if the cat fixates a stimulus projected in some defined region of space (for instance, right of the body axis). They seem to be "looking through a viewfinder" (that is, their receptive field) and opening a gate for an eye position signal if, and only if, they "see" a target. Another group, likewise eye-position dependent, has eccentric receptive fields (Figure 2C). The signals conveyed by cells of the last two groups (also encountered in monkey cortex) could represent

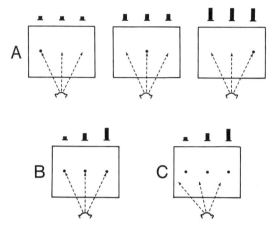

Figure 2. Schematic representations of neuronal firing patterns (black bars, response intensity) related to the spatial position of a target (black circle) displayed on a screen (rectangle) in complete darkness. The subject's head–body axis is fixed with respect to the screen. Gaze direction is indicated by dashed lines. Three trials are illustrated in separate frames for A and condensed in one frame for each B and C. Type A response intensity depends exclusively on target position in space and is shown invariant with changes of eye position. Type B and C responses vary with retinal location of target and with eye position in orbit.

an intermediate step in the elaboration of a true "space-constant" signal uniquely coding space, regardless of eye position.

In monkeys, no "space-constant" cells have been found in the central thalamus, although there is some evidence for their presence in cerebral cortex (see Gentilucci, Scandorlara, Pigarev, & Rizzolatti, 1983). Visual cells contributing to spatial coding have been recorded from two cortical areas involved in gaze control and cognitive functions: The posterior parietal cortex (Mountcastle, Lynch, Georgopoulos, Sakata, & Acuna, 1975; Sakata, Shibutani, & Kawano, 1980; Andersen & Mountcastle, 1983; Andersen, Essick, & Siegel, 1985) and the supplementary eye field (Schlag & Schlag-Rey 1987).

The parietal units of interest lie in a region long presumed important for visual space perception: in man, the destruction of the corresponding area causes mislocalization. These parietal units have retinotopic receptive fields; however, when the fields are tested with gaze pointed in different directions, the intensity of the responses varies systematically. Andersen et al. (1985) argued that eye position provides a gain by which receptive field responses are multiplied. Each unit taken individually would be incapable of specifying target location in space, since its activity is not independent of eye position. But target location may be coded by an ensemble of such cells with different receptive field properties and different optimal angles of gaze.

Recently, Zipser and Andersen (1988) tested the validity of this assumption by constructing a model fed separately by receptive field information and eye position signals. The inputs to the network carry signals copied from those recorded from some real parietal cells. The model has three layers, and all the units are connected from each layer to the next. Learning is imposed by backward propagation of output error (Rumelhart, Hinton, & Williams, 1986) to modify connection strength. The significant results of this simulation are, first, that output units can be led to produce a signal representing target position in space but, perhaps more interestingly, in the process hidden units (those of the intermediate layer) acquire the properties of neurons actually recorded in the inferior parietal lobe (that is, receptive field response multiplied by eye position).

The supplementary eye field is a dorsomedial frontal oculomotor area situated just rostral to the classical supplementary motor area (Schlag & Schlag-Rey, 1987). Some of its visually sensitive cells modulate their responses as a function of eye position, as do parietal cells in monkey or thalamic cells in cat. Some of its saccade-related cells appear to encode an intended position rather than an intended movement, since activation is maximal when eye movements, in a broadly tuned direction, terminate at a given point in orbit (Schlag-Rey & Schlag, 1985).

It is tempting to view the input to intended position units in the supplementary eye field as originating in the parietal cortex. The existence of connections between these areas has been established by anatomic tracing (Petrides & Pandya, 1984). Parietal neurons could provide the signal of target location from which the supplementary eye field would derive the signal specifying a goal. The two signals carry the same information but differ by the time of their occurrence: one occurs at stimulus onset, the other at saccade onset.

The finding of units coding target location in spatial coordinates is in agreement with the production of goal-directed saccades by electrical stimulation. The direction of such movements varies as a function of the initial position of the eyes with respect to the goal, and the amplitude depends on the proximity to the goal. No saccade is produced if the eyes are already within, or close to, the goal area. Goal-directed saccades have been electrically elicited from the central thalamus in cat (Maldonado, Joseph, & Schlag, 1980), from the posterior parietal lobule in monkey (Shibutani, Sakata, & Hyvarinen, 1984), and from the supplementary eye field in monkey (Schlag & Schlag-Rey, 1987).

In all the brain regions mentioned, receptive fields are usually very large. This seems to be the rule beyond the primary visual cortex, as if neuronal processing, at further levels of visual analysis, relied on population ensembles. Another common observation is the absence of evident topographical organization, typical of most visual areas. The inadequacy of the methods of neurophysiological exploration is probably not at fault, since units that represent a given locus in space are often found in several patches throughout a given area, separated by units representing a quite different locus. In the same way, the effects of stimulation do not reveal a clear continuum, for instance, in terms of the direction of movements induced. Should it be surprising that spatial maps would not be spatially organized? In their simulation study already mentioned, Zipser and Andersen (1988) note that target localization is successfully achieved despite the lack of organization in the network. It should be realized that spatial maps are not representing elemental features such as oriented lines, colors, contrast, or texture. Such properties are extracted by comparing the input from adjacent retinal receptors. At the early stage of visual processing, topographical organization seems to be the substrate of an important algorithm that Schwartz (1977) calls "computational geometry." Maps of the environment are different. They concern entities identified as objects that, like words or concepts, may be treated as symbols and represented by connections between cells rather than by cells themselves.

In this section, we have dealt with egocentric frames of reference. They affect not ony our capacity to interact with our environment but also our perception of it. Artificially altering motor feedback can create the false impression that objects move (Matin et al., 1982; Biguer, Donaldson, Hein, & Jeannerod, 1986). It is tempting to visualize our relationship with the surroundings as specified by a pointer in an internal map (Zipser, 1983). The map is robust, the pointer fugacious. It is displaced continually as we move around, and in the dark it fades away within a few seconds, leaving us helpless (Thomson, 1980).

TIME: SIMULTANEITY IN THE WORLD AND IN THE BRAIN

In the preceding section we were concerned with the calculation of spatial coordinates of a target, and we saw that the brain performs this operation by summing two parameters: retinotopic target location and eye position in orbit. In normal activity, the values of these parameters change frequently, which introduces a problem of synchronization. Obviously, the values to be summed are those existing at the instant of target presentation. Were the processing of neural signals uniformly fast in the nervous system, there would be no problem because signals corresponding to simultaneous events would reach the brain simultaneously. However, this is not the case. Signal conduction and processing are very slow, particularly in the visual system. Initial visual processing consumes a considerable amount of time, much of it spent in the retina. In comparison, information on eye position, obtained from either corollary discharge or proprioception, is transmitted faster. The difference in delay is large enough for the gaze to have shifted to a new place before the brain has yet accessed the visual information captured at the previous place.

The problem is not trivial, as can be seen in the example in Figure 3. A target (26 msec duration) is flashed in front of a monkey at time t_0. Let us assume that the visual signal reaches, at time t_1, the summing point where target spatial coordinates are calculated in the monkey's brain. We need not make any assumption about where this place may be. A minimum value of 40 msec for the interval t_0–t_1 seems realistic, since it takes approximately that much time for the retinal input to arrive to the brain. At t_1 the retinal error signal pertaining to an event that has occurred at t_0 should be referred to the eye position that existed at t_0.

Meanwhile, however, the eyes moved spontaneously, carrying with them the reference retinal point (fovea) from which the retinal error was measured. Such interference is not rare in an active animal exploring its environment. Note that the animal could not yet be aware of the flash when the movement started. Nevertheless, Figure 3 shows that the perturbating gaze shift does not prevent the monkey from aiming correctly at the site where the flash has appeared. This suggests that the eye position value used to calculate the correct saccade vector is indeed that which existed at t_0.

If this interpretation is correct, it should also be valid in the case where the retinal signal is generated artificially by electrical stimulation. Electrical stimulation applied in certain brain structures evokes fixed-vector saccades (so called because of their constant amplitude and direction). Each stimulation site is characterized by a particular vector. In Figure 4B, we assume that the stimulation is delivered at t_1 and that it mimics a visual target (imagine a phosphene). To facilitate the comparison with the effect of presenting a real target (Figure 4A), the trajectories of ongoing and evoked saccades and the timing of events are supposed to be identical. If the brain treats the "pseudotarget" as a real one, it should refer its location to an eye position preceding the stimulation by a time equal to the delay t_0-t_1.

Practically, the test can be performed by delivering the stimulation during a natural eye movement (spontaneous or visually guided). When the eyes are steady, such a stimulation drives the eyes to a goal at a certain distance in a certain direction. In this case, the saccade vector corresponds to the retinal error generated. But, if the eyes are already moving at stimulation onset, the starting point of the evoked saccade is displaced, and its termination point should be the location of the pseudotarget in space, as computed by the brain. In other words, the saccade vector should be modified in a predictable way to compensate for the

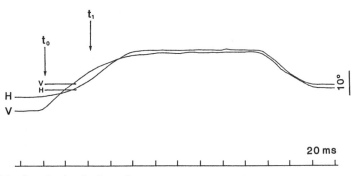

Figure 3. Monkey in the dark performs a correct saccade to the site of a flashed target despite the occurrence of a spontaneous eye movement that diverts its eyes away from the position where the retinal error is measured. Vertical (V) and horizontal (H) coordinates of eye and flash positions are plotted as a function of time. Target flashed at time t_0. Arrow at t_1 indicates hypothetical time when retinal error signal becomes available to the brain.

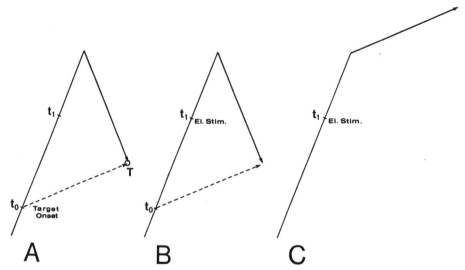

Figure 4. Results of "colliding saccade" test (B and C) compared to equivalent situation with real visual target (A). Two-dimensional representations of spontaneous saccade trajectories (thin lines) followed by evoked saccade trajectories (thick lines) are shown. (A) Arrangement corresponds to condition illustrated in Figure 3. Target at location T is flashed when eye is at position t_0. Retinal error signal reaches the brain at time t_1. (B and C) Electrical stimulation is delivered at t_1. Such a stimulus applied when the eyes are steady would produce the saccade vector shown by dashed line (in B) similar to retinal error (in A). (B) The eyes are driven to the retinal location as registered from eye position at time t_0. (C) Stimulation is of deep layer of superior colliculus, and the eyes are driven by motor error signal from wherever the evoked saccade begins.

eye displacement since time t_0. The correctness of this prediction was tested by electrical stimulation of various structures.

First, with this paradigm, it is possible to recognize structures carrying a retinal error from those carrying a motor error signal. In the latter case (Figure 4C), the vectors of evoked saccades are the same as controls, as expected if the command is to execute a movement of a given amplitude and a given direction. This is what is found by stimulating in deep layers of the superior colliculus (Schlag-Rey, Schlag, & Shook, 1989). In contrast, vectors of evoked saccades vary in the former case, since the eyes tend to reach the same goal point from wherever the movements start. This difference arises from the fact that a retinal error specifies a goal, not a vector. Stimulation in superficial layers of the superior colliculus and in several forebrain structures produces modified saccade trajectories when "collision" occurs with ongoing eye movements (Schlag, Schlag-Rey, & Dassonville, 1989).

However, an important difference exists among structures carrying a retinal error signal. If all our assumptions are correct, the eyes should be driven to a goal whose location in space is calculated with respect to the eye position at hypothetical time t_0 (Figures 3 and 4). We have obtained estimates of t_0 with respect to stimulation onset. For saccades evoked from the central thalamus and supplementary eye field, the reference time t_0 is 35 to 65 msec prior to stimulation. This range of values for the t_0-t_1 interval is realistic (in Figure 3 that interval is assumed to be 40 msec). The results are consistent with the hypothesis that the stimulation evokes a retinal error signal and the latter is then used to calculate target position in space. The calculation is not necessarily carried at the sites that were stimulated. However, the recording of units with spatial properties, described above, makes it a strong possibility. Furthermore, stimulation at some points of the same structures evokes goal-directed saccades (terminating at a particular position of the eye in orbit).

In contrast, the estimations of t_0 are around 0 msec prior to stimulation in superficial layers of the superior colliculus. The implication is that no eye position is sampled, and saccades are driven directly by the retinotopic vector. The collicular reflex would thus be unable to aim the gaze correctly at a target if any eye movement interfered during the saccade reaction time.

These observations illustrate a paradoxical situation caused by characteristics of the cerebral hardware. For some neural processing, the time scale is in the same range as for movement. Pellionisz and Llinas (1982) have suggestively compared this situation to "an attempt of coordinating the position of speeding battle tanks from the headquarters, not with instantaneous radio signals but by cavalry messengers." Simultaneity in the outside world is not necessarily imaged in the nervous system. Time, as well as space, may have to be reconstructed internally.

REFERENCES

Andersen, R. A., Essick, G. K., & Siegel, R. M. (1985). Encoding of spatial location by posterior parietal neurons. *Science, 230,* 456–458.

Andersen, R. A., & Mountcastle, V. B. (1983). The influence of the angle of gaze upon the excitability of the light-sensitive neurons of the posterior parietal cortex. *Journal of Neuroscience, 3,* 532–548.

Biguer, B., Donaldson, I. M. L., Hein, A., & Jeannerod, M. (1986). La vibration des muscles de la nuque modifie la position apparente d'une cible visuelle. *Comptes-Rendus de l'Académie des Sciences, Paris, 303,* 43–48.

Gentilucci, M., Scandolara, C., Pigarev, I. N., & Rizzolatti, G. (1983). Visual responses in the postarcuate cortex (area 6) of the monkey that are independent of eye position. *Experimental Brain Research, 50,* 464–468.

Hallett, P. E., & Lightstone, A. D. (1976). Saccadic eye movements towards stimuli triggered by prior saccades. *Vision Research, 16,* 99–106.

Jeannerod, M. (1983). How do we direct our actions in space? In A. Hein & M. Jeannerod (Eds.), *Spatially oriented behavior* (pp. 1–13). New York: Springer-Verlag.

Maldonado, H., Joseph, J.-P., & Schlag, J. (1980). Types of eye movements evoked by thalamic microstimulation in the alert cat. *Experimental Neurology, 70,* 613–625.

Matin, L., Picoult, E., Stevens, J. K., Edwards, M. W., Young, D., & MacArthur, R. (1982). Oculoparalytic illusion: Visual-field dependent spatial mislocalizations by humans partially paralyzed with curare. *Science, 216*, 198–201.

Mountcastle, V. B., Lynch, J. C., Georgopoulos, A., Sakata, H., & Acuna, C. (1975). Posterior parietal association cortex of the monkey: Command functions for operations within extrapersonal space. *Journal of Neurophysiology, 38*, 871–908.

Paillard, J. (1986). Cognitive versus sensorimotor encoding of spatial information. In P. Ellen & C. Thinus-Blanc (Eds.), *Cognitive processes and spatial orientation in animals and man* (pp. 1–35). Dordrecht, The Netherlands: M. Nijhoff.

Pellionisz, A., & Llinas, R. (1982). Space–time representation in the brain. The cerebellum as a predictive space–time metric tensor. *Neuroscience, 7*, 2949–2970.

Petrides, M., & Pandya, D. N. (1984). Projections to the frontal cortex from the posterior parietal region in the Rhesus monkey. *Journal of Comparative Neurology, 228*, 105–116.

Rumelhart, D. E., Hinton, G. E., & Williams, R. J. (1986). Learning representations by back-propagating errors. *Nature, 323*, 533–536.

Sakata, H., Shibutani, H., & Kawano, K. (1980). Spatial properties of visual fixation neurons in posterior parietal association cortex of the monkey. *Journal of Neurophysiology, 43*, 1654–1672.

Schiller, P. H., & Koerner, F. (1971). Discharge characteristics of single units in superior colliculus of the alert rhesus monkey. *Journal of Neurophysiology, 34*, 920–936.

Schlag, J., & Schlag-Rey, M. (1987). Evidence for a supplementary eye field. *Journal of Neurophysiology, 57*, 179–200.

Schlag, J., Schlag-Rey, M., & Dassonville, P. (1989). Interactions between natural and evoked saccades. II. At what time is eye position sampled as a reference for the localization of a target? *Experimental Brain Research, 76*, 537–547.

Schlag, J., Schlag-Rey, M., Peck, C. K., & Joseph, J.-P. (1980). Visual responses of thalamic neurons depending on the direction of gaze and the position of targets in space. *Experimental Brain Research, 40*, 170–184.

Schlag-Rey, M., & Schlag, J. (1985). Presaccadic units in the supplementary eye field of monkey, head fixed and free. *Society for Neuroscience Abstracts, 11*, 82.

Schlag-Rey, M., & Schlag, J. (1989). The central thalamus. In R. H. Wurtz & M. E. Goldberg (Eds.), *Neurobiology of saccadic eye movements* (pp. 361–390). New York: Elsevier.

Schlag-Rey, M., Schlag, J., & Shook, B. (1989). Interactions between natural and evoked saccades. I. Differences between sites carrying retinal and motor error signals in monkey superior colliculus. *Experimental Brain Research, 76*, 548–558.

Schwartz, E. L. (1977). Afferent geometry in the primate visual cortex and the generation of neuronal trigger features. *Biological Cybernetics, 28*, 1–14.

Shibutani, H., Sakata, H., & Hyvarinen, J. (1984). Saccade and blinking evoked by microstimulation of the posterior association cortex of the monkey. *Experimental Brain Research, 55*, 1–8.

Sparks, D. L., & Mays, L. E. (1983). Spatial localization of saccade targets. I. Compensation for stimulation-induced perturbations in eye position. *Journal of Neurophysiology, 49*, 45–63.

Thomson, J. A. (1980). How do we use visual information to control locomotion? *Trends in Neurosciences, 3*, 247–250.

Wiersma, C. A. G. (1966). Integration in the visual pathway of crustecea. *Symposium of the Society for Experimental Biology, 20*, 151–177.

Zipser, D. (1983). The representation of location. *Institute for Cognitive Science Report 8301*, University of California, San Diego.

Zipser, D., & Andersen, R. A. (1988). A back-propagation programmed network that simulates response properties of a subset of posterior parietal neurons. *Nature, 331,* 679–684.

DISCUSSION

JOAQUIN FUSTER: In both the frontal eye fields and the supplementary motor cortex you find cells that seem to relate to two basic cognitive functions that are important for integration of behavior in the temporal domain. One is short-term memory, and the other one is preparatory set. Both functions, I think, are paradigmatic of what happens in frontal areas at large. The only things that are different are the nature of the stimuli, the nature of the response, and of course the time scale. The basic principle operates the same way I think in these little areas for eye movement as it operates in the frontal cortex at large, for the larger action.

ERIC HALGREN: I remember Bjorn Merker used to have a sign in your lab that said "free the head," and he was referring to the possibility of recording units or stimulating when the head was free as well as the eyes so that you could get even better support for the idea that these are gaze-related or location-related cells, goal-related cells, and spatial cells. Has anyone freed the head?

JOHN SCHLAG: Yes of course we have freed the head, but you know it adds another dimension of difficulty. You can do this experiment, and then you will need a lot of time to analyze the data. We had started to do that, and we do have cells that are showing their activity as a function of the eye position. And others that show their activity as a function of gaze position, gaze being the eye plus head. But it will take some time to have the complete story.

THE ONTOGENY OF ANATOMIC ASYMMETRY: CONSTRAINTS DERIVED FROM BASIC MECHANISMS

GLENN D. ROSEN, PhD, ALBERT M. GALABURDA, MD,
and GORDON F. SHERMAN, PhD

Beth Israel Hospital and Harvard Medical School

INTRODUCTION

In this chapter we discuss the development of anatomic asymmetry in the brain. Our interest in this topic arose from our studies on the neuroanatomy of developmental dyslexia. We have shown that the dyslexic brain is distinguished from that of the nondyslexic by the presence of anomalous cortical migration in conjunction with brain symmetry. Specifically, dyslexics exhibit symmetry in a presumptive language area (the planum temporale) that is ordinarily asymmetrical in favor of the left hemisphere (Galaburda & Kemper, 1979; Galaburda, Sherman, Rosen, Aboitiz, & Geschwind, 1985). The understanding of the mechanisms involved in the development of symmetrical and asymmetrical brains might enable greater understanding of the ways in which the development of the brain of a dyslexic differs from that of normal readers. We have therefore generated a number of questions concerning the ontogenesis of asymmetry: Do brain regions start off as symmetrical from the earliest moment of cerebral development, or is asymmetry the natural case? Is asymmetry the result of side differences in cell production or of cell death or transformation? How does the development of the brain of the dyslexic differ from that of a nondyslexic?

In order to begin to answer these questions, we have first sought to delineate some of the underlying biological mechanisms that distinguish symmetrical from asymmetrical brains in adulthood—specifically the gross morphometric, cellular morphometric, and connectional characteristics of symmetrical and asymmetrical brains. Information gleaned from these studies has enabled us to evaluate critically the possible mechanisms for the development of cerebral asymmetry and to plan experiments to test these hypotheses. Before we discuss these issues, however, we cursorily review first the evidence for anatomical asymmetry and functional lateralization in humans and, because much of our work involves animal models, subhuman animals. From there we move to a discussion of the ontogeny of lateralization and then onto a discussion of our experiments on the mechanisms of cerebral asymmetry.

CEREBRAL LATERALIZATION AND ANATOMIC ASYMMETRIES

Functional Lateralization

HUMANS

Beginning with the discovery by Broca in 1861 of the left hemisphere's role in the production of language (Broca, 1865), lateralization of function has been an area of active research. Lateralization of language to the left hemisphere in most dextral individuals has been clearly demonstrated in aphasic populations (LeCours, Lhermitte, & Bryans, 1983), in split-brain patients (Sperry, 1974), and in stimulation experiments during surgery (Ojemann, 1983; Ojemann, Cawthon, & Lettich, this volume; Penfield & Roberts, 1959). In addition, this pattern of language lateralization can be seen in intact subjects through the use of dichotic listening (cf. Kimura, 1961), tachistoscopic lateralized presentation (Springer, 1977), regional cerebral blood flow (Larsen, Skinhoj, & Lassen, 1978), evoked potentials (Anderson, 1977), and positron emission tomography (Phelps, Hoffman, & Mazziota, 1981).

Although the left hemisphere is predominantly involved in language processing, a role for the right hemisphere in this function is also evident. For example, Ross and colleagues (Ross, 1984; Ross & Mesulam, 1979) have found that prosodic function is localized to the right hemisphere. Moreover, Ross has hypothesized that damage to areas homologous to those producing aphasia result in analogous behavioral deficits. For example, damage to the homologue of Broca's area results in a deficit in the production of prosody. Aside from the emotional aspects of speech, Zaidel has shown that some split-brain patients have significant amounts of language in their right hemisphere (Zaidel, 1977, 1979; Zaidel, Clarke, & Suyenobu, this volume). More traditionally, the right hemisphere is shown to be the repository for spatial, constructional, emotional, and perhaps musical functions (see Springer & Deutsch, 1981).

ANIMALS

Until the early 1970s, lateralization of function was thought to be a human characteristic only most likely because language, a function not seen in animals, was the most prominent example of this characteristic. However, Nottebohm and colleagues (Nottebohm, 1970, 1977; Nottebohm, Stokes, & Leonard, 1976) elegantly demonstrated that the left hemisphere of the zebra finch and canary was preferentially involved in the production of bird song. Specifically, damage to any portion of the neural pathway for song in the left hemisphere resulted in profound disturbances in song production, whereas lesions to homologous areas in the opposite hemisphere had little effect on this function. Thus, communicative function of birds is lateralized to the left hemisphere. In a similar vein, Japanese macaques have a right ear advantage (indicating left hemisphere preference) in the processing of species-specific vocalizations (Peterson, Beecher, Zoloth, Moody, & Stebbins, 1978).

However, as with the human, there are functions in some animals that appear to be preferentially processed in the right hemisphere. Denenberg and colleagues have shown that the hemispheres of the rat process affective information differentially (Denenberg, Garbanati, Sherman, Yutzey, & Kaplan, 1978; Denenberg, 1981), with the right hemisphere purported to be dominant for these classes of functions. Spatial asymmetries in the rat (as measured by preferred direction of turning) also seem to be under the control of the right hemisphere in at least one strain of rats (Sherman, Garbanati, Rosen, Yutzey, & Denenberg, 1980). Interestingly, neonatal tail posture asymmetries in these animals predict their adult pattern of spatial preference (Denenberg et al., 1982; Rosen, Finklestein, Stoll, Yutzey, & Denenberg, 1984; Ross, Glick, & Meibach, 1981), thereby indicating that lateralization is present at birth in these animals. Numerous other examples of behavioral lateralization in animals have been documented, and the reader is referred to Denenberg (1981) for a comprehensive review.

Anatomic Asymmetries in Humans

PLANUM TEMPORALE AND SYLVIAN FISSURE

The search for anatomic asymmetries has naturally centered about the classical language areas. Although evidence has accumulated since the time of Broca's original discovery, it was not until 1968, with the report of Geschwind and Levitsky (1968), that this area of research entered the modern era. They examined the outside border of the planum temporale (an area on the posterior superior temporal plane bordered anteriorly by Heschl's gyrus and laterally by the Sylvian fissure and purported to be involved in language processing) and found that 65 of the 100 brains they examined had a larger left planum, whereas only 11 had the reverse asymmetry and 24 had no bias. They also found that the planum was, on average, 33% longer on the left than on the right. In their examination of 100 adult brains, Wada, Clarke, and Hamm (1975) reported that 82% were leftward biased, 10% were rightward biased, and 8% showed no asymmetry. Witelson and Pallie (1973) found that 69% of the brains they examined had a larger left planum, with 31% having the reverse asymmetry. Other investigators have since looked at anatomic asymmetries of the planum temporale by direct measurement of histological material (Chi, Dooling, & Gilles, 1977; Rubens, Mahowald, & Hutton, 1976; Teszner, Tzavaras, Gruner, & Hécaen, 1972), direct measurements of intact brains through computerized axial tomography (Galaburda, LeMay, Kemper, & Geschwind, 1978; Pieniadz & Naeser, 1984), and indirect measurement by radiological techniques (LeMay & Culebras, 1972; Hochberg & LeMay, 1975). Length of the Sylvian fissure has also been assessed directly (Yeni-Komshian & Benson, 1976; Rubens et al., 1976) as well as indirectly through measurements of endocranial casts and skulls (LeMay & Geschwind, 1975; LeMay, 1976; Gundara & Zivanovic, 1968). These studies have conclusively demonstrated that the left planum is larger and the left Sylvian fissure longer in the majority of individuals.

It is of particular importance with regard to our interest in the ontogeny of asymmetry that these asymmetries are documented in infants as well. Wada et al. (1975) examined the brains of 85 infants and found that 56% had a leftward biased asymmetry, whereas only 12% were rightward biased. Witelson and Pallie (1973) found a larger left planum in 79% of the 14 infants examined, a larger right planum in 14%, and 7% with no difference between left and right. Thus, this anatomic asymmetry is present at least from the time of birth.

Cytoarchitectonic asymmetries have also been demonstrated in the superior temporal plane. Galaburda, Sanides, and Geschwind (1978) measured both the planum temporale and cytoarchitectonic area Tpt (an auditory association cortex located partially within the planum temporale) in four brains from the Yakovlev collection. They found striking asymmetries in area Tpt, with the left up to 620% larger than the right. Moreover, ranking the specimens by degree of cytoarchitectonic asymmetry perfectly correlated with the ranking by degree of planum asymmetry. Thus, asymmetry in the temporal lobe has been demonstrated at the one-dimensional (length) as well as the two- (area) and three-dimensional (volume) levels.

AREAS OUTSIDE THE SUPERIOR TEMPORAL PLANE

Wada et al. (1975) found in their sample of 100 adult and 85 infant brains that the surface area of the right frontal operculum was greater than that on the left. Given their impression of greater fissuration on the left, they stated that the asymmetry could well be in the opposite direction. Indeed, evidence from arteriograms (LeMay & Culebras, 1972) that give an indirect measure of the frontal operculum indicate a larger left frontal operculum than the right. Galabruda (1980) measured architectonic area 42 within the frontal operculum and found an asymmetry in favor of the left in the majority of the brains examined.

The parietal lobe has also been shown to be anatomically asymmetrical. Eidelberg and Galaburda (1984) parceled the parietal lobe and found that area PEG, an area structurally similar to the visually related cortices of the posterior superior temporal region, was larger on the right in seven of the eight brains studied. When the asymmetry in the planum temporale was leftward biased, area PG (an area corresponding to area 39 of Brodmann) asymmetry also favored the left. In addition, there was a significant positive correlation between asymmetry of the planum temporale and PG, although there was no relationship between asymmetry in PEG and any language-related areas.

Anatomic Asymmetries in Subhuman Animals

APES AND MONKEYS

Functional lateralization has clearly been demonstrated in a number of animals ranging from mouse to monkey. For the most part, this lateralization is less directionally biased at the population level than in the human, yet individual animals are significantly lateralized (Denenberg, 1981). Anatomic asymmetries are widespread throughout the animal kingdom as well. Yeni-Komshian and Benson (1976) measured Sylvian fissure lengths in chimpanzees and found a significantly greater left length in 80% of the specimens, with 12% having no asymmetry and 8% exhibiting the reversed asymmetry. Yeni-Komshian and Benson (1976) found significant laterality differences of skull size in one species of gorilla. The left was larger than the right in 17 of the 38 specimens of *Gorilla gorilla beringie*, and the remaining 21 skulls had equal lengths. LeMay (1976) found no asymmetry in the lesser apes and monkeys but did find a longer Sylvian fissure length on the left in great apes.

Studying baboon brains, Cain and Wada (1979) found the right frontal pole longer in six of seven brains, with the seventh brain having poles of equal length. These are similar to the findings in humans that the right frontal pole protrudes farther (Hadziselimovic & Cus, 1966).

Cerebral morphological asymmetries have also been found in Old World monkeys. Falk (1978) analyzed the endocasts of 88 skulls representing eight genera. These endocasts revealed details of external brain morphology including sulcal patterns. She found, contrary to reports in humans and great apes, that the right temporal sulcus and Sylvian fissure were larger than the left. She hypothesized that the expanded frontal and parietal cortices on the left side obscured the Sylvian and temporal sulci in that hemisphere.

LIZARDS AND AMPHIBIANS

It has long been known that there are asymmetries in the habenular nuclei of amphibians and reptiles (Braitenberg & Kemali, 1971). Some species of frogs, for example have two nuclei on the left and one on the right. In addition, there are connectional as well as morphological differences between the two nuclei in at least one species of lizard (Engbretson, Reiner, & Brecha, 1981). Thus, the left habenula of *Uta stansburiana* (slide-blotched lizard) has two distinct morphological areas, a pars dorsolateralis and a pars ventromedialis, whereas the right habenula lacks these subdivisions. Furthermore, the centripetal fibers of the parietal eye ganglion cells project only to the pars dorsolateralis of the left habenular nucleus. There is no projection to the right habenular nucleus.

RATS

Diamond, Johnson, and Ingham (1975) examined the forebrains of male Long–Evans rats at a variety of ages ranging from 6 to 300 days of age and found that the right neocortex was thicker than the left at all ages. Female rats had slightly thicker left neocortices than right, although not significantly so (Diamond, Young, Singh, & Johnson, 1983). Females ovariectomized at birth had significantly thicker right neocortices than left—the same asymmetric pattern seen in male rats.

Others have found that the right hemisphere had a larger wet weight than the left in both adult and 15-day-old Long–Evans rats. The right hemisphere was found to be larger than the left in length, width, and height (Kolb, Sutherland, Nonneman, & Whishaw, 1982). They also found a 5% difference in cortical thickness in favor of the right hemisphere.

We have found, similar to Diamond et al., that male rats have a larger volume of neocortex on the right, whereas females have a nonsignificant bias to the left. Architectonic parcellation of the cortex indicated that the primary visual and sensorimotor cortices tended to be larger on the right side, whereas the motor region was symmetrical (unpublished observations).

Summary

Anatomic cerebral asymmetry is common to all animals that have been examined. Anatomic asymmetries have been documented throughout the human brain, some having intuitively obvious links to functional lateralization (e.g., the planum temporale) and others (e.g., area PEG) with a less obvious relationship to function. In subhuman animals, asymmetry has been noted in a wide variety of species, and in some a link between structural and functional asymmetry is evident. Yet, what is clear from studies of animal asymmetry is that the pattern of asymmetry seen in subhuman animals is much less skewed than that seen in the human. Thus, whereas approximately 99% of dextral individuals have language localized to the left hemisphere and 80–90% of humans are right handed, such a strong bias at the level of the population is rare in subhuman animals. It might therefore be helpful at this point to introduce the notion of individual versus population asymmetry. An individual animal can exhibit a strong side bias in a certain behavioral function or anatomic region while another animal of the same species might have an asymmetry of a similar magnitude but in the opposite direction. This species would be said to be strongly asymmetrical at the individual level but exhibit no population asymmetry. The mechanisms whereby asymmetry exists at the individual but not the population level are not known, but it is likely that there are forces at work in the creation of the former that are quite different from those that direct the latter. It has therefore proven useful, especially in the study of the mechanisms of anatomic asymmetries in subhuman animals, to consider individual asymmetries rather than population asymmetries. One is thus able to generalize principles involved in making an individual brain symmetrical or asymmetrical without the confounding effects of directional bias.

We have therefore chosen to investigate issues of symmetry and asymmetry without consideration of directional bias at the population level. Thus, we have been addressing issues involved in the differentiation of symmetrical and asymmetrical brains—specifically at the level of gross architectonic volume, cellular arrangement, connectivity, and ontogeny.

However, before turning to the investigation of the biological mechanisms of cerebral asymmetry, we next turn to discussion of the ontogeny of lateralization.

Ontogeny of Lateralization

Most of the early work involving the ontogeny of laterality was the result of investigations into the functional effects of early unilateral brain damage. Basser (1962) found that lesions of the right hemisphere in early life resulted in speech deficits much more often than comparable lesions in adulthood. In addition, the aphasias seen in early childhood were less severe, whereas aphasia acquired sometime after the eighth year of life approached the severity of aphasia acquired in adulthood. The greater recovery of function following lesions to the left hemisphere during development was attributed by Basser to greater right hemisphere involvement in speech and language during early life. These findings led Lenneberg (1967) to conclude that language lateralization develops from a stage of equipotentiality to the adult stage of full lateralization of function.

The first and most obvious problem with the comparison of infant and adult lesions is the role of recovery of function and plasticity in the developing brain. Major reorganization of structure is possible when lesions take place during critical stages of brain development. It is possible to restructure the architecture of the cortex as well as the architecture of connections following early interference. It is reasonable to suspect that with such a degree of structural reorganization, there will be accompanying changes in function. Because similar strategies are not available to the adult brain, direct comparisons should be handled cautiously.

There are additional problems with the use of developmentally brain-damaged children as a primary source of data on the development of language lateralization in the normal case. Conclusions derived from these individuals must be considered with regard to the biological characteristics of acquired disease at different ages. In children, right or left hemisphere damage is normally the result of either infection, trauma, stroke, or tumor. However, the interpretation of data derived from these subjects is tainted by the nature of the disease process. Thus, infection, normally the result of brain abscess, often has bilateral mass effect, and localization has always been difficult to document in cases of trauma, especially in closed-head trauma where bilateral injury is commonly seen. Although localization of damage from stroke might appear to be less problematic, differences in the etiology of stroke in children and adults inhibit generalization from these subjects. For example, stroke in childhood, unlike the usual adult pattern of localized infarction from progressive vascular degeneration, is more often the result of hemorrhage into brain tissue. These hemorrhages are the result of abnormal blood vessels embedded within abnormal brain tissue. Because this type of malformation occurs around midgestation, it is possible that the underlying brain connections would reorganize in an unpredictable pattern of language representation. It is difficult, therefore, to generate hypotheses concerning the development of language lateralization in individuals whose brain organization is possibly not "normal" even before the damage itself. Tumors, which often have bilateral mass effects, may also arise from neuronal or glial remnants representing developmental anomalies capable of altering brain organization, again precluding the possibility of comparing deficits in childhood to those acquired in the adult.

The theory of equipotentiality of the hemispheres at birth must be viewed in light of demonstrable functional lateralization in early life. Evidence that infants might be lateralized came indirectly from work involving infant speech perception. Eimas and colleagues (Eimas, Siqueland, Jusczyk, & Vigorito, 1971; Eimas, 1985) found that 1- to 4-month-old infants could perceive and distinguish various speech sounds. Using the high-amplitude sucking paradigm, they demonstrated that infants dishabituated to the stimulus when it changed from a /ba/ to a /pa/ sound or vice versa—a finding that has since been replicated (Moffit, 1971; Morse, 1972). Infants discriminate speech much in the same way that adults do in that they discriminate differences in temporal order information (Jusczyk, Pisoni, Walley, & Murray, 1980; Jusczyk, 1985).

Because the infant could discriminate speech, it was hypothesized that the brain might therefore be lateralized at birth. Molfese, Freeman, and Palermo (1975) recorded auditory evoked potentials over homologous areas of the left and right hemispheres of infants during the presentation of speech and musical stimuli. They found that the left hemisphere was more activated during the presentation of the speech stimulus and that the right hemisphere was more active during the musical stimulus. Further studies (Molfese, 1977; Molfese & Molfese, 1986) demonstrated that although the infant was lateralized, the patterns of the auditory evoked potentials were not the same as those of adults.

The results of dichotic listening procedures in infancy have also supported the notion that the initial state of the infant is lateralized (Entus, 1977). Entus combined the techniques of a high-amplitude sucking paradigm with dichotic listening to demonstrate that infants had a left ear advantage for music and nonspeech sounds and a right ear advantage for speech. This is the same pattern of ear advantage that is seen in the adult. However, others (Vargha-Khadem & Corbalis, 1979) failed to replicate these results, but the differences in procedure between the two experiments make it difficult to indicate exactly why the replication was unsuccessful. Others have found that speech stimuli delivered to an infant disproportionately affected right limb movement—a purported indicator of greater left hemisphere involvement in speech processing (Segalowitz & Chapman, 1980).

Finally, there is evidence to indicate that lesions of the left hemisphere early in development (1 year of age) may have profound effects on later language abilities (Dennis, 1983). Dennis examined two subjects who received lesions to the left hemisphere at 1 year and a subject who received a comparable lesion to the right hemisphere at the same time. Those subjects with left hemisphere damage exhibited deficits in the verbal sections of the ITPA, whereas the right-hemisphere-damaged subject was deficient in spatial aspects of the test. This suggested that hemispheric specialization was present at 1 year of age. It has also been demonstrated that there is no change in "degree" of lateralization over the developmental time span of an individual. Again, one must consider these data with caution, because children undergoing hemispherectomy are also likely to have dramatic reorganization of brain structure and function, as these operations are done for congenital disorders or for tumors of great severity.

Mechanisms of Brain Asymmetry

It is therefore evident that lateralization of function does not develop over time but, rather, is present at least from the time of birth. The presence of anatomic asymmetries in the planum temporale in the 29-week-old fetus reinforces this idea. The question of how lateralization of function begins is still not known. What we consider in the remaining sections of this chapter are the mechanisms of brain asymmetry and how what we know about the adult state of the organism can help us to understand better the process of the development of asymmetry.

Thus, our goal in the experiments described below is to examine systematically the ways in which symmetrical and asymmetrical brains differ. As discussed above, by establishing principles of asymmetry in the "final state" (adulthood), we would then be better able to determine the constraints involved in the development of either a symmetrical or asymmetrical brain. Toward that end, we began our investigations at the level of gross volumetric asymmetry, moving next to the cellular and finally to the level of connectivity.

The Characteristics of Gross Volumetric Asymmetry

The research discussed in this section concerns the comparison of areal measure of asymmetrical and symmetrical brain regions, in particular the planum temporale. Through this comparison, we hope to gather preliminary evidence concerning the mechanisms involved in the production of symmetrical or asymmetrical brain regions. The three *a priori* hypothetical predictions and possible outcomes based on this comparison are illustrated in Figure 1. Symmetrical brains can result from either an increase in size of the normally smaller side, a decrease in the usually larger side, or a combination of a decrease in the larger side and increase in the smaller side. In the first case, the total brain area of symmetrical brain regions would be larger than their asymmetrical counterparts, whereas the opposite would be true in the second case. Brain areas would be similar if the third scenario were true.

To test these hypotheses, we examined the same 100 brains used by Geschwind and Levitsky (1968) and measured instead the total planum area in the left

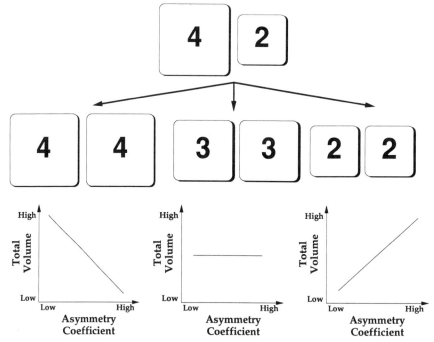

Figure 1. Schematic illustration of the three hypothetical possibilities when comparing an asymmetrical brain (top) to symmetrical brains (middle). The symmetrical brain can be made up of two large sides (left), two small sides (right), or two medium-sized sides (middle). Each of these possibilities carries with it predictable outcomes based on the comparison of the total (right + left) area (or volume) of a region to the asymmetry coefficient $[(R -L)/(0.5)(R + L)]$. Thus, when the symmetrical brain region is made up of two large sides, one would expect a negative correlation between these two variables, whereas a positive correlation would be predicted if symmetrical brain regions were composed of two smaller sides. In the case of the medium-sized symmetrical brain region, there would be no change in total volume with changes in asymmetry coefficient.

and the right side (Galaburda, Corsiglia, Rosen, & Sherman, 1987). Similar to the findings of Geschwind and Levitsky, we found a leftward-biased asymmetry in 63%, while 21% were rightward biased, and 16% had no bias. When we plotted the total planum area (right + left) against a measure of directionless asymmetry, a significant negative correlation was found, indicating that as asymmetry increased, the total planum area decreased (Figure 2A). Moreover, the area of the smaller of the two plana significantly predicted asymmetry, whereas there was no correlation between the degree of asymmetry and the larger planum area (Figures 2B and 2C). These results, then, support the hypothesis that symmetry is caused by two large planum areas in each hemisphere—as asymmetry increased, the total planum area decreases as a result of the decrease in size of the smaller of the two plana.

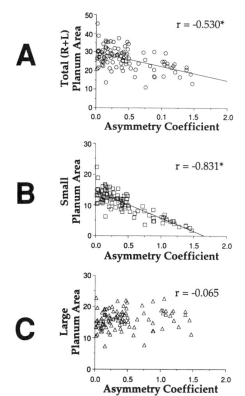

Figure 2. Scatterplot showing relationship of asymmetry coefficient and (A) total area of the planum temporale, (B) the area of the smaller of the two plana, and (C) the area of the larger of the two plana in 100 brains previously examined by Geschwind and Levitsky (1968). r = Pearson product–moment correlation coefficient ($^{*}p < .001$).

Morphometric Cellular Basis of Asymmetry

The previous study demonstrated that a symmetrical brain region is made up of two large areas when compared to its asymmetrical counterpart. The question we next wished to address was the morphometric cellular basis of this difference. When considering this question, one has to be aware that there are only two parameters of cellular arrangement that determine architectonic volume: cell-packing density and cell numbers. Given this fact, one is left with three hypothetical possibilities to explain the difference between asymmetrical and symmetrical brains: (1) smaller volumes may be the result of a decrease in cell numbers without any change in cell-packing density, (2) smaller volumes may result from changes in cell-packing density with the numbers of cells constant between the larger and the smaller area, or (3) a combination of an increase in cell-packing density and a decrease in the number of cells may occur (see Figure 3).

For methodological reasons, it was determined that the rat would be the proper animal model to study this problem. However, before we could use the rat, we had to determine whether characteristics of asymmetry and symmetry generated from the previous experiment—that there was an inverse relationship between total area volume and degree of asymmetry—held true for this species.

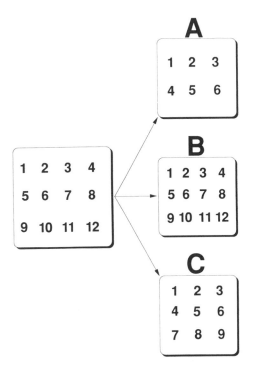

Figure 3. Schematic diagram demonstrating the three hypothetical possibilities of morphometric cellular differences between the two sides of an asymmetrical brain region. Changes could occur in (C) cell numbers with no changes in cell-packing density, (B) cell-packing density with no changes in cell number, or (A) changes in both cell-packing density and cell number.

We therefore measured the volume of cortical area 17, the primary visual cortex, of this animal. We chose that region because previous research had indicated that this area was anatomically asymmetrical. We found, analogous to the results seen in the human planum temporale, that there was a negative correlation between total area 17 volume and asymmetry coefficient. In addition, the smaller of the two sides was also inversely related to degree of asymmetry, whereas there was no relationship between the larger side and total volume asymmetry (Figure 4). Thus, rats with asymmetrical brain regions have, like the human, smaller brain regions than those that are symmetrical. This having been established, we could then proceed to test the three alternatives offered above.

We counted the cells within area 17 of these animals and found that there was no relationship between cell-packing density and volumetric asymmetry. Because any changes in cortical volume can only reflect differences in cell-packing density or cell numbers, it was clear that any change in asymmetry must be related to changes in total cell numbers (Galaburda, Aboitiz, Rosen, & Sherman, 1986). That changes in cell numbers and not cell-packing density are related to asymmetry is not surprising. For example, changes in cell-packing density large enough to account for the volumetric asymmetries would clearly disturb the cytoarchitectonic appearance of the areas and thus make recognition of these areas impossible. Others have shown (Rakic & Williams, 1986) that changes between cytoar-

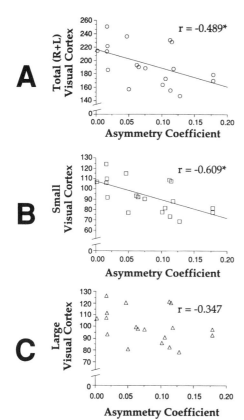

Figure 4. Scatterplot showing relationship of asymmetry coefficient and (A) total area of the primary visual cortex, (B) the area of the smaller of the sides, and (C) the area of the larger of the sides in 19 rat brains. $r =$ Pearson product–moment correlation coefficient ($*p < .05$).

chitectonic intrahemispheric borders are subject to the same mechanism, specifically, changes in cell numbers not cell-packing density.

The finding that symmetrical brain regions are larger than asymmetrical brain regions acts to constrain the possible biological mechanisms involved in the development of asymmetry. Thus, if the earliest state of the organism is asymmetrical, then one would have to explain the appearance of a symmetrical brain in adulthood by the addition of cells to the now larger side. On the other hand, if the initial state is symmetrical, then the asymmetrical final status would have to be explained by cell loss (Figure 5). Thus, one would be able to determine the initial state of the organism by demonstrating either instructionist (cell addition) or selectionist (cell loss or transformation) mechanisms. Alternatively, if exploration of the initial state of the organism revealed symmetry, then one would have to conclude that a selectionist mechanism operates, whereas an asymmetrical initial state would suggest the instructionist method. Thus, the results of the experiments described above, although not directly applicable to the development of asymmetry, clearly delimit the possible mechanisms through which asymmetry can develop and, as such, dictate the types of questions needing to be resolved.

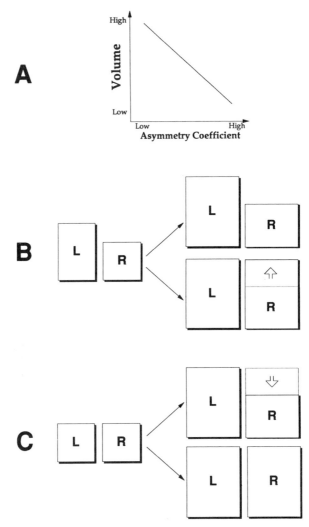

Figure 5. Schematic diagram to show the constraints on the possible mechanisms for the development of asymmetry given that (A) there is a negative relationship between total (right + left) area (or volume) of a brain region and the asymmetry coefficient [(R −L)/ (0.5) (R + L)]. One can start from an initial state of asymmetry (B), so that symmetry is the result of increased growth of one side, or from a symmetrical initial state (C), such that asymmetry in the adult would have to be accounted for by a reduction of one side.

Interhemispheric Connectivity

The next question we wished to address was whether interhemispheric connections differ between asymmetrical and symmetrical brains. It has long been speculated that the mechanism for cerebral dominance might lie in the callosal connectivity—that the dominant hemisphere exerts control over its homologue through the corpus callosum (Weiskrantz, 1977). By this reasoning, one might expect that the larger, dominant brain region, which has more cells than its homologue, would send more projections across the corpus callosum. Alternatively, it could be that symmetrical and asymmetrical brains have *patterns* of connections that are both qualitatively and quantitatively different.

We sought to investigate this problem by severing the corpus callosum of the rat and looking at the pattern of axonal terminal degeneration. Thus, the corpus callosum of 15 90-day-old Wistar rats was sectioned. One week following surgery, the animals were perfused, and the brain was removed from the skull and serially sectioned in the coronal plane at 30 μm. One series of every 10th section was stained using modifications of the Fink–Heimer method for demonstrating degenerating axon terminals (Fink & Heimer, 1967). An adjacent series was mounted onto slides and stained with cresyl violet for Nissl substance.

Of the 15 surviving animals, eight were determined to have nearly complete damage of corpus callosum with a minimum of extracallosal involvement and were included in the study. The first stage of the analysis was performed on our image acquisition and analysis system. The images of slides were captured using a video camera attached to a stereomicroscope and interfaced to a digitizing device. This device is capable of converting the analog signal from the video camera to a digital image made up of a 512×512 array (262,144 pixels), with each pixel assigned a value from 0 to 255 depending on its gray value—0 being black and 255 white. For this study, we digitized the dark-field images from the series of sections stained for axonal terminal degeneration and saved them to disk. The somatosensory–somatomotor cortex (SM-I; areas 3, 1, and 2) was parceled on the Nissl-stained sections and these sections were then overlaid with the adjacent silver-stained sections and the borders traced onto the latter. The percentage degeneration (a measure that corrects for background staining and artifact) of SM-I for each image was computed by first setting a gray-level cutoff level determined by sampling obvious regions of degeneration for ranges of gray-level values. The number of pixels with gray-level values greater than the cutoff level divided by the total number of pixels in the parceled region yielded a measure, percentage degeneration. In addition, the directionless asymmetry coefficient (δ) was computed for SM-I ($\delta = |R - L| / [(R + L) (0.5)]$.

There was a negative correlation between δ and total (right + left) volume of SM-I ($r = -.780$, $t = 3.05$, $df = 6$, $p < .05$), indicating that as the degree of asymmetry of the architectonic region increased, the total volume of the region decreased (Figure 6a)—a finding previously reported for other brain regions (see above). In addition, there was a significant inverse relationship between δ and percentage of callosal terminal degeneration ($r = -.889$, $t = 4.76$, $df = 6$, $p < .05$), indicating that in SM-I, symmetrical regions had a greater percentage of callosal terminations than did more asymmetrical regions (Figure 6b).

Because callosal projections in the rat are segregated into patches of termination, these results—that symmetrical brains have a greater density of callosal connections than do asymmetrical brains—suggest a number of possible interpre-

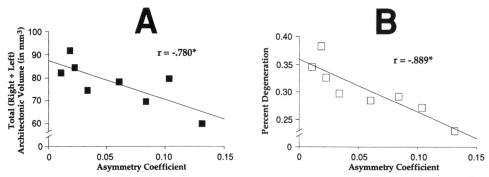

Figure 6. (A) Scatterplot of total (right + left) architectonic volume of SM-I (in mm³) versus the asymmetry coefficient of that region. (B) Scatterplot of percentage degeneration versus asymmetry coefficient of SM-I. *$p < .05$.

tations, as illustrated in Figure 7. It could be that there are more patches of termination in symmetrical brains as compared to asymmetrical. Alternatively, if there were similar numbers of patches of degeneration in symmetrical and asymmetrical brains, the density of these projections would be greater in the symmetrical cases. A third possibility is that there are more patches of callosal termination in asymmetrical brains but that the callosal terminations of symmetrical brains are more diffuse.

Each of the abovementioned alternatives carries with it certain predictable outcomes. For example, if symmetrical brains simply have more patches of termination than asymmetrical brains, then one should see a negative correlation between the number of patches and volume asymmetry. On the other hand, one would expect a positive correlation between these two variables if asymmetrical brains had more patches of termination. Finally, if the number of columns were the same in symmetrical and asymmetrical brains, only the width of terminations within the columns would be different, and there would be no correlation between δ and the number of columns.

In order to distinguish among these possibilities, we counted the number of discrete columns and the laminar distribution of the callosal terminations in all brains using a computer-based algorithm (see Rosen, Sherman, & Galaburda, in press). We found a negative relationship between the number of patches of callosal termination and δ ($r = -.857$, $t = 4.07$, $df = 6$, $p < .05$) indicating that there are more patches of callosal termination in the symmetrical, as opposed to asymmetrical, brain regions.

Our results are compatible with the notion that more symmetrical brains have relatively greater numbers of callosal fibers. Moreover, there are more patches of termination in symmetrical brains, thus introducing an additional dimension to the comparison of symmetrical to asymmetrical brains. Therefore, if the detailed architecture of connections, as well as their number, affects

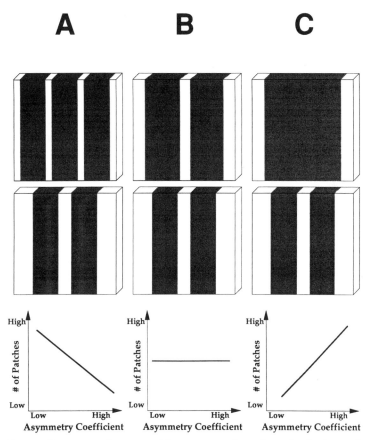

Figure 7. Figure illustrating three possible outcomes based on the finding of an inverse relationship between volume asymmetry and percentage degeneration. (A) Symmetrical brains (top row) could have more patches of termination than asymmetrical brains (middle row); this would also produce a negative correlation between number of patches and asymmetry coefficient (bottom row). (B) Symmetrical brains could have the same number of patches of termination as asymmetrical brains, but they would be wider in the former; in this case there would be no correlation between numbers of patches and asymmetry coefficient (bottom row). (C) Finally, there could be fewer patches of termination in the symmetrical brain, but they would occupy a greater proportion of the region. In this case, a positive correlation would be found between the asymmetry coefficient and number of patches of termination (bottom row).

functional capacity, symmetrical and asymmetrical brains may differ in their preferred cognitive strategies as well as in their extent of hemispheric lateralization. For example, Witelson (1985) has demonstrated a difference in the midsagittal area of the corpus callosum between left and right handers whereby left handers, whose brains are more likely to be symmetrical (LeMay & Culebras, 1972), had larger midsagittal corpus callosum areas (the result of more and/or thicker fibers) than did their right-handed counterparts. It is possible that the greater cross-sectional area of the corpus callosum in left handers reflects cerebral symmetry.

Variability in the pattern and number of callosal terminations may be considered with regard to the ontogeny of the callosal connections. During early development, callosal cells of origin are diffusely represented throughout the cerebral cortex (Ivy & Killackey, 1981, Ivy, Akers, & Killackey, 1979; Innocenti & Clarke, 1983; Wise & Jones, 1976). As the brain matures, callosal cells of origin are seen only in discrete laminar and columnar locations (Jacobson & Trojanowski, 1974; Zaborsky & Wolff, 1982). Likewise, the axonal terminations of these cells are distributed diffusely beneath the cortical plate until they penetrate it in discrete bundles and terminate on their appropriate targets (Olavarría & van Sluyters, 1985; Zaborsky & Wolff, 1982). The progressive restriction of callosal cells of origin and terminations is thought to result from axonal pruning rather than from the death of neurons (Ivy & Killackey, 1981; Ivy et al., 1979; O'Leary, Stanfield, & Cowan, 1981). The present findings of decreased callosal connections in SM-I in brains with asymmetrical architectonic regions are consistent with an increased pruning of callosal axons and maintenance of ipsilateral cortical projections during development of this region, as has been previously demonstrated (Ivy & Killackey, 1981).

As described above, an increase in volumetric architectonic asymmetry reflects an asymmetrical decrease in the numbers of neurons (Galaburda et al., 1985). If callosal connections also decrease, and proportionally so, then one would expect no change between symmetrical and asymmetrical brains in the percentage of terminal degeneration. However, the present study shows that this percentage is less in the asymmetrical than in the symmetrical cases, thus suggesting that they diminish out of proportion to cell numbers. This relative deficit of callosal connections with increasing hemispheric asymmetry may reflect the possibility that with increasing asymmetry, some neurons withdraw their callosal axons during development with maintenance of those within the ipsilateral hemisphere. Alternatively, there may be a disproportionate loss of callosally related as compared to noncallosal cells in the asymmetrical case. However, we have failed to demonstrate any differences in proportions of cell types wholly or within specific laminae in symmetrical and asymmetrical brains. Specifically, we assessed the proportions of pyramidal and nonpyramidal cells by Nissl appearance in layer II–VI in the rat cortex (A. M. Galaburda et al., unpublished observations, 1986) and found no differences between brains with symmetrical and asymmetrical areas. In addition, others have shown that neuronal death is not a major factor in the development of callosal projections in SM-I (Ivy & Killackey, 1981; O'Leary et al., 1981). However, we have no direct evidence for either hypothesis at present.

Summary

It is clear that there are a number of biological differences between asymmetrical and symmetrical brains. We know that as asymmetry increases, the total area of the region decreases, suggesting that when a brain is symmetrical, it is the result of two large sides rather than two small sides. We also know that these volume differences are caused by changes in the number of cells, not changes in cell-packing density. These results, as discussed above, clearly constrain the possible ways in which an asymmetrical brain can develop. Furthermore, the pattern of callosal connections differs between symmetrical and asymmetrical brains, with differential axonal pruning being implicated.

Thus, we have begun to indirectly address issues of the development of brain asymmetry in the research detailed above, and more direct investigation is currently in progress in our laboratory. We know that any hypothesis on the ontogenesis of anatomic asymmetry must take into account these basic mechanisms of cerebral asymmetry in adulthood. What remains unanswered at present, however, are the questions that originally motivated the research, specifically, how does the development of asymmetrical and symmetrical brains differ? Are brain regions symmetrical or asymmetrical from the time of cell proliferation or do later genetic and/or epigenetic events (such as cell loss or transformation) play a role in the formation of symmetry or asymmetry? It is clear that the answers to these questions hold profound implications for the understanding of the mechanisms of brain development in general and, perhaps, abnormal brain development in dyslexia.

REFERENCES

Anderson, S. W. (1977). Language-related asymmetries of eye-movement and evoked potentials. In S. Harnad, R. W. Dotty, L. Goldstein, J. Jaynes, & G. Krauthamer, (Eds.), *Lateralization in the nervous system* (pp. 403–428). New York: Academic Press.

Basser, L. S. (1962). Hemiplegia of early onset and faculty of speech with special reference to the effects of hemispherectomy. *Brain, 85,* 427–460.

Braitenberg, V. & Kemali, M. (1971). Exceptions to bilateral symmetry in the epithalamus of lower vertebrates. *Journal of Comparative neurology, 138,* 137–146.

Broca, P. (1865). Sur la faculté de langage articulé. *Bulletin de la Société Antropologique (Paris), 6,* 337–393.

Cain, D. P., & Wada, J. A. (1979). An anatomical asymmetry in the baboon brain. *Brain, Behavior and Evolution, 16,* 222–226.

Chi, J. G., Dooling, E. C., & Gilles, F. H. (1977). Gyral development of the human brain. *Annals of Neurology, 1,* 86–93.

Denenberg, V. H. (1981). Hemispheric laterality in animals and the effects of early experience. *Behavioral and Brain Sciences, 4,* 1–49.

Denenberg, V. H., Garbanati, J., Sherman, G. F., Yutzey, D. A., & Kaplan, R. (1978). Infantile stimulation induces brain lateralization in rats. *Science, 201,* 1150–1152.

Denenberg, V. H., Rosen, G. D., Hofmann, M., Gall, J., Stockler, J., & Yutzey, D. A. (1982). Neonatal postural asymmetry and sex differences in the rat. *Developmental Research, 2,* 417–419.

Dennis, M. (1983). The developmentally dyslexic brain and the written language skills of

children with one hemisphere. In U. Kirk (Ed.), *Neuropsychology of language, reading, and spelling* (pp. 185–208). New York: Academic Press.

Diamond, M. C., Johnson, R. E., & Ingham, C. A. (1975). Morphological changes in the young, adult, and aging rat cerebral cortex, hippocampus, and diencephalon. *Behavioral Biology, 14*, 163–174.

Diamond, M. C., Young, D., Singh, S. S., & Johnson, R. E. (1983). Age-related morphologic differences in the rat cerebral cortex and hippocampus: Male–female; right–left. *Experimental Neurology, 81*, 1–13.

Eidelberg, D., & Galaburda, A. M. (1984). Inferior parietal lobule: Divergent architectonic asymmetries in the human brain. *Archives of Neurology, 41*, 843–852.

Eimas, P. D. (1985). Constraints on a model of infant speech perception. In J. Mehler & R. Fox (Eds.), *Neonate cognition: Beyond the blooming buzzing confusion* (pp. 185–197). Hillsdale, NJ: Lawrence Erlbaum.

Eimas, P. D., Siqueland, E. R., Jusczyk, P., & Vigorito, J. (1971). Speech perception in infants. *Science, 171*, 303–306.

Engbretson, G. A., Reiner, A., and Brecha, N. (1981). Habenular asymmetry and the central connections of the parietal eye of the lizard. *Journal of Comparative Neurology, 198*, 155–165.

Entus, A. K. (1977). Hemispheric asymmetry in processing of dichotically presented speech and nonspeech stimuli by infants. In S. J. Segalowitz & F. A. Gruber (Eds.), *Language development and neurological theory* (pp. 63–73). New York: Academic Press.

Falk, D. (1978). Cerebral asymmetry in old world monkeys. *Acta Anatomica, 101*, 334–339.

Fink, R. P., & Heimer, L. (1967). Two methods for selective silver impregnation of degenerating axons and their synaptic endings in the central nervous system. *Brain Research, 4*, 369–374.

Galaburda, A. M. (1980). La région de Broca: Observations anatomiques faites un siècle après la mort de son découvreur. *Revue Neurologique (Paris), 136*, 609–616.

Galaburda, A. M., Aboitiz, F., Rosen, G. D., & Sherman, G. F. (1986). Histological asymmetry in the primary visual cortex of the rat: Implications for mechanisms of cerebral asymmetry. *Cortex, 22*, 151–160.

Galaburda, A. M., Corsiglia, J., Rosen, G. D., & Sherman, G. F. (1987). Planum temporale asymmetry, reappraisal since Geschwind and Levitsky. *Neuropsychologia, 25*, 853–868.

Galaburda, A. M., & Kemper, T. L. (1979). Cytoarchitectonic abnormalities in developmental dyslexia: A case study. *Annals of Neurology, 6*, 94–100.

Galaburda, A. M., LeMay, M., Kemper, T. L., & Geschwind, N. (1978). Right–left asymmetries in the brain. *Science, 199*, 852–856.

Galaburda, A. M., Sanides, F., & Geschwind, N. (1978). Human brain: Cytoarchitectonic left–right asymmetries in the temporal speech region. *Archives of Neurology, 35*, 812–817.

Galaburda, A. M., Sherman, G. F., Rosen, G. D., Aboitiz, F., & Geschwind, N. (1985). Developmental dyslexia: Four consecutive patients with cortical anomalies. *Annals of Neurology, 18*, 222–233.

Geschwind, N., & Levitsky, W. (1968). Human brain: Left–right asymmetries in temporal speech region. *Science, 161*, 186–187.

Gundara, N., & Zivanovic, S. (1968). Asymmetry in east African skulls. *American Journal of Physical Anthropology, 28*, 331–338.

Hadziselimovic, H., & Cus, M. (1966). The appearance of internal structures of the brain in relation to configuration of the human skull. *Acta Anatomica, 63*, 289–299.

Hochberg, F. H., & LeMay, M. (1975). Arteriographic correlates of handedness. *Neurology, 25,* 218-222.

Innocenti, G. M., & Clarke, S. (1983). Multiple sets of visual cortical neurons projecting transitorily through the corpus callosum. *Neuroscience Letters, 41,* 27-32.

Ivy, G. O., Akers, R. M., & Killackey, H. P. (1979). Differential distribution of callosal projection neurons in the neonatal and adult rat. *Brain Research, 173,* 532-537.

Ivy, G., & Killackey, H. (1981). The ontogeny of the distribution of callosal projection neurons in the rat parietal cortex. *Journal of Comparative Neurology, 195,* 367-389.

Jacobson, S., & Trojanowski, J. Q. (1974). The cells of origin of the corpus callosum in the rat, cat and rhesus monkey. *Brain Research, 74,* 149-155.

Jusczyk, P. W. (1985). On characterizing the development of speech perception. In J. Mehler & R. Fox (Eds.), Neonate cognition: Beyond the blooming buzzing confusion (pp. 199-229). Hillsdale, NJ: Lawrence Erlbaum.

Jusczyk, P. W., Pisoni, D. B., Walley, A., & Murray, J. (1980). Discrimination of relative onset time of two-component tones by infants. *Journal of the Acoustical Society of America, 67,* 262-270.

Kimura, D. (1961). Cerebral dominance and the perception of verbal stimuli. *Canadian Journal of Psychology, 15,* 166-171.

Kolb, B., Sutherland, R. J., Nonneman, A. J., & Whishaw, I. Q. (1982). Asymmetry in the cerebral hemispheres of the rat, mouse, rabbit, and cat: The right hemisphere is larger. *Experimental Neurology, 78,* 348-359.

Larsen, B., Skinhøj, E., & Lassen, N. A. (1978). Variations in regional cortical blood flow in the right and left hemispheres during automatic speech. *Brain, 101,* 193-209.

LeCours, A. R., Lhermitte, F., & Bryans, B. (1983). *Aphasiology.* London: Balliere Tindall.

LeMay, M. (1976). Morphological cerebral asymmetries of modern man, fossil man, and non-human primate. *Annals of the New York Academy of Sciences, 280,* 349-366.

LeMay, M., & Culebras, A. (1972). Human brain: Morphological differences in the hemispheres demonstrable by carotid arteriography. *New England Journal of Medicine, 287,* 168-170.

LeMay, M., & Geschwind, N. (1975). Hemispheric differences in the brains of great apes. *Brain Behavior and Evolution, 11,* 48-52.

Lenneberg, E. H. (1967). *Biological foundations of language.* New York: John Wiley & Sons.

Moffit, A. R. (1971). Consonant cue perception by 20-24-week-old infants. *Child Development, 42,* 717-731.

Molfese, D. L. (1977). Infant cerebral asymmetry. In S. J. Segalowitz & F. A. Gruber (Eds.), *Language development and neurological theory* (pp. 21-25). New York: Academic Press.

Molfese, D. L., Freeman, R. B., & Palermo, D. S. (1975). The ontogeny of brain lateralization for speech and nonspeech stimuli. *Brain and Language, 2,* 356-368.

Molfese, D. L., & Molfese, V. J. (1986). Psychophysiological indices of early cognitive processes and their relationship to language. In J. E. Obrzut & G. W. Hynd (Eds.), *Child neuropsychology: Theory and research* (pp. 95-115). New York: Academic Press.

Morse, P. A. (1972). The discrimination of speech and nonspeech stimuli in early infancy. *Journal of Experimental Child Psychology, 14,* 477-492.

Nottebohm, F. (1970). Ontogeny of bird song. *Science, 167,* 950-956.

Nottebohm, F. (1977). Neural lateralization of vocal control in a passerine bird. *Journal of Experimental Neurology, 177,* 229-262.

Nottebohm, F., Stokes, T. M., & Leonard, C. M. (1976). Central control of song in the canary, *Serinus canarius. Journal of Comparative Neurology, 165,* 457-486.

Ojemann, G. A. (1983). The intrahemispheric organization of human language, derived with electrical stimulation techniques. *Trends in Neuroscience, 6*, 184–189.

Olavarría, J., & van Sluyters, R. (1985). Organization and postnatal development of callosal connections in the visual cortex of the rat. *Journal of Comparative Neurology, 239*, 1–26.

O'Leary, D., Stanfield, B., & Cowan, W. (1981). Evidence that the early postnatal restriction of the cells of origin of the callosal projection is due to the elimination of axonal collaterals rather than to the death of neurons. *Brain research, 227*, 607–617.

Penfield, W., & Roberts, L. (1959). *Speech and brain mechanisms.* Princeton: Princeton University Press.

Petersen, M. R., Beecher, M. D., Zoloth, S. R., Moody, D. B., & Stebbins, W. C. (1978). Neural lateralization of species-specific vocalizations by Japanese macaques (*Macaca fuscata*). *Science, 202*, 324–327.

Phelps, M. E., Hoffman, E. J., & Mazziota, J. C. (1981). A new high resolution positron computed tomograph (PCT) for mapping cerebral glucose metabolism: Studies in normal and sensory stimulated subjects. *Society for Neuroscience Abstracts, 7*, 243.

Pieniadz, J. M., & Naeser, M. A. (1984). Computed tomographic scan cerebral asymmetries and morphologic brain asymmetries: Correlation in the same cases post mortem. *Archives of Neurology, 41*, 403–409.

Rakic, P., & Williams, R. W. (1986). Thalamic regulation of cortical parcellation: An experimental perturbation of the striate cortex in rhesus monkeys. *Society for Neuroscience Abstracts, 12*, 1499.

Rosen, G. D., Finklestein, S., Stoll, A. L., Yutzey, D. A., & Denenberg, V. H. (1984). Neonatal tail posture and its relation to striatal dopamine asymmetry in the rat. *Brain Research, 297*, 305–308.

Rosen, G. D., Sherman, G. F., & Galaburda, A. M. (in press). Interhemispheric connections differ between symmetrical and asymmetrical brain regions. *Neuroscience.*

Ross, D. A., Glick, S. D., & Meibach, R. C. (1981). Sexually dimorphic brain and behavioral asymmetries in the neonatal rat. *Proceedings of the National Academy of Sciences of the United States of America, 78*, 1958–1961.

Ross, E. D. (1984). Right hemisphere's role in language, affective behavior, and emotion. *Trends in Neuroscience, 7*, 342–346.

Ross, E. D., & Mesulam, M.-M. (1979). Dominant language function of the right hemisphere? Prosody and emotional gesturing. *Archives of Neurology, 36*, 144–148.

Rubens, A. B., Mahowald, M. W., & Hutton, J. T. (1976). Asymmetry of lateral (Sylvian) fissures in man. *Neurology, 26*, 320–324.

Segalowitz, S. J., & Chapman, J. S. (1980). Cerebral asymmetry for speech in neonates: A behavioral measure. *Brain Language, 9*, 281–288.

Sherman, G. F., Garbanati, J. A., Rosen, G. D., Denenberg, V. H., & Yutzey, D. A. (1980). Brain and behavioral asymmetries for spatial preference in rats. *Brain Research, 192*, 61–67.

Sperry, R. W. (1974). Lateral specialization in the surgically separated hemispheres. In B. Milner (Ed.), *Hemispheric specialization and interaction.* Cambridge: MIT Press.

Springer, S. P. (1977). Tachistoscopic and dichotic-listening investigations of laterality in normal human subjects. In S. Harnad, R. W. Doty, L. Goldstein, J. Jaynes, & G. Krauthamer, (Eds.), *Lateralization in the nervous system* (pp. 325–336). New York: Academic Press.

Springer, S. P., & Deutsch, G. (1981). *Left brain, right brain.* San Francisco: W. H. Freeman.

Teszner, D., Tzavaras, A., Gruner, J., & Hécaen, H. (1972). L'asymmétrie droite–gauche du planum temporale: A propos de l'étude anatomique de 100 cervaeux. *Revue Neurologique (Paris), 126,* 444–449.

Vargha-Khadem, F., & Corballis, M. C. (1979). Cerebral asymmetry in infants. *Brain and Language, 8,* 1–9.

Wada, J. A., Clarke, R., & Hamm, A. (1975). Cerebral hemispheric asymmetry in humans. *Archives of Neurology, 32,* 239–246.

Weiskrantz, L. (1977). On the role of cerebral commissures in animals. In I. S. Russell, M. W. van Hof, & G. Berlucchi (Eds.), *Structure and function of cerebral commissures* (pp. 475–478). Baltimore: University Park Press.

Wise, S. P., & Jones, E. G. (1976). The organization and postnatal development of the commissural projection of the rat somatic sensory cortex. *Journal of Comparative Neurology, 168,* 313–343.

Witelson, S. F. (1985). The brain connection: The corpus callosum is larger in left-handers. *Science, 229,* 665–668.

Witelson, S. F., & Pallie, W. (1973). Left hemisphere specialization for language in the newborn: Neuroanatomical evidence of asymmetry. *Brain, 96,* 641–646.

Yeni-Komshian, G. H., & Benson, D. A. (1976). Anatomical study of cerebral asymmetry in the temporal lobe of humans, chimpanzees, and rhesus monkeys. *Science, 192,* 387–389.

Zaborsky, L., & Wolff, J. R. (1982). Distributional patterns and individual variations of callosal connections in the albino rat. *Anatomy and Embryology, 165,* 213–232.

Zaidel, E. (1977). Unilateral auditory language comprehension on the token test following cerebral commissurotomy and hemispherectomy. *Neuropsychologia, 15,* 1–18.

Zaidel, E. (1979). Lexical organization in the right hemisphere. In P. Buser & A. Roreul-Buser (Eds.), *Cerebral correlates of conscious experience* (pp. 177–197). Amsterdam: Elsevier.

DISCUSSION

ISAK PROHOVNIK: I like your first conclusion. I think it makes sense to think that asymmetry is due to one side being smaller than expected rather than to one side being larger than expected. I think that's certainly what we would expect in the clinical context whenever we find asymmetries. It's most usually the case that one side is atrophied or smaller rather than the other side being hypertrophic. So that makes sense, and I think we've demonstrated that, although I'm not sure about the generalizability, but within the context of this I think it is true. The second conclusion I don't really understand, and I didn't see that you documented it. You've shown that it's not cell-packing density, but have you presented data showing that it is changes in cell numbers, or are you concluding that that's inevitable?

GLENN ROSEN: I only know of two factors that can affect the volume of the hemisphere—either cell-packing density or cell numbers.

PROHOVNIK: Have you counted cell numbers?

ROSEN: Well that's how we got the cell-packing density, but the problem is that you're counting cells within a specific field or a specific area, and you would have to get an estimate of total cell numbers, which is based on the volume that you've already measured. If you're going to try to compare those two, you have a correlated measure, so you can't do that comparison. The only way to do it would be to count every cell within that area, which is a technically difficult if not impossible task. So, I think the key issue here is if there's something else that is going to affect cell architectonic volume besides cell number or cell-packing density, then we would have to consider that, but there isn't to my knowledge, so we're left with the idea that it has to be cell numbers that change.

PROHOVNIK: The reason for the question that I raised is this. Your idea to deal with area 17 is very interesting, and I think you have a very interesting model to study the issue of asymmetries. What you lose, however, in this is the idea that asymmetry observed in humans is a very specific pheonomenon caused by some mechanism that has specific features as opposed to presumably mere random asymmetries that you find in the lab model, which may well be caused by a different mechanism and have different effects from that in the human temporal cortex.

ROSEN: I think you're bringing up a couple of interesting points, and I think it's probably useful right now to talk about the issue of individual versus population asymmetry. There is no doubt that animals and humans exhibit asymmetry at the individual level; that is, one side is bigger than the other in anatomic areas. The issue of a population asymmetry may in fact be quite different. In other words, the mechanisms that force the majority of humans to have a larger left planum may be quite different from the mechanisms that control whether one side is bigger than the other. That is why we are concerned with mechanisms of asymmetry, and directionless measures of asymmetry at that. Then we are not getting into issues of which factors are determining the asymmetry of the population level.

MARIAN DIAMOND: Are you familiar with the recent work that indicates that when the pregnant female is stressed, the male pups at birth don't show right dominance. What has been shown is that the left side comes up to the level of the right. Since this happened prenatally, it would be interesting to see whether the number of cells was increased or decreased during this period of time.

ROSEN: Or, alternatively, it could be that the normal cell loss that occurs during development is prevented from occurring.

DIAMOND: It is an interesting experiment.

JACKSON BEATTY: It didn't necessarily follow, but it would be very nice evidence of small-side control.

ROSEN: So what you're saying is perhaps the small side is determining the . . .

BEATTY: And a mechanism by which that could take place is if there were some kind of a restriction that said all callosal pathways had to be reciprocal.

ROSEN: Right, and that's a very intriguing idea.

DENDRITIC CORRELATES OF HIGHER
COGNITIVE FUNCTION

ARNOLD B. SCHEIBEL, MD
University of California, Los Angeles

INTRODUCTION

Contemporary neuroscience has become an intensely pragmatic discipline, an observation that would have been of the greatest interest to both Charles Sherrington and Sigmund Freud. Toward the end of a long and committed life, the English physiologist looked almost with despair at the "magic shuttle" of the mind, which "goes more ghostly than a ghost" (Sherrington, 1937). From a very different vantage point, the first psychoanalyst accepted the conceptual limitations of his time but looked forward with confidence to some future period when behind the psychiatrist would stand "the man with the syringe," providing biological correlates for even the most subtle manifestations of the psyche (Freud, 1946). For many of us today, the mind–brain dichotomy is a dead issue, and "monism" and "emergent properties" have become part of the "pop" vocabulary of neurobiologists and cognitive psychologists alike.

Once arrived at this point, however, there is substantially less agreement as to how and where we can begin to identify the biological correlates of mental activity. Fortunately, the structures and processes involved may eventually turn out to be substantially less subtle than we had originally feared (or hoped!). Variations in the quality and quantity of input to the central nervous system are now known to produce remarkably large-scale changes in the overall dimensions of the forebrain, including neocortical thickness, dendrite branching, neuronal somal dimensions, numbers of oligodendroglia, DNA/RNA ratios, neurotransmitter levels, etc. (Diamond, this volume). The activities of neurons, individually and in small clusters, are now being related to certain types of cortical operations (Fuster, this volume; Schlag & Schlag-Rey, this volume), and somewhat larger domains of bioelectrical activity evoked by presumptive cognitive activities are also being described (Mangun & Hillyard, this volume; Pahl, this volume). Exploration of the exposed and wakeful human brain is now possible and seems to

Acknowledgments: These studies were supported by the David Murdock Foundation for Advanced Human Brain Studies. I am grateful to my young colleagues and students for their untiring work in the development of these data.

provide evidence for highly idiosyncratic localization of discrete "language points," although the meaning of these data is not yet clear (Ojemann, Cawthon, & Lettich, this volume).

Our own interest in neural substrates of higher cognitive function extends back to a memorable week in 1954 spent in the Brain Research Institute of Professors Oscar and Cecile Vogt at Neustadt in the Black Forest. At that time, the Vogts had accumulated an impressive collection of clinically documented human brain specimens, including a number from individuals with specific talents. Among the many Nissl-stained sections they demonstrated, two were especially noteworthy. In one case, the brain of a distinguished Belgian violinist who was reported to have been born with the gift of perfect pitch, layer IV of the primary auditory receptive cortex was approximately twice as thick as that of the cortices of ungifted control individuals. In the second, derived from a prominent artist who was said to have maintained his capacity for intense eidetic imagery throughout his life, layer IV of his primary visual cortex was similarly enhanced in depth. No quantitative studies had been done on this material, but I can recall that, to casual visual examination at least, the numbers of nerve cell bodies seemed approximately equal in the index subjects and in the controls. The only obvious difference appeared to lie in the lower density of neurons in the former. From this, one might deduce the presence of a more elaborate neuropil in these gifted subjects' brains, thereby accounting for the decreased packing density in the thicker cortical lamina.

In the years that followed, these observations were not forgotten, and the possibility of seeking correlations between human cognitive activity and neuropil patterns remained attractive. As exciting as these observations were, we had little success in obtaining brain tissue from unusually talented men and women. It gradually became apparent that it would be more practical to consider specific, functionally characterizable parts of the human brain that did become available to the laboratory, using each cortical zone (somesthetic, auditory, sensory association, etc.) as an area uniquely endowed in its own right, relative to the rest.

In the following material, quantitative aspects of dendritic morphology are emphasized, not because the patterns of presynaptic structures are considered of less import but rather because postsynaptic elements are structurally more robust and usually better impregnated (visualized). Examination by light microscopic techniques represents a necessary first step for preliminary evaluation, to be followed ultimately by higher-resolution studies with electron microscopy.

PROBLEMS AND HYPOTHESES

By using relatively uncomplicated quantitative histological and statistical techniques, a number of questions can be put directly to the tissue. Are there discernible differences in organization and/or complexity among dendrite systems of diverse functionally characterized areas of neocortex? Do the demands of neural processing in a somesthetic receptive zone differ sufficiently from those of a sensory associative zone to manifest themselves in variations in dendrite patterns? Are the processing requirements involved in homologous expressive language areas of the two hemispheres sufficiently different to be reflected in the structure of the dendrite ensembles? And, if they are, can the development of such variations be traced sequentially as the young individual gains language competence? These are representative of the kinds of problems we are addressing in the laboratory.

Final answers are difficult to come by, and the problems of working exclusively with human brain tissue are well known. Nevertheless, sufficient data have been collected to indicate directions for further research and to provide bases for a group of working hypotheses. They include the following: (1) relationships appear to exist between the complexity of a neural computational task and the organization of the neuronal dendritic ensemble; (2) generally, the more complex the subsumed neural computation, the more extensive is the dendrite system; (3) the more peripheral portions (later-order dendrites) of the dendritic tree appear to be those that reflect most closely the level of the mature neural operation; (4) the more central portions of the dendritic tree (the earlier-order dendrites and therefore the ones that are first to appear in ontogenetic development) probably reflect processing loads in the earlier phases of life; and (5) there is at least some evidence for the possibility that these early-order dendrites may "shorten," either by secondary branching or by partial resorption, during the process of maturation.

METHODOLOGY

In the studies described below, we had recourse to two major modes of data acquisition. In each case, the first step involved removing appropriate tissue blocks as soon as possible after death and immersing them in a preliminary fixative such as 4% neutral buffered paraformaldehyde or 10% buffered formalin. One of the many problems inherent in research on human cortical tissue is the time between death and preliminary fixation. Our shortest elapsed time periods were 5–6 hours, but many were 18 to 24 hours old before preliminary fixation, and in the case of our developmental study, a few samples from "young" brains were not available for fixation until 30 hours or more had elapsed. Such periods of postmortem autolysis are potentially destructive of dendritic tissue and compromise the experimental results (Williams, Ferrante, & Caviness, 1978; Buell, 1982). It should be pointed out that removal of tissue blocks from the postmortem brain naturally precludes precise functional characterization of the area. One is forced to rely on cortical maps of the relevant areas (Penfield & Boldrey, 1937; Penfield & Rasmussen, 1950). However, the well-known variability of human cortical topography and functional representation inevitably adds an element of uncertainty to this procedure.

Following preliminary fixation, the tissue blocks were refixed in 0.33% osmium tetroxide for 3–4 days, impregnated in 0.75% silver nitrate solution, shelled in paraffin, and sectioned at 120 μm. Following dehydration and clearing, the tissue sections were mounted sequentially on glass slides under coverslips and allowed to dry in darkness for 1–2 weeks. All slides were coded so that the investigator was unaware of the source of cortical derivation, the hemisphere involved, or the identity of the patient.

Following the establishment of criteria for cell selection, dendrite ensembles were described in quantitative terms by one of two methods. In the technique of Sholl (1956), a group of concentric circles inscribed in the ocular was superimposed and centered over the middle of the neuronal soma. The number of dendrite–ring intersections for each circle was then counted, thereby providing a measure of the complexity or "branchiness" of the ensemble. This method does not provide discrete data about dendritic branch number, branch length, or total dendrite length. Such information can be obtained by a second measuring technique, which is based on accurate camera lucida drawings of the entire dendrite tree. These drawings are then transposed to an electronic digital pad, by means of which they are entered into a computer and are thereafter available for a number of different types of analyses.

Dendrite Patterns in Four Selected Cortical Areas

Using the Sholl method, we analyzed the dendrite patterns of eight randomly selected pyramidal neurons in layers II–III in the gyral crowns of each of four cortical areas: the trunk receptive and hand–finger receptive zones of the primary sensory somesthetic area (primarily areas 3 and 1), the sensory associative zone of the supramarginal gyrus (area 40), and the superior frontal gyrus of the frontal lobe approximately 2 cm posterior to the frontal pole (area 9) in the left hemispheres of 10 patients (Figure 1) who died in a Veterans Administration Hospital (A. B. Scheibel & T. Conrad, unpublished data). These areas were chosen with the hope that they would represent a broad range of cortical processing patterns. Although both trunk and hand–finger zones were obviously sensory receptive in function, we assumed that the considerable differences in grain and pattern of sensory information that they received might make them useful areas for comparison. The supramarginal area was selected as an example of a higher-level sensory associative field subject to already highly processed information converging from several adjacent sensory areas. Area 9 was selected as an example of superior lateral prefrontal cortex with its broad range of higher cognitive activities built around "attention and intention" (Pribram, 1987). In this study our working hypotheses led us to predict that dendrite systems of the primary receptive area for trunk sensation might show the simplest level of organization, the hand–finger area an intermediate level of complexity, and the prefrontal and parietal association areas the highest levels of dendritic complexity. Data analysis provided

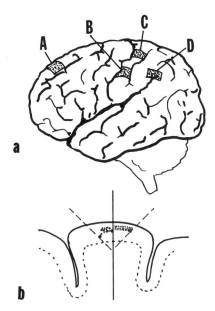

Figure 1. (a) Lateral surface of the human left cerebral hemisphere showing the approximate locations for selection of cortical tissue blocks: A, superior frontal gyrus of prefrontal cortex (area 9); B, hand–finger area; C, trunk receptive zones of postcentral gyrus (primary sensory receptive areas 3 and 1); D, supramarginal gyrus of the parietal lobe (area 39). (b) Section through gyral crown showing the areas explored for neuron–dendrite measurements.

partial support for these expectations but emphasized the undoubted presence of a number of other variables including the importance of acquired skills and lifestyles in modifying neural structure (Scheibel, Conrad, Perdue, Tomiyasu, & Wechsler, in press).

Table 1 summarizes our information about the 10 patients on whom the study is based. With the exception of one case for whom no data were available, note that all except one were right handed and that approximately two-thirds would probably have depended professionally on some degree of finger dexterity. Their ages ranged from 53 to 74 years (mean age 63.7), and only one of the nine for whom we have data was female.

Despite extensive variation in the profile and complexity of the dendrite ensembles, certain patterns emerge from examination of even so limited a number of cases as these. Superimposition of values for dendrite–ring intersection frequencies of all cases for each of the four areas studied are shown in Figures 2 through 5. Note that dendrite systems from trunk receptive zones provide on the average the narrowest profiles. The area of peak values centers on ring 8, and the number of counts then decreases so sharply that at ring 12 all values are below the 15-intersections index line. A much broader and more varied pattern is generated by the dendrite systems of the hand–finger area. Peak intersection values are spread more widely over the figure, and the declining slope is more gradual. This undoubtedly reflects enhanced branching patterns in the outer half of the dendrite tree of the hand–finger neurons compared to those of the trunk area. Mean dendrite "profiles" for each of the association areas are also quite broad, the parietal association area appearing to have more sustained peaks and gradually declining slopes. This may be a function of the powerful presynaptic

TABLE 1
TABULAR SUMMARY OF THE 10 SUBJECTS USED IN THIS STUDY

Case number	Age, sex	Handedness	Education	Occupation
A-20-85	66, male	RH	H.S. graduate	Civil service/salesman
A-104-85	67, male	RH	10th grade	Mechanic
A-59-84	53, male	RH	H.S. graduate	Machine operator
A-135-84	62, male	RH	H.S. graduate	Chef/cook
A-55-85	73, male	RH	H.S. graduate	Clerk–receptionist–typist
A-38-85	66, male	RH	H.S. graduate	Major appliance repairman
A-178-84	74, male	RH	H.S. graduate	Tailor
A-108-85	61, male	LH	2 years college	Radio operator/repairman
A-169-84	60, female	RH	H.S. graduate	Office work–typist
A-113-84			No historical data	

convergence from adjacent sensory receptive cortical zones (somesthetic, visual, auditory, etc.) and the extensive postsynaptic surface that develops to handle this influx. Individual assessment of the neurons in each area shows that 20% of those in the prefrontal area and 60% of those in the trunk receptive zone do not reach the 15 dendrite–ring intersection level at any point in their arborizations. We do not yet know whether these values simply reflect our sample size or whether they also indicate the degree or "intensity" of neuronal use in each area.

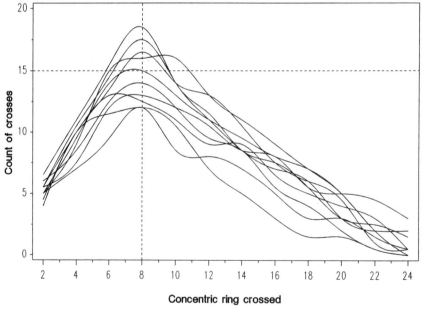

Figure 2. Mean values for counts of ring crossings by dendrite branches from all 10 cases in the trunk receptive area. Each case is represented by a separate line without symbols.

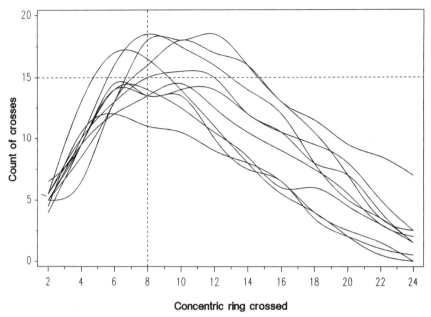

Figure 3. Mean values for counts of ring crossings by dendrite branches from all 10 cases in the hand–finger receptive area. Each case is represented by a separate line without symbols.

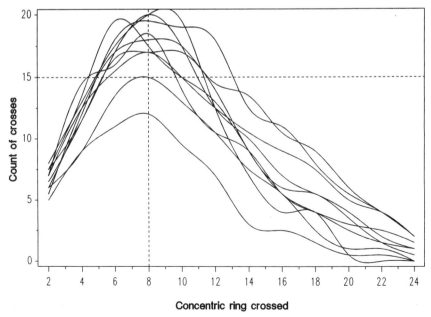

Figure 4. Mean values for counts of ring crossings by dendrite branches from all 10 cases in the prefrontal region. Each case is represented by a separate line without symbols.

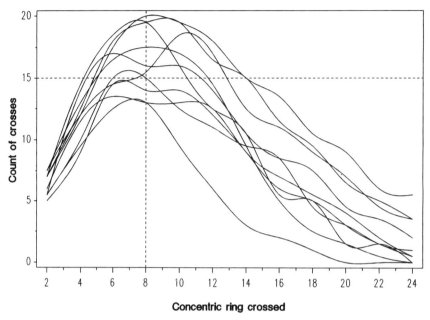

Figure 5. Mean values for counts of ring crossings by dendrite branches from all 10 cases in the supramarginal gyrus. Each case is represented by a separate line without symbols.

When mean values of dendrite profiles from trunk and hand–finger areas of case 59 were compared graphically, significant differences were noted. The number of hand–finger dendrite–ring intersections exceeded those of the trunk at every point except at ring 4, often by more than 100% (Figure 6). Similar analysis of the nine remaining cases (Figure 7) reveals equivalent patterns in several, although there is loss of the hand–finger "advantage" to varying degrees in three cases. Subsequent investigation revealed that one of these individuals (case 108) was a life-long left hander.

Comparisons were also made between values for dendritic arbors from the hand–finger area of the sensory strip and the supramarginal gyrus of case 59 (Figure 8). In this instance the latter shows a modest (and nonsignificant) advantage over the former at each data point except one (ring 20). Figure 9 shows similar comparisons in the remaining nine individuals. A very broad range of patterns is apparent here, attesting to the high degree of interindividual variation between the levels of dendritic complexity in these two areas.

One final measure of comparative dendritic complexity is shown in Figure 10, which illustrates cumulative counts of dendrite–ring crossings. With case 59 as a model once more, the dendrite arbor of the trunk area has the smallest total number of intersections (67), the hand–finger area has almost twice as many (119), and the supramarginal gyrus has the highest number (132). When data from the other nine cases are similarly arranged (Figure 11), a very large degree of interindividual variation is apparent, not only in the patterns of dendrite complex-

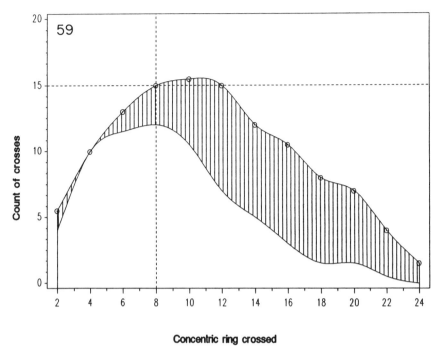

Figure 6. Mean values for counts of ring crossings by dendrite branches for case 59, comparing trunk receptive area (line without symbols) and hand–finger area (line with circles). The shaded area represents the amount of area under curve by which the former exceeds the latter.

ity but in the degree of difference among the four areas. For instance, in case 55, the mean value for the number of dendrite–ring intersections of the supramarginal area (the most complex dendrite system in this individual) is almost 130% greater than that of the prefrontal area, whereas in case 135 the total spread between most and least complex systems (hand–finger versus trunk) is less than 30%. The most consistent pattern is shown by dendrite systems of the trunk area, which generate (with one exception, case 108, the single left-handed individual in our study) a consistently lower level of ring intersection counts than most of the other areas studied.

Viewed within the broadest perspective, these data seem noteworthy primarily for their variability. But this is not so surprising when one considers our effrontery in asking an inconsequentially small fraction of neurons to reveal structural floor plans that may be idiosyncratic to certain types of neural processing paradigms. It seems sufficiently remarkable to note even a suggestion of a pattern in the dendrite profiles we have explored. Pyramidal neurons in the supragranular layers of primary sensory cortex receiving thoracic inputs do seem, on the whole, to be endowed with less extensive basilar dendritic envelopes than those of other areas studied. The relative "deprivation" seems most obvious among the higher-order (later appearing) dendrite segments (Figures 2–5), the

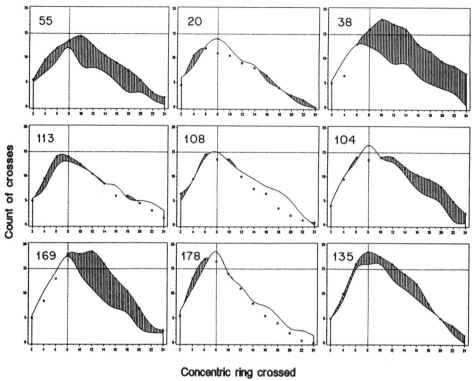

Figure 7. Mean values for counts of ring crossings by dendrite branches for nine cases (case identification in upper left corner of each panel) comparing trunk receptive area (line without symbols) and hand–finger area (line with circles). The shaded area represents the amount of area under curve by which the former exceeds the latter.

elements where we would have reason to expect the most growth if processing loads expand incrementally as the organism matures. Figures 6 and 7, which summarize comparisons between thoracic and hand–finger receptive zones, are generally supportive to this notion, although cases 22, 108, and 178 are not. However, patient 108 was a life-long left hander, suggesting that maximal tactile sensitivity might reasonably have been vested in the other hemisphere. The occupation of case 20 is listed as civil service/salesman, work areas that might arguably provide fewer tactile challenges than those of the more manually oriented majority of the rest (machinists, typists, repairmen, etc.), and yet there is virtually no difference in dendritic profiles between trunk and finger–hand zones in case 178, whose lifetime work is listed as "tailor." We have no explanation for this apparent deviation from our hypothesis. Either the hypothesis is entirely wrong (always the most likely possibility), or else it has some degree of validity, but we are unaware of all of the variables in the case. Quite apart from the degree of validity of the hypothesis, there can be no doubt as to the latter point. We are

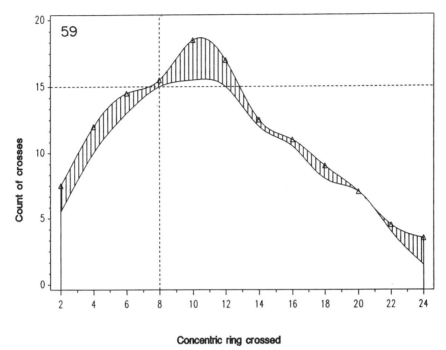

Figure 8. Mean values for counts of ring crossings by dendrite branches for case 59 comparing hand–finger receptive area with supramarginal gyrus (line with triangles). The shaded area represents the amount of area under curve by which the latter exceeds the former.

learning that any attempted correlational study of this type must have the fullest possible information about the individual's life, the details of his work, his interests, avocations, period and quality of retirement years, details of final illness(es), length of agonal period, etc.

DIFFERENTIAL DENDRITIC PATTERNS IN CORITICAL AREAS FOR EXPRESSIVE SPEECH

The preceding study emphasizes the variability of dendrite patterning among individual brains and the consequent difficulties in data interpretation. This problem might be mitigated to some degree in an experimental paradigm in which each brain served as its own control. Such a situation can be approximated in the case of the language-related areas of the human cerebral cortex because of well-recognized differences in contribution by the two hemispheres.

In the example that follows, we examined dendritic structure in cortical samples from the expressive speech area of the left frontal cortex, that is, the opercular and triangular zones of the inferior frontal gyrus (Broca's area), and its homologous area on the opposite hemisphere. In addition, cortical zones directly posterior to these at the foot of the precentral gyrus were similarly examined.

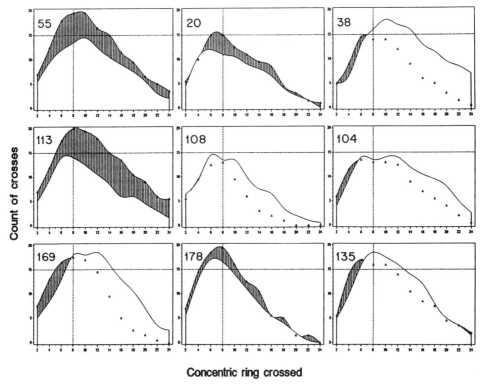

Concentric ring crossed

Figure 9. Mean values for counts of ring crossings by dendrite branches for nine cases (case identification in upper left corner of each panel) comparing hand–finger receptive area with supramarginal gyrus. The shaded area represents the amount of area under curve by which the latter exceeds the former.

These latter areas constitute motor control areas for orofacial musculature, that is, the face and tongue area of the cortical motor homunculus (Penfield & Boldrey, 1937; Penfield & Rasmussen, 1950). The opercular and triangular portions of the inferior frontal gyrus were considered the "strategic area" for language function, and the orofacial zone of the motor strip area the "tactical area" (Scheibel, Fried, et al., 1985; Scheibel, Paul, et al., 1985).

Since the initial observations of Dax (1865) and Broca (1865), it has been generally accepted that the left inferior frontal lobe is primarily responsible for expressive (motor) activity. This appears to be true for virtually all right-handed individuals and, somewhat surprisingly, for the majority of left handers, although the degree of lateralization of function varies among individuals. The right inferior frontal area seems much poorer in its ability to handle a number of semantic and syntactic aspects of language, although it is considered important in capturing the emotional nuances of incoming speech patterns and in identifying or creating overall linguistic patterns and intonations (Gardner, Brownell, Wapner, & Michelow, 1983; Zaidel, 1985).

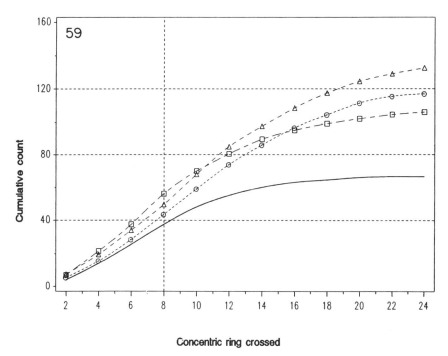

Figure 10. Mean value of cumulative counts of ring crossings by dendrite branches for four areas of the brain in case 59. The solid line without symbols is the trunk area, the line with circles is the hand–finger area, the line with triangles is the supramarginal gyrus, and the line with squares is the prefrontal area.

These clinically well-documented functional differences appeared to provide a satisfactory setting in which to extend our exploration of postulated differences in dendritic patterning. Once again our working hypotheses were based on putative correlations between complexity of the computational task and the extent and intricacy of the dendritic ensemble. We assumed that left- and right-sided operations differed not only in the "difficulty" of the computations involved (obviously a dangerous assumption in itself) but also in the ontogenetic sophistication of the task. Central to this notion was the inference that the more holistic and emotional capabilities of the nondominant hemisphere represented neural operations more "primitive" in nature and derivation than the lexical and syntactic functions of the dominant side. On the basis of these working ideas, we predicted that dendritic systems of neurons in the "strategic" language areas would be more complex and extensive than those in "tactical" areas and, further, that those in the language-dominant hemisphere would exceed those of the opposite side. As will be seen, certain aspects of these working assumptions appeared to have some degree of validity, although they would turn out to be overly simplistic and often incorrect in detail (Scheibel, Paul, et al., 1985).

The study was based on examination of brain tissue from eight male patients with an age range of 58 to 77 years (mean age 65.9, S.D. 6.4). All were known to

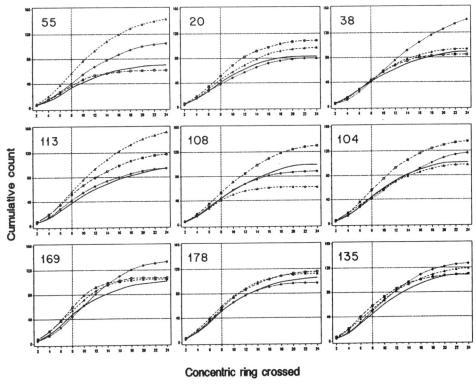

Concentric ring crossed

Figure 11. Mean values of cumulative counts of ring crossings by dendrite branches for four areas of the brain in nine cases (case identification numbers in upper left corner of each panel). The solid line without symbols is the trunk area, the line with circles is the hand-finger area, the line with triangles is the supramarginal gyrus, and the line with squares is the prefrontal area.

be free of neurological disease, and all came to autopsy within 5 to 28 hours after death. Tissue samples were selected from left and right opercular and precentral areas (Figure 12), impregnated by the rapid Golgi method, sectioned at 120 μm, mounted under coverslips, and coded to prevent investigator bias. From each of the four regions selected for study—left opercular (LOP), right opercular (ROP), left precentral (LPC), and right precentral (RPC)—six neurons were selected from each subject according to a group of predetermined criteria, which included (1) a depth beneath the cortical surface of 400–1,200 μm, (2) position of the cell body approximately midway between upper and lower surfaces of the tissue section, and (3) presence of at least three well-stained primary basilar dendrites and their complement of dendritic branches.

A Sholl-type analysis of these data resulted in the graphs of Figure 13. Here the number of dendrite–ring intersections plotted against the ring number (ring interval 28 μm) provides in aggregate a profile of the complexity or "branchiness" of the dendritic tree. Note that in cases 1, 2, and 4, the values for neurons in

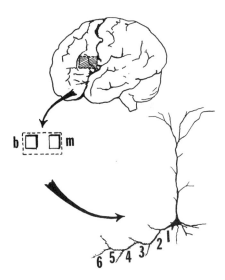

Figure 12. Site of removal of tissue specimens from each hemisphere, which includes the inferior portion of the motor strip area and the posterior portion of the inferior frontal gyrus. Division of the larger block into a posterior part made up of the orofacial motor zone (m) and the pars opercularis and triangularis of Broca's area (b). The cortical pyramidal cell shows the elements of the basilar dendrite system with centrifugal designation of its branching pattern. First-, second-, and third-order branches (1, 2, 3) make up the proximal system; fourth-, fifth-, and sixth-order branches (4, 5, 6) make up the distal system. From R. J. Simonds & A. B. Scheibel, 1989. The postnatal development of the motor speech area: A preliminary study. *Brain and Language, 37,* 42–58. Copyright 1989 by Academic Press. Reprinted by permission.

Broca's area (LOP) appear appreciably higher than those for any of the other areas. The unexpected reversal in case 5, where values for ROP exceeded all others, became more reasonable when we learned at the conclusion of the study that this patient was one of two non-right-handers in the study. As already indicated, the majority of left handers are also now believed to be "left brained," but it is clear from the clinical studies that approximately 15% of such individuals are, in fact, right hemisphere dominant for language function, and patient 5 was undoubtedly one of these.

The second method of data analysis was based on computer-aided measurements of the camera lucida drawings already alluded to. This technique provides us with a good deal of discrete, quantitative information about each dendrite ensemble including total dendrite length (*tdl*), the average length of dendrite segments of each order (*asl*), and the average number of dendrite segments for each order of dendritic branches (*asn*). After all of the data had been collected and processed, information about the patients' handedness was sought in addition to any other meaningful behavioral or linguistic characteristic.

Several findings emerged from the study that appear relevant to the problem of language and verbal behavior. The bar graph of Figure 14 compares total dendrite length of neurons from the left opercular (LOP) with right opercular (ROP) areas and, in turn, those of left precentral (LPC) with right precentral (RPC) areas. We were surprised that there was no significant difference in TDL between left and right hemispheres, either for strategic speech (LOP = 2,714.5 μm versus ROP = 2,540.8 μm) or for tactical speech (LPC = 2,208.3 μm versus RPC = 2,540.8 μm) areas. According to our *a priori* hypotheses, we would have expected *tdl* values for opercular neurons on the propositional speech-dominant

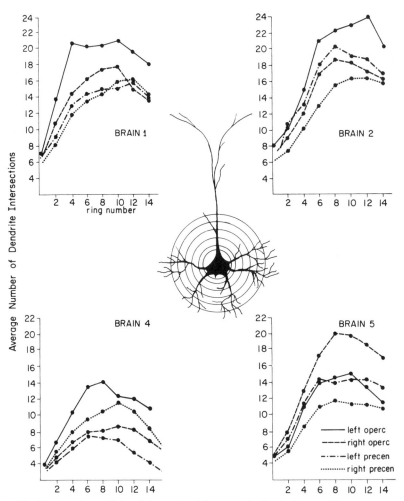

Figure 13. Comparison of dendrite ensemble complexity in four subjects as revealed by Sholl-type evaluation (center diagram). Average number of dendrite intersections (ordinate) is plotted against concentric ring number (abscissa) for tissue specimens from four cortical areas: left opercular, right opercular, left precentral, and right precentral. Values for the left opercular zone are highest in brains 1, 3, and 4, whereas those for right opercular are highest in brain 5. This subject was non-right-handed. From A. B. Scheibel, 1988. Dendritic correlates of human cortical functions. *Archives Italiennes de Biologie,* *126,* 347–357. Copyright 1988 by Università degli Studi di Pisa. Reprinted by permission.

side to exceed those of the opposite hemisphere because of the presumably greater processing load consequent to speech strategy activities.

Analysis by segment order, however, revealed idiosyncratic patterns that appeared to reflect both ontogenetic development and hierarchies of plasticity. In summary, a larger fraction of the dendrite arbors in the right hemisphere were made up of lower-order (first, second, and third) branches, whereas in the left hemisphere, a larger proportion of each dendrite ensemble consisted of higher-

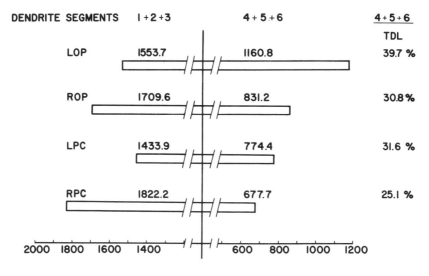

DENDRITE SEGMENTS

Figure 14. Comparison of dendrite lengths and proportion of dendritic branching systems made up of lower-order (1, 2, 3) and higher-order (4, 5, 6) branches in left opercular (LOP), right opercular (ROP), left precentral (LPC), and right precentral (RPC) areas. Figures on the extreme right indicate the percentage of total dendritic length (TDL) making up the higher-order dendrite branches in each region. From A. B. Scheibel, I. Fried, et al., 1985. Differentiating characteristics of the human speech cortex: A quantitative Golgi study. In D. F. Benson & E. Zaidel (Eds.), *The dual brain* (pp. 65–74). New York: Guilford Press. Copyright 1985 by The Guilford Press. Reprinted by permission.

order (fourth, fifth, and sixth) branches. Additionally, these differences also gained expression in a distinctive manner. Lower-order branches were longer on the right side; higher-order branches were more numerous on the left side. It was particularly interesting to find that this pattern of values was partially reversed in the two non-right-handers in our study, thereby suggesting that the histological differences might bear a relationship to behavior. The apparent importance of higher-order dendrite branches in neurons of the language-dominant hemisphere is emphasized in Figure 15.

In this graph, where total basal dendritic length (*tbdl*) of LOP is maintained at a value of 1.0 for each branch order and compared with that of similar branch orders for ROP, LPC, and RPC, note how the value for higher-order dendrite segment orders in the three other areas rapidly falls away when compared to the values for LOP. In combination, these data suggest that it is not so much the total length (and therefore membrane surface area) of the dendrite tree but rather the topographic and electrotonic organization of the ensemble that may be significant.

Organizational patterns of dendrite systems reflect in some measure the life history of the neuron. In fact, the complex admixture of genetic and epigenetic

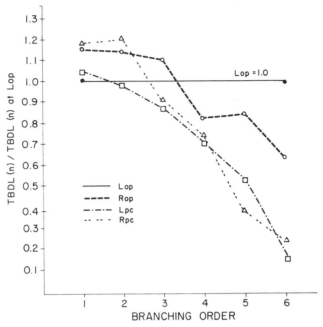

Figure 15. Comparison of total basilar dendritic length of each branch order [TBDL(n)] compared to values in the left opercular region (Lop) in six right-handed subjects. The value of Lop is maintained at 1.0. Note that as the more distal branching order segments are approached, values for Lop progressively increase relative to right opercular (Rop), left precentral (Lpc), and right precentral (Rpc) cortical zones. From A. B. Scheibel, 1988. Dendritic correlates of human cortical functions. *Archives Italiennes de Biologie*, *126*, 347–357. Copyright 1988 by Università degli Studi di Pisa. Reprinted by permission.

factors that constitutes the ontogenetic history of the cell should be readable in the structure and function of the mature element. Dendrite development follows a time-linked progression during the pre- and postnatal stages of life, idiosyncratic to the neural site, paced by the particular level of need for that neural function, and modulated by the demands or limitations posed by the external and internal milieu. Although developmental and maturative patterns differ appreciably among the various cortical areas (Conel, 1939–1959), primary sensory developing appreciably earlier than sensory associative cortices, an overall pattern is discernible. Cortical dendritic elaboration usually begins during the early part of the third trimester. By the time of birth, most cortical neurons have first- and second-order dendrite systems and, in some cases, the rudiments of third-order branches. Following birth, there is marked extension of these branch orders with the subsequent addition of higher-order branches, resulting in an increasingly complex neuropil whose density may augment progressively for a number of years.

Just as climatic history can be read retrospectively in the rings of a felled tree trunk, so can the duration and activity levels of discrete neuroontogenetic epochs be inferred from the length and/or number of various dendrite segment orders. To a limited extent, then, the specific dendrite patterns we found might be considered as a fossilized history of early dendrite growth, modified by the now-recognized capacity of dendrite systems to prune and restructure themselves to shifting patterns of input (Connor, Melone, Yuen, & Diamond, 1981).

Operating on this inference, we drew several tentative conclusions from the differentially patterned dendrite systems of the two hemispheres. The presence of longer dendrite segments of lower (first, second, and third) order on the side nondominant for propositional speech was considered as possibly indicative of greater functional activity during the early postnatal period. During this first year or so of life, the nonverbal sensory–motor period of Piaget (1954), the infant depends on sensory impressions of a highly concrete nature and is limited to relatively large-scale, undifferentiated action patterns. It is emotionally responsive, vocal, and increasingly sensitive to inflection and nuance in the human voice, faculties that are believed to be significantly supported by right hemispheric activity. The marked increase in the number of higher-order (fourth, fifth, and sixth) branches on the language-dominant side compared to the opposite hemisphere suggested enhanced dendritic growth at a somewhat later time, that is, the second year and beyond, when the beginnings of internalization and conceptualization mark the onset of language competence in the child. On the basis of these suppositions, a second set of inferences was that during the first year of postnatal development, organization of opercular (and perhaps precentral) cortex on the right side might be more advanced than that on the left, as expressed by the number and total length of early-order dendrite branches. Thereafter, it was postulated that language-involved areas in the left hemisphere might begin to catch up with and finally exceed those on the right as the use and complexity of language increased.

In order to examine these possibilities more directly, we have attempted a quantitative analysis of dendritic development in the anterior speech and orofacial motor zones of a group of age-graded infant brains ranging from 3 months to 6 years of age (Simonds & Scheibel, 1989). Our primary goal was to chart the course of development of dendrite ensembles in these areas during the period of language acquisition and to see whether inferences about developmental patterns drawn from the dendritic structure of mature dendrite systems might be borne out in sequential observations.

PATTERNS OF POSTNATAL DEVELOPMENT IN ANTERIOR SPEECH-RELATED CORTICES

Tissue specimens from left and right opercular (motor speech) and left and right precentral motor areas (the orofacial zone at the foot of the precentral gyrus) from 17 age-graded subjects were used in this study. Ages ranged from 3 months to 6 years and represented the eventually acceptable distillate from a much larger group (75 cases) originally chosen for the study. Postmortem state of the tissue and problems with impregnation resulted in the drastic decrease in number of cases finally available for the study. The small n with which we were forced to work also resulted in a highly asymmetric age distribution of the case material. Table 2 shows the age groupings we used and the number of subjects, gender, source, and postmortem interval for each subject. We took as our task a description of the sequential growth patterns of cortical pyramidal cells similar to those we had examined in adults. Unfortunately, problems with impregnation of most neurons in the cortical supragranular layers made it necessary for us to transfer our efforts to the infragranular pyramids of layer V. All comparisons between this body of data and the previous one accordingly should be made with this constraint in mind.

In this preliminary study, four cells satisfying a group of predetermined criteria were drawn with the camera lucida from each of the four areas in each of the cases to be studied. A total of 276 cells, accounting for 941 primary dendrites and their branch systems, formed the basis of the study. In the statistical analysis, numbers of segments of each order, segment lengths, and summed proximal (first, second, and third) and distal (fourth, fifth, and sixth) orders constituted some of the dependent variables. For each dependent variable, several independent measures were used, including (1) age of the individual, (2) hemisphere, (3) cortical area (opercular versus motor), and (4) identifiers for particular brains and cells. These identifying markers were used as random components in mixed analysis of variance models generated by the computer program BMDP3V (BMDP Statistical Software, University of California Press, 1985). t-tests were also provided to investigate mean differences between brain regions with age groups (Tables 2, 3, and 4).

Examination of these data reveals a series of changes in the structure of dendritic envelopes in each of the four cortical zones studied. A few salient events are emphasized in each of the five epochs examined, followed by some reflections on the possible functional consequences of such changes.

At 3 months of age, the right motor (RM) area shows a significant advantage in total dendrite length over both of the presumptive motor speech areas (LB and RB) and the opposite orofacial area (LM). This advantage is expressed almost entirely within the proximal orders. Both LB and RB show approximately equal dendritic development at this time, suggesting that in the first few months of life, there is relatively little differential activity in motor speech areas.

In the 5- to 6-month period, differential changes in dendritic ensembles become obvious in the increased length of proximal and distal segments in both areas of the right hemisphere and an increase in the numbers of distal segments in the left hemisphere, especially in LB. Of particular interest here is an apparent developing difference in growth strategies in the two hemispheres: more numerous distal dendrites on the left side versus longer but fewer distal dendrites on the right (Table 3).

TABLE 2
TABULAR SUMMARY OF THE 17 SUBJECTS USED IN THIS
DEVELOPMENTAL STUDY OF LANGUAGE CORTEX

Age group	Brain age	Sex	Source	DTO
3 months	3 months	Female	LACC	16 hr
	3 months	Male	LACC	27 hr
	3 months	Male	LACC	25 hr
	3 months	Male	LACC	24 hr
5–6 months	5 months	Male	LACC	28 hr
	6 months	Female	LACC	19 hr
	6 months	Male	LACC	24 hr
12–15 months	12 months	Male	LACC	62 hr
	15 months	Male	LACC	27 hr
24–36 months	24 months	Male	LACC	57 hr
	24 months	Female	LACC	17 hr
	36 months	Female	LACC	24 hr
	36 months	Female	LACC	48 hr
42–72 months	42 months	Male	CHS	24 hr
	48 months	Female	LACC	27 hr
	60 months	Male	CHS	22 hr
	72 months	Male	LACC	60 hr

Note. DTO, time from death until osmic acid fixation; LACC, Los Angeles County Coroner; CHS, Center for Health Sciences, UCLA.

During the 12- to 15-month period there is a substantial increase in total dendritic length in both areas of the left hemisphere compared to those on the right. However, motor areas on both sides continue to exceed the presumptive speech areas in total dendritic length and distal segment lengths, and those on the left now exceed those on the right.

Between 24 and 36 months, an enhanced pace of dendritic growth in LB and RB now enables these areas to exceed that of the motor zones, particularly LM. However, maximal distal segment length is now found in RB, which exceeds that of all other areas, suggesting that functions of the right opercularis–traingularis zone may be expanding more rapidly at this time.

In the oldest group that we studied (42 to 72 months), development of both motor speech zones (LB and RB) are preeminent. The LB exceeds all others in total dendritic length, distal segment length exceeds proximal in both speech areas, and both LB and RB exceed their respective motor areas in total dendritic length. From this, we infer that the process of lateralization of speech function is now well advanced, and the computational demands of maturing language function exceed those imposed by the control of orofacial musculature.

SOME THOUGHTS ON CORTICAL DEVELOPMENT

Although the problematic nature of these data is clear, several tentative conclusions can nevertheless be drawn, conclusions that must be considered

TABLE 3

Tissue Specimen Analysis by Grouped Segment Length

	Segment length		
	Proximal	Distal	Overall
3 months	N.S.		
Brain	N.S.	N.S.	N.S.
Hemisphere	RM > LB°°°°°	N.S.	RM > LB°°°°
Region			RM > LM°°°°
			RM > RB°°°°
5–6 months	Distal > proximal for LB, LM, RB		
Brain	RH > LH°°°°	N.S.	N.S.
Hemisphere	RM > LB°°	N.S.	N.S.
Region	RM > RB°°		
	RM > LM°°°		
	LM > LB°°		
12–15 months	N.S.	N.S.	N.S.
Brain	N.S.	N.S.	N.S.
Hemisphere	LM > RB°°		RM > RB°
Region	RM > RM°°°°		LM > RB°
	LB > RB°°		LM > LB°°
	LM > LB°°		LB > RB°°°°
24–36 months	Distal > proximal for LM, RB, RM		
Brain	N.S.	N.S.	N.S.
Hemisphere	RB > LM°°	N.S.	LB > LM°°°°
Region	LB > LM°°°°		RB > LM°°°°°
	RM > LM°°		
42–72 months	Distal > proximal for LB, RB		
Brain	N.S.	N.S.	N.S.
Hemisphere	N.S.	LB > RM°	LB > LM°
Region		LB > LM°	LB > RM°
		RB > RM°°	RB > RM°
		RB > LB°°°°°	LB > RB°°°°
			RB > LM°°°°

Note. *t*-test analysis: °p < .005; °°p < .01; °°°p < .02; °°°°p < .05; °°°°°p < .1; N.S., not significant. Values for left Broca area only become significantly greater than all other areas in the 42- to 72-month period. LH, left hemisphere; RH, right hemisphere; LB, left Broca; RB, right Broca; LM, left motor; RM, right motor. From R. J. Simonds & A. B. Scheibel, 1989. The postnatal development of the motor speech area: A preliminary study. *Brain and Language, 37*, 42–58. Copyright 1989 by Academic Press. Reprinted by permission.

available for reshaping as a more extensive and definitive range of data becomes available. As the dimensions and topography of dendritic ensembles are followed through the first 6 years of life, the complex and multifaceted nature of dendritic growth is emphasized. Not only do neurons in adjacent but functionally diverse cortical areas follow different development schedules but, even more dramatically, similarly situated pyramidal cells in the two hemispheres may show different growth strategies. Thus, anatomic and physiological asymmetries undoubtedly develop as part of a multimodal process during the early life of the organism.

TABLE 4

RELATIONSHIP BETWEEN THE PRESENCE (+) AND ABSENCE (−) OF DISTAL DENDRITE SEGMENTS
TO THE LENGTH (MEAN ± S.D.) OF PROXIMAL DENDRITE SYSTEMS

	(+) Distal segments		(−) Distal segments			
	n	Length of proximal system	n	Length of proximal system	t	p
3 months						
LB	32	203.62 ± 92.84	20	331.35 ± 154.20	3.37	<.001
LM	33	215.18 ± 92.28	17	403.64 ± 124.85	6.05	<.001
RB	38	220.60 ± 98.75	12	376.25 ± 145.21	4.22	<.001
RM	34	238.73 ± 91.67	16	386.25 ± 92.45	5.29	<.001
5–6 months						
LB	36	216.11 ± 112.34	2	342.00 ± 90.50	1.55	.129
LM	34	218.41 ± 94.91	6	421.50 ± 160.03	4.33	<.001
RB	31	230.29 ± 113.93	9	285.00 ± 99.75	1.30	.201
RM	31	289.67 ± 104.61	10	386.60 ± 115.61	2.48	.017
12–15 months						
LB	18	220.05 ± 73.92	10	285.70 ± 102.34	1.96	.060
LM	18	273.72 ± 138.11	7	341.00 ± 138.93	1.09	.286
RB	14	193.28 ± 58.35	11	209.09 ± 76.77	0.58	.563
RM	21	233.19 ± 80.03	3	406.66 ± 146.15	3.18	.004
24–36 months						
LB	52	282.07 ± 130.27	9	379.55 ± 155.38	2.01	.048
LM	51	222.37 ± 95.68	10	363.50 ± 161.04	3.77	<.001
RB	43	269.37 ± 129.86	14	407.57 ± 104.34	3.61	<.001
RM	45	260.13 ± 127.44	13	395.30 ± 139.46	3.29	.001
42–72 months						
LB	54	279.77 ± 103.37	10	373.70 ± 198.97	2.23	.028
LM	46	264.30 ± 119.50	17	324.17 ± 108.21	1.80	.075
RB	47	267.25 ± 113.15	10	414.30 ± 167.55	3.41	.001
RM	47	251.85 ± 114.03	10	345.00 ± 226.80	1.92	.059

Note. There is a strong trend, often at significant levels, for mean proximal dendrite length values to be smaller where distal dendrite systems exist. From R. J. Simonds & A. B. Scheibel, 1989. The postnatal development of the motor speech area: A preliminary study. *Brain and Language, 37,* 42–58. Copyright 1989 by Academic Press. Reprinted by permission.

A significant part of this process seems to consist of continuous plastic reshaping even as the basic sequence of lengthening and branching proceeds. The dimensions of proximal and distal branches appear to bear a complementary relationship to each other. In the absence of distal segments, proximal segments appear to be longer, individually and collectively (Table 4). The growth of distal branches adds significantly to the total length of the dendritic ensemble, but individual proximal segments appear shorter. The possibility that proximal branches may continue to change in length (and diameter?) long after their own terminal bifurcations have generated further orders of peripheral segments underlines the concept of the entire dendritic arbor as a dynamic structural entity.

There are, as yet, no definitive studies on the differential functional roles of proximal and distal dendrites. It does seem quite clear, however, that distance from the soma and initial segment is not a significant determinant of the weight that synapses will play in determining neuronal output. In fact, it has been suggested that special membrane characteristics of the distal dendrite branches or amplification mechanisms situated along the dendrite shafts may actually enhance the effectiveness of distally derived p.s.p. *vis-à-vis* those developing close to the perikaryon (Llinas, 1985; Bras, Destombes, Gagan, & Tyc-Dumont, 1987).

Be that as it may, it seems clear from our two studies of speech cortex that proximal systems and distal systems relate differently to language in both temporal and functional contexts. Proximal systems appear earlier, whereas distal systems appear later. Quantitatively, proximal dendrite segments, both individually and collectively, appear to be longer on the right side than on the left, a situation that seems to be maintained throughout life in right handers. The primacy of proximal segments bilaterally during the first 6 months to 1 year of postnatal life, and their continued primacy on the nondominant speech area, provides suggestive correlations with the affective and prosodic elements of communicative behavior. These are the only "language" components available to the infant during the first year of life and probably continue to represent a major contribution of the right hemisphere to expressive speech in the vast majority of individuals. Conversely, distal segments develop later and reach their ultimate expression in the left hemisphere, which almost always harbors propositional and syntactic speech.

A correlation of this type clearly says nothing about the mechanisms involved. It seems reasonable to hope that with the development of higher-resolution techniques providing more detailed information about the chemical structure and electrodynamics of dendrite membrane, we can develop better insights into these correlations. At present, it may be sufficient to point out that a reasonable amount of information is already available about the structural and electrotonic characteristics of dendrite ensembles. Diameter and taper of dendrite shafts, the number and arrangement of dendrite bifurcations, the distribution and individual morphology of dendrite spines, and the topographical source, functional characteristics, and terminal arrangement of synaptic terminals are all significant in determining the nature of dendritic operations and, presumably, the kind of neural computations subserved (Rall, 1977; Segundo, 1986).

Functional lateralization of the motor speech cortices is one of the most thoroughly established facts of clinical neurology (Broca, 1865; Penfield & Roberts, 1959; Brain, 1961). The temporal sequence for development of this asymmetry, however, has come increasingly under question. Initial equipotentiality of the left and right motor speech cortices has been a generally accepted fact for many years. This position was strongly supported by Lenneberg (1967), who maintained that processes of language acquisition and hemispheric lateralization developed apace, with the final lateralization of language function occurring shortly before puberty. A study of aphasic children led Krashen (1973) to suggest a more rapid pace for the process, with complete lateralization occurring by the sixth year of life. Unilateral hemispherectomy or hemidecortication in very young infants, however, may lead to permanent linguistic defects that are sufficiently robust to raise questions about both of these suggested patterns of differential hemispheric development (Dennis & Kohn, 1975; Dennis & Whitaker, 1976, 1977; Day & Ulatowska, 1979; Dennis, 1980). When either male or female infants were subject to left hemisphere injury or removal, the resulting range of deficits was found to include a number of aspects of spoken language with particular emphasis on the processing and production of complex syntactic units. Curtiss (1985) has concluded that ". . . disruption of the preset specialization of the left hemisphere for language appears to permanently affect linguistic development, even if it occurs in infancy before the process of language acquisition has begun."

Corollary to these findings are data that have come from study of a relatively small number of "wolf" children whose process of language acquisition did not begin until after childhood (Curtiss, 1977; Fromkin, Krashen, Curtiss, Rigler, & Rigler, 1974). In such children, normal language patterns and lateralization of speech function appear to have been seriously and permanently affected. According to Curtiss (1985), language achievements in young adulthood for such patients seem limited to "structural (or computational) linguistic knowledge." Expressed differently, these subjects eventually developed a workable vocabulary but were unable to generate a sentence structure matrix for the words they had learned. Furthermore, when hemispheric function was investigated using event-related potentials, dichotic listening, and tachistoscopic language tasks, it became evident that these right-handed individuals were using their right hemispheres for both language and non-language-related processing. Such data seem to suggest that both language acquisition and normal hemispheric specialization might suffer in the absence of development of language competence in the child.

The notion that structural maturation develops concomitantly with, and may in fact depend on, functional activity is not without precedent. Hubel and Wiesel showed in a number of classic experiments that visual experience is vital to the postnatal maturation of visual cortex (Hubel & Wiesel, 1963; Wiesel & Hubel, 1974) and that such sensory exposure must occur during a well-defined time window (critical period) to be effective. Similarly, Curtiss (1985) suggests that the process of language acquisition—and "more specifically the acquisition of the computational component—may be a crucial trigger for the development of lateralization. If language acquisition is prevented, lateral asymmetries may never be established."

This conception of maturation of speech-related cortex seems somewhat at variance with ideas about hemispheric asymmetries centered about the Sylvian fissure that have received wide acceptance over the past two decades. Geschwind and Levitsky (1968) reported the presence of robust anatomic asymmetries centering on the planum temporale and lateral fissure and related these putatively to language function. In the years that followed, there has been abundant documentation of these observations by a number of investigators (LeMay & Culebras, 1972; Witelson & Pallie, 1973; Wada, Clarke, & Hamm, 1975; Rubens, Mahowald, & Hutton, 1976). Interestingly, such asymmetries are also present in the neonate (Witelson & Pallie, 1973) and have been identified in skull endocasts of Neanderthal and Peking man (Holloway, 1980; Holloway & De La Costa-Lareymondie, 1982). Similar observations have also been reported in the brains of great apes (LeMay & Geschwind, 1981) and Old World monkeys (LeMay, Billig, & Geschwind, 1982). A strong body of evidence accordingly argues not only for the early development of hemispheric asymmetry in human ontogeny but for its long history in primate lineage. From these data it appears that gross cortical asymmetries (the cortical macroenvironment) in what are presumed to be language-involved areas appear both phylogenetically and ontogenetically before the appearance of human language function.

In contradistinction, the process of lateralization of language function and its biological substrate at the neurohistological level (the cortical microenvironment) does not seem to develop until well after birth and then, presumably, only during a critical postnatal time window. This suggests that the maturation of the cortical macroenvironment and microenvironment represent disparate processes with different time scales and different controlling mechanisms. Control of macroenvironmental events might well be genetic, and that of the microenvironment largely epigenetic. Some support for this notion comes from the Diamond group (Lin, Greer, & Diamond, 1987), who have shown a positive correlation between the amount of environmental enrichment and the pace of anatomic lateralization from right hemisphere to left.

Data such as these can only hint at the complexity of maturative processes involved in the development of so complex a cognitive ability as language competence. Indeed, the suggestive evidence for what might be termed a "two-tiered process" for speech cortex maturation could serve as a template for future studies, which may eventually reveal multitiered idiosyncratic developmental sequences at many levels of resolution including synaptic arrays, neurotransmitters, neuronal and glial surface markers, etc.

CONCLUSIONS

The studies summarized here represent a group of early attempts to relate the cortical neurohistological substrate to a few selected elements of cognitive activity. The problematic aspects of this report are, in part, those that inevitably accompany the exclusive use of human material, compounded by the importance and difficulty of obtaining satisfactory background information. Brain tissue is so sensitive a reflector of the genetic inheritance, moods, activities, skills, and challenges of the individual involved that it is almost impossible to have too fine-grained a history of the subject if satisfactory correlations are to be attempted. In a sense, the neurostructural and neurochemical milieu are at once the cause and effect of the history of the individual . . . an organic autobiography.

For a number of reasons, technical, ethical, and compassionate, it has been very difficult in these first studies to obtain more than a bare minimum of information about each individual. In the first study we were able in most cases to learn about handedness and job or profession. But nothing was available about personality, avocation, and life relationships, and even information about the final illness and length of premortem hypoxia was minimal. Aside from handedness, available information was even more meager for the second study, and in the case of the third, literally nothing could be learned about the lives of the accident and acute illness victims whose brain tissue provided information about speech cortex during the first 6 years of life. In the majority of cases, we could not establish the levels of language competence for each of the individuals studied nor even the nature of the primary language (i.e., English, Spanish, Chinese).

Limitations of this sort are unfortunate, especially where the focus of the study is based in attempted correlations between structure and function. Quite clearly, a more effective level of information must be available if our understanding of the substrates of cognitive activities is to increase. This should entail more complete clinical chart records, a more understanding attitude about the nature and importance of basic research on human tissue by pathologists and coroners, and the opportunity to involve families as colleagues in the pursuit of knowledge.

Summary

The purpose of this group of studies was to seek correlations between dendritic structure in selected areas of the cerebral cortex and human behavior at several levels of complexity. Despite the inevitable problems that arise in human studies of this type, several initial impressions deserve to be noted.

1. Correlation appears to exist between the pattern and complexity of dendrite ensembles and the nature of the computational task involved.

2. This correlation may be expressed in total length of dendrite tree, in "branchiness" of the dendrite ensemble, or in the relative proportion of the dendrite system made up of lower-order versus higher-order dendrite segments.

3. Dendrite systems are plastic in nature. In addition to growth (or loss) of peripheral (higher-order) segments, there is some evidence that central (lower-order) segments may also lengthen or shorten even in the presence of extensive branching at their peripheral termini.

4. Dendrite systems from cortical areas presumably supporting different functions show idiosyncratic structural patterns.

5. Comparison of cortical pyramidal cells in the left opercular (Broca's area) and right opercular areas of the frontal lobe reveal differences in organization of the dendritic ensemble, probably related to their qualitatively different contributions to expressive speech.

6. Study of the left and right opercular ("motor speech") zones in an age-graded series of human infants (3 months to 6 years) indicates that dendrite

systems on the right side initially exceed those on the left. After the first 6 to 12 months of postnatal life, higher-order dendrite systems on the left (speech-dominant) side begin to exceed those of the right. Differential patterns of development of the two sides proceed somewhat unevenly during the next 5 years, but by 72 months dendrite systems on the left appear generally more complex than those on the right and begin to approximate in appearance those described in the Broca area of adult human cortex.

7. Patterns of gross hemispheric asymmetry (the cortical macroenvironment) and histological asymmetry (the cortical microenvironment) appear to have a vastly different time scale. The former is tentatively associated with genetic factors; the latter largely with epigenetic factors. This putative two-tiered pattern of cortical differentiation is suggested as a possible model for even more complex developmental sequences, each with its own time scale. It also underlines the importance of a suggested "critical window" for the development of language competence, a period during which functional (language acquisition) activity is essential to maturation of the language brain.

REFERENCES

Brain, W. R. (1961). *Speech disorders, aphasia, apraxia, and agnosia.* London: Butterworths.

Bras, H., Destombes, J., Gogan, P., & Tyc-Dumont, S. (1987). The dendrites of single brain-stem motoneurons intracellularly labelled with horseradish peroxidase in the cat. An ultrastructural analysis of the synaptic covering and the microenvironment. *Neuroscience, 22,* 971-981.

Broca, P. (1865). Du siège de la faculté du langage articulé. *Bulletin et Mémoire de Société d'Anthropologie, Paris, 6,* 377-393.

Buell, S. J. (1982). Golgi-Cox and rapid Golgi methods as applied to autopsied human brain tissue: Widely disparate results. *Journal of Neuropathology and Experimental Neurology, 41,* 500-507.

Conel, J. (1939-1959). *The postnatal development of the human cerebral cortex* (Vols. 1-6). Cambridge: Harvard University Press.

Connor, J. R., Melone, J. H., Yuen, A. R., & Diamond, M. C. (1981). Dendritic length in aged rats' occipital cortex. An environmentally-induced response. *Experimental Neurology, 73,* 827-830.

Curtiss, S. (1977). *Genie: A psycholinguistic study of a modern-day "wild child."* New York: Academic Press.

Curtiss, S. (1985). The development of human cerebral lateralization. In D. F. Benson & E. Zaidel (Eds.), *The dual brain* (pp. 97-116). New York: Guilford Press.

Dax, G. (1865). Lésions de la moitié gauche de l'encéphale coincidant avec trouble des signs de la pensée. *Gazette Hebdomadaire Médical et Chirurgical, 2nd Series, 2,* 259.

Day, P. S., & Ulatowska, H. K. (1979). Perceptual, cognitive and linguistic development after early hemispherectomy. Two case studies. *Brain and Language, 7,* 17-33.

Dennis, M. (1980). Capacity and strategy for syntactic comprehension after left or right hemidecortication. *Brain and Language, 10,* 287-317.

Dennis, M., & Kohn, B. (1975). Comprehension of syntax in infantile hemiplegics after cerebral hemidecortication: Left hemisphere superiority. *Brain and Language, 2,* 472–482.

Dennis, M., & Whitaker, H. (1976). Language acquisition following hemidecortication: Linguistic superiority of the left over the right hemisphere. *Brain and Language, 3,* 404–433.

Dennis, M., & Whitaker, H. (1977). Hemispheric equipotentiality and language acquisition. In S. Segalowitz & F. Grular (Eds.), *Language development and neurological theory* (pp. 93–106). New York: Academic Press.

Freud, S. (1946). *Collected papers* (Vols. I–V). London: Hogarth Press.

Fromkin, V., Krashen, S., Curtiss, S., Rigler, D., & Rigler, M. (1974). The development of language in Genie: A case of language acquisition beyond the "critical period." *Brain and Language, 1,* 81–107.

Gardner, H., Brownell, H. H., Wapner, W., & Michelow, D. (1983). Missing the point: The role of the right hemisphere in the processing of complex linguistic material. In E. Perecman (Ed.), *Cognitive processing in the right hemisphere* (pp. 169–191). New York: Academic Press.

Geschwind, N., & Levitsky, W. (1968). Human brain left–right asymmetries in temporal speech region. *Science, 161,* 186–187.

Holloway, R. L. (1980). Indonesian "Solo" [Ngandong] endocranial reconstructions: Some preliminary observations and comparisons with Neanderthal and *Homo erectus* groups. *American Journal of Physical Anthropology, 53,* 285–295.

Holloway, R. L., & De La Coste-Lareymondie, M. C. (1982). Brain endocast asymmetry in Pongids and Hominids: Some preliminary findings on the paleontology of cerebral dominance. *American Journal of Physical Anthropology, 58,* 101–110.

Hubel, D. H., & Wiesel, T. N. (1963). Receptive fields of cells in striate cortex of very young, visually inexperienced kittens. *Journal of Neurophysiology, 26,* 994–1002.

Krashen, S. (1973). Lateralization, language learning and the critical period: Some new evidence. *Language Learning, 23,* 63–74.

Le May, M., Billig, M. S., & Geschwind, N. (1982). Asymmetries of the brains and skulls of non-human primates. In E. Armstrong & A. Falk (Eds.), *Primate brain evolution: Methods and concepts.* New York: Plenum Press.

Le May, M., & Culebras, A. (1972). Human brains: Morphological differences in the hemispheres demonstrable by carotid arteriography. *New England Journal of Medicine, 287,* 168–170.

Le May, M., & Geschwind, N. (1981). Morphological cerebral asymmetries in primates. In B. Preilowsky & C. Engele (Eds.), *Is there cerebral hemispheric asymmetry in non-human primates?* Tübingen: University of Tübingen.

Lenneberg, E. H. (1967). *Biological foundations of language.* New York: John Wiley & Sons.

Lin, J. C., Greer, E. R., & Diamond, M. C. (1987). Altered patterns of cerebral cortical lateralization in male rats with increased levels of environment complexity. *Society of Neuroscience Abstracts, 13,* 1594.

Llinas, R. (1985, September 8). Role of dendritic excitability in neuronal integration. In *The function of dendrites,* IBRO Satellite Symposium, Oxford.

Penfield, W., & Boldrey, E. (1937). Somatic motor and sensory representation in the cerebral cortex of man as studied by electrical stimulation. *Brain, 60,* 389–443.

Penfield, W., & Rasmussen, T. (1950). *The cerebral cortex of man: A clinical study of localization of function.* New York: Macmillan.

Penfield, W., & Roberts, L. (1959). *Speech and brain mechanisms.* Princeton, NJ: Princeton University Press.

Piaget, J. (1954). *The construction of reality in the child*. New York: Basic Books.

Pribram, K. H. (1987). The subdivisions of the frontal cortex revisited. In E. Perecman (Ed.), *The frontal lobes revisited* (pp. 11–40). New York: IRBN Press.

Rall, W. (1977). Core conductor theory and cable properties of neurons. In J. M. Brookhart, V. B. Mountcastle, & E. R. Kandel (Eds.), *Handbook of physiology. The nervous system* (Vol. 1, Part 1, pp. 39–97). Bethesda: American Physiological Society.

Rubens, A. B., Mahowald, M. W., & Hutton, J. T. (1976). Asymmetry of the lateral (Sylvian) fissures in man. *Neurology, 26,* 620–624.

Scheibel, A. B. (1988). Dendritic correlates of human cortical functions. *Archives Italiennes de Biologie, 126,* 347–357.

Scheibel, A. B., Conrad, T., Perdue, S., Tomiyasu, U., & Wechsler, U. (in press). A quantitative study of dendrite complexity in selected areas of the human cerebral cortex. *Brain and Cognition.*

Scheibel, A. B., Fried, I., Paul, L., Forsythe, A., Tomiyasu, U., Wechsler, A., Kao, A., & Slotnick, J. (1985). Differentiating characteristics of the human speech cortex: A quantitative Golgi study. In D. F. Benson & E. Zaidel (Eds.), *The dual brain* (pp. 65–74). New York: Guilford Press.

Scheibel, A. B., Paul, L. A., Fried, I., Forsythe, A. B., Tomiyasu, U., Wechsler, A., Kao, A., & Slotnick, J. (1985). Dendritic organization of the anterior speech area. *Experimental Neurology, 87,* 109–117.

Segundo, J. P. (1986). What can neurons do to serve as integrating devices? *Journal of Theoretical Neurobiology, 5,* 1–59.

Sherrington, C. S. (1937). *Man on his nature. The Gifford lectures*. Edinburgh/New York: Macmillan.

Sholl, D. A. (1956). *The organization of the cerebral cortex*. New York: John Wiley & Sons.

Simonds, R. J., & Scheibel, A. B. (1989). The postnatal development of the motor speech area: A preliminary study. *Brain and Language, 37,* 42–58.

Wada, J. A., Clarke, R. C., & Hamm, A. (1975). Cerebral hemispheric asymmetry in humans. *Archives of Neurology, 32,* 239–246.

Wiesel, T. N., & Hubel, D. H. (1974). Ordered arrangement of orientation columns in monkeys lacking visual experience. *Journal of Comparative Neurology, 158,* 307–318.

Williams, R. S., Ferrante, R. J., & Caviness, V. S., Jr. (1978). The Golgi rapid method in clinical neuropathology: The morphological consequences of suboptimal fixations. *Journal of Neuropathology and Experimental Neurology, 37,* 13–33.

Witelson, S. F., & Pallie, W. A. (1973). Left hemisphere specialization for language in the newborn: Neuroanatomical evidence of asymmetry. *Brain, 96,* 641–646.

Zaidel, E. (1985). Language in the right hemisphere. In D. F. Benson & E. Zaidel (Eds.), *The dual brain* (pp. 205–231). New York: Guilford Press.

DISCUSSION

SANDRA WITELSON: I understand that you're suggesting that initially in the immature state the cortical systems may be more advanced on the right than on the left side. In other words, at the microscopic level it may not be the same very early in life, as is the case at maturity. If I understand you correctly, then the psychological data are completely in agreement with your hypothesis that the two hemispheres really are neither the same nor equivalent. There may be some equipotentiality following brain damage, but that doesn't mean that the receptive substrate is equivalent. The concept of plasticity doesn't rule out specialization right from the beginning. There may be specialization plus plasticity. In the psychological data, for example, the electrophysiological work using evoked potentials in 2- or 3-month-old infants showed that phonemic discrimination is better in the dichotic listening situation when it is delivered to the right than left ear, just as in the adult. Everything suggests that there is functional asymmetry as early as it has been able to be tested.

ARNOLD SCHEIBEL: Much of that, of course, may depend on the level of perception and discrimination and on the response we're examining. But it's very possible. You know, a cell with second- and third-order dendrites is already a fairly complex unit, and since we usually have this much on both sides at term birth, it may well be that there are no problems. When we come to the much more difficult problems of language comprehension and utilization, it may be that by that time we need a great deal more dendritic tissue. No one knows what the computational schemes are that occur along these dendrite systems. I can't directly answer, but I don't see it as a limitation at this point. I think there are lots of other problems with the idea, but I don't think that that is necessarily a limiting parameter.

DEEPAK PANDYA: In which layer are these pyramidal neurons?

SCHEIBEL: That's a very good question; I'm sorry I didn't speak to that. That's another problem with our study. In the analysis of the adult Broca regions, we used supragranular cells, that is to say, cells in deep layer 2 and all of layer 3. These were what we wanted because of their late maturation. In the developmental study, we could not get dependable staining of supragranular elements, so we had to shift down to the layer 5 pyramidal cells. That is another serious constraint. We're not comparing the same cell systems.

GLENN ROSEN: This is just a follow-up on the point that Sandra made. One of the things that impressed me about the data is that the areas you're measuring are primarily concerned with the articulation of speech. What would you expect to see if you were to move into a more posterior language area? I am asking this because we know that infants can distinguish language quite early in life. Some studies by Mehler and colleagues found that newborn infants could distinguish between two languages spoken by a bilingual person, one of the languages being the mother tongue. So we know that they're doing something with language at that age, even though it may not include articulation.

SCHEIBEL: I want you to know that George Ojemann is laughing at us both as you articulate that question. That's precisely what we want to do now. A new student of mine, who is a linguist, has joined the laboratory to work with me on the progressive development of the Wernicke area. Our problem is going to be to figure out exactly where we shall work, because George's data show that no one spot will always be a Wernicke-relevant zone. That is the next step. But now, in addition to the morphology, we want to do some cytochrome oxidase studies and, if possible, look at one long-lingering neurotransmitter to see if we can see anything else. Again it's like looking for your keys in a dark parking lot. You look under the lights.

ISAK PROHOVNIK: What do we know about the correlation between dendritic proliferation and morphology and the consequences of the enriched environment in rats that we heard about yesterday. Are those two phenomena highly correlated? The other less serious question is this: I don't know if the controversy has yet been settled whether apes can develop language or not, but if it has, and if there are talking apes, is somebody looking at their brains when they die?

SCHEIBEL: I might answer the second one first. The number of talking apes is, of course, much smaller than the number of talking humans. We would not be adverse to looking at the brains of talking apes, but we do have to get them, and we'll have to wait and see. With regard to the first question, it's extremely relevant. It would be great fun to get the brain of a great orator, for example. As a matter of fact, one of our problems is chicken or egg. In the gifted typist or the great pianist, do they have magnificent hand–finger areas because they were born that way and developed the skills, or did they develop the skills and produce the structural changes secondarily? Marian's work would suggest that the second is equally important. I suspect that it may be even more important.

ROSEN: What are the inputs to the dendrites that expand? And my other question is how can you be sure that the decrease in length of the left proximal dendrite branches occurs because they sprout peripheral branches?

SCHEIBEL: As to the nature of the input to them, we haven't studied them and don't yet know them. That's a very powerful question. I don't know how to address it. So far as the lengthening and shortening of dendrites, that's a very interesting subject. Our data suggest the following: if you study cells that have only early-order dendrites, that is, first, second, and third order, and then you study companion cells of roughly the same size but that also have fourth- and fifth- and maybe sixth-order branches, you find in *every* case that the first- and second- and third-order dendrites are much shorter in the second group. Some years ago, Bob Lindsay and I did a rather careful computer-based developmental analysis of dentate granule cells. It strongly suggested that dendrites seem to have an increasing tendency to bifurcate as they approach a certain length; in other words, a kind of minimax range of values beyond which the likelihood of bifurcation becomes very high. It may be that there are certain constraints on the total length of any dendrite order. Our new data could be interpreted now as suggesting that there is secondary shortening as the more peripheral branch orders develop, so the accordion effect can't be totally ignored.

ELECTROPHYSIOLOGICAL STUDIES OF VISUAL SELECTIVE ATTENTION IN HUMANS

GEORGE R. MANGUN, PhD, and STEVEN A. HILLYARD, PhD
University of California, San Diego

INTRODUCTION

The processing of sensory information by a human observer begins with transduction of physical stimuli at peripheral receptors and continues through multiple stages of neural analysis that lead to perception and awareness. A key element in this processing sequence is the selection of relevant environmental events for further analyses and/or the attenuation of irrelevant events. One means of selection involves the directing of sensory receptors toward relevant stimuli. For example, foveation of a visual stimulus aligns it with retinal regions of highest acuity. In addition to movements of the head and eyes, stimulus selection is achieved via powerful covert mechanisms of attention that differentially influence the neural processing of relevant and irrelevant stimuli. Both psychological and physiological theories concerning these attentional mechanisms have emphasized the distinction between early and late stimulus selection. From a psychological perspective, "early" refers to selection of a relevant event that occurs before its properties are fully analyzed; such selection is possible when an easily discriminable feature of the stimulus (e.g., location, color) allows it to be distinguished from irrelevant stimuli (Adrian, 1954; Broadbent, 1958, 1971; Treisman, 1964). "Late" selection theories of attention specify that all features of a stimulus be analyzed fully before selection is possible (Deutsch & Deutsch, 1963; Norman, 1968).

Although the psychological distinction between early and late selection is generally not specified in neural terms, it has a counterpart in physiological theories of selective attention. In principle, the flow of sensory information could be regulated at the relatively early subcortical levels of the afferent pathways or sensory cortices or, alternatively, at the relatively late stages of processing in cortical association areas. One possible mechanism for early selection would be

Acknowledgments: This research was supported by grants from the National Institute of Mental Health (MH 25594) and National Institutes of Health (NS17778) and by Office of Naval Research contract N00014-86-K-0291. G.R.M. was supported by NIMH Research Service Award 1 F31 MH09360.

the differential processing of relevant and irrelevant information in the ascending sensory pathways via the modulatory influence of descending neural systems. Theoretically, such a sensory "gating" or filtering mechanism could operate in cortical sensory areas, thalamic relay nuclei (Skinner & Yingling, 1977; Singer, 1977), or at the sensory receptors themselves (Hernandez-Peon, 1966). As used here, sensory gating refers to selective descending control over the gain of sensory transmission in an afferent pathway that does not involve the activation of additional populations of sensory neurons.

PHYSIOLOGICAL STUDIES OF VISUAL–SPATIAL ATTENTION IN HUMANS

Physiological mechanisms of selective attention can be investigated in humans by recording event-related brain potentials (ERPs) elicited by attended and ignored stimuli (e.g., Eason, Harter, & White, 1969; Van Voorhis & Hillyard, 1977). ERPs are voltage fluctuations recorded from the scalp that are time-locked to sensory, motor, or cognitive processes and are resolved from the ongoing EEG using signal averaging. ERPs can index stages of neuronal processing beginning as early as a few milliseconds post-stimulus and continuing as long as several hundreds of milliseconds. The successive positive and negative voltage deflections in the ERP are characterized by a latency that indicates the timing of underlying neuronal activity, a scalp distribution determined by the anatomic orientation of the neuronal generator(s), and an amplitude determined by the net synaptic activity in the participating neuronal population(s). These properties of the ERP are typically sensitive to the physical parameters of the eliciting stimulus and may be influenced by the attentive state of the experimental subject as well. Thus, ERPs can be used to study the timing, neural locus, and functional properties of stimulus selection processes as subjects attend to different classes of stimulus features (Hillyard & Kutas, 1983; Hillyard & Picton, 1987).

The primary focus of the present chapter is on reviewing recent evidence from ERP studies of visual–spatial attention. It is well established that attention can be voluntarily directed toward particular locations in the visual field and that stimuli falling at or near attended locations are processed more efficiently. This facilitated processing is evident in the improved detectability or discriminability of attended-location stimuli and/or in speeded reaction times for stimulus identification (Bashinski & Bacharach, 1980; Eriksen & Yeh, 1985; Jonides, 1981; Posner, Snyder, & Davidson, 1980; Prinzmetal, Presti, & Posner, 1986). One basic issue that remains unresolved concerns the locus of this selectivity of processing— whether spatial attention influences the amount or quality of perceptual information that is received or whether it only impacts subsequent decision processes (Downing, 1988; Muller & Findlay, 1987; Shaw, 1984). In other words, is sensory transmission modulated at an early, "intraperceptual" level (Johnston & Dark, 1982), or does sensory information build up automatically, outside of attentional control. The present chapter considers this question of early versus late selection from the perspective of electrophysiological studies of visual ERPs in human subjects.

The basic paradigm used to study visual–spatial attention is shown in Figure 1, where stimulus-evoked electrical activity from the occipital scalp is amplified and signal averaged to produce the visual ERP. In this design, stimuli are flashed one at a time in a rapid sequence to left and right visual field locations in a randomized order. Subjects maintain fixation of their eyes on a central point while attending exclusively to the stimuli on one side at a time. The assigned task is to detect and respond to infrequent target stimuli embedded in the stream of

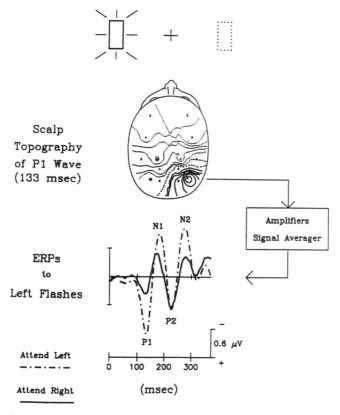

Figure 1. Visual ERP changes in a typical spatial attention task. Stimuli (top) were bars flashed on a video screen in random order to locations 5° to the left and right of fixation (+); ISIs were randomized between 250 and 500 msec. The subjects' task was to attend to and discriminate the height of the bars at one location (ignoring the other) and to press a button on detection of a slightly shorter bar (target) that occurred 10% of the time. Attention is sustained on one location for the duration of a 1 to 2-minute run. The predominant response to a left flash begins as a positive voltage shift (P1 wave) over the contralateral occipital scalp onsetting at 90–100 msec latency (topographic voltage map, middle). Overlaid (bottom) are ERPs to left flashes when attended (dot-dash) and ignored (attend right; solid).

stimuli at that location; the stimuli that occur on the other side are to be ignored. Attention is sustained to one or the other side for the duration of each 1- to 2-minute run in a counterbalanced order. Thus, ERPs are recorded to both left and right stimuli when attended and when ignored. Since the eyes remain fixed on the same central location, and the stimuli are identical in the attend-left and attend-right conditions, differences in the ERPs to a lateral stimulus when attended versus when ignored can be interpreted in terms of stimulus selection processes.

The visual ERP elicited by stimuli such as the flashed bars shown in Figure 1 consists of a series of positive and negative voltage fluctuations over the posterior scalp. The main attention-sensitive components include the P1 (peaking at 100–140 msec), N1 (160–200 msec), P2 (220–250 msec), and N2 (260–300 msec) waves. Shown in Figure 1 are the ERPs elicited to left-field flashes when attended (dot-dash line) and ignored (solid line). The ERP elicited by the stimulus when attended contains enhanced P1, N1, and N2 peaks (and sometimes P2 as well) as compared to the ERP elicited by the same stimulus when ignored (i.e., when attending the opposite-field stimuli). The effect of attention is manifest as an amplitude modulation of these peaks without any changes in their latencies, polarities, or wave shapes. Such a result is consistent with a mechanism of sensory gating, since it implies that the principal effect of attention on the neural generators of these sensory-evoked components is simply to increase or decrease their level of activation. These attention-related changes in activity are presumed to be the result of descending neural influences on either the inputs to the early ERP generators or the activity of the generators themselves.

Evidence from mappings of ERP scalp distributions also supports this sensory gating interpretation (Hillyard & Mangun, 1987; Mangun & Hillyard, 1988). If the mechanism of spatial attention involved a simple amplitude modulation of the activity of those neural elements coding a particular stimulus, then it would be expected that the scalp topography of the associated ERP components would be invariant across attention conditions. Topographic voltage maps showing isopotential contour lines for the P1 component (at 133 msec) to left flashes are presented in Figure 2 as a function of attention condition. The scalp location of the positive voltage maximum to the same physical stimulus does not change as a function of whether the stimulus is attended or ignored, indicating that the same neural elements are being activated; only the amplitude of the evoked signal is changed with attention. Thus, these ERP results are consistent with the hypothesis that the earliest effects of spatial attention involve a mechanism of sensory gain control.

The precise location in the visual pathway of this gain control mechanism is uncertain, but the timing and topographical distribution of the attention-sensitive P1 component provide some clues. In accordance with the anatomic projection of the geniculostriate pathway to visual cortex, the location of the attention-sensitive P1 scalp maximum is located over the occipital scalp contralateral to the visual field of the stimulus. Figure 3 shows the typical scalp topography of the P1

P1 Scalp Topography To Left Flashes

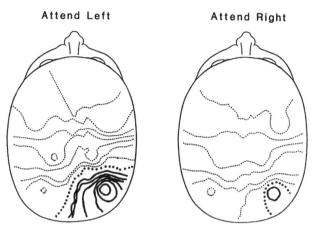

Figure 2. Isopotential contour plots show the distribution of the P1 component of the visual ERP over the scalp at 133 msec latency. Shown are the plots for bars flashed in the left visual field when attended (left) and ignored (right). The scalp location of the positive maximum is over the lateral occipital region contralateral to the visual field of the stimulus. Dotted line, zero voltage; broken lines, negative voltage values; solid lines, positive voltage values. Voltage increments 0.16 μV for each line traversed.

component (Mangun & Hillyard, 1988) juxtaposed with a sketch of the underlying cortical areas based on recent anatomic studies of the correspondence between cortical anatomy and surface electrode sites (Homan, Herman, & Purdy, 1987). The location of the P1 scalp maximum is over the lateral occipital scalp (at electrode site F), which approximately overlies the extrastriate visual cortex (areas 18 and 19). Although it is not possible to localize the neural generator of the P1 component precisely on the basis of the evidence presented here, these data are in line with a radially oriented dipole generator located in extrastriate cortex. Such a finding is of interest given the recent work in monkey visual cortex using single-unit recording techniques that have demonstrated neurons in extrastriate area V4 that are attention sensitive (Boch & Fischer, 1983; Fischer & Boch, 1985; Moran & Desimone, 1985; Spitzer, Desimone, & Moran, 1988). Thus, the ERP evidence suggests that spatial attention involves a mechanism of sensory gain control that operates at or before the level of extrastriate visual cortex.

Although the P1 component is almost certainly of cortical origin, the attention-related changes in P1 activity could possibly reflect modulations of inputs to the P1 generator at earlier cortical or even thalamic levels as well (Eason et al., 1969; Skinner & Yingling, 1977). It should be noted that this pattern of early ERP change suggestive of sensory gain control appears to be uniquely characteristic of visual–spatial attention. Selections based on other visual features such as color or

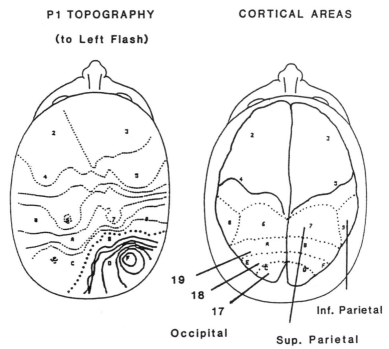

Figure 3. Schematic representation of the relationship between scalp surface electrode sites and underlying cortical areas. Electrode F (left), the site of the amplitude maximum of the attention-sensitive P1 component, overlies the extrastriate cortex near the area 18–19 border (right).

shape are associated with very different ERP patterns; these effects are discussed in a subsequent section.

The Attentional "Spotlight"

A basic property of spatial selective attention is the size of the visual field region that receives facilitated processing. Is the influence of spatial attention confined to a circumscribed zone immediately surrounding the attended stimulus, or is it distributed more broadly? Some authors have described the distribution of attention in space in terms of a narrow "spotlight" (e.g., Posner et al., 1980). In the spotlight analogy, attention facilitates the processing of objects that lie within the boundaries of the attentional "beam," leaving stimuli located outside the beam unfacilitated (or suppressed) to the same extent regardless of their proximity to the attended location. In contrast, others have suggested that spatial attention is more broadly distributed in the form of a "gradient" across visual space (Downing & Pinker, 1985; Shulman, Wilson, & Sheehy, 1985; Shulman, Sheehy, & Wilson, 1986). Such a gradient of attention would yield a maximal enhancement of perceptual processing at the attended location, dropping off gradually with distance away from that location. In some accounts, the distribution of attention may be so broad as to involve the facilitation or inhibition of an entire visual hemifield (Hughes & Zimba, 1987).

The behavioral evidence for attentional gradients has come from studies in which simple reaction time (RT) is the dependent measure. Unfortunately, the RT measure does not readily distinguish between changes in sensory processing and the biasing of decision and/or response processes. Thus, for example, in the studies showing gradients of attention, RTs could be prolonged for stimuli farther from the attentional focus because of elevated decision criteria for those events rather than as a consequence of attentional influences on perceptual processing. An additional confounding factor with the RT method is that responses must be directed toward nominally unattended events. This might cause the subject's attention to be partially divided rather than strictly focused on the attended locations. Using ERPs to study the spatial distribution of attention allows the examination of sensory processes separately from decision/response processes and also allows the measurement of the processing of stimuli to which no overt response is required.

In a preliminary approach to this question we used ERPs to task-irrelevant probe flashes to index the processing of events occurring at varying distances from an attended location (Mangun & Hillyard, 1985). If the spotlight metaphor is accurate, and the attentional beam is narrowly focused, then ERPs to irrelevant probe stimuli should not differ as a function of whether they are located near (3–4°) or far (8–9°) from an attended location. On the other hand, a more extensive zone of visual facilitation during focused attention should result in ERP differences between probes located near versus far from the attended locus.

Figure 4 shows the stimulus array presented to the subjects. Stimuli consisted of task-relevant and irrelevant (probe) stimuli flashed on a video monitor (white on black). Task-relevant flashes consisted of vertically oriented bars (3° × 1°) located in mirror-image positions 2.5° to the left and right of a central fixation point on the horizontal meridian. Targets consisted of shorter bars (2.5° × 1°) that were flashed unpredictably at the task-relevant locations 15% of the time. Irrelevant probe stimuli were small squares (1° × 1°) located 6.0° to the left and right of the central fixation point. The task-relevant and irrelevant probe stimuli were flashed one at a time in random order to the left and right fields with the ISI varying from 300 to 600 msec; all were 100 msec in duration. Separate ERPs were obtained for each of the four stimuli under the two attention conditions: on half of the runs subjects directed their attention solely to the right task-relevant bars, and on the remaining runs they attended the left bar stimuli. The task was to detect and respond to the infrequent targets at the attended location. Thus, in this experiment the task and stimuli were very similar to those described in Figure 1, with the addition of the laterally placed task-irrelevant probe stimuli.

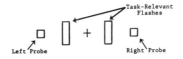

ERPs To

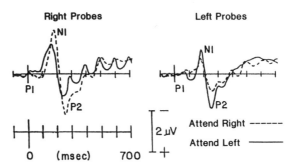

Figure 4. Event-related potentials to irrelevant probe stimuli. Subjects fixated a central point (+) and attended to the task-relevant bar stimuli on one side while ignoring all other stimuli. The task was to detect a shorter "target" bar occurring at the attended location. Subjects maintained attention to one location for the duration of each 1- to 2-minute run, attending the left or right task-relevant bars in different runs in counterbalanced order. The irrelevant probe stimuli were never attended. Grand average ERPs over eight subjects to task-irrelevant probe stimuli are shown when attending the right (dashed line) and left (solid) task-relevant bar stimuli. The ERPs were recorded from occipital scalp sites contralateral to the visual field of the stimulus.

Attention effects for the task-relevant bar stimuli were essentially the same as those described for the related situation in Figure 1. The ERPs to the irrelevant probe stimuli are of primary interest here. The probes occurring in the same hemifield as the attended bars elicited enlarged P1 (P110), N1 (N190), and P2 (P250) components as compared to when the bars were in the opposite visual hemifield (Figure 4). Thus, there was an influence of attention that extended to irrelevant stimuli located some 3–5° away from the attended location. Such a result is not consistent with the idea of a narrowly focused spotlight but instead implies a broader attentional distribution. Thus, the probe technique can provide an index of attentional facilitation for various regions of the visual field independently of the requirement of overt response.

GRADIENTS OF ATTENTION IN SPACE

The results of the above-described probe study do not reveal whether attention was distributed in space as a sloping gradient in this type of task or as an all-or-none zone of facilitataion, perhaps extending over as much as an entire visual hemifield. To get at this question we examined ERP changes as subjects shifted attention among three stimulus locations (Mangun & Hillyard, 1987, 1988). In these studies, bar stimuli were flashed in random order to one of three upper field locations: one in each of the lateral visual fields 5.3° to the left and right of fixation and one on the vertical midline. Subjects attended to the stimuli at one of these three locations for the duration of each 1- to 2-minute run, with their direction of gaze always remaining fixed on a same central spot; each location was attended in turn in a counterbalanced order. The task was to detect and respond to difficult infrequent targets (slightly shorter bars) at the attended location. If visual attention was distributed in a gradient fashion across the visual field, then the ERP amplitude to a stimulus located in the lateral visual field would be expected to decrease progressively as attention was focused first 5° and then 10° from that location.

Figure 5 shows the progressive decline in amplitude of the sensory evoked P1 and N1 components that was observed as attention was directed to flashes at increasing distances from the location of the evoking stimuli. These graded amplitude changes are summarized in the line graphs plotted at the top of Figure 6 (Mangun & Hillyard, 1987). The later N2 component (Figure 5, not plotted in Figure 6) was only elicited by the attended location stimuli and did not show a graded response pattern. These findings suggest that spatial selective attention is distributed as a rather broad gradient across the visual fields at the level of early visual processing but that subsequent stages of selection (indexed by N2) become more narrowly focused to the attended region.

A second study (Mangun & Hillyard, 1988) investigated the perceptual significance of these early graded amplitude changes by obtaining behavioral as well as ERP measures of the attentional gradient. The same stimuli were used as in the previous study, but with a slightly different task assignment. As before, subjects were asked to devote all of their efforts to the "primary" task of detecting infrequent shorter target bars at the attended location and reporting them by pressing a button. This time, however, a "secondary task" was also assigned. Subjects were asked to push a second button in response to shorter target bars in either of the two *unattended* locations if they "happened to notice them" without actively trying to detect them. Secondary target detections would thus give a behavioral measure of perceptual processing in the to-be-ignored stimulus locations.

As in the previous experiment, the amplitudes of the sensory evoked P1 and N1 waves decreased progressively as attention was directed to locations increasingly distant from an evoking lateral stimulus (Figure 6, bottom line graphs). In parallel with this ERP amplitude gradient, the d' measures indicated that a gradient of target detectability was also present. This finding is in line with that of Downing (1988), who showed that d' scores for luminance detection tended to drop off in a graded fashion with increasing separation between expected and actual stimulus locations.

Regression analyses revealed significant between-subject correlations between d' scores for detecting lateral targets and early ERP amplitudes; correla-

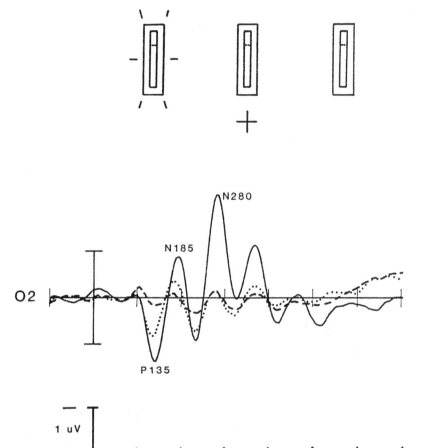

Figure 5. Event-related potential gradients during spatial attention. Subjects fixated a central location (+) while directing their attention to one of the three positions in order to detect infrequent shorter target bars. Overlaid are the ERPs to left flashes recorded from right occipital scalp under attend-left (solid line), attend-midline (dotted line), and attend-right (dashed line) conditions. Both the P1 (P135) and N1 (N185) peaks showed progressive amplitude reductions as attention was focused at increasing distance from the evoking (left) stimulus. In contrast, the N2 (N280) peak was elicited only by the stimulus when attended.

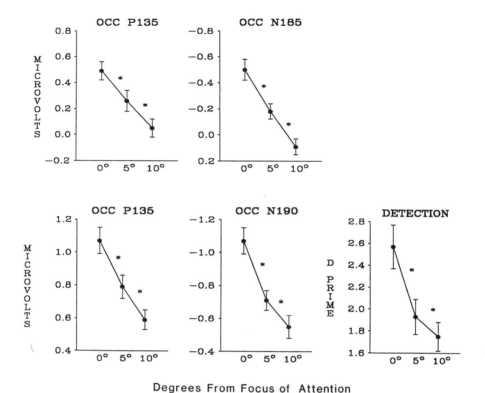

Figure 6. Behavioral and ERP gradients during spatial attention from two experiments. (Top) Line graphs showing that the P1 and N1 waves to lateral flashes were largest when attended, smallest when attending rights (10° away), and of intermediate amplitude when attending midline (5° away). (Bottom) This pattern is replicated in a second experiment for P1 and N1, and in addition, these ERP gradients were paralleled by a gradient of signal detectability.

tions were greatest for the P1 (P135) peak and slightly lower for the N1 peak. This relationship was significant for d' and P1 amplitudes to unattended lateral stimuli (i.e., while subjects attended the midline or opposite-field stimuli) and approached significance for attended stimuli (Figure 7). Such a relationship between measures of perceptual sensitivity and the P1 and N1 peaks is consistent with the hypothesis that the amplitudes of these occipital components are an index of sensory information utilized by the perceptual system.

Despite the significant correlation between d' scores and P1 amplitudes for a given attention condition, the changes in subjects' d' scores between attention conditions did not correlate with the corresponding changes in their P1 amplitudes. Thus, although there was a general increase in both d' scores and P1 amplitudes as attention was moved nearer the evoking stimuli, the ratio of d' change to P1 change was variable among subjects. This variation may reflect differences among individuals in the quantitative scaling relationship between

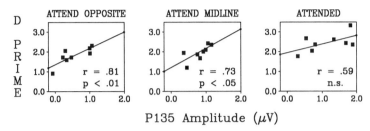

Figure 7. Scatter plots of d' scores and corresponding P135 (P1) amplitudes to lateral stimuli for eight subjects in study by Mangun and Hillyard (1988). Data were collapsed across left and right field flashes and plotted separately for the three attention conditions: attend opposite (top), attend midline (middle), and attended (bottom). The regression lines are indicated along with the correlation coefficient (r) and significance level.

physiological and behavioral variables or may result from subjects adopting different detection strategies *vis-à-vis* the unattended locations.

Another consideration in relating target detection performance to early ERP amplitudes is that accuracy of discriminating the shorter bars may not be a simple function of sensory pathway gain. Although detection accuracy would certainly depend in part on adequate sensory inflow, it would also depend on accurate maintenance of internal target representations (i.e., "templates") and the matching of sensory inputs against them. Thus, variations in d' could result from individual differences in target-matching accuracy that could be partially dissociable from the amount of sensory inflow, which we propose to be indexed initially by P1 amplitude. Nonetheless, the general qualitative relationship between d' increase and P1 increase across the two unattended conditions is in line with the proposition that P1 amplitude indexes sensory input to the perceptual system.

ATTENTION IN SPACE: INTRA-HEMIFIELD MAPPINGS

A further experiment attempted a more extensive mapping of the distribution of visual attention in space (G. R. Mangun & S. A. Hillyard, unpublished results). Several recent behavioral studies have suggested that natural boundaries such as the horizontal and vertical meridians may constrain the distribution of attention (Hughes & Zimba, 1987; Rizzolatti, Riggio, Dascola, & Umiltà, 1987; Tassinari, Aglioti, Chelazzi, Marzi, & Berlucchi, 1987). Since the stimulus displays used in our previous studies could not have revealed within-hemifield patterns, four stimulus locations were used in the present experiment, two in each hemifield.

The four stimulus locations included two "far lateral" stimulus positions located 6.0° to the left and right of the midline and two "near lateral" stimulus positions located 2.0° to the left and right of the midline. All four stimulus locations were in the upper visual field, such that subjects fixated a point in the center of the display, approximately 2.0° below the lower edge of the stimuli.

The four locations were continuously demarcated by vertically oriented gray rectangles (4.6° × 1.1°) on which the flashed stimuli were superimposed. Stimuli consisted of vertically oriented white bars (3.0° × 0.4°) flashed for 67-msec durations one at a time in random order to the four locations, with ISIs varying randomly from 250 to 500 msec (rectangular). Target stimuli consisted of shorter white bars (2.2° × 0.4°) that occurred randomly 10% of the time at a given location. With their eyes fixated centrally, subjects directed their attention to one of the four locations for the duration of a run with the task of detecting the infrequent and unpredictable shorter target stimuli occurring at that location. Each location was attended in turn (counterbalanced order) so that ERPs to each of the eight stimuli (four targets and four nontargets) could be recorded when they were attended as well as when each of the other three locations was attended.

Figure 8 (top) shows grand average ERPs (over 14 subjects) to the far lateral (6°) stimuli in the left (lvf) and right (rvf) visual fields as a function of attention condition. Substantial attention effects were observed for the P1, N1, and N2 components of the ERPs to attended far lateral stimuli recorded over contralateral occipital scalp; these components were largest in amplitude when that location was attended and smallest when attention was directed to the opposite-field far lateral stimuli. Of greatest interest here is the form of the dropoff in amplitude of the P1 and N1 components as attention was shifted at increasing distances away from the lateral stimuli in 4° intervals. Over contralateral scalp the P1 component showed a progressive amplitude decrement as attention was focused at locations progressively farther from the evoking stimuli.* In sharp contrast, the N1 component to the far lateral stimuli did not show a progressive amplitude decrement; instead, the N1 amplitude was similarly enlarged when evoking stimulus was attended and when the focus of attention was directed 4° away to the near lateral stimuli in the same half-field. A sharp drop in N1 amplitude to far lateral stimuli occurred when attention was directed to either of the stimulus locations in the opposite visual half-field.

The N1 amplitude pattern for the far lateral stimuli suggests an all-or-none effect of the vertical meridian. The ERPs to the near lateral stimuli (2°), however, did not support such a straightforward picture. Figure 8 (bottom) shows ERPs to the near lateral stimuli under the four attention conditions. The N1 waves evoked by these stimuli were not of equivalent amplitude when attention was directed to different locations in the same hemifield. Instead, N1 was largest in amplitude for attended near lateral stimuli and was sharply reduced when attention was directed to any of the other three locations. (Note that for stimuli at all positions the N2 component was elicited only by attended stimuli, a general pattern found in all spatial attention studies of this type.)

---

*The mean P1 peak amplitudes to far lateral stimuli (collapsed across left and right stimuli) when attended and for increasing separations between evoking and attended locations were as follows: 1.61, 1.24, 1.16, and 0.93 μV. The corresponding N1 amplitudes were 1.89, 1.67, 0.39, and 0.24 μV.

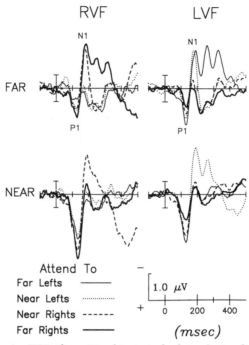

Figure 8. Grand average ERPs from 14 subjects to far lateral stimuli (6° eccentricity; top) and near lateral stimuli (2° eccentricity; bottom). Overlaid are the ERPs recorded under the four attention conditions: attend far left (thin solid), attend near left (dotted), attend near right (dashed), and attend far right (thick solid). The ERPs were recorded from lateral occipital sites contralateral to the visual field of stimulation (RVF, right visual field; LVF, left visual field).

These initial results reveal an interesting dissociation between the P1 and N1 components of the visual ERP that was not evident in previous studies of the spatial distribution of visual attention (Mangun & Hillyard, 1987, 1988). Although the P1 component to lateral stimuli showed progressive, gradient-like amplitude decrements as attention was directed to increasingly more distant loci in the visual field, the N1 component displayed a more complicated response pattern. One possible way to interpret the differing behavior of the P1 and N1 waves would be to suggest that the P1 indexes a tonic, preset spatial gating process, whereas the N1 wave (or wave forms overlapping in time with the N1 peak) is a sign of active orienting to relevant or potentially relevant events (Hillyard, Münte, & Neville, 1985).

In this framework, the difference in N1 response pattern to near versus far lateral stimuli suggests that such an active attentional orienting is more automatic or robust for events occurring peripheral to the focus of attention, whereas stimuli located medially to the focus of attention could be more effectively ignored. Accordingly, the far lateral flashes would elicit an N1 of enhanced amplitude either when they were attended or when the near laterals (in the same hemifield) were attended, but the latter stimuli would not produce an enlarged N1 when the far laterals were attended. The division of a visual hemifield into medial and lateral regions may be relative to the focus of attention just as the left and right visual fields are defined relative to the point of eye fixation. Thus, the point at which attention is focused may define a boundary in visual space that serves as a reference for subsequent attentional orienting.

In previous experiments using three stimulus positions (e.g., Mangun & Hillyard, 1987), the intermediate size of the N1 component to lateral flashes while attending midline may have resulted from an averaging of the attended and unattended field amplitudes. An alternative possibility, however, is that lateral stimuli do not elicit an automatic orienting response so readily when attention is directed toward foveal or near-foveal stimuli; perhaps lateral field stimuli can be more effectively ignored when attention and fixation are aligned. In any case, the ERP evidence reviewed above implies that attending a location 2° eccentric to the vertical midline is significantly different in this regard from attending to a midline stimulus.

Event-Related Potential Amplitudes Indicate the Allocation of Attention

The relationship between attention-related changes in ERP amplitudes and the accuracy of perceptual discriminations is of central importance to the interpretation of these physiological responses. What is the perceptual significance of the enhancement of an ERP peak? So far we have suggested that attention-related increases in P1 and N1 amplitudes are indicative of enhanced sensory input from and orienting toward the region of the evoking stimulus. Such an interpretation would be strengthened by establishing that the amplitudes of these early ERPs were reliable indicators of the graded allocation of attention among multiple spatial locations.

This relationship was investigated using a letter search task in which semicircles of four letters each (Figure 9) were flashed in random order to the left or right visual field at a rapid rate (interstimulus intervals of 300–450 msec) (Mangun, 1987). The subjects' task was to detect and respond to infrequent sets that contained a single letter "T" located in any of the four letter positions. Left-field targets were registered by left-hand button presses and right field by right-hand responses. The attentional "allocation policy" of the subjects was manipulated according to the method used by Kinchla (1980) and Sperling (1984), wherein the relative percentages of attentional effort being dedicated to the left versus right letter displays were varied systematically. Five separate conditions were employed, with the left/right allocation of attention being 100%/0%, 75%/25%, 50%/50%, 25%/75%, and 0%/100%. After a bit of practice subjects did not find it difficult to allocate attention according to these numerical instructions, as can be seen in their behavioral target detection and reaction time tradeoff curves (Figure 10).

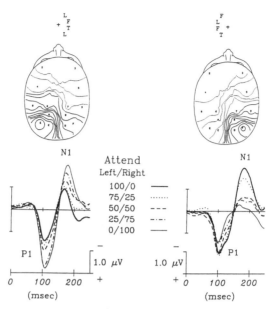

Figure 9. Event-related potential amplitudes parallel attentional allocation policy. Subjects fixated a central location (+) and were instructed to attend exclusively to either the left (thick solid) or right (thin solid) letter arrays or to divide their attention between the two sides in designated proportions: 75% left/25% right (dotted), 50% left/50% right (dashed), and 25% left/75% right (dot-dash). Grand average ERPs to left and right visual field stimuli are shown below. Recordings are from the lateral occipital scalp site contralateral to the visual field of stimulation.

Figure 9 shows the strong modulation of the early ERPs by attention, with P1 and N1 amplitudes to right-field letters showing a progressive increase with greater attentional allocation to the right (left tracings) and a converse pattern for the P1 and N1 peaks to left-field stimuli (right tracings). This reciprocal tradeoff is plotted for P1 amplitude in Figure 10. Note that the increases in P1 amplitude with higher percentages of allocation bear a monotonic relation with improved target detectability and decreased RTs. This orderly relationship provides a validation of these early ERP components as indices of attentional allocation policy.

The quantitative relationship between early ERP amplitudes and detection performance raises some interesting interpretive issues. In general, as attention was withdrawn from stimuli in one field, the amplitudes of the P1 and N1 components elicited by those stimuli showed a steeper decline than did the corresponding performance measures. Thus, although these ERP indices of signal strength decreased monotonically, performance remained relatively high, suggesting that performance was not limited at the early processing stage(s) indexed by P1 and N1. Such a result is not surprising given that the letter stimuli were well above threshold in intensity and were presented in close proximity to the fovea.

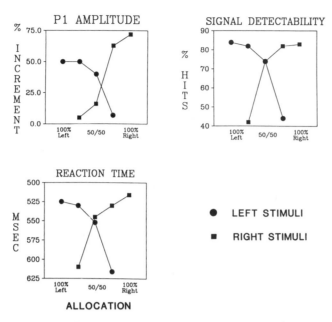

Figure 10. Line graphs of ERP and performance values as a function of attentional allocation. P1 amplitude (plotted as percentage increment over the unattended amplitude) is shown at the top left for the left (dots) and right (squares) field stimuli as a function of allocation (100% left, through 50/50 to 100% right conditions; 75/25 conditions not indicated on abscissa). Signal detectability (top right; the percentage of total targets detected) and reaction times (msec) are also plotted for the five attention conditions.

Under these conditions, the perceptual demands of detecting T's on one side would not be so great as to require a full (100%) commitment of early processing capability (i.e., sensory gain) in order to achieve a high level of performance. Presumably, changes in sensory gain across the visual field would have important consequences for other forms of perceptual processing (e.g., threshold-level detection); further work is needed to determine which aspects of visual perception are most sensitive to these presumed changes in sensory input gain.

VISUAL–SPATIAL PRIMING AFFECTS EARLY SENSORY PROCESSING

Although the evidence is strong that sensory gain control (as indexed by modulation of P1 and N1) is involved in spatial selective attention to rapidly presented sequences or "streams" of flashes, the role of such a mechanism in trial-by-trial cued attention tasks remains to be demonstrated. For example, Posner and colleagues (1980) have argued that the speeded reaction times observed to stimuli that occur in expected versus unexpected locations (as cued by a prior attention-directing stimulus) are the result of facilitated perceptual processing.

Although the RT data are consistent with this interpretation, the question has been raised as to whether such RT modulations might actually result from various nonsensory factors that could play a role. Among the latter would be differences in decision criteria for responding to targets at cued and uncued locations (Shaw, 1984; Sperling, 1984). By recording ERPs to the task stimuli in the spatial priming paradigm developed by Posner, we examined the hypothesis that target flashes at expected (cued) locations show an early sensory facilitation as indexed by the P1 and N1 component amplitudes (Mangun, Hansen, & Hillyard, 1987).

Each trial began with a centrally located arrow that pointed to either the left or right visual field. Following this spatial cue by 800 msec was a target located in either the left or right visual field. The spatial cue correctly indicated the location of the subsequent target stimulus with a 75% probability (validly cued stimulus); on 25% of the trials the arrow pointed to the side opposite to where the target stimulus would occur (invalidly cued stimulus). Trials were presented at approximately 3-second intervals. Subjects had to make a moderately difficult discriminative RT judgment, pressing one button for "tall" bars and a second button for "short" bars. If the validly cued targets (e.g., arrow left, stimulus left) elicited enhanced early sensory components over the contralateral occipital lobe, this would provide support for the view that sensory pathway facilitation was operative in cued spatial attention.

The waveforms in Figure 11 show that an enhancement of both the P1 and N1 components occurred for the valid flashes, whether they occurred in the left visual field (lvf) or right visual field (rvf). As expected, reaction times to valid targets were speeded as compared to invalid targets—566 msec versus 592 msec. Thus, these data support the view that spatial priming results in a facilitation of sensory processing that might contribute to the RT effects observed here and in numerous behavioral studies. Further, it appears that the early selection mechanisms that operate during tasks where spatial attention is cued on a trial-by-trial basis are similar to those engaged when attention is sustained throughout a sequence of stimuli (e.g., as in Figures 1, 5, and 9).

EVENT-RELATED POTENTIALS INDEX HIERARCHICAL SELECTION OF STIMULUS FEATURES

Thus far we have only considered ERP changes brought about by attending to spatial locations. Although location is perhaps the most effective cue for selecting visual stimuli, strong effects of perceptual and response selectivity can also be achieved using other cues such as color, spatial frequency, orientation, shape, or various conjunctions of these features (Kahneman & Treisman, 1984). Studies to date indicate that the pattern of early P1/N1 enhancement is unique to spatial attention and that selection based on other stimulus features is associated with quite different ERP patterns. In most cases the predominant response to an

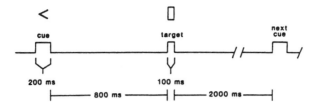

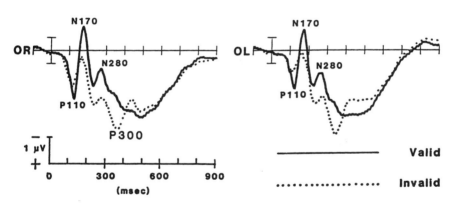

Figure 11. Event-related potentials in a spatial cuing paradigm. Each trial began with a central cue (arrow) that was followed 800 msec later by a lateralized target bar to which a discriminative height judgment response was required. Grand average ERPs to left (LVF) and right (RVF) stimuli are shown at bottom. Recording sites shown are contralateral occipital right (OR) and left (OL). Overlaid are ERPs to validly precued target bars (solid) and invalidly precued targets (dotted). The P1 (P110) and N1 (N170) components of the ERPs to validly cued stimuli were significantly larger in amplitude over contralateral occipital scalp.

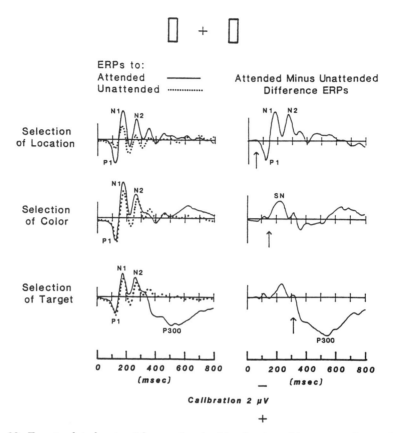

Figure 12. Event-related potentials associated with selection of location, color, and shape (target). Stimuli consisted of red and blue bars flashed in random order to the left and right visual fields. Subjects attended to bars of a particular color at one location and responded to slightly shorter target bars that occurred infrequently at the attended location. Grand average ERPs recorded from occipital scalp to all stimuli (red and blue) occurring at a particular location are shown in the top tracing. When that location was attended, there was an enhancement of the P1, N1, and N2 components of the ERPs to stimuli occurring there as compared to when the opposite side was attended. The ERPs averaged separately for attended versus unattended colors (collapsed over red and blue bars) showed a different pattern of ERP change (middle), consisting principally of a slow negative component beginning at 150 msec and lasting until about 300 msec. Finally, when the correct combination of location, color, and bar height (i.e., a target) is detected, a P300 component is elicited by the target (bottom).

attended nonspatial cue is a broad negative component ("selection negativity") beginning at 150–200 msec and extending until 300–400 msec (Harter, Aine, & Schroeder, 1982; Harter & Aine, 1984). Since selection based on a spatial cue produces an ERP signature that is distinctive from that based on a nonspatial cue such as color, it is possible to visualize the sequence of cue selections from a multidimensional stimulus as they take place. From the hierarchy of early and late

ERP changes, information can be gleaned about the primacy of one type of feature selection over another.

This approach is illustrated in an experiment (Hillyard & Münte, 1984) in which the task stimuli were red and blue bars flashed in random order to right and left visual field locations. Each of these four stimulus classes was equiprobable, and interstimulus intervals were 350–500 msec. The task was to attend to one of the four color–location combinations at a time (e.g., to red bars on the right) and to respond to target bars of that type that were slightly shorter than the more frequent standard bars.

The ERPs were averaged separately according to whether the stimulus had the attended location, the attended color, both features, or neither. Further, averages were obtained for both target (taller) and nontarget (shorter) stimuli. As shown in Figure 12, all stimuli at the attended location elicited enlarged P1 and N1 (and N2) waves in relation to all stimuli at unattended locations. This early selection for location proceeded independently of whether a stimulus was of the attended color, and its timing can be visualized in the attention "difference waves" formed by subtracting the ERPs to the stimulus when ignored from the ERP to the stimulus when attended (right column). In contrast, selection for color was manifested in a broader negative component ("selection negativity" or SN) that began at around 150 msec. Significantly, the SN was much larger in response to attended-color stimuli when they occurred at the attended location (not shown in figure). This indicates that selection of the attended color is hierarchically dependent on the prior selection for location; in other words, the early suppression of unattended location inputs prevents their being processed further in regard to their color attributes. This ERP pattern provides strong support for early selection models of attention and fits with recent evidence that spatial attention can gate the registration of simple feature information (Kahneman & Treisman, 1984; Prinzmetal et al., 1986).

The ultimate recognition of the task-relevant targets (bars of the proper location, color, and height) triggers a P300 component that onsets at 200–250 msec and is absent if the target is "missed." Thus, in this situation and many others (Coles, Gratton, Bashore, Eriksen, & Donchin, 1985; Hansen & Hillyard, 1983; Harter et al., 1982; Kramer, Schneider, Fisk, & Donchin, 1986; Wijers et al., 1987), the ERPs provide a window on the entire pattern of early and later stimulus selections throughout the range 75–300 msec, far earlier than the ultimate motor responses to the targets that form the main data base of behavioral investigation.

REFERENCES

Adrian, E. D. (1954). The physiological basis of perception. In J. F. Delafresnaye (Ed.), *Brain mechanisms and consciousness* (pp. 237–248). Blackwell: Oxford.

Bashinski, H. S., & Bacharach, V. R. (1980). Enhancement of perceptual sensitivity as the result of selectively attending to spatial locations. *Perception and Psychophysics*, 28, 241–248.

Boch, R., & Fischer, B. (1983). Saccadic reaction times and activation of the prelunate cortex: Parallel observations in trained rhesus monkeys. *Experimental Brain Research*, 50, 201–210.

Broadbent, D. E. (1958). *Perception and communication*. London: Pergamon Press.

Broadbent, D. E. (1971). *Decision and stress* (pp. 132–213). New York: Academic Press.

Coles, M. G. H., Gratton, G., Bashore, T. R., Eriksen, C. W., & Donchin, E. (1985). A psychophysiological investigation of the continuous flow model of human information processing. *Journal of Experimental Psychology: Human Perception and Performance*, 11, 529–553.

Deutsch, J. A., & Deutsch, D. (1963). Attention: Some theoretical considerations. *Psychological Review*, 70, 80–90.

Downing, C. J. (1988). Expectancy and visual–spatial attention: Effects on perceptual quality. *Journal of Experimental Psychology: Human Perception and Performance*, 14, 188–202.

Downing, C. J., & Pinker, S. (1985). The spatial structure of visual attention. In M. I. Posner & O. S. Marin (Eds.), *Attention and performance XI* (pp. 171–187). Hillsdale, NJ: Lawrence Erlbaum.

Eason, R. G., Harter, M. R., & White, C. T. (1969). Effects of attention and arousal on visually evoked cortical potentials and reaction time in man. *Physiology and Behavior*, 4, 283–289.

Eriksen, C. W., & Yeh, Y. (1985). Allocation of attention in the visual field. *Journal of Experimental Psychology: Human Perception and Performance*, 11, 583–597.

Fischer, B., & Boch, R. (1985). Peripheral attention versus central fixation: Modulation of the visual activity of prelunate cortical cells of the rhesus monkey. *Brain Research*, 345, 111–123.

Hansen, J. C., & Hillyard, S. A. (1983). Selective attention to multidimensional auditory stimuli. *Journal of Experimental Psychology: Human Perception and Performance*, 9, 1–19.

Harter, M. R., & Aine, C. J. (1984). Brain mechanisms of visual selective attention. In R. Parasuraman & D. R. Davies (Eds.), *Varieties of attention* (pp. 293–322). Orlando: Academic Press.

Harter, M. R., Aine, C., & Schroeder, C. (1982). Hemispheric differences in the neural processing of stimulus location and type: Effects of selective attention on visual evoked potentials. *Neuropsychologia*, 20, 421–438.

Hernandez-Peon, R. (1966). Physiological mechanisms in attention. In R. W. Russell (Ed.), *Frontiers in physiological psychology* (pp. 121–147). New York: Academic Press.

Hillyard, S. A., & Kutas, M. (1983). Electrophysiology of cognitive processing. *Annual Review of Psychology*, 34, 33–61.

Hillyard, S. A., & Mangun, G. R. (1987). Sensory gating as a physiological mechanism for visual selective attention. In R. Johnson, Jr., R. Parasuraman, & J. W. Rohrbaugh (Eds.), *Current trends in event-related potential research* (pp. 61–67). New York: Elsevier.

Hillyard, S. A., & Münte, T. F. (1984). Selective attention to color and location: An analysis with event-related brain potentials. *Perception and Psychophysics*, 36, 185–198.

Hillyard, S. A., Münte, T. F., & Neville, H. J. (1985). Visual–spatial attention, orienting and brain physiology. In M. I. Posner & O. S. Marin (Eds.), *Attention and performance XI* (pp. 63–84). Hillsdale, NJ: Lawrence Erlbaum.

Hillyard, S., & Picton, T. W. (1987). Electrophysiology of cognition. In F. Plum (Ed.),

Handbook of physiology: The nervous system (Vol. V, Part 2, pp. 519–584). Bethesda: American Physiological Society.

Homan, R. W., Herman, J., & Purdy, P. (1987). Cerebral location of international 10–20 system electrode placement. *Electroencephalography and Clinical Neurophysiology, 66*, 376–382.

Hughes, H. C., & Zimba, L. D. (1987). Natural boundaries for the spatial spread of directed visual attention. *Neuropsychologia, 25*, 5–18.

Johnston, W. A., & Dark, V. J. (1982). In defense of intraperceptual theories of attention. *Journal of Experimental Psychology: Human Perception and Performance, 8*, 407–421.

Jonides, J. (1981). Voluntary versus automatic control over the mind's eye's movement. In J. B. Long & A. D. Baddely (Eds.), *Attention and performance IX* (pp. 187–203). Hillsdale, NJ: Lawrence Erlbaum.

Kahneman, D., & Treisman, A. (1984). Changing views of attention and automaticity. In R. Parasuraman & D. R. Davies (Eds.), *Varieties of attention* (pp. 29–62). Orlando: Academic Press.

Kinchla, R. A. (1980). The measurement of attention. In R. S. Nickerson (Ed.), *Attention and performance VIII* (pp. 213–237). Hillsdale, NJ: Lawrence Erlbaum.

Kramer, A. F., Schneider, W., Fisk, A., & Donchin, E. (1986). The effects of practice and task structure on components of the event-related brain potential. *Psychophysiology, 23*, 33–47.

Mangun, G. R. (1987). *Mechanisms of visual selective attention: Analyses with event-related brain potentials in humans.* Doctoral dissertation, University of California, San Diego.

Mangun, G. R., Hansen, J. C., & Hillyard, S. A. (1987). The spatial orienting of visual attention: Sensory facilitation or response bias? In R. Johnson, Jr., J. W. Rohrbaugh, & R. Parasuraman (Eds.), *Current trends in event-related potential research* (pp. 118–124). New York: Elsevier.

Mangun, G. R., & Hillyard, S. A. (1985). Event-related brain potentials reveal processing gradients during visual–spatial selective attention in man. *Society for Neuroscience Abstracts, 11*, 879.

Mangun, G. R., & Hillyard, S. A. (1987). The spatial allocation of visual attention as indexed by event-related brain potentials. *Human Factors, 29*, 195–211.

Mangun, G. R., & Hillyard, S. A. (1988). Spatial gradients of visual attention: Behavioral and electrophysiological evidence. *Electroencephalography and Clinical Neurophysiology, 70*, 417–428.

Moran, J., & Desimone, R. (1985). Selective attention gates visual processing in the extrastriate cortex. *Science, 229*, 782–784.

Muller, H. J., & Findlay, J. M. (1987). Sensitivity and criterion effects in the spatial cuing of visual attention. *Perception and Psychophysics, 42*, 383–399.

Norman, D. A. (1968). Toward a theory of memory and attention. *Psychological Review, 75*, 522–536.

Posner, M. I., Snyder, C. R. R., & Davidson, B. J. (1980). Attention and the detection of signals. *Journal of Experimental Psychology: General, 109*, 160–174.

Prinzmetal, W., Presti, D. E., & Posner, M. I. (1986). Does attention affect visual feature integration? *Journal of Experimental Psychology: Human Perception and Performance, 12*, 361–369.

Rizzolatti, G., Riggio, L., Dascola, I., & Umiltà, C. (1987). Reorienting attention across the horizontal and vertical meridians: Evidence in favor of a premotor theory of attention. *Neuropsychologia, 25*, 31–40.

Shaw, M. L. (1984). Division of attention among spatial locations: A fundamental difference between detection of letters and detection of luminance increments. In H. Bouma & D. G. Bouwhuis (Eds.), *Attention and performance X: Control of language processes* (pp. 109–121). Hillsdale, NJ: Lawrence Erlbaum.

Shulman, G. L., Sheehy, J. B., & Wilson, J. (1986). Gradients of spatial attention. *Acta Psychologica, 61,* 167–181.

Shulman, G. L., Wilson, J., & Sheehy, J. B. (1985). Spatial determinants of the distribution of attention. *Perception and Psychophysics, 37,* 59–65.

Singer, W. (1977). Control of thalamic transmission by corticofugal and ascending reticular pathways in the visual system. *Physiological Reviews, 57,* 386–420.

Skinner, J. E., & Yingling, C. D. (1977). Central gating mechanisms that regulate event-related potentials and behavior. In J. E. Desmedt (Ed.), *Attention, voluntary contraction and event-related cerebral potentials. Progress in clinical neurophysiology* (Vol. 1, pp. 30–69). Basel: S. Karger.

Sperling, G. (1984). A unified theory of attention and signal detection. In R. Parasuraman & D. R. Davies (Eds.), *Varieties of attention* (pp. 103–181). Orlando: Academic Press.

Spitzer, H., Desimone, R., & Moran, J. (1988). Increased attention enhances both behavioral and neuronal performance. *Science, 240,* 338–340.

Tassinari, G., Aglioti, S., Chelazzi, L., Marzi, C. A., & Berlucchi, G. (1987). Distribution in the visual field of the costs of voluntarily allocated attention and of the inhibitory aftereffects of covert orienting. *Neuropsychologia, 25,* 55–71.

Treisman, A. M. (1964). Selective attention in man. *British Medical Bulletin, 20,* 12–16.

Van Voorhis, S., & Hillyard, S. A. (1977). Visual evoked potentials and selective attention to points in space. *Perception and Psychophysics, 22,* 54–62.

Wijers, A. A., Okita, T., Mulder, L. J. M., Lorist, M. M., Poiesz, R., & Scheffers, M. K. (1987). Visual search and spatial attention: ERPs in focussed and divided attention conditions. *Biological Psychology, 25,* 33–60.

DISCUSSION

JOAQUIN FUSTER: From where do these influences come that actually modulate or gate that information? I can think of only one process or direction, and that is that they come from upstream parts of the cortical hierarchy. We have some old data suggesting that in some situations, the reticular formation didn't seem to affect the arousal level and didn't seem to affect the evoked potential at the geniculate level, but it did affect potentials at the visual cortical level. The information that the individual uses for gating that input is semantic and so must come down from higher cortical levels.

STEVEN HILLYARD: Certainly when one decides to attend to something, the information's got to start out at the cortical level. I think this type of question can really be answered more directly with PET information, and I've been trying to get various PET scan groups interested in this type of attention experiment.

FUSTER: Are they listening?

HILLYARD: This paradigm of presenting repeated flashes over a period of a couple of minutes is eminently suited to a PET scan technique, and preliminary results from the St. Louis group, which used a somewhat different paradigm than this, indicate that visual cortex does show enhanced blood flow during spatial attention. But as to where this selectivity originates, it seems to me that all of the forward projections from V1 to V2 to V4 to IT have their own backward projections, and I think those projections would be the most likely candidates for shutting off unattended inputs at lower levels.

ERIC HALGREN: Do you have any feeling about what may come first, that is, gating versus some sort of system of identification or an initial coarse processing of information?

HILLYARD: The spatial aspect of a stimulus is certainly one of its most fundamental features in evolutionary terms. When something happens out there in the environment, the first thing one needs to do is orient toward it. Since all the stimuli in the world do have a spatial aspect to them, it seems reasonable that a whole separate system would have evolved to deal with space. And this appears to be the case.

HALGREN: But do you think that these later selection negativities might also represent sensory gating? I think the early spatial-sensitive components are pretty clearly representative of sensory gating, but some of the other monkey studies indicate that higher-order selections also involve sensory gating. We've seen from the monkey studies of Joaquin, for example, that a lot of these relevant stimuli trigger very long, slow, unitary bursts. So I think some of these later, slower negativities could also represent a gating type of mechanism, but at a higher level.

JOHN SCHLAG: Did you consider the possibility of eye-movement-related potentials?

HILLYARD: Yes, we did a number of controls. We have been paranoid about eye movements all along, so one of our control manipulations was to actually have the person move the eyes over part way to the stimulus or all the way to the stimulus, and the pattern of changes in the evoked potential is quite a bit different from the changes produced by attention. The P1 effect is larger than the N1 effect, and the scalp distribution shifts over the posterior scalp as a function of where the eyes are looking. But maybe you're asking about orienting the eyes over to a position, whether that implies a kind of attention to that location. Clearly, if the eyes are deviated, there will be a different set of pathways activated and a different pattern of potentials evoked across the scalp. We once did an experiment to see whether moving the eyes over toward a loudspeaker would in itself increase the auditory evoked potentials. Since looking directly at the speaker sometimes helps auditory detection, we wondered whether that would increase the attention effect on the evoked potentials. It didn't, and that was the last experiment in which we tried moving the eyes. We've kept the eyes fixated at the center ever since. But it would be an interesting thing to try.

HEMISPHERIC INDEPENDENCE: A PARADIGM CASE FOR COGNITIVE NEUROSCIENCE

ERAN ZAIDEL, PhD, JEFFREY M. CLARKE, MA, and BRANDALL SUYENOBU, MA
University of California, Los Angeles

INTRODUCTION

Assumptions and Beliefs

This chapter reflects the position that the organization of the brain is responsible for the structure of the mind. Ontologically, we take a reductionist and monist–materialist stance on the mind–body problem. Epistemologically, we propose that a neuroscientifically informed approach to higher cognitive functions offers substantial methodological advantages over the strictly behavioral approach of most cognitive psychologists or the functional approach of many cognitive neuropsychologists. The advantages include particularly an arsenal of physiological and anatomic methods that can test interpretations, provide converging evidence, and constrain possible models of cognitive functions.

TRANSPARENCY

Our approach presupposes that cognitive deficit resulting from brain damage is transparent to normal function. That is, brain damage simplifies cognitive functioning by eliminating some processing components, reducing processing resources, and slowing down speed of processing. This reduces the opportunity for alternative strategies. Complications introduced by diaschysis, release of function, and release of functional inhibition are all lawful and predictable.

SIMULATION

We further believe that it is possible in principle to simulate in the normal brain various cognitive deficits by appropriate application of load, stress, and

Acknowledgments: This work was supported by NIH grant NS-20187, by an NIMH RSDA MH-00179, and by a UCLA Biomedical Research Support Grant. Thanks to J. Rayman for comments and to S. Spence and J. Bogen for critical readings of the manuscript.

selective activation and inhibition. This describes much of what distinguishes cognitive neuropsychology from traditional cognitive psychology and may be regarded as a paradigmatic research program of cognitive neuroscience.

FIRMWARE

Brain damage is not merely a "hardware" malfunction; it also involves software errors. Software modules come to be embodied in distinct cortical areas since neural architecture has evolved to be changed by the acquisition of cognitive operations. That is why cognitive neuroscience is a viable field, why a neuroscientific approach to cognition is possible.

CONVERGENCE

A successful cognitive neuroscience has to account for both normal functions and cognitive deficits. Different subject populations afford particular advantages and disadvantages so that convergent evidence using different experimental paradigms is necessary for a successful theory. In the case of hemispheric specialization, normal subjects offer the ultimate testing ground for any theory, but their brains are fast and complex. Hemisphere-damaged patients reveal functional specialization by inference from deficit, but cognitive deficit may reflect both loss of function and cognitive reorganization. (Reorganization could include pathological inhibition of intact homologous regions on the other side as well as compensatory takeover by other undamaged circuits on the damaged side.) Commissurotomy patients offer a direct comparison between the positive competence of matched right and left hemispheres, but this competence may reflect reorganization resulting from early brain damage as well as unusual deficit or exceptional ability arising from absence of normal interhemispheric interaction.

Modularity

Traditional neuroscientific conceptions of information processing distinguish two basic structures: localized gray cell assemblies for representing and processing cognitive information and white communicating fibers for information transfer between assemblies. Moreover, in this view there is directionality of information flow from primary sensory areas, through secondary association areas and tertiary amodal regions that integrate information, and eventually to output areas that control motor function. Similar conceptions underlie information-processing psychology: information undergoes sequential transformations through a series of independent stages from sensory analysis through decision to motor response. Functional independence of information-processing stages is the theoretical precursor of the recent concept of modularity (Fodor, 1983).

But the Fodorian version of functional independence embodied in the concept of a module is too restrictive. In Fodor's view, two pairwise functionally independent units have to be automatic or resource-independent of each other and have to communicate exclusively through their input–output pathways without mutual access to internal structure. In our view, instead, it is sufficient to show partial independence where parallel function is possible and where communication is restricted to certain times and to the results of limited stages of processing. We believe that the cognitive operation of the two cerebral hemispheres illustrates such partial independence in the normal brain. Underlying our belief is the observation that the two cerebral hemispheres represent two fairly complete cognitive systems, each capable of processing most of the information from the environment and of controlling the behavior of the organism as a whole. At the same time, their processing strategies and competencies differ and complement each other.

A Paradigm Case for Cognitive Neuroscience

The study of hemispheric independence can serve as a paradigm case for present-day cognitive neuroscience because it instantiates some basic theoretical issues in a particularly simple and dramatic way.

REPRESENTATION

The two hemispheres exemplify the concept of dual representation. Each hemisphere appears to represent the self and the environment differently. Most left hemispheres (LHs) may emphasize digital linguistic representation, whereas most right hemispheres (RHs) may emphasize analog perceptual representation. Asymmetric dual representation, in turn, dictates dual and complementary processing strategies. For example, the LH may excel at feature extraction and analysis, whereas the RH may excel at form recognition including gestalt completion, feature integration, and synthesis.

MODULARITY

For most people, the two hemispheres are not only functionally different and anatomically distinct, but they also represent modular computational systems in the sense that they can operate in various degrees of functional independence of each other.

PARALLELISM

Hemispheric independence posits parallel and independent computational systems. The parallelism here does not refer to the parallel operation of numerous nonoverlapping components whose interaction is controlled by probabilistic rules, as in connectionist models of cognition. Rather, we analyze the parallel operation of only two overlapping systems whose interactions are deterministic and hence more wieldy to analysis by traditional information-processing methodology.

INTERMODULAR COMMUNICATION

Cross-callosal communication between the hemispheres is selective and illustrates intermodular communication. Communication can consist of raw sensory data, partially or fully processed information, or control signals in the form of facilitation or inhibition. Hemispheric independence may be maintained at many levels ranging from sensory isolation by suppression of callosal transfer to response inhibition in one hemisphere following parallel computation. Since different callosal regions probably serve to communicate different types and levels of information, it is possible to study intermodular communication in this case behaviorally, anatomically, and physiologically.

MONITORING AND CONTROL

Since the two hemispheres may carry out parallel computations, their activities need to be coordinated by some overall monitoring and control process. The control system may be built in as an integrated part of stimulus processing, resulting in "implicit" control. Alternatively, there may be a separate control module so that priority is "decided" at a particular stage in the information-processing sequence. This is required in order to maintain hemispheric independence when necessary, effect cooperation when needed, resolve conflict when it arises, and monitor the accuracy of critical computations.

The following discussion of hemispheric independence is in the nature of a progress report. Some of the basic concepts were introduced in Bogen (1969), Sperry (1968), and Zaidel (1983, 1986).

The next three sections of this chapter* discuss in turn (1) how hemispheric independence implements modularity of representation and processing in the normal brain, (2) how the corpus callosum implements interhemispheric interaction, and (3) how control is established in this parallel system.

FOOTPRINTS OF MODULARITY: HEMISPHERIC INDEPENDENCE IN THE NORMAL BRAIN

The Split Brain as a Model

The split brain illustrates the potential for hemispheric independence in a dramatic form: each hemisphere can separately and simultaneously perceive, cognize, recall, and emote; and each seems separately and simultaneously con-

---

*The following abbreviations are used throughout the rest of the chapter: LH, left hemisphere; RH, right hemisphere; LVF, left visual hemifield; RVF, right visual hemifield; LE, left ear; RE, right ear; Lh, left hand; Rh, right hand; RVFA, right visual hemifield advantage; REA, right ear advantage; RhA, right hand advantage; RT, reaction time; CUD, crossed–uncrossed difference; CC, corpus callosum. For figures, ° = statistically significant at the .05 level of confidence; °°= significant at the .01 confidence level; °°°= significant at the .001 confidence level.

scious. One possible criticism of split-brain research is that callosal disconnection exists solely as a pathological state and does not generalize to the normal brain. However, it is the radical thesis of this chapter that neocommissural disconnection simulates, albeit nonreversibly, a common normal state wherein the corpus callosum serves to effect hemispheric independence by maintaining interhemispheric separation. In fact, the most notable feature of the chronic split-brain syndrome is the apparent normality of these patients in everyday behavior; they show an apparent lack of any gross cognitive deficits, with the possible exception of memory and certain pragmatic deficits involving language use in social situations. Extensive interhemispheric communication can occur even in the absence of the neocortical commissures. Such communication includes simple sensory and motor signals on the one hand (cf. Clarke & Zaidel, 1989) and highly processed abstract concepts on the other (cf. Cronin-Golomb, 1986; Sergent, 1987; Zaidel, 1976a; Zaidel, Zaidel, & Bogen, in press) as well as control signals in the form of inhibition (Zaidel, 1978; Zaidel, Rayman, Letai, & White, 1989). It is even likely that the disconnected hemispheres share resources (cf. Holtzman, Sidtis, Volpe, Wilson, & Gazzaniga, 1981) so that temporary paralysis of one disconnected hemisphere at a time would yield a different pattern of hemispheric specialization from the classic disconnection syndrome.

A likely resolution of this apparent paradox is the conclusion that hemispheric independence is a common and ubiquitous state in the normal brain and that much of the interhemispheric communication needed to support and modulate it can be accomplished through noncallosal routes.

Some outstanding conflicts persist between the pattern of hemispheric specialization inferred from the disconnection syndrome in comparison with hemispheric damage syndromes, on the one hand, and in comparison with patterns of laterality in normal subjects, on the other. For instance, localized LH damage can result in global aphasia, which contrasts with the substantial linguistic competence of the disconnected RH, and localized RH damage can result in neglect and denial or prosopagnosia, which contrast with intact control of left half of space or of face perception in the disconnected LH. The simplest explanation is that hemispheric damage results in loss of function both of damaged tissue and of inhibited regions in the intact side. By the same token, our data suggest that the disconnected RH underestimates the apparent linguistic competence of the normal RH (Zaidel et al., in press). It appears that in the normal brain hemispheric independence is associated with recruitment of resources from the other side, which is prevented in the disconnected brain. In this view, the scope of hemispheric independence in the normal brain is even wider than in the split brain: independent actions can be supplemented by interhemispheric interactions.

Of course, alternative explanations of the relationship between disconnection syndrome and hemisphere-damage syndromes are possible. One possible explanation is that the split-brain syndrome represents unusual compensatory adjustment to long-term epilepsy and to the surgery by having developed more bilat-

eral competence of lateralized functions. However, there are several arguments
against this viewpoint. (1) There is no anatomical, physiological, or behavioral
evidence for massive early lesions in the key commissurotomy patients of the
California series, such as would cause language or cognitive reorganization.
(2) Patients in the California series vary widely in neurological history yet exhibit
a common syndrome. (3) In general, the predominant hemisphericity of extracallosal damage in these patients does not correlate with laterality effects, be they
visual or auditory, linguistic or nonlinguistic, with the possible exception of
stereognosis (Zaidel, 1978). (4) New neuropsychological evidence from other
clinical populations, such as dominant hemispherectomy for late lesions or right
hemisphere damage, is in greater general support of the thesis of hemispheric
independence than originally realized. (5) Most importantly, emerging evidence
from the normal brain is most parsimoniously explained by extensive hemispheric
independence and rich bilateral competencies in the presence of the neocortical
commissures.

Hemispheric Independence in the Normal Brain:
Dynamic Modularity

The strong thesis of hemispheric independence or hemispheric modularity
argues for two fairly complete, though not identical, cognitive systems, each
subsuming most stages of processing. Thus, it may not make sense to look for a
single stage of processing, early or late, when behavioral laterality effects emerge
(cf. Moscovitch, 1979). Instead, the thesis of hemispheric independence suggests
that hemispheric differences can emerge at any stage of processing. Then, the
absence of a difference between the hemispheres does not mean shared or
interactive processing; it could mean independent but similar processing in each
hemisphere or different processes that yield the same results. Indeed, we have
shown that there exists hemispheric independence in many stages of a lateralized
lexical decision task, ranging from perceptual input stages through central decision stages to response programming and even monitoring stages (Zaidel, 1989).

The model proposed here is of multiple dynamic independence. Several
parallel processes are initiated simultaneously in each hemisphere, and the two
communicate with each other at different stages of processing. But control
resides in only one process, depending on the nature of the task. Thus, different
tasks result in different degrees of independence, depending on the process in
control. Priority may reside in one process either implicitly or explicitly, before
the computation is initiated or on the basis of intermediate results. When priority
is determined prior to computation, it may result in sensory isolation in one
hemisphere; when priority is determined in midprocessing, it may result in
arrested computation in one hemisphere; and when priority is determined just
prior to completion, it may merely cause response inhibition in one hemisphere.

Models

DIRECT ACCESS VERSUS CALLOSAL RELAY TASKS

Interhemispheric Transfer. Anatomic interpretations of behavioral laterality effects presuppose that callosal transfer results in measurable loss of speed as well as in loss of stimulus quality, which in turn results in loss of accuracy. We may expect delay and degradation to depend on the nature of the information transferred and the channel used to transfer it. Unfortunately, we do not yet possess detailed information about the distribution of channels in the corpus callosum and their efficiency of transfer. But we do know that callosal fibers differ in myelinization and diameter, so that even one synaptic transmission may result in delays anywhere from 1 to 300 msec or more. Of course, a behavioral laterality effect need not reflect only callosal transfer; considerable independent processing may proceed before relevant transfer occurs.

Significant laterality effects may occur even if the task logically requires only the transfer of a 1-bit sensory or motor signal, which, in principle, could transfer in as little as 1–5 msec through large myelinated fibers. That is, latency differences between conditions in which stimulus perception and response generation are controlled by the same hemisphere [uncrossed: left visual hemifield–left hand (LVF-Lh), right visual hemifield–right hand (RVF-Rh)] and conditions in which stimulus perception and response generation are controlled by opposite hemispheres (crossed: LVF-Rh, RVF-Lh) could logically be as small as required for a simple sensory or motor signal to traverse the callosum. From the crossed-uncrossed difference (CUD) in simple RT tasks we know that such transfer takes about 2 msec. And yet the brain apparently does not adopt such a seemingly optimal strategy. For example, numerous two-choice reaction time tasks with stimuli lateralized to one or the other visual hemifield and responses lateralized to one or the other hand show "interhemispheric transfer time" on the order of 30 msec. The actual longer CUDs may reflect a strategy that is more adaptive on the average for a larger class of problems, or it may reflect the evolutionary adaptation of vestigial cortical–thalamic design principles, which served different purposes in previous evolutionary stages.

Hemispheric Independence versus Exclusive Specialization. A behavioral laterality effect is ambiguous. It suggests that one hemisphere is superior, but it does not by itself specify the competence of the inferior hemisphere. Two limit cases are conceivable. First, the "inferior" hemisphere may be unable to process the information at all. In that case, the superior hemisphere is exclusively specialized for the task, and the laterality effect reflects callosal transfer from the incompetent to the competent hemisphere. Second, the inferior hemisphere may be able to process the information independently but uses less efficient strategies. In that case, the laterality effect reflects the difference in competence between the two independent hemispheres. We refer to the first limit case as the "callosal relay model" and to the second limit case as the "direct access model" (Zaidel, 1983, 1986).

MODEL-FITTING CRITERIA

A set of behavioral criteria can be developed to test which model, if either, applies to a particular laterality experiment with normal subjects. The criteria presuppose merely that the task involves lateralized stimuli and lateralized responses. For the sake of exposition we will assume henceforth that the task involves hemifield tachistoscopic presentations and unimanual button-press responses in a two-choice decision experiment that emphasizes both speed and accuracy. Suppose further that the task shows a right hemifield advantage (RVFA).

Correlation between Left Hemifield and Right Hemifield Scores. Perhaps the simplest outcome of pure callosal relay is that LVF and RVF scores should be positively and significantly correlated as difficulty changes and that the correlation coefficient is not significantly lower than the split-half reliability of the test in either VF. Here, each within-hemifield reliability can be interpreted as measuring the correlation of the hemisphere with itself and should be significant for the results to be meaningful. This method was proposed by Dr. J. Rayman (personal communication). The rationale is that if the LH processes the input from both VFs, then responses to LVF presentations should simply add a constant delay or error increment from callosal relay of the stimuli to the specialized hemisphere prior to processing. A high positive correlation between the VFs is necessary but not sufficient for inferring callosal relay. It could be that the processing strategies in the two hemispheres are similar though independent. On the other hand, a low correlation between VFs combined with high reliabilities within the VFs *does* uniquely point to the direct access model, from which we can infer hemispheric independence.

Interaction between an Experimental Parameter and Hemifield of Presentation. The simplest pattern for inferring direct access or hemispheric independence is shown in Figure 1a. If there is no hemispheric difference at either level of the experimental variable, then each hemisphere must be processing both levels and each shows the same difference between levels. The zero slope implies that no callosal transfer is involved, given our initial assumption that callosal relay decreases accuracy and speed.

The pattern in Figure 1b is ambiguous. On the one hand, the pattern is logically consistent with direct access. Both hemispheres may show the same difference between level I and level II, but the RH may be slower by a constant amount corresponding to the slope in Figure 1b, left. On the other hand, the pattern is also consistent with callosal relay. The LH may be exclusively specialized for the task, and the slope represents callosal transfer, which is the same for level I and level II stimuli. In the absence of further information about the actual costs of callosal transfer for specific stimuli in a particular test, it is not possible to determine whether the slope represents callosal relay or hemispheric independence.

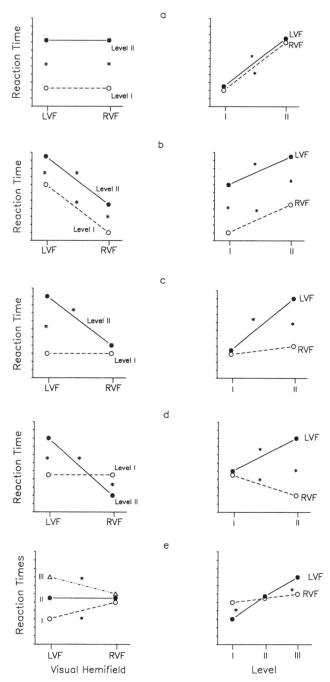

Figure 1. Patterns of possible interactions between visual hemifield of stimulus presentation and one experimental variable with two or three levels (I, II, III) in a lateralized tachistoscopic experiment. The column on the left plots the pattern with hemifield on the *x* axis; the column on the right plots the same data with the experimental variable on the *x* axis. *Statistically significant difference in a planned comparison.

The pattern in Figure 1c is common and includes a significant interaction of the experimental variable with VF ("processing dissociation"; cf. Zaidel, 1983). It is clear that level I stimuli are processed independently by either hemisphere. The interpretation of processing level II stimuli is ambiguous for the same reasons that apply to Figure 1b. Thus, it is possible that the RH can process level 1 stimuli independently but relays level II stimuli to the LH for processing. In that case the RH "makes" an explicit or implicit distinction between level I and level II stimuli and may be said to discriminate between, or recognize, them. However, the RH may not itself have access to that information and thus may not make the discrimination or act on it.

Another difficulty with pattern 1c is that the interaction may reflect the choice of scale used to represent performance. It may be that the scale that underlies the psychological reality of the phenomenon is a nonlinear transformation of accuracy or latency that would not yield an interaction with VF (cf. Hellige, 1983). This difficulty is avoided in interactions that show a crossover pattern similar to the one in Figure 1d. However, here too, level II stimuli could be processed by callosal relay.

The ambiguity of the pattern in Figure 1c as evidence for direct access is a special case of Dunn and Kirsner's (1988) admonition that double dissociation does not ensure the independence of two processes. In the case of laterality effects, the likelihood of correctly inferring direct access can be increased by choosing at least three levels of the experimental variable. Then, if the scores of each VF yield a monotonic curve, the likelihood of having separate processes becomes greater. The likelihood increases with the number of levels of the experimental variable. Moreover, the separate processes must reflect direct access if at some level of the experimental variable, the difference in performance between the two hemifields is zero (Figure 1, right).

The ambiguity of direct access in pattern 1c can also be partly resolved through "bootstrapping," that is, by demonstrating another processing dissociation in an orthogonal experimental variable.

Interaction between Response Hand and Hemifield of Presentation. The anatomical model predicts that when the processing and the response programming take place in the same hemisphere, responses should be faster and more accurate than when they take place in opposite hemispheres because the latter requires callosal transfer of the motor command (Moscovitch, 1973). Thus, the hand (h) $\times$ VF interaction can differentiate between direct access and callosal relay. Direct access predicts an ipsilateral hand advantage (hA) in each VF, that is, a significant h $\times$ VF interaction, superimposed, perhaps, on an overall VFA (Figure 2b). By contrast, callosal relay predicts a significant main effect of response hand; that is, responses should be faster with the hand contralateral to the hemisphere that controls processing, together with a significant main effect of VF showing an advantage in the ipsilateral hemifield (Figure 2a).

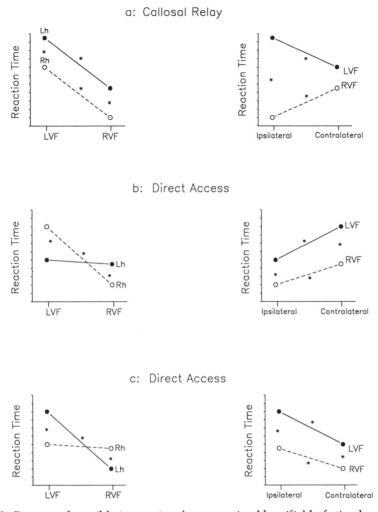

Figure 2. Patterns of possible interactions between visual hemifield of stimulus presentation and response hand in a lateralized tachistoscopic experiment. The figures on the left show h × VF plots; the figures on the right show plots of VF × condition. Condition has two levels: ipsilateral (RVF-Rh, LVF-Lh) and contralateral (RVF-Lh, LVF-Rh). (A) Callosal relay pattern reflecting exclusive specialization in the left hemisphere. (B) Direct-access pattern reflecting independent processing in each hemisphere. (C) Direct-access pattern with interference between central decision and response programming, reflecting hemispheric independence.

The statistical tests for callosal relay (VFA together with an ipsilateral hA) require more power than the corresponding tests for direct access (h × VF interaction). This imbalance can be "adjusted" by considering "ipsilateral" versus "contralateral" combinations instead of response hands (T. Wickens, personal communication). With this manipulation, direct access requires a main effect of VF (Figure 2b, right column), whereas callosal relay requires a condition (ipsi, contra) $\times$ VF interaction (Figure 2a, right). As Figure 2 makes clear, the two complementary tests are not quite equivalent. A significant but asymmetric h $\times$ VF interaction (Figure 2b, left) may translate into significant main effects of condition and of VF without an interaction (Figure 2b, right). Similarly, the main effects of h and VF (Figure 2a, left) may translate into a significant condition $\times$ VF interaction but without a crossover (Figure 2a, right).

As was noted above, the interhemispheric pathways that mediate the contra-lateral hand–hemifield responses in simple and choice RT tasks are probably not the same, although *a priori* they could use the same sensorimotor routes. As mentioned, in the normal brain, the mean CUD in simple RT to a light flash shows a small effect of about 2 msec (Clarke & Zaidel, 1989), whereas the CUD in choice RT to lexical decision shows a large effect of about 30 msec. Con-versely, in the split brain, the CUD in simple RT varies from 30 to 90 msec, but there is no CUD in choice RT to lexical decision; that is, contralateral h-VF responses are made just as fast as ipsilateral h-VF responses in the absence of the corpus callosum. Together, these results suggest that the signal that mediates the h-VF coordination in choice RT tasks is abstract rather than sensory or motor.

When resources are limited, central decision processes can interfere with response programming in the same hemisphere. In that case, better performance will result from pairing the decision in one hemisphere with the response in the other, since interference within the hemispheres is greater than between the hemispheres (Zaidel, White, Sakurai, & Banks, 1988; Zaidel et al., 1989). Such shifts of control can occur spontaneously and dynamically, and a significant interaction between response hand and visual hemifield of presentation, such that contralateral combinations show an advantage, would then signal direct access (Figure 2c). Thus, a h $\times$ VF interaction can signal direct access either with an ipsilateral (Figure 2b) or a contralateral (Figure 2c) advantage.

It may be argued that since both the "ipsilateral" and "contralateral" patterns signal direct access, so do intermediate patterns, including the callosal relay pattern of Figure 2a. However, there is no evidence that there is a continuity between the contralateral and ipsilateral patterns or that intermediate patterns can be assigned dynamically. Thus, if the callosal relay pattern does occur, it probably, in fact, reflects an assignment of control that corresponds to callosal relay or exclusive specialization.

Dual Task Interference. A definitive method for determining the degree of involvement of a hemisphere in processing a task would be to paralyze the hemisphere, administer the task, and measure the deficit relative to normal performance. This method can be approximated or partly simulated by pairing the task in question with another whose laterality is known and then observing the degree of mutual interference between them. In order to demonstrate resource sharing beyond time sharing cost, it is usually necessary to show that increasing the difficulty of one task increases the degree of interference or performance deficit of the other. Suppose that the secondary task is exclusively specialized in the LH and that the primary task in question is direct access, hence sharing no resources with the unstimulated hemisphere. In this case, a pattern showing interference with the primary task when presented to either VF would signal callosal relay where the primary task is exclusively specialized in the LH (Table 1, condition 1). On the other hand, if there is interference with RVF but not with LVF presentations of the primary task, then the task can be processed independently by either hemisphere, direct-access fashion (Table 1, condition 2). If there is no interference with presentation of the primary task to either VF, then there must be differentiation of resources within the LH, and the task could be either direct access or callosal relay specialized in the LH (Table 1, condition 3). This model includes conditions for its own refutation. If a situation matching condition 4 on Table 1 is encountered, then some of the assumptions of the model must be wrong. The entire interpretation of the four conditions can be confirmed by pairing the primary task with another secondary task that is specialized in the RH.

J. Rayman proposed a special case of the dual-task interference test for direct access in which laterality effects with unilateral and bilateral presentations are compared. Consider a paradigm in which unilateral presentations are interspersed with bilateral presentations that include a central mark signaling which hand should be used to respond. Suppose that both hemispheres respond similarly to the change in difficulty involved in shifting from unilateral to bilateral presentations. Then a difference in laterality effect between unilateral and bilateral presentations would signal a callosal relay task, whereas no difference would signal direct access. In the case of a callosal relay task, say specialized to the LH, bilateral stimuli with LVF targets would be delayed and degraded because of occurrence of RVF stimuli. Thus, the increased laterality effect with bilateral presentations would reflect a decrease in LVF scores while RVF targets show no difference relative to the unilateral condition (Rayman & Zaidel, 1989).

Speed–Accuracy Relations. It is customary to regard accuracy and latency as equivalent and interchangeable indices of hemispheric performance. In fact, however, experience in our lab suggests that accuracy is a more sensitive index of laterality. This is especially surprising since the more intuitive interpretation of the anatomical model of laterality effects is that callosal relay takes time. The

TABLE 1

PATTERNS OF INTERFERENCE BETWEEN A CALLOSAL RELAY SECONDARY TASK SPECIALIZED IN THE LH AND A PRIMARY TASK PRESENTED IN THE RVF AND, IN TURN, IN THE LVF

Condition	RVF	LVF	Interpretation
1	I[a]	I	Primary task is callosal relay, specialized in the LH
2	I	No I	Primary task is direct access
3	No I	No I	?(Resource differentiation within the LH)
4	No I	I	Impossible

[a]I = Interference that is sensitive to difficulty of primary task.

explanation may be that subjects performing the tasks emphasize accuracy rather than speed even though instructions usually call for both. Consequently, latency may be longer, it may have a larger variance, and it may reflect factors other than callosal relay. This pattern of no correlation or a small positive correlation between speed and accuracy reflects a condition intermediate between data- and resource-limited processing.

We summarized the significant statistical effects of 17 lateralized tachistoscopic experiments carried out in our lab in the past 2 years. Every significant main effect and two-way and three-way interaction was tallied from separate analysis of variance (ANOVA) tests with accuracy and latency as dependent variables. Altogether there were 50 significant effects for accuracy and 44 significant effects for latency, and of those only 23 were common to both dependent variables. A separate count for effects involving VF disclosed 33 significant effects for accuracy, 17 effects for latency, and only 12 common to both. Thus, accuracy seems to be a more sensitive measure than latency, but the two variables seem to be sensitive to different experimental variables and not interchangeable.

When processing is data limited and accuracy as well as speed is emphasized, the two dependent variables should be positively correlated and should exhibit the same laterality effects both within subjects, with trials as a random variable, and between subjects, with subjects as the random variable. On the other hand, when processing is resource limited, spontaneous tradeoffs between speed and accuracy, which signal choices of processing strategy, can occur and may differ between the hemispheres. Such a difference was observed, for example, in lexical decision of concrete and abstract nouns, where both VFs showed the same accuracy pattern but diverged in latency (Eviatar, Menn, & Zaidel, 1989).

In the same experiment, which also varied the emotionality of words, male subjects who showed a trend toward an interaction between noun concreteness and VF in latency $[F(1, 30) = 3.7, p = .061]$ also showed a significant emotionality $\times$ VF interaction in accuracy $[F(1,26) = 4.9, p < .05$ for all subjects] (Eviatar et al., 1989). Thus, one independent variable (noun concreteness) gave rise to direct access in latency, whereas an orthogonal independent variable (emotionality) resulted in direct access in accuracy. Apparently, subjects did not simply emphasize speed or accuracy to the exclusion of the other. Rather, the accuracy–latency relationship appears to index relatively local hemispheric strategic deployment. In order to study further hemispheric difference in accuracy–latency relations, we are planning to plot speed–accuracy tradeoff functions in the two hemifields of normal subjects using the deadline method during the performance of a direct access task (Z. Eviatar, personal communication).

Yet another observation made in the same lexical decision experiment was that the disconnected RH of a patient (L.B.) with complete cerebral commissurotomy showed the emotionality $\times$ VF interaction in latency [no RVFA for emotional words, significant RVFA for neutral words: matched $t(44) = 2.32$, $p < .05$], whereas normal subjects showed a similar interaction with accuracy.

The difference between the patterns suggests that the normal and disconnected hemispheres operate with different resource assignment, that is, that the normal RH, say, shares different resources with the normal LH than does the disconnected RH with the disconnected LH. Consequently, the disconnected RH and the normal RH are expected to use somewhat different processing strategies.

Comparing the Split to the Normal Brain. In principle, pure direct-access tasks involve no callosal relay and therefore should show the same laterality pattern in the split brain and in the normal brain. Callosal relay tasks, on the other hand, should show a massive laterality effect in the split brain, with one hemisphere exhibiting full competence, the other no competence. By contrast, callosal relay tasks should show significant but small laterality effects in the normal brain because callosal transfer allows effective processing by the specialized hemisphere of stimuli projected to the ipsilateral VF.

In this view, tasks that show similar laterality patterns in the split and in the normal brains are probably direct access; tasks that show a large laterality effect in the split brain and a moderate one in the normal brain are probably callosal relay. However, this will not hold for a version of hemispheric independence that permits resource sharing between the normal hemispheres even while control is maintained separately in each hemisphere. In that case, shared resources can serve to increase "hemispheric" competence in the normal relative to the split brain even for direct-access tasks. Resource sharing could also serve to attenuate or somewhat increase the laterality effect in the normal relative to the split brain if sharing is asymmetric. But in either case, bilateral competence, consistent with direct access, is maintained.

DYNAMICS

Sequences. Consider a complex task that consists of a sequence of two-component simple tasks, each one being either direct access or callosal relay. The usual simplifying assumptions and a systematic enumeration of all the possible combinations yield the surprising theoretical result that if either component task is callosal relay, then the final h $\times$ VF pattern is callosal relay as well, with the direction of VFA determined by the first callosal relay component and the direction of the hA determined by the last callosal relay component (Zaidel, 1986; cf. Moscovitch, 1986). Any direct-access component does affect the slope or the laterality effect, but without prior knowledge about the actual contribution of callosal relay to the slope, it is not possible to factor out an observed laterality effect into its direct-access and callosal relay components.

The same argument can be generalized by induction to an arbitrary sequence of direct-access and callosal relay tasks. Since even one callosal relay component would result in a net effect of callosal relay, a complex task that exhibits a net direct-access pattern must be completely direct access, that is, be processed independently by either hemisphere *in toto*. In that case, the slope reflects the additive laterality effects from all the component direct-access patterns.

Shifts. It is well known that laterality effects can shift as a function of experience. Novel tasks tend to show a LVFA that shifts to a RVFA with familiarity and, presumably, the application of more analytic strategies (Bradshaw & Nettleton, 1983; Goldberg & Costa, 1981; Zaidel, 1979). Turkewitz and Ross-Kossad (1984) described a three-step shift from a LVFA when the task is novel to a RVFA when it is familiar and back to a LVFA when it becomes automatic. Hellige, Cox, and Litvac (1979) and others described shifts from one hemifield advantage to another with hemispheric load using dual-task interference paradigms, and T. Landis and M. Regard (personal communication) described such shifts as a function of lateralized epileptic activity. In all these cases, shift can only occur with direct-access tasks.

We may expect that, with experience, tasks that initially show a callosal relay pattern can shift to a direct-access pattern. Indeed, it is likely that some individuals with greater hemispheric competencies may show a direct-access or hemispheric independence pattern for tasks that appear to be processed callosal relay fashion, that is, are exclusively specialized, in others (J. Rayman, personal communication). Moreover, we have observed dynamic shifts of lexical decision from direct access to callosal relay (with LH control) accompanied by RH dominance for error correction (Stein & Zaidel, 1989). We have also observed shifts from direct access to callosal relay and back from trial to trial as a function of item difficulty in comparative judgment (Zaidel et al., 1988). Similar shifts as a function of item difficulty can occur spontaneously from a direct-access h × VF pattern showing an ipsilateral advantage to a direct-access h × VF pattern showing a contralateral advantage because of limited resources and interference between central processing and response programming (Zaidel et al., 1988).

HIERARCHIES AND REFUTATIONS

In general, based on our own experience, which is largely but not exclusively with linguistic tasks, an overall VFA is the most robust finding and is more likely to occur than an interaction of an experimental variable with VF (processing dissociation). A VFA may occur in one dependent variable but not in the other. Occasionally accuracy shows one laterality effect, such as a RVFA in lexical decision, while latency shows other laterality effects, such as an interaction between an independent variable (wordness) and VF (Measso & Zaidel, in press). Not all behavioral criteria that identify a task as direct access or callosal relay are equally likely to occur, and most have not been assessed comprehensively or compared systematically to others (but see Zaidel, 1989). Callosal relay predicts a VFA in both accuracy and latency. Thus, the total absence of a VFA in one dependent variable suffices to establish direct access. When the task is direct access, processing dissociation is more likely to occur than a h × VF interaction. An interaction of dependent variables (accuracy, latency) with VF of presentation is quite common as an index of direct access, especially in conjunction with gender differences (Eviatar & Zaidel, 1989).

Not all combinations of patterns of results can co-occur, so the models provide ample opportunity for refutation. It is, of course, logically impossible for a task to show a direct-access pattern according to one behavioral criterion and a callosal relay pattern according to another. Such a combination would therefore signal that either the behavioral criteria or the theoretical model distinction is wrong. In particular, it should not be possible to observe direct access with one dependent variable and callosal relay with another. It is not clear whether the h × VF test could ever reveal an overall VFA together with an overall contralateral hand advantage; that pattern would be inconsistent with callosal relay with interference, but it may also reflect an intermediate step between a direct-access pattern with an ipsilateral advantage and one with a contralateral advantage, provided a continuous shift is neuropsychologically coherent, that is, well defined. As condition 4 in Table 1 shows, the dual-task method of model testing predicts that certain patterns of results are impossible. Specifically, it should not be possible for any primary task, whether direct access or callosal relay, when paired with a secondary callosal relay LH task, to show interference when the primary task is presented to the LVF but not when it is presented to the RVF.

As mentioned above, the temporal interpretation of callosal relay remains problematic. Laterality effects caused by presumed callosal relay may occur in accuracy but not in latency. Moreover, temporally advancing the stimuli presented to the inferior VF in bilateral presentations does not erase the laterality effect (cf. Zaidel, 1986). It is possible to explain this apparent paradox by reference to a preferred strategy that emphasizes accuracy at the expense of latency. This account could be tested by creating speed emphasis and showing the predicted reduced laterality effects of delaying the stimuli presented to the superior VF. However, this possibility dilutes the predictive power of the callosal relay model and makes it more difficult to refute by empirical counterevidence.

Reality of Direct-Access and Callosal Relay Models

The direct-access and callosal relay models are limit cases of a continuum of tasks with varying degrees of interhemispheric interaction, and yet there are surprisingly many tasks that show evidence of direct access or hemispheric independence. The sample is limited by the standard methodology of hemifield tachistoscopy largely to tasks where RT lasts less than 1 second, but we have seen evidence for hemispheric independence in tasks that last as long as 3–4 seconds with several lateralized stages (B. Rothwell, personal communication), and the upper limit is unknown.

HEMISPHERIC INDEPENDENCE IN LEXICAL DECISION

There is now ample evidence that lexical decision of concrete nouns and orthographically regular nonwords can be direct access (Zaidel, 1989). The stimuli are processed independently in each hemisphere, although the LH is superior.

The controversy concerning the information-processing locus of lexical decision notwithstanding, the task allows us to tap the structure of the lexicon in each hemisphere (Zaidel, 1989). The classic result includes an overall advantage of word over nonword decisions, an overall RVFA, and a wordness × VF interaction. Usually, there is no VFA or even LVFA for nonwords but a significant RVFA for words (Chiarello, 1988; Zaidel, 1989). Moreover, the advantage of words over nonwords is usually significant in the RVF but often not in the LVF, where there may even be an advantage for nonwords. This pattern of interaction between an experimental variable (wordness) and VF of presentation is consistent with direct access, at least for nonwords.

Figure 3 shows the wordness × VF interaction for accuracy and for latency in a computerized lateralized lexical decision experiment that assessed the influence of response mode on the laterality effects (Measso & Zaidel, in press). The stimuli consisted of four- and five-letter concrete nouns and orthographically regular nonwords. Stimuli were presented for 80 msec to one or the other VF on a CRT monitor controlled by an IBM-PC-compatible computer. Response programming was a between-subject factor: half of the subjects used a two-choice button press with the index finger of one hand signaling one choice (i.e., either a word or nonword decision) and the middle finger signaling the other (counterbalanced); the other half of the subjects responded in a go/no-go paradigm, some responding by a unimanual button press to words and some responding to nonwords. Response hand was changed halfway through a session, and initial response hand was counterbalanced across subjects.

Accuracy (plotted in Figure 3 as percentage errors) and latency showed what might be considered complementary results. Accuracy revealed an overall RVFA, an overall advantage for words, but no wordness × VF interaction. Moreover, there was no significant main effect of response mode nor any signifi-

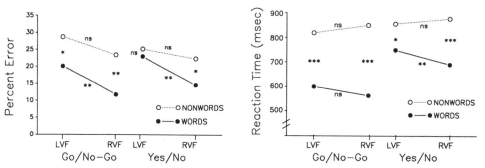

Figure 3. Results of lexical decision of concrete nouns and orthographically regular nonwords. Response mode was a between-subject variable: Go/No-Go required button presses to words by some subjects and to nonwords by others. Yes/No required pressing one button in response to words and another button in response to nonwords (Measso & Zaidel, in press). *Statistically significant at the .05 level of confidence; **.01 level; ***.001 level.

cant interactions involving response mode. Latency revealed a significant overall advantage for words, no RVFA, a significant overall advantage of go/no-go over word/nonword responses, and a significant wordness × VF interaction (RVFA for words but not for nonwords). Moreover, there were no significant interactions involving response mode. There were also no significant main effects or interactions involving response hand. Thus, this experiment illustrates that the processing dissociation criterion of direct access (in this case a wordness × VF interaction) is a more sensitive index of hemispheric independence than the h × VF interactions. Moreover, the experiment illustrates the nonequivalence of accuracy and latency measures of performance, although both showed no VFA for nonwords, thus verifying independent hemispheric processing at least for this variable.

In another experiment, we compared a very similar go/no-go lateralized lexical decision task to one that incorporated lateralized associated or unassociated primes preceding the target stimuli (Radant, 1981). The primes and half of the targets were all highly imageable, concrete, and frequent words. The other half of the targets were orthographically regular nonwords. Half of the word targets were highly associated with their primes, and half were not. Equal numbers of associated target word pairs (eight), unassociated target word pairs (eight), and target nonword pairs (16) were assigned to each of four presentation conditions: (1) prime in the LVF and target in the LVF (LL), (2) prime in the RVF and target in the LVF (RL), (3) prime in the left and target in the right (LR), and (4) prime in the right and target in the right (RR). In this version of the task, prime and target lists were counterbalanced between left and right hemifields. The lateralized primes appeared for 100 msec, and the lateralized targets were presented for 50 msec following an interstimulus interval of 500 msec. The targets alone, without the primes, were given to another group of subjects as a control task. Here too, a go/no-go paradigm was used, requiring speeded right-hand button presses to word targets.

An ANOVA of RTs to target words in the priming experiment with association (A−, A+), prime VF, and target VF as within-subject factors showed main effects of association (associated targets were decided faster than unassociated targets) and target VF (RVF targets were decided faster than LVF targets) and a significant interaction of prime VF by target VF. The same interaction occurred for associated and for unassociated primes (Zaidel, 1983). In each of the four conditions (LL, LR, RL, RR) the difference between the "targets only" and "primes plus targets" conditions includes inhibition of the target by the unassociated prime and facilitation of the target by the associated prime. The inhibition may be caused by semantic interference as well as resource depletion, whereas the priming may result from nonspecific activation of lexical analysis systems. Figure 4 plots the difference in RT between the "targets only" and "primes plus targets" in the A− and A+ conditions as a function of processing hemisphere (LL = RH, RR = LH). The figure shows that there is no inhibition and little

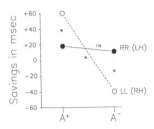

Figure 4. Facilitation and inhibition in lateralized lexical decision with associated and unassociated primes, respectively. The *y* axis shows the latency difference between decision of targets preceded by primes and targets presented alone. RR, prime in RVF and target in RVF; LL, prime in LVF and target in LVF. A⁺, associated prime-target pairs giving rise to facilitation; A⁻, unassociated prime-target pairs giving rise to inhibition. Positive savings show facilitation, and negative savings shows inhibition.

facilitation in the normal LH but strong inhibition and even greater facilitation in the normal RH. This result is consistent with direct access. Thus, for this test at least, the primary locus of both the priming and interference effects is the normal RH. Automatic spreading activation for these associative/semantic relationships appears stronger in the lexical semantic network of the RH. Put together, evidence from both lateralized lexical decision tasks—targets only and primed targets—suggests that targets are processed independently in each hemisphere by direct access.

CALLOSAL RELAY IN DICHOTIC LISTENING

Dichotic listening to simultaneous auditory pairs of stop consonant–vowel syllables that differ in place of articulation and voicing (Ba, Da, Ga, Pa, Ta, Ka) consistently shows a right ear advantage (REA) in accuracy of verbal report by normal subjects and is taken to reflect LH specialization for phonetic perception (Studdert-Kennedy & Shankweiler, 1970). Anatomical interpretations of the REA assume (1) that the LH is exclusively specialized for processing these phonetic stimuli, (2) that during dichotic listening the ipsilateral auditory pathways (left ear to LH, right ear to RH) are functionally suppressed, and (3) that the left ear (LE) signal is somewhat degraded as a result of the circuitous transmission from the RH through the corpus callosum to the LH (i.e., callosal relay), and hence the LE signal is dominated by the direct contralateral RE signal (Figure 5).

These assumptions were verified by analyzing performance on this task by split-brain patients (Zaidel, 1976b, 1983). Figure 5 shows the accuracy of verbal reports of dichotic stimuli in each ear in normal subjects and in commissurotomy patients. Normal subjects show a small but statistically significant REA, whereas patients with complete cerebral commissurotomy show a massive REA with chance reports of LE stimuli. Since only the LHs of these patients have verbal output, the data verify ipsilateral suppression of the LE in the LH.

In order to determine directly the separate competence of each disconnected hemisphere on the task, we used lateralized visual probes immediately following the dichotic pair. We also constructed auditory pairs consisting of the syllables Bee, Dee, Gee, Pee, Tee, and Kee so that the meaningfulness of the stimuli could be manipulated while maintaining their highly coded phonetic structure. Probes consisted of either a capital letter (B, D, G, P, T, K) or a simple line drawing [a

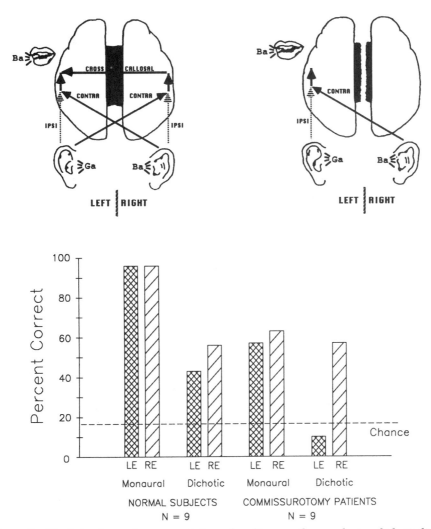

Figure 5. (Top) A schematic representation of auditory pathways during dichotic listening in normal (left) and split (right) brains. (Bottom) Accuracy of reports of dichotic perception of stop-consonant CVs by normal subjects and by commissurotomy patients. LE, left ear; RE, right ear.

bee, a girl named Dee, a boy named Guy (French pronunciation), a pea pod, a tea cup, and a key]. Ipsilateral suppression is known to be sensitive to the acoustic overlap between the members of the dichotic pair (Zaidel, 1976b); hence, the stimuli consisted of natural speech tokens aligned by a special computer program at Haskins Laboratories in New Haven, Connecticut.

Each dichotic pair was followed by a picture or a letter probe flashed briefly and randomly either to the left or to the right of a central fixation dot. The probe corresponded equally often to the LE signal, to the RE signal, or to neither ear. The patient then pointed with the hand ipsilateral to the stimulated half-field to the words "yes" or "no" in order to indicate whether the visual probe did or did not match the sound heard in either ear. This cross-modal lateralized task allowed each disconnected hemisphere to respond separately. Monaural and binaural control conditions were also administered.

The task was administered to five completely sectioned and two partially sectioned (splenium intact) patients. The RVF (i.e., LH) performance in commissurotomy patients showed a large REA that varied with performance level across subjects and was higher for letter than for picture probes. The LVF (i.e., RH) scores were consistently above chance for the LE in only one patient (L.B.), and occasionally in another (N.G.). Thus, LH specialization for the task was verified.

An ANOVA was performed on the five patients' data with VF of probe (LVF, RVF), ear (LE, RE), and probe type (consonant, picture) as independent within-subject variables and with d', the bias-free signal detection measure of sensitivity, as the dependent variable. The measure d' was generated from the accuracy data for each subject in all conditions by pairing the probability of hits with the probability of false alarms. The ANOVA disclosed a significant REA, confirming hemispheric specialization and a significant VF $\times$ ear interaction. Furthermore, although d' for the LE in the LVF was significantly above zero, it was not significantly above chance, confirming RH incompetence for this task. At the same time, d' for the RE in the LVF was not significantly different from zero, confirming ipsilateral suppression of the RE in the RH. Similarly, d' for the LE in the RVF was essentially zero, confirming ipsilateral suppression of the LE in the LH. No significant effects or interactions related to probe type occurred (Kashdan, 1979; Zaidel, 1983).

Separate ANOVAs were performed for patients L.B. and N.G. because they were the only ones showing some, albeit minimal, RH competence. Both patients showed a (nonsignificant) trend for a VF $\times$ probe interaction. However, patient L.B., who showed an equally massive REA for both picture and letter probes in the RVF, also showed a significant LEA for pictures but a nonsignificant REA for letters in the LVF. This suggests RH control of responses to picture probes but LH cross-cueing and control of responses to letter probes, with poor ipsilateral visual transfer of LVF stimuli to the LH. Thus, some RH perception can occur in rare cases, when the stimuli are perhaps interpreted as acoustic labels for the pictures, but LH perception appears to dominate (even when the probe is restricted to the LVF).

Thirty-six of 40 (90%) right-handed normal subjects showed a REA on the dichotic listening task using visual probes. Similar laterality effects were observed in the LVF and in the RVF. Letter probes yielded a slightly larger REA than did picture probes, especially in the RVF. Thus, the test seems unusually valid and reliable. An ANOVA of the accuracy data (VF $\times$ ear $\times$ probe type) for the normal subjects revealed only a significant REA. An ANOVA of the latency data showed that letters were recognized significantly faster than pictures and that LVF probes were recognized significantly faster than RVF probes. Thus, it would seem that accuracy data emphasized the LH advantage in processing the auditory stimuli, whereas latency data emphasized RH superiority in processing the visual probes, even though the latter have linguistic associations.

In a second validation study (Kashdan, 1979) with 16 normal right-handed subjects, an ANOVA with d' as the dependent variable disclosed a significant REA but no effect of probe type or VF. In a third validation study (Kashdan, 1979), letter and picture probes were introduced as between-subject variables with identical results. The failure of the REA in normal subjects to be affected by probe type, that is, stimulus meaningfulness, parallels the pattern observed in the disconnected LH but not in the RH. This confirms again exclusive LH specialization and callosal relay to the LH on this task.

THE CORPUS CALLOSUM AS A SYSTEM OF CHANNELS FOR COMMUNICATION AND CONTROL

Functional Decomposition

Research with monkeys shows that the corpus callosum is organized by sensory modality (motor, somatosensory, auditory, visual) (Pandya & Seltzer, 1986) and by function (Hamilton, 1982). Partial callosum section in humans can show selective visual, auditory, and somatosensory disconnection (e.g., Bogen, 1987), and physiological stimulation of the corpus callosum while recording responses from the exposed cortex during neurosurgery in humans shows a substantially orderly homotopic representation, with anterior callosal regions interconnecting anterior cortical areas, etc. (B. Chen, Beijing Neurosurgical Institute, personal communication). Thus, the corpus callosum appears to house a set of communication channels; each channel may be represented in a different anatomical part and may integrate different cortical regions, and each then transmits modality- or function-specific messages in different codes. The transmission in each channel has a definite rate, capacity, and measurable information loss. In this view, interhemispheric interaction requires translation to and from a callosal code prior to or following callosal transmission, and messages that cannot be so coded must remain locked in one hemisphere, even in the intact brain. Moreover, each channel would include separate routes for transferring information and for transferring control signals. Further, there is a striking absence of disconnection symptoms following cerebral commissurotomy sparing the splenium (Gordon, Bogen, & Sperry, 1971; Purves et al., 1988). Thus, the commissural system seems to be a dynamic set of channels with both facilitatory and inhibitory effects and with the ability to recode certain information for transmission through alternate channels. Indeed, callosal connectivity may depend on the integrity of certain noncallosal control structures as well. This is suggested by the observation that disconnection syndrome caused by stroke is often accompanied by dramatic interhemispheric conflict rarely observed in the surgical syndrome. Consequently, we posit that hemispheric autonomy is sometimes maintained by suppression of callosal transfer. At other times, the commissural system helps maintain dominance by inhibiting computation or response in one hemisphere (Cooke, 1986). Occasionally, pathological states involve callosally mediated inhibition of residual competence in the intact hemisphere by diseased tissue on the other side (Zaidel, 1986). In principle, competence can be released experimentally from pathological inhibition in several ways, including by cognitive loading of the inhibiting system.

In this anatomical view, the neocortical commissures mediate both interhemispheric communication and interhemispheric control. Alternative conceptualizations of callosal function deemphasize its communicative role. Kinsbourne (1975) formulated an attentional model that retains only the control functions of the callosum, which is said to equilibrate interhemispheric activation. Callosal section then results in reduced resources and a generally reduced level of performance. Brown (1988) formulated a microgenetic model that discards both the communicative and the control functions of the callosum. He believes that the disconnection syndrome reflects early and shared bilateral processing that has not reached the level of verbal awareness. However, Brown's model fails to account for complex RH cognitions not available to the disconnected LH, and Kinsbourne's model fails to account for the presence of hemispheric activation in the absence of interhemispheric exchange (Zaidel, 1986).

In the following experiments we set out to determine whether regional callosal size is a measure of the effectiveness of the transfer of information or of control signals from one hemisphere to the other.

Anatomical Correlates of Callosal Relay and Direct Access

In collaboration with Dr. Robert Lufkin of the Department of Radiological Sciences at UCLA we have been investigating the relationship between anatomical measures of the corpus callosum (CC) and behavioral measures of hemispheric specialization and of interhemispheric transfer (cf. Clarke, Zaidel, & Lufkin, 1989). To date, 43 UCLA graduate students (males and females, left and right handers) have undergone magnetic resonance imaging (MRI) and have participated in a dichotic listening task as well as a lexical decision task with associative priming.

SEX AND HANDEDNESS DIFFERENCES IN CORPUS CALLOSUM MEASURES

The 43 graduate students (23 are females, 21 are left-handed) are from a variety of academic departments. A modified version of the Edinburgh Handedness Inventory was used to determine handedness, and none of the right handers had left-handed parents or siblings. Midsagittal magnetic resonance images of the CC were obtained from a 0.3-T field with the following parameters using a spin-echo sequence: TR = 500 msec and TE = 28 msec. The images were digitally enlarged to between 1.4X and 1.8X life size, a line representing the maximum anterior–posterior CC distance was drawn, and a Microcomp Planar Morphometry digitizing system was used to measure the entire CC area as well as the areas of the following subdivisions based on the line length: (1) the anterior third of the CC, (2) the region between the anterior third and the midline (anterior mid-body), (3) the region between the midline and the posterior third of the CC (posterior midbody), (4) the region between the posterior midbody and the posterior fifth of the CC (isthmus), and (5) the posterior fifth of the CC (splenium) (Figure 6). This partitioning of the CC has been adapted from Witelson and Kigar (1987). Since there are no overt anatomical landmarks within the CC as seen on the MRI that would implicate anatomically distinct regions, these partitions have been arbitrarily chosen as representative of different topographically arranged sections of the CC. Additionally, three distance measures were determined for each CC: (1) the maximum anterior–posterior CC length, (2) maximum splenial width, and (3) minimum width of the body. All measurements were made twice, by two different experimenters, without knowledge of the subjects' sex or handedness.

Midsagittal measures of the CC have been reported to differ as a function of sex (e.g., de Lacoste-Utamsing & Holloway, 1982) and handedness (e.g., Witelson, 1989). In the present study, we found only a significant sex difference in minimal body width: this measure was larger in females than in males. Byne, Bleier, and Houston (1988) also found the minimum CC body width to be significantly larger in females than in males and also did not find sex differences in any other CC measure. Contrary to these findings, S. Clarke, Kraftsik, Van der Loos, and Innocenti (1989) made several width measures of the CC body and found them all to be larger in males than in females, although they used a radial rather than a vertical measure and so did not consider minimum body width *per se*. The present study did not find significant sex or handedness differences in maximum splenial width, splenial area, or the ratio of splenial area to total CC area. Although several researchers report a sex difference in splenial measures

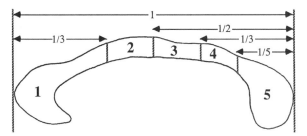

Figure 6. Scheme for partitioning the corpus callosum from midsagittal MRI views based on the maximum anterior–posterior length (Witelson & Kigar, 1987). The total madsagittal corpus callosum area was measured in addition to the following five subdivisions: 1, anterior third; 2, anterior midbody; 3, posterior midbody; 4, isthmus; 5, splenium.

(S. Clarke et al., 1989; de Lacoste-Utamsing & Holloway, 1982; Holloway & de Lacoste, 1986; Reinarz, Coffman, Smoker, & Godersky, 1988), the majority of studies fail to find such sex differences (Byne et al., 1988; Demeter, Ringo, & Doty, 1988; O'Kusky et al., 1988; Oppenheim, Lee, Nass, & Gazzaniga, 1987; Weber & Weis, 1986; Witelson, 1985). Similarly, whereas Witelson (1985) reports larger CC areas in mixed handers than in consistent right handers, other studies, including the present one, have failed to find handedness differences in CC measures (Kertesz, Polk, Howell, & Black, 1987; O'Kusky et al., 1988; Reinarz et al., 1988). Interestingly, Witelson (1989) reports that the isthmus area varies as a function of sex and handedness, while we and Byne et al. (1988) find a sex difference in minimum body width, which is usually located within the isthmus. The apparent consensus from the above studies is that there is great individual variation in the size and shape of the corpus callosum, which in turn is a more striking finding than differences between groups.

In order to examine whether behavioral data in callosal relay tasks and direct-access tasks are related to individual differences in CC measures, our subjects were given dichotic listening and lateralized lexical decision tests in addition to receiving MRI.

DICHOTIC LISTENING

The dichotic listening task was comprised of 120 trials consisting of dichotic pairs of the six consonant–vowel (CV) syllables Bee, Dee, Gee, Pee, Tee, Kee. Subjects indicated the sound(s) they had heard by pointing to a response sheet containing the capital letters B, D, G, P, T, K. Separate tests with commissurotomy patients showed the same right ear advantage (REA) with pointing responses (either hand) and with verbal report. As expected, an overall significant REA was found. Group differences were examined using the laterality index f, which corrects for overall accuracy; $f = (Rc - Lc)/(Rc + Lc) \times 100$ if $Lc + Rc < 100\%$ (maximum $Rc + Lc = 200\%$), and $f = (Rc - Lc)/(Re + Le) \times 100$ otherwise, where Rc is the percentage of correct responses for right ear (RE) stimuli, Le is the percentage of incorrect responses for left ear (LE) stimuli, etc. (Marshall, Caplan, & Holmes, 1975). Although main effects of sex and handedness were not significant,

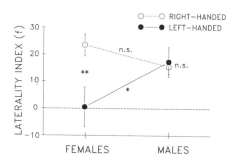

Figure 7. Mean laterality index scores (f) and standard error bars for each sex and handedness group for dichotic listening to consonant–vowel syllables. A positive f indicates a right ear advantage, and a negative f indicates a left ear advantage.

the sex × handedness interaction was significant. As can be seen in Figure 7, only the left-handed females did not show an overall laterality effect.

Scores on the dichotic listening task were correlated with the two sets of anatomical measures (i.e., tracings from the two experimenters). The behavioral scores used were LE performance, RE performance, and the laterality index *f*. As several correlations were analyzed, the cutoff probability level for statistical significance was set at .01 (two-tailed), and a result was considered significant only if this level was reached by the anatomical measures of both experimenters. Correlations were determined across all subjects and then separately for males, females, right handers and left handers.

A significant effect was found only for right handers. The total CC area correlated negatively with RE performance. Correlations were also determined for all subjects combined excluding left-handed females, since this was the only group that did not exhibit a behavioral laterality effect (see Figure 7). For this combined group of subjects ($N = 31$) the RE performance correlated negatively with total CC area and with the two anterior CC areas (see Figure 6). Here, the larger anterior CC areas probably resulted in the larger total CC area. Again, LE performance did not correlate with any CC measure.

Because dichotic listening to CV syllables is a callosal relay task with CV identification being exclusively specialized in the LH for most right-handed subjects, one might predict that left, rather than right, ear performance should be positively correlated with CC size. This prediction is based on the conclusion that LE inputs reach the LH via callosal transfer, whereas RE inputs reach the LH directly, without callosal transfer. The ease with which LE auditory inputs transfer from the RH to the LH might be a function of the size of the region of the CC that subserves this auditory transfer, perhaps the isthmus or posterior body (cf. Alexander & Warren, 1988; Degos et al., 1987; de Lacoste, Kirkpatrick, & Ross, 1985; Pandya & Seltzer, 1986; Risse, Gates, Lund, Maxwell, & Rubens, 1989). On the contrary, we did not find a relationship between LE performance and any CC area. Instead, our finding that RE performance tends to be worse when callosal size is large suggests that the RH may be exerting competing or inhibiting influences that selectively affect early processing of RE inputs in the LH. Since the inhibition does not affect LE scores, it could not modulate either callosal transfer or ipsilateral suppression of the LE in the LH, nor could it modulate the phonetic processing module in the LH. The conclusion that this inhibitory effect is probably independent of competition from interhemispheric transfer of LE auditory inputs is supported by the fact that the RE performance did not correlate with CC regions involved with auditory transfer but rather with anterior CC regions.

Although RE performance correlated negatively with callosal size, neither LE accuracy nor the laterality index *f* correlated significantly with any CC measure. Furthermore, RE and LE performances were not significantly correlated across subjects. Since dichotic listening is a callosal relay task with exclusive LH specialization in most subjects, one might expect a significant correlation between RE and LE accuracy. This follows since both the RE and LE inputs are presumably processed by the same LH structures. However, as the above findings suggest, interhemispheric factors also play a role. The lack of a significant correlation between RE and LE performance is probably related to individual differences in interhemispheric connectivity. Notice that a significant and positive correlation between RE and LE performance would be expected if the correlation was determined across stimulus items rather than across subjects. In this manner, stimulus items that are more difficult to discern (i.e., by the LH) should result in poorer performance than easier items, whether they are presented to the RE or the LE. Of course, this assumes that within each subject interhemispheric influences are constant across item difficulty. The validity of this assumption has yet to be determined.

Kertesz et al. (1987) reported that the midsagittal CC area from 104 subjects was uncorrelated ($r = .03$) with a laterality index derived from dichotic listening performance. However, O'Kusky et al. (1988) did find a significant negative correlation between total CC area and a dichotic listening index in 50 normal subjects ($r = .31$, $p < .05$). O'Kusky et al. propose that individuals with larger corpus callosums tend to have greater RH speech representation. Implicit in their conclusion is the assumption that the signal from each ear is processed in the contralateral hemisphere, direct-access fashion, and then the LE score reflects RH language ability. In the present study, the total CC area did not correlate significantly with the laterality index f ($r = .21$, $p > .05$), although the correlation was in the same direction as in the O'Kusky et al. study. Unlike the present study, Kertesz et al. and O'Kusky et al. did not report the relationship between callosal size and the performance of each ear separately. Apparently, RE performance is associated with callosal size independent of LE performance, and exclusive LH specialization for this task in right handers would then imply inhibition of RE perception prior to phonetic analysis. Because we found a relationship between RE accuracy and callosal size only in those groups demonstrating a strong RE advantage (i.e., exclusive LH specialization), we believe that this relationship represents interhemispheric inhibition rather than varying degrees of RH speech ability as proposed by O'Kusky et al. Our interpretation is based on dichotic listening findings from split-brain subjects that suggest exclusive LH specialization for this task. However, we used nonsense CV syllables known to produce strong ipsilateral suppression and to be processed exclusively in the LH, whereas O'Kusky et al. used monosyllabic words, which may result in weaker ipsilateral suppression and may also make possible greater RH involvement. It is unclear whether the O'Kusky et al. findings represent the effects of interhemispheric inhibition, RH linguistic processing, or reduced ipsilateral suppression, which may be proportional to callosal size.

LEXICAL DECISION WITH ASSOCIATIVE PRIMING

The lexical decision task consisted of lateralized primes, all concrete nouns, and lateralized targets, half of which were concrete nouns and half of which were orthographically regular nonwords (cf. Radant, 1981). Of the targets that were words, half were associatively related to the respective prime words (as determined by free-association norms), and half were unrelated (see above). Each of the 128 trials consisted of the following sequence: 100-msec lateralized prime, 500-msec interstimulus interval, 60-msec lateralized target, and a 3-second period to respond if the target was a word, before commencement of the next trial.

Because the overall hit rate for words was 75%, accuracy was considered a more suitable dependent variable than reaction time. The expected RVFA for target words was found, although there was no significant visual field effect for primes. Apparently, the prime information was transferred successfully between the hemispheres during the 500-msec interval that preceded target presentation. Thus, the lexicons of both hemispheres were probably influenced by each prime presentation. The associative priming manipulation was successful, as accuracies were higher when primes and targets were associated than when they were unassociated.

The response hand × target visual field interaction was significant. As can be seen in Figure 8, the RVFA was greater when responses were made with the left hand than with the right hand. This interaction is indicative of direct access together with effects of intrahemispheric resource limitations (Zaidel, 1985). When the response hand and the target stimuli are on the same side (i.e., Lh-LVF or Rh-RVF), the hemisphere that first receives the stimulus input presumably carries out both the linguistic processing and the response programming. Intrahemispheric resource limitations then cause performance to be poorer than when load is shared between the hemispheres, as would occur during crossed hand–visual field conditions (i.e., Lh-RVF or Rh-LVF). In the crossed conditions, the hemisphere that first receives the stimulus input presumably carries out the linguistic processing while the contralateral hemisphere is responsible for response programming. Therefore, the interaction shown in Figure 8 reflects an overall RVFA caused by the LH's greater competence with linguistic stimuli, with the additional effects of augmented performance for crossed hand–VF condi-

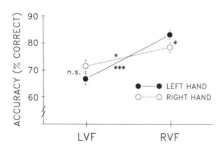

Figure 8. Mean accuracies and standard error bars during a lexical decision task with associated priming for left visual hemifield (LVF) and right visual hemifield (RVF) target presentations and left- or right-hand responses.

tions and diminished performance for uncrossed hand–VF conditions. This results in a larger RVFA for left than right hand responses.

A difference in the pattern of performance between right and left handers was evident in a significant handedness × association × target VF interaction. Simple effects were tested at $p < .01$, and as can be seen in Figure 9, right handers displayed a RVFA for unassociated targets and no VFA for associated targets. Left handers displayed an opposite pattern, with the RVFA apparent only for associated targets. Both of these association × target visual field patterns are consistent with a direct-access interpretation. For the right handers, an effect of association occurred only in the LFV (see Figure 9). Thus, the results in right handers replicate previous findings of greater facilitation of lexical decision by associated primes and greater inhibition by unassociated primes in the normal RH than in the LH (Radant, 1981; Zaidel, 1983). The left handers, on average, appear to have partly reversed lexical semantic hemispheric roles in this task.

Correlations were determined between the anatomical measures of the CC and three accuracy measures: percentage correct for RVF targets, for LVF targets, and the difference between these (i.e., RVF − LVF). The criterion for significance was again set at the .01 level of confidence, which had to be obtained by both experimenters' measures. For all subjects combined, the maximum splenial width correlated negatively with LVF performance and correlated positively with the VF difference score. The correlations between the callosal measures and the RVF score were not significant. Thus, subjects who had larger splenial widths tended to have lower LVF accuracies and greater RVFA than did subjects with smaller splenial widths. Significant positive correlations were also apparent between the VF difference score and two other CC measures: anterior midbody area and isthmus area. When right handers, left handers, males, and females were examined separately, only the left handers demonstrated a significant effect. For left handers, the VF difference score correlated positively with maximum splenial width.

A commonly held view is that a larger CC allows for greater interhemispheric communication and consequently results in smaller laterality effects. The above findings, however, suggest just the opposite. Across all subjects, three CC measures (maximum splenial width, anterior midbody area, and isthmus area) tended to be larger when the VF difference (i.e., RVF − LVF) was also larger. Why these three CC measures correlate with the laterality score and the other CC measures do not is unclear. However, there is a trend for all the CC area measures, except the anterior third, to correlate positively with the VF difference score (i.e., $p < .05$ for both sets of CC measures). We propose that these findings reflect an inhibitory role of the CC, with the linguistically competent LH exerting inhibitory control influences on the RH. In contrast to the topographic arrangement of CC fibers that convey modality-specific information, CC fibers responsible for control information may be more diffusely represented throughout the CC. Our interpretation does not deny a role of the CC in transmitting sensory

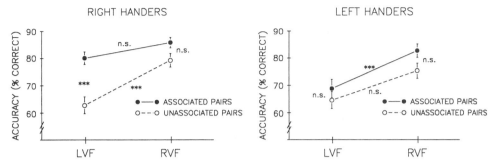

Figure 9. Mean accuracies and standard errors for left-handed ($N = 21$) and right-handed ($N = 22$) subjects for lexical decision to associated and unassociated prime–target pairs when the target appeared in the left visual hemifield (LVF) and in the right visual hemifield (RVF).

information from one hemisphere to the other. However, such transmission of information, unlike inhibitory control, does not correlate with callosal size in this task.

Correlations were also determined between the CC measures and laterality scores (i.e., RVF − LVF) for associated and unassociated targets separately. In right handers, only the anterior midbody CC area correlated significantly and positively with the laterality score for associated targets. Furthermore, there was a trend ($p < .05$) for a negative correlation between anterior midbody area and accuracy for LVF-associated targets, whereas RVF scores did not correlate with any part of the CC. For left handers, the maximum splenial width was the only measure that correlated significantly with the laterality score for associated targets. Similarly, maximal splenial width correlated negatively with accuracy for LVF-associated targets but not for RVF-associated targets. The findings from the two handedness groups suggest that interhemispheric inhibitory channels may have different regional CC distributions in right and left handers. This may in turn represent qualitatively different types of inhibitory influences (e.g., affecting early versus late processing) in these two groups.

Recall that the behavioral data also indicated different laterality effects for right and left handers. For right handers, there was no significant VF difference for associated targets but there was a RVFA for unassociated target, whereas in left handers the RVFA only occurred for associated targets (Figure 9). It is interesting that in right handers the laterality score is correlated with callosal size for associated pairs, which do not show a significant overall laterality effect, that is, no RVFA, whereas there is no correlation between the laterality score and callosal size for unassociated pairs, which do show a significant RVFA. This apparent paradox may be explained by noting that associated pairs are most probably processed independently in each hemisphere, direct-access fashion (Figure 1a), whereas unassociated pairs are consistent with either direct access or callosal relay to the LH. If this is indeed the case, then the laterality effect for associated pairs depends on a RH contribution during LVF target presentations, which is sensitive to cross-callosal inhibition by the LH, and thus the laterality effect is negatively correlated with callosal size. It follows that the laterality effects in direct-access tasks may not reflect the true difference in hemispheric competence. On the other hand, if the laterality effect for unassociated pairs does not depend on a RH contribution (i.e., callosal relay), it should not be sensitive to cross-callosal inhibition and should, in turn, not correlate positively with callosal size. In effect, then, a positive correlation between the behavioral laterality effect and callosal size and/or a negative correlation between the LVF score and callosal size become indices for direct access (i.e., hemispheric independence).

Put together, the behavioral–anatomical correlations observed in the dichotic listening and lexical decision tasks suggest that callosal size is related more to the capacity for interhemispheric inhibition than to the capacity for interhemispheric transfer of information. In the dichotic listening experiment, which involves callosal relay of the left ear signal to specialized phonetic processors in the LH, there is no correlation between the left ear score and the size of any callosal region. On the other hand, for those subjects exhibiting a laterality effect, there is a significant negative correlation between callosal size and right ear scores, even though right ear signals do not undergo callosal transfer. The effect of callosal size on right ear scores may be interpreted as RH inhibition of phonetic processing in the LH. By the same token, in the lexical decision task, which is presumed to be processed independently in each hemisphere, decision of associatively related pairs (those showing unequivocal evidence for direct access since they exhibit no VFA) gives rise to a significant positive correlation of the RVFA with anterior midbody CC area as well as a negative correlation of LVF but not RVF scores with anterior midbody callosal size. The effect of callosal size of LVF processing may be interpreted as LH inhibition of lexical analysis in the RH. Furthermore, such inhibitory effects may have different regional distributions in right and left handers.

Inhibition may originate in either the dominant or nondominant hemisphere, and it appears to be mediated by different channels for different tasks and in different subjects. The inhibition serves to decrease the behavioral laterality effect in a callosal relay task but to increase the laterality effect in a direct-access task. Thus, it is not true in general that a larger callosum implies a smaller laterality effect because of more effective information transfer from the nondominant to the dominant hemisphere. Nor do our data support the hypothesis that the ontogenesis of hemispheric specialization is mediated by a decrease in callosal size through axonal elimination (Rosen, Galaburda, & Sherman, this volume).

It is important to note that although callosal size may be related to the sizes and signs of behavioral laterality effects, this relationship between anatomy and lateralized behavior can occur independently of the presence of an actual overall laterality effect in a particular experiment. For example, in right handers there is an overall REA in the dichotic listening task and no RVFA for associated pairs in the primed lexical decision task, yet both show an effect of anatomy on lateralized behavioral (i.e., RE performance in one case, and RVF − LVF performance as well as LVF performance in the other). Conversely, in the same subjects there is a significant RVFA for unassociated pairs in the lexical decision task, yet no effect of callosal size on lateralized behavioral performance (i.e., no correlation with accuracy for unassociated targets in the LVF, RVF, or RVF − LVF).

We hypothesize that callosal size is more sensitive to the presence of inhibitory callosal channels than to channels that transmit information because callosal fibers that mediate interhemispheric control might be larger in diameter and occur with fixed densities so that a greater number of them would require a larger cross-sectional area. We would expect such fibers to be more abundant in callosal areas that interconnect association cortex than in areas that interconnect primary sensory cortex (Aboitiz, Zaidel, & Scheibel, 1989).

Modulation of Callosal Connectivity

There is some evidence that callosal connectivity increases with age (e.g., Galin, Johnstone, Nakell, & Herron, 1979; Salamy, 1978) and that it may be impaired in certain pathological states such as schizophrenia (Gruzelier, 1987). However, there has been little or no definitive work on short-term modulation of callosal connectivity in normal subjects as a result of changes in either exogenous or endogenous states. The critical step is to distinguish effects on hemispheric activation from effects on callosal transfer. Direct-access and callosal relay models of behavioral laterality effects provide the requisite methodology. These models suggest that modulation of callosal connectivity of channels that mediate information transfer should have a very different effect than modulation of callosal connectivity of channels that mediate control signals. Suppose callosal transfer is automatic rather than optional. Then a larger splenium may help performance on visuospatial tasks that require interhemispheric integration of visual information but may hurt performance on visuospatial tasks specialized in one hemisphere. By the same token, tasks that are optimized by independent hemispheric contributions may benefit from smaller callosal control channels so that inhibitory interhemispheric interference effects are minimized.

Radant (1981) used the lateralized lexical decision task with associative priming in order to study the effect of anxiety on callosal transfer. He measured transfer for visual or semantic information by comparing latencies for prime-target pairs when primes and targets appeared in opposite fields to latencies when primes and targets appeared in the same field. He found a significant negative correlation between state anxiety (measured by the Spielberger State-Trait Anxiety Inventory; Spielberger, Gorsuch, & Lushene, 1970) and left-to-right hemisphere transfer of facilitation but not with right-to-left transfer. Since hemispheric activation appears to facilitate information transfer out of the hemisphere but to inhibit transfer into it (cf. Inouye, Yagasaki, Takahashi, & Shinosaki, 1981), Radant's data suggest selective RH activation during anxiety (cf. Inouye et al., 1981). Different results apply to intermanual transfer in a motor learning task, where high trait anxiety is associated with greater LH-to-RH transfer for "quiet" conditions but with greater disruption of such transfer for "noise" conditions (Thakur, 1977). Thus, different factors may selectively modulate different callosal channels.

EFFECTS OF HYPNOSIS ON THE RIGHT EAR ADVANTAGE IN DICHOTIC LISTENING

Frumkin, Ripley, and Cox (1978) found a reduction in the REA in right-handed subjects during dichotic listening to nonsense CVCs with hypnosis. They concluded that their "results support the view that hypnosis facilitates greater participation of the right cerebral hemisphere in cognition" (p. 741). However, their data do not clearly support this specific interpretation, say, by demonstrating a specific increase in LE score. Indeed, our demonstration that the RH is not normally involved in this task suggests that the effect results instead from either a reduction in LH activation or an increase in callosal connectivity. Earlier, we have shown that dichotic listening to nonsense CV syllables is a callosal relay task that requires perceptual phonetic processes, which are exclusively specialized in the LH. Therefore, assuming a complete or constant ipsilateral suppression, a change in the REA that is affected by manipulating some experimental variable may reflect (1) a corresponding change in LH competence, (2) a change in callosal connectivity from the RH to the LH, or (3) a change in ipsilateral suppression of the LE in the LH. This ambiguity reflects the fact that the RE and LE scores may not be independent of each other, and an increase in LE accuracy may be associated with a decrease in RE accuracy.

The hypnosis experiment was carried out by B. Suyenobu. In order to increase the likelihood of finding an effect of hypnosis on the REA, subjects who were moderately and highly hypnotizable were selected, that is, those subjects who scored 4–12 on the Harvard Group Scale of Hypnotic Susceptibility (HGSHS). The hypnotic induction and termination procedures were from the Stanford Hypnotic Susceptibility Scale, Form C, prerecorded on audio tape. Subjects were audiometrically screened for normal hearing (Grason–Stadler model 1704 audiometer) and also for handedness using a modified version of the Edinburgh Handedness Inventory. Forty-nine subjects completed the experiment. They included 16 right-handed females, 11 right-handed males, 10 left-handed females, and 12 left-handed males. The stimuli consisted of the same dichotic pairs of consonant–vowel nonsense syllables from the set Bee, Dee, Gee, Pee, Tee, and Kee described above. Subjects were required to report verbally the sounds they had heard. Subjects participated in both the hypnosis and neutral conditions during a single session. The conditions were separated by 5 minutes of walking and conversation, and the order of the conditions were counterbalanced across subjects.

The laterality coefficient f served as the dependent variable, hypnosis was a within-subject variable (hypnosis versus neutral condition), and handedness and gender were between-subject variables. An ANOVA disclosed a significant main effect of handedness, with right handers showing a greater laterality effect [$f = 19.6$ versus 9.1, $F(1,45) = 6.24$, $p < .025$] (Figure 10). There was also a main effect of gender, with males showing a greater REA than females [$f = 18.7$ versus 10.1, $F(1,45) = 4.2$, $p < .05$]. But there was no significant main effect, nor any significant interactions with hypnosis (Figure 10). Further analysis of the data from the most susceptible subjects (HGSHS 9–12) still showed no shifts in the laterality effect with hypnosis. Indeed, there were no significant differences in the effect of hypnosis on the laterality index between highly susceptible (HGSHS 9–12) and moderately susceptible (HGSHS 4–8) subjects. Although the handedness $\times$ hypnosis interaction was not significant ($p = .12$), the results demonstrated a trend for the right handers to have a greater laterality index in the neutral condition ($f = 21.4$) than in the hypnosis condition ($f = 17.8$), whereas left handers tended to have a greater laterality index in the hypnosis condition ($f = 10.6$) than in the neutral condition ($f = 7.7$). Thus, hypnosis seems to have an opposite modulatory effect on left and right handers.

An ANOVA using accuracy of verbal report as the dependent variable with ear of report as a within-subject variable disclosed a significant REA but no main effects of hypnosis, handedness, or gender. The hypnosis $\times$ handedness interaction approached significance, with hypnotized left handers obtaining the highest scores [$F(1,45) = 3.75$, $p = .056$]. Planned comparisons showed a surprising trend for a higher RE score by left-handed males in the hypnosis than in the neutral condition [56.9% correct versus 52.4%, respectively, $F(1,45) = 4.75$, $p = .05$]. Also, in the neutral condition, female right handers had higher RE scores than female left handers [53.8% versus 42.2%, $F(1,45) = 7.37$, $p < .01$]. These group differences in RE rather than LE scores suggest that the effects of handedness in females and of hypnosis in left-handed males may be related to modulation of phonetic specialization in the LH or to ipsilateral suppression of the LE signal in the LH rather than to

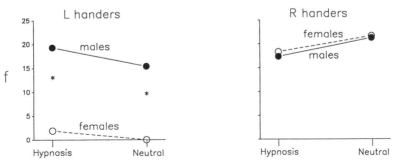

Figure 10. Mean laterality index f as a function of handedness, gender, and hypnosis condition. A positive f means a REA.

modulation of callosal transfer of the LE signal to the LH. Modulation of callosal connectivity by hypnosis is not supported by these data.

Thus, hypnosis failed to have an overall effect on the normal laterality pattern even though the experiment was sensitive enough to show differences in laterality index as a function of handedness and gender.

EFFECTS OF RELAXATION ON THE RIGHT EAR ADVANTAGE
IN DICHOTIC LISTENING

Crawford, Crawford, and Koperski (1983) have suggested that relaxation may be responsible for the reduced REA in dichotic listening during hypnosis. The following experiment was carried out by B. Suyenobu in an attempt to test this claim. Forty-seven UCLA undergraduates (including 25 females, 24 left-handed) served as subjects. Relaxation was induced by a modified version of the Jacobson Progressive Relaxation Procedure (Braud & Braud, 1973) recorded in the examiner's voice. Subjects in the control or neutral condition heard an essay on states of consciousness also recorded in the examiner's voice. Subjects participated in relaxation and neutral conditions on separate days. The order of conditions was counterbalanced across subjects. At three points during the procedure subjects rated the degree of their experienced relaxation in two ways: (1) raising the nondominant hand and (2) verbally reporting a number between 1 and 10, with an increase in height or number indicating greater relaxation.

An ANOVA with handedness and gender as between-subject independent variables, with relaxation condition as a within-subject independent variable, and with the laterality index f as the dependent variable showed a significant main effect of handedness, with lower scores for left handers ($f = 7.4$) than for right handers ($f = 17.6$) [$F(1,43) = 4.89$, $p < .05$]. There were no significant main effects of relaxation or gender or any significant interactions. However, a planned comparison considering the relaxation effect for left-handed women showed a trend toward these subjects exhibiting a significantly lower laterality effect in the relaxed condition ($f = 0.06$) than in the neutral condition ($f = 8.6$) [$F(1,43) = 3.8$, $p = .055$] (Figure 11).

Based on their performance in the procedure, subjects were classified into two groups: those whose laterality index decreased with relaxation ("shifters," $N = 27$) and those whose laterality index stayed the same or increased ("non-shifters," $N = 20$). Independent t-tests showed that shifters tended to be left handed [$t(45) = 2.61$, $p = .025$]. There were no sex differences or differences in overall accuracy in either the relaxed or neutral condition between shifters and nonshifters. However, whereas there were no significant differences between shifters and nonshifters in LE accuracy as measured by hits in 90 trials (mean 39% and 41% correct, respectively) or RE accuracy (mean 51% and 50%, respectively) in the neutral condition, shifters were significantly more accurate in reporting LE items (mean 44% and 36%, respectively) and significantly less accurate in reporting RE items (mean 47% and 54%, respectively) than nonshifters in the relaxation

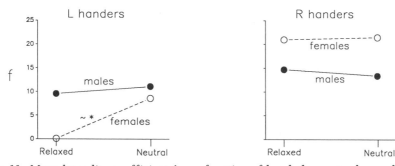

Figure 11. Mean laterality coefficient f as a function of handedness, gender, and relaxation condition. ~*$p = .055$.

condition. Moreover, the shifters had significantly higher final nonverbal self-ratings of relaxation than nonshifters [$t(30)$ 2.66, $p = .012$] though not higher verbal self-ratings [$t(39) = 0.19$, $p = .85$]. Thus, the relaxation that is related to laterality effects is better monitored by a nonverbal report with the nondominant hand, which may reflect judgment mediated by the nondominant hemisphere, than by a verbal report, which may reflect judgment by the dominant hemisphere.

An ANOVA with ear of report as an additional within-subject independent variable and with accuracy as a dependent variable yielded a significant main effect of ear, with significantly more correct RE reports (45.45) than LE reports (35.87) [$F(1,43) = 29.04$, $p < .001$] and a significant interaction between ear and handedness [$F(1,43) = 4.4$, $p < .05$]. *Post hoc* comparisons showed that this interaction resulted from right handers obtaining significantly higher RE than LE accuracy, whereas left handers showed no significant difference between RE and LE accuracy. There were no other significant main effects or interactions.

As in the hypnosis study reported above, relaxation failed to show an overall effect on the normal laterality pattern, although the procedure was sensitive enough to show a difference in the laterality index as a function of handedness.

Taken together, the experiments on modulation of callosal connectivity by hypnosis and by relaxation are at best inconclusive. There are hints that hypnosis increases the RE score in left-handed males and that relaxation increases the LE scores and decreases the RE scores in left-handed females. The group differences in LE scores suggest that these laterality differences result from variations in effectiveness of callosal transfer of the LE signal from the RH to the LH or from variations in RH competence in processing some LE stimuli. Conversely, group differences in RE scores suggest that these laterality differences may be caused by variations in LH competence or ipsilateral suppression. Thus, if in fact hypnosis and relaxation do modulate the laterality effect, they do so by very different mechanisms. Indeed, although both appear to modulate the laterality effect more in left handers than in right handers, hypnosis serves to increase the laterality effect, whereas relaxation seems to decrease it in these subjects. Our data do not support the speculation of Crawford et al. (1983) that relaxation is the factor that affects the reduced REA in hypnosis.

PARALLELISM, MONITORING, AND CONTROL

Parallelism

RATIONALIST, AI, AND NEUROSCIENTIFIC MODELS OF COGNITION

Classical models of information processing, both in neuroscience and in cognitive science, assume independent and sequential centers or stages of processing. This view was reinforced by the logic of programming on the von Neumann digital computer and by rationalist, logical models of computation, such as Post's, Turing's, and Gödel's. However, the relationship between brain and mind in humans does not respect the difference between hardware and software on a digital computer. In the brain, the physical layout of the processing machinery has everything to do with the functions computed by it. Moreover, rationalist, logical models of artificial intelligence, however useful in applications, may be quite misleading as models of human cognition for two reasons. First, when computer scientists construct programs that imitate a human in a limited domain, they typically dedicate the program exclusively to the task and gain efficiency at the expense of generality. But the human cognitive components serve multiple functions not all related nor all apparent to the cognitive scientist. Thus, what appears to be an optimal solution for a specific problem may be suboptimal for a domain of problems, whose scope is initially unknown. Second, the design of the human cognitive system is dictated by evolution, which, as Jacob has aptly said, is a tinkerer, not an engineer. Even if evolution reflects optimal solutions to environmental selection pressures, the precise nature of those pressures and the goals of specific adaptation still largely elude us. Consequently, a logical analysis of the problem space is unlikely to lead to the solution actually implemented in the human brain. Instead, effective scientific research remains closely bound to empirical data, where the hidden design is revealed as if reluctantly. As pointed out by Crick, in cognitive neuroscience, unlike physics, the formal simplicity and beauty of a theory may not be faithful guides to accuracy or validity. This does not mean that rationalist models of cognition are impossible or even dispensable. Rather, it means that such top-down models are unlikely to succeed as processing accounts of actual cognitions unless they are closely guided by detailed observations and bottom-up unfolding of underlying brain organization.

PARALLEL COMPUTATIONS

Cognitive processes that seem intuitively to be serial appear in fact to be implemented in the brain as parallel processes. This illustrates the weakness of our rational modeling intuitions. The following examples show dramatically that it is misleading to infer implementation from logical design principles but fruitful to infer design principles from actual implementation. The examples of parallelism that we have encountered, stumbled on as it were, are of two deterministic macro processes that operate redundantly and in parallel. They contrast with the massive microparallelism at the level of numerous separate atomic nodes that characterize recent connectionist models of cognition.

Multiple Parallel Interhemispheric Pathways. Clarke and Zaidel (1989) measured simple unimanual reaction times to lateralized light flashes in normal subjects, commissurotomy patients, and one case of callosal agenesis. Differences in reaction time between crossed (LVF-Rh, RVF-Lh) and uncrossed (LVF-Lh, RVF-Rh) combinations of visual field of input and hand of response (crossed-uncrossed differences or CUDs) provide estimates of interhemispheric transfer time. Stimulus light intensity and eccentricity were manipulated in order to determine whether they affect the CUD, thus implicating a visual pathway. Normal subjects exhibited the smallest CUD, ranging from a nonsignificant 1 msec in one experiment to a significant 3 msec in a second experiment (Table 2). Although both stimulus intensity and eccentricity affected overall reaction time, neither affected the CUD in normal subjects (relevant work by others is discussed in Clarke & Zaidel, 1989). Clarke and Zaidel concluded that nonsensory callosal pathways mediated interhemispheric integration in these subjects.

Patients with complete cerebral commissurotomy exhibited both quantitative and qualitative individual differences in interhemispheric transfer. Their mean CUDs varied from 39 to 74 msec (Table 2). One patient (L.B.) exhibited no effect of stimulus intensity or eccentricity on the CUD. We attributed "interhemispheric transfer" in this case to ipsilateral corticospinal motor tracts. The

TABLE 2

SUMMARY OF SIMPLE REACTION TIME RESULTS FOR NORMAL SUBJECTS ($N = 20$ PER EXPERIMENT),
FOUR COMMISSUROTOMIZED PATIENTS, AND AN ACALLOSAL BOY (M.M.), FOR EXPERIMENT 1
IN WHICH STIMULUS INTENSITY (I) IS MANIPULATED AND FOR EXPERIMENT 2
IN WHICH STIMULUS ECCENTRICITY (E) IS MANIPULATED

	Main effect of visual parameter?		Effect of I or E on CUD?		Mean size of CUD (msec)
	I	E	I	E	
Normals	+	+	−	−	1.9
L.B.	+	+	−	−	39.4
N.G.	+	+	−	+	49.0
A.A.	+	+	−	+	63.8
R.Y.	+	+	+	+	73.5
M.M.	+	+	−	−	16.1

Note. CUD = crossed–uncrossed difference in reaction time. A "+" signifies "yes" while a "−" signifies "no." Data from Clarke and Zaidel (1989).

CUDs of two other patients (N.G., A.A.) varied with stimulus eccentricity but not intensity, suggesting some visual transfer. There are at least two neural routes incorporating the superior colliculus that could account for the visual transfer. The first is a direct ipsilateral visual projection in which midline transfer, presumably via the superior colliculi, occurs prior to cortical processing. The second possible route involves an interhemispheric subcallosal pathway, in which some sensory processing is accomplished in the contralateral cerebral hemisphere prior to subcortical transfer. Unlike patients with blind sight who presumably also have the ipsilateral visual pathway available to them and yet are unaware of stimuli presented in their scotomas, our patients were aware of stimuli in either hemifield, presumably because of cortical processing. Consequently, it was concluded that in these cases a subcortical interhemispheric visual route rather than an ipsilateral visual pathway mediated crossed responses in these patients and that this route is more sensitive to stimulus eccentricity than to stimulus intensity.

The CUD of the last commissurotomy patient (R.Y.) was sensitive to both stimulus intensity and eccentricity, implicating a somewhat different pathway than that used by N.G. and A.A. He had the slowest and least accurate responses to stimuli presented in the RVF during left-hand but not right-hand responses. An asymmetry in subcortical visual interhemispheric communication caused by a lesion in the left visual association area that affected the transfer of visual information from the LH to the RH might explain the results in this patient. R.Y. exhibited a paradoxical increase in latency with brighter stimuli in the RVF-Lh condition, presumably because of a greater activation of the malfunctioning system.

The callosal agenesis case (M.M.) exhibited an intermediate CUD that varied from 12 to 20 msec across the two experiments and was insensitive to stimulus intensity or eccentricity (Table 2). We suppose that this subject used the anterior commissure or ipsilateral motor pathways. It could not be determined from the data whether these pathways are normally available as effectively as this or whether they reflect functional reorganization consequent to congenital agenesis. The advantage of the CUD of this subject over that of patients with complete cerebral commissurotomy suggests that the pathways available to him are weaker or not present in the surgically sectioned and normal brains.

The following information-processing model accounts for the apparent variety of interhemispheric transfer routes. Visual information reaches both hemispheres through direct contralateral as well as indirect ipsilateral projections. However, full awareness of a visual stimulus can only be achieved via the contralateral visual system. Moreover, visual information transfers interhemispherically across the corpus callosum, anterior commissure, and subcortical commissures. Following visual analysis, information undergoes cognitive elaboration, and again abstract cognitive information transfers, perhaps across more anterior parts of the corpus callosum. Finally, information flows into the motor-programming stage, and motor commands can again transfer between the two

hemispheres via cortical and/or subcortical commissures. In addition, each hemisphere has direct contralateral and indirect ipsilateral corticospinal motor control
systems. In this model, all possible connections are activated simultaneously and
result in multiple parallel processes, often terminated horse-race fashion by the
one that completes processing first.

In sum, two general observations emerge. First, assuming that the pathways
available to the commissurotomy patients are also available to cases of callosal
agenesis and to normal subjects, it appears that a "horse-race" model applies and
that the fastest available process/route dominates the responses that require
interhemispheric integration. However, this is not always the case. Other examples show exhaustive completion of all available parallel processes, and yet others
show dominance by a suboptimal process that controls the final behavior (Zaidel,
1978, and see below). Also, each of the four commissurotomy patients apparently
used one of several different pathways, all presumably available to each. The
case of R.Y. is especially interesting because it may illustrate dominance by a
suboptimal system that is malfunctioning yet remains in control, presumably
because of a lesion.

Parallel Hemispheric Processing: Hemispheric Independence. Parallel processing in the two hemispheres, at least for divided input, is demonstrated by the
existence of direct-access tasks (see above). Remarkably, it is not necessary to
present simultaneous bilateral and conflicting inputs to the two hemifields for
independence to occur, and independent processing can persist for at least 2 to
3 seconds. Lexical decision of concrete nouns and orthographically regular nonwords illustrates such independent hemispheric processing in the normal brain
(see above). Elsewhere (Zaidel, 1989) we have shown that hemispheric independence extends to all stages of the task, from perceptual analysis through semantic,
orthographic, phonological, morphological, and grammatic stages of lexical analysis, to response programming and even error monitoring.

Binary Choice Tasks: Parallel Processes within the Hemispheres. Consider a
binary choice task such as lexical decision or same–different judgment with two
response codes. An intuitive and logical strategy is to search for a match in one
category and then choose its response code if a match is found or choose the
alternative code if a match is not found. For example, in a lexical decision task,
the classical lexical search model yields "word" responses if an exhaustive search
through an appropriate part of the lexicon results in a match and "nonword"
responses otherwise. Of course, the "one category match" strategy can apply to
either category, and thus its application involves a choice between two available
strategies corresponding to the two categories. Surprisingly, it appears that independent processing of binary choice tasks within each hemisphere often involves
simultaneous activation of separate category match searches for each of the
categories. Thus, whereas lexical decision in the RVF of normal subjects usually
shows the classic significant advantage of words over nonwords, decisions in the
LVF of normals often do not (Figure 3, accuracy for yes–no responses) and

occasionally yield a significant nonword advantage. A "one category match" lexical search strategy would produce responses to the second category (in this case nonwords) that should be on the average worse by a fixed amount than responses to the "unmarked" (first-searched) category (in this case words). Logically, that amount need only reflect a decision of the form "if not A then B" and "not A" implies "B" and so should be quite small, in contrast with the large typical word advantage. Rather, it appears that in both hemispheres each category is matched separately, and responses of one category reflect the results of a match strategy in that category. For example, if the response is "nonword," then the search reflects a nonword match strategy, whereas if the response is "word," then the search reflects a word match strategy. This seemingly suboptimal, redundant strategy pattern suggests that responses are programmed into decision processes rather than constituting independent decision stages.

A second example of the parallel match principle was provided in a lateralized rhyming judgment task (Rayman & Zaidel, 1989). Subjects determined whether two successively presented and orthographically different words rhymed. The first word was presented at fixation, and the second was presented either to the left or to the right of fixation, either alone or accompanied by a distracter word in the other visual hemifield, with an arrow at fixation indicating the target. Overall, subjects were more accurate when the words did not rhyme and when presentation was to the RVF, but the RVFA was stronger when the words rhymed. In fact, the classical nonrhyme advantage was significant in the LVF but not in the RVF (Figure 12). Most importantly, accuracy on nonrhyming trials was predicted by word frequency, whereas accuracy on rhyming trials was predicted by the length of the first word. This pattern was the same in each hemifield. Thus, rhyme judgments and nonrhyme judgments appear to use quite different strategies, both strategies are applied in parallel, and this is done independently in each hemisphere. A similar argument was advanced to explain the paradoxical finding that "same" decisions are usually faster than "different" decisions in pattern pair comparison tasks. It has been suggested that two separate processes are involved in the comparison: a fast holistic process for "same" judgments and a slower analytic feature comparison process for "different"

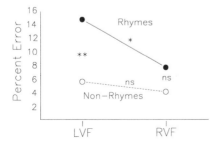

Figure 12. Results from a lateralized rhyming judgment task (Rayman & Zaidel, 1989).

judgments (Farell, 1985). Taking together our data on parallel processing between and within the hemispheres, we may conclude that macro parallel processing is ubiquitous throughout the brain and occurs at multiple levels of the hierarchical organization of human cognitive functioning.

"Parallel Stages." The experiment by Measso and Zaidel (in press) described above was designed to compare the effects of response programming on laterality effects in lexical decision. Some subjects were to make word/nonword binary decisions, others only a response to words in a go/no-go paradigm, and yet others only a response to nonwords in a go/no-go paradigm. The data revealed a significant overall RVFA in accuracy and sensitivity and a significant interaction between VF and wordness in latency but no significant interactions with response condition. However, planned comparisons revealed two interesting differences related to response condition. First, there was a significant RVFA for latency of word decisions in the word/nonword binary condition but not in the go/no-go conditions. Second, there was a significant word advantage for accuracy in the LVF with the go/no-go conditions but not in the word/nonword binary condition (Figure 3). Thus, response programming appeared to interact with hemispheric lexical access in this previously demonstrated direct access task. Measso interpreted the interaction to reflect an overlap between lexical decision stages and motor-programming stages of the task. That interpretation supports a continuous rather than a discrete stage model of human information processing, since response preparation can begin before stimulus identification is complete (Miller, 1982). However, the overlapping stages of interpretation contrast with our earlier observation that response programming is packaged together with the process that leads to it.

Illusions. B. Rothwell presented lateralized tachistoscopic length estimation tasks to normal subjects and a split-brain patient in order to compare the susceptibility of the two hemispheres to the Oppel–Kundt illusion of filled extent (Rothwell & Zaidel, 1990) (Figure 13b). The results showed that the susceptibility of the LVF/RH declined more than that of the RVF/LH as illusion processing time increased. In one experiment with normal subjects, the RH was more susceptible when the subjects responded quickly, whereas when they responded slowly there was no VF difference in susceptibility (Figure 13a). The authors interpreted the results as reflecting the net effect of two parallel processes available to both hemispheres. One process is fast, uses feature extraction to analyze the illusion figure, and is performed more effectively in the LH, thus rendering it less susceptible. The second process is slow, uses visuospatial analysis to compute distances between parts of the illusion figure, and is performed more effectively in the RH, reducing its susceptibility. In this view, susceptibility to the illusion depends on the relative state of completion of the two processes. However, in this case, the decision to respond is neither controlled by the faster process, as a horse-race model would predict, nor is it necessarily delayed until both processes are

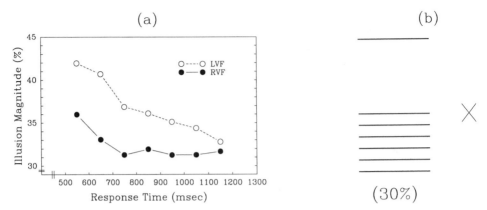

Figure 13. Susceptibility to the Oppel–Kundt illusion in the two hemifields as a function of processing time (a). Subjects were shown a single figure containing both filled and unfilled extents whose heights had to be compared with each other. In this example (b), the unfilled extent is 30% longer than the filled extent. The responses were collapsed across all subjects and then divided into bins according to the response times (Rothwell & Zaidel, 1990).

completed. Instead, some responses are made quickly so that the fast process dominates, whereas others are made slowly so that the slow process dominates. The variables that control the decision to respond are presently unknown.

In sum, parallelism introduces a need for coordination and control. In the examples presented above, control is implicit rather than explicit. Priority is built into the process rather than decided by an independent process. In the case of interhemispheric pathways, control is largely determined by speed, although localized lesions appear capable of derailing it. In the case of binary decisions, control is built into the decision process; each process controls its own response program. This model implies that the two independent decision processes may conflict when one is in error. Such a conflict may be expected to be revealed as response competition or as self-corrections. We have not observed a substantial proportion of changes of mind, but it may be possible to develop tests for the occurrence of otherwise hidden response competition. The illusion experiment suggests a variable criterion for decision to respond, controlled neither by speed nor by exhaustive processing. Rather, some trials are quick and are dominated by a fast process, whereas others are slow and are dominated by a lengthier parallel process.

Monitoring within and between the Hemispheres

HEMISPHERIC INDEPENDENCE AND MODULARITY OF ERROR CORRECTION

Given hemispheric independence in lexical decision, does independence extend to error monitoring and correction? Does each hemisphere include its own executive control? If so, is error monitoring functionally independent of decisions; that is, is it modular? In order to address these questions, R. Stein used a version of the same lexical decision task discussed above, which showed a direct-access pattern. Here, however, the task was made more difficult by flashing the lateralized stimuli for only 40 msec using a projection tachistoscope. Word/nonword responses were signaled on a two-way toggle switch. Subjects were induced to correct their own errors by appeal to a special reward system that heavily penalized uncorrected errors but partially rewarded self-corrected errors. They were instructed to be both fast and accurate and to correct themselves by pushing the switch in the opposite direction to the initial response. Accuracy of initial performance was compared to accuracy of self-corrections (Stein & Zaidel, 1989; Zaidel, 1987).

Initial responses showed the usual significant effects: a RVFA, an advantage of words over nonwords, and an interaction of wordness by VF (Figure 14). There was a significant RVFA for words but not for nonwords, and the word advantage was significant in the RVF but not in the LVF. This direct-access pattern verifies hemispheric independence. By contrast with initial responses, accuracy of self-corrections showed no overall hemifield advantage and a massive advantage of nonwords over words. Thus, initial responses and self-corrections appear to be processed by separate modules. Self-corrections also showed a significant wordness × VF interaction with no VFA for nonwords but a surprising LVFA for words, consistent with direct access in error monitoring. Therefore, each hemisphere has its own lexical access and decision module as well as its own error correction module. The LH is superior in initial decisions, but the RH is superior in correcting those decisions.

MONITORING BETWEEN THE HEMISPHERES

Males and females had somewhat different patterns of h × VF interactions. Initial word decisions by females showed a callosal relay pattern with LH specialization indicated by a RVFA ($p < .01$) and a RhA ($p < .01$) (Figure 15). Self-corrections of word decisions, however, showed a LhA ($p < .01$), and Rh responses were at chance for both VFs (Figure 15). Thus, RVF stimuli appear to be

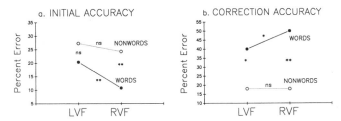

Figure 14. Lateralized lexical decision with unimanual self-corrections. (a) Accuracy of initial word/nonword decisions. (b) Accuracy of manual self-corrections indicated by changing the response (Stein & Zaidel, 1989).

decided more accurately in the LH but appear to be corrected more accurately in
the RH. Similarly, initial word decisions by males show a pattern consistent with a
callosal relay pattern and LH specialization, and self-corrections of word decisions show a pattern consistent with direct access, although neither pattern is
statistically significant (Figure 15). It thus appears that for the males, even though
both hemispheres were capable of initial decisions, the LH was assigned the role
of deciding not only RVF stimuli but also LVF stimuli at the same time that the
RH was assigned the role of correcting errors made in deciding these same LVF
stimuli. Here, then, one hemisphere is temporarily assigned the role of a monitor
for a task specialized in the other. Error correction seems to be optimized by
parallel computation wherein the LH may proceed bottom up and the RH may
check the response top down. A discrepancy would signal an error that can be
resolved by implicit control when the confidence estimates of the two hemispheres reach certain combined thresholds.

Dynamic Shifts in the Control Status of the Two Hemispheres

RESOURCE SHARING

It has been proposed that the two cerebral hemispheres have completely
independent and dedicated resource pools, each limited and undifferentiated,
which cannot be shared (Friedman, Polson, Dafoe, & Gaskill, 1982). This view
appears to be consistent with hemispheric independence and the view that each
normal hemisphere is a complete cognitive system. Their view of the hemispheres as independent limited resource pools claims that processes in opposite
hemispheres should not interfere with each other, whereas any two processes in
the same hemisphere should interfere with each other. Counterexamples to both
claims exist (Zaidel et al., 1989). Thus, the Friedman–Polson hypothesis overesti-
mates intrahemispheric connectivity and underestimates interhemispheric connectivity.

By contrast, one can posit a cognitive cerebral network (Kinsbourne &
Hiscock, 1983) of basic neurocognitive modules that are localized in different
parts of the brain and interact both through input–output information transfer
and through control operations consisting of facilitation and interference. Module–module interaction may shift continuously from facilitation to interference
according to the Yerkes–Dodson law: performance on a task would increase with
moderate increases in the level of arousal or priming but would decrease as the
information-processing load becomes too great. Moreover, in this scheme there is
greater module–module connectivity within than between the hemispheres. Consistent with the foregoing, Zaidel et al. (1980) have found that resource differentiation can exist within each hemisphere, that there is less interference across than
within the hemispheres, and that processing modules in the two hemispheres can
interact even in the absence of the corpus callosum. Thus, some modules within a
hemisphere are independent, some modules across the hemispheres are not, and

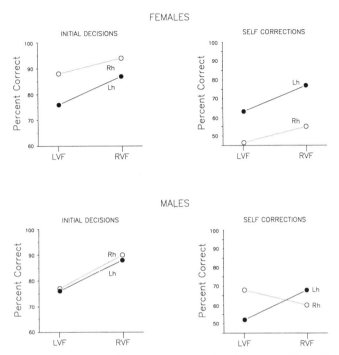

Figure 15. Patterns of interactions between response hand and visual hemifield of presentation shown separately for initial decisions and for self-corrections, for males and for females (Stein & Zaidel, 1989).

modules within a hemisphere may or may not interact, depending on processing load.

Also consistent with this approach, Hellige et al. (1979) showed a shift in hemispheric superiority from the LH to the RH in a lateralized same–different judgment involving nonsense geometric shapes, presumably direct access, with increasing difficulty of a secondary task involving verbal recall, which presumably engaged the LH. A direct-access task can then shift from a LH dominance to a RH dominance and vice versa. Dividing the labor by assigning different task components to opposite hemispheres can optimize performance in processing as well as in control. Conversely, maintaining hemispheric independence by inhibiting callosal connectivity may improve the processing of specialized tasks. In fact, resource assignment in the normal brain appears to be flexible and dynamic (Zaidel et al., 1989) as a function of subject, task, or stimulus. This may help explain the frequent inconsistencies between different experiments in the literature.

SHIFTS BETWEEN DIRECT ACCESS AND CALLOSAL RELAY

Zaidel et al. (1988) illustrated three types of dynamic shifts in hemispheric control status as a function of stimulus complexity. The experimental paradigm involved symbolic comparative judgment. In two experiments subjects saw (experiment 3) a central comparative adjective (BIGGER or SMALLER) or heard it read aloud (experiment 1) followed by two lateralized animal names (e.g., HIPPO above WHALE) taken from a size-graded series (e.g., ant, . . . , whale). Subjects were required to push a button corresponding to that member of the lateralized pair of animal names that matched the central or heard adjective. Thus, the sequence BIGGER followed by HIPPO, WHALE would require the subject to press the button corresponding to WHALE. In half the trials the comparative adjective and animal sizes represented the same pole of the dimension, for example, BIGGER—HIPPO, WHALE (congruent pairs), and in half the trials the comparative adjective represented the opposite pole of the animal size, for example, BIGGER—MOUSE, RAT (incongruent pairs). In experiment 2 digits from 1 to 9 were used. Pairs were lateralized pseudorandomly to the left and right visual hemifields, and the response hand was varied within subjects in counterbalanced blocks. The complete results are reported in White, Banks, and Zaidel (1989).

The classic congruity effect was observed in all three experiments: congruent pairs were processed faster and more accurately than incongruent ones. In all three experiments there were significant response hand × visual hemifield interactions (with an ipsilateral advantage, i.e., best performance in the RVF-Rh and LVF-Lh conditions) for congruent pairs. This suggests direct-access processing of congruent trials. However, incongruent pairs showed variable hand × field patterns. In experiment 1 (animal names, I), the h × VF pattern for incongruent pairs was consistent with callosal relay to an exclusive processor in the RH (Figure 16a). In this case there was a shift of control for RVF trials from direct access for congruent pairs to callosal relay (to the RH) for incongruent pairs. In experiment 2 (digits), the h × VF pattern for incongruent pairs was consistent with callosal relay to an exclusive processor in the LH (Figure 16b). Thus, the shift from congruent to incongruent trials resulted in a shift of control of LVF pairs from the RH to the LH, that is, from direct access to callosal relay. Experiment 3 (animal names, II) showed a direct-access h × VF pattern with a contralateral advantage resulting from interference between central processing and response programming for the incongruent pairs, that is, best performance in RVF-Lh and LVF-Rh conditions (Figure 16c). Thus, the random trial-to-trial shift from congruent to incongruent pairs resulted in a spontaneous shift of resource allocation to response programming modules in the hemisphere opposite to the one controlling the decisions. Still, central processing maintained hemispheric independence for all pairs. In sum, the three experiments demonstrate that hemispheric dominance shifted as a function of item congruity within each experiment and as a function of task between the experiments.

SHIFTS OF DOMINANCE FOR ERROR CORRECTION
AS A FUNCTION OF EXPERIENCE

Data in the experiment on lexical decision with self-corrections were analyzed for the effect of practice. Accuracy of initial decisions and of self-

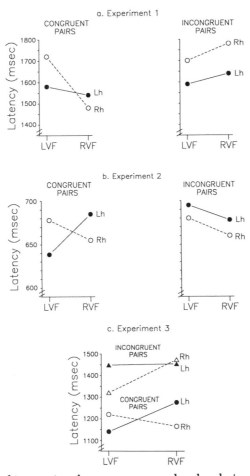

Figure 16. Patterns of interactions between response hand and visual hemifield of stimulus presentation in three lateralized comparative judgment tasks shown separately for congruent and incongruent trials (White et al., 1989). Experiment 1 involved animal names; experiment 2 involved digits; and experiment 3 involved animal names, but the procedure was somewhat different from experiment 1.

corrections in the first and second halves of the test was compared. An ANOVA of initial decisions revealed no significant main effects or interactions involving test half (Stein & Zaidel, 1989). Thus, the RVFA and word advantage were similarly significant in both test halves. However, an ANOVA of self-corrections showed a significant interaction of test-half × VF (Figure 17). Accuracy of self-corrections in the RVF increased in the second half, and accuracy of self-corrections in the LVF decreased in the second half. Indeed, there was a significant LVFA for correction accuracy in the first half but an insignificant superiority of the RVF in the second half. Thus, unlike other experiments that show a shift from RH dominance to LH dominance in processing (Zaidel, 1979), here we see a

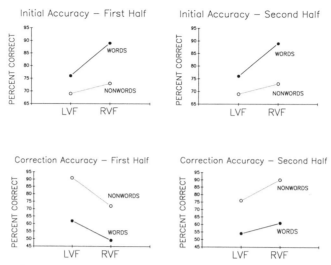

Figure 17. Initial accuracy and accuracy of self-corrections of lateralized lexical decision with unimanual responses, shown separately for the first and second halves of the test (Stein & Zaidel, 1989).

parallel shift from RH dominance to LH dominance in error correction without a corresponding shift in initial decisions, which shows a consistent RVFA.

Conclusion: Dynamic Modularity

Cognitive modularity refers to functional specialization in components of the cognitive system that can process information independently of each other. Fodor (1983) proposed the following strong criteria for modules: (1) they are domain-specific; (2) they are innately specified and not assembled from more basic elements; (3) they are hard wired; (4) they are computationally autonomous; that is, they do not share attention, memory, or other general-purpose processes with other modules; (5) they are informationally encapsulated, that is, they have very restricted access to information in the rest of the system, usually through fixed input channels; (6) they are impenetrable; that is, the rest of the system does not have access to their internal structure but only to the results of their computations, usually through fixed output channels; and (7) they have a characteristic pattern of development (Shallice, 1988).

This view is too strong. A more useful concept of modularity for neuropsychology admits of degree: two functional systems can vary in the degree of interaction between them and thus in their degree of modularity or independence (Marr, 1982; Zaidel et al., 1989). One functional system could operate independently of the other, although not necessarily as efficiently. It should be possible to change the level of performance of one functional system without affecting the other, and they should process information using different principles (Tulving, 1983).

Hemispheric independence shares some features with Fodor's definition but fits better the Marr–Tulving conception. First, we have shown that the two hemispheres can and often do operate independently of each other and that such independence can be computationally advantageous. Moreover, there are clues that the level of performance of the two hemispheres can be modulated independently of each other. Some of Fodor's criteria still apply to hemispheric independence. (1) Hemispheric independence subsumes complementary hemispheric specialization, which includes at least some domain specificity (Zaidel, 1978). (2) Hemispheric specialization appears to be innately specified and hard wired (Zaidel, 1979). (3) The two hemispheres may have different patterns of development (Bradshaw & Nettleton, 1983). However, all the other criteria of Fodor's definition are possible rather than necessary features of the hemispheres. The hemispheres often do not but sometimes do share general processing resources with each other (Zaidel et al., 1989). Moreover, although they are potentially modular at any level of the system, the two hemispheres can and often do maintain autonomy at any level of information processing (Zaidel, 1989). That is one sense in which the two hemispheres are dynamically modular: they change in their degree of functional independence and thus go beyond the conception of Marr and Tulving.

There is another important sense in which hemispheric independence goes beyond Fodor's conception: neither hemisphere is primitive; each is a cognitive system with a complex structure of component processes. Indeed, some believe that the overall cognitive structure of each hemisphere is different. For example, LH structure may be more hierarchical yet localized, whereas RH structure may be more heterarchical yet diffuse (Zaidel, 1978).

The importance of hemispheric independence as a neuropsychological design principle is that it introduces parallel modularity into the highest level of cognitive complexity rather than into a hierarchical sequence of control. This arrangement makes possible three basic modes of hemispheric function. First, there is independent hemispheric computation of domain-specific material by specialized processors. We have shown that there is modularity of control in each hemisphere, with separate processing, error-detection, and error-correction subsystems. A similar internal modularity of control has been implemented in Sussman's computer program for skill acquisition, HACKER, which learns from mistakes (cf. Shallice, 1988). However, the anatomical basis for modularity of intrahemispheric control is still unknown, partly because there is little systematic research on the neuropsychology of error monitoring (Zaidel, 1987). A second mode of hemispheric function is process interactive: each hemisphere contributes to a different stage of processing. For example, the RH may be specialized when the information is novel or unfamiliar during initial stages, the LH during later, analytic stages (Goldberg & Costa, 1981; Zaidel, 1979). A third mode is made possible by shifting the role of one hemisphere from that of an independent processor to that of a monitor for the other (Stein & Zaidel, 1989; Zaidel, 1987).

The modes are not mutually exclusive and can proceed in parallel. In particular, parallel independent computations in the two hemispheres can be used for error detection by cross-comparing the results. Moreover, parallel computational packages that include complete information-processing sequences from sensory registration to programmed behavior can underlie decisions and give the illusion of choice.

In sum, the design advantage of hierarchical modularity is its adaptability to error and to change, so that the whole system can be adapted by local repair. The design advantage of parallel modularity is flexibility in cognitive control. Such flexibility is particularly well illustrated by the dynamics of hemispheric independence.

REFERENCES

Aboitiz, F., Zaidel, E., & Scheibel, A. A. (1989). Variability in fiber composition in different regions of the posterior corpus callosum in humans [Abstract]. *American Association of Anatomists Anatomical Record, 224,* 6a.

Alexander, M. P., & Warren, R. L. (1988). Localization of callosal auditory pathways: A CT case study. *Neurology, 38,* 802–804.

Bogen, J. E. (1969). The other side of the brain—II. An appositional mind. *Bulletin of the Los Angeles Neurological Society, 34,* 135–162.

Bogen, J. E. (1986). Mental duality in the intact brain. *Bulletin of Clinical Neurosciences, 51,* 3–29.

Bogen, J. E. (1987). Physiological consequences of complete or partial commissural section. In M. L. J. Apuzzo (Ed.), *Surgery of the third ventricle* (pp. 175–194). Baltimore: Williams & Wilkins.

Bradshaw, J. L., & Nettleton, N. C. (1983). *Human cerebral asymmetry.* Englewood Cliffs, NJ: Prentice-Hall.

Braud, W. G., & Braud, L. W. (1973). Preliminary explorations of psi-conducive states: Progressive muscular relaxation. *Journal of the American Society for Psychical Research, 67,* 26–46.

Brown, J. W. (1988). *The life of the mind.* Hillsdale, NJ: Lawrence Erlbaum.

Byne, W., Bleier, R., & Houston, L. (1988). Variations in human corpus callosum do not predict gender: A study using magnetic resonance imaging. *Behavioral Neuroscience, 102,* 222–227.

Chiarello, C. (1988). Lateralization of lexical processes in the normal brain: A review of visual half-field research. In H. A. Whitaker (Ed.), *Contemporary reviews in neuropsychology* (pp. 36–76). New York: Springer-Verlag.

Clarke, J. M., & Zaidel, E. (1989). Simple reaction times to lateralized light flashes: Varieties of interhemispheric communication routes. *Brain, 112,* 849–870.

Clarke, J. M., Zaidel, E., & Lufkin, R. B. (1989). Visuospatial performance is related to the size of the splenium of the corpus callosum in normal subjects [Abstract]. *Journal of Clinical and Experimental Neuropsychology, 11,* 74.

Clarke, S., Kraftsik, R., Van der Loos, H., & Innocenti, G. M. (1989). Forms and measures of adult and developing human corpus callosum: Is there sexual dimorphism? *Journal of Comparative Neurology, 280,* 213–230.

Cooke, N. D. (1986). *The brain code: Mechanisms of information transfer and the role of the corpus callosum*. London: Methuen.

Crawford, H. J., Crawford, K., & Koperski, B. J. (1983). Hypnosis and lateral cerebral function as assessed by dichotic listening. *Biological Psychiatry, 18*, 415–427.

Cronin-Golomb, A. (1986). Subcortical transfer of cognitive information in subjects with complete forebrain commissurotomy. *Cortex, 22*, 499–519.

Degos, J. D., Gray, F., Louarn, F., Ansquer, J. C., Poirier, J., & Barbizet, J. (1987). Posterior callosal infarction. Clinicopathological correlations. *Brain, 110*, 1155–1171.

de Lacoste, M. C., Kirkpatrick, J. B., & Ross, E. D. (1985). Topography of the human corpus callosum. *Journal of Neuropathology and Experimental Neurology, 44*, 578–591.

de Lacoste-Utamsing, C., & Holloway, R. L. (1982). Sexual dimorphism in the human corpus callosum. *Science, 216*, 1431–1432.

Demeter, S., Ringo, J. L., & Doty, R. W. (1988). Morphometric analysis of the human corpus callosum and anterior commissure. *Human Neurobiology, 6*, 219–226.

Dunn, J. C., & Kirsner, K. (1988). Discovering functionally independent mental processes: The principle of reversed association. *Psychological Review, 5*, 91–101.

Eviatar, Z., Menn, L., & Zaidel, E. (1989). *Right hemisphere contribution to lexical analysis*. Manuscript submitted for publication.

Eviatar, Z., & Zaidel, E. (1989). *The effects of word length and emotionality on hemispheric contribution to lexical decision*. Manuscript submitted for publication.

Farell, B. (1985). Same–different judgments: A review of current controversies in perceptual comparisons. *Psychological Bulletin, 98*, 419–456.

Fodor, J. (1983). *The modularity of mind*. Cambridge: MIT Press.

Friedman, A., Polson, M. C., Dafoe, C. E., & Gaskill, S. J. (1982). Divided attention within and between hemispheres: Testing a multiple resources approach to limited-capacity information processing. *Journal of Experimental Psychology: Human Perception and Performance, 8*, 625–650.

Frumkin, L. R., Ripley, H. S., & Cox, G. B. (1978). Changes in cerebral hemispheric lateralization with hypnosis. *Biological Psychiatry, 13*, 741–750.

Galin, D., Johnstone, J., Nakell, S., & Herron, J. (1979). Development of the capacity for tactile information transfer between hemispheres in normal children. *Science, 204*, 1330–1332.

Goldberg, E., & Costa, L. D. (1981). Hemispheric differences in the acquisition and use of descriptive systems. *Brain and Language, 14*, 144–173.

Gordon, H. W., Bogen, J. E., & Sperry, R. W. (1971). Absence of deconnexion syndrome in two patients with partial section of the neocommissures. *Brain, 94*, 327–336.

Gruzelier, J. H. (1987). Cerebral laterality and schizophrenia: A review of the interhemispheric disconnection hypothesis. In A. Glass (Ed.), *Individual differences in hemispheric specialization* (pp. 357–376). New York: Plenum Press.

Hamilton, C. R. (1982). Mechanisms of interocular equivalence. In D. J. Ingle, M. A. Goodale, & R. J. W. Mansfield (Eds.), *Analysis of visual behavior* (pp. 693–717). Cambridge: MIT Press.

Hellige, J. B. (1983). Hemisphere × task interaction and the study of laterality. In J. B. Hellige (Ed.), *Cerebral hemisphere asymmetry* (pp. 411–443). New York: Praeger.

Hellige, J. B., Cox, J. P., & Litvac, L. (1979). Information processing in the hemispheres: Selective hemisphere activation and capacity limitations. *Journal of Experimental Psychology: General, 108*, 251–279.

Holloway, R. L., & de Lacoste, M. C. (1986). Sexual dimorphism in the human corpus callosum: An extension and replication study. *Human Neurobiology, 5*, 87–91.

Holtzman, J. D., Sidtis, J. J., Volpe, B. T., Wilson, D. H., & Gazzaniga, M. S. (1981). Dissociation of spatial information for stimulus localization and the control of attention. *Brain, 104*, 861–872.

Inouye, T., Yagasaki, A., Takahashi, H., & Shinosaki, K. (1981). The dominant direction of interhemispheric EEG changes in the linguistic process. *Electroencephalography and Clinical Neurophysiology, 51*, 265–275.

Kashdan, B. (1979). *Speech perception and cerebral asymmetry.* Honors undergraduate thesis, Dartmouth College, Department of Psychology.

Kertesz, A., Polk, M., Howell, J., & Black, S. E. (1987). Cerebral dominance, sex, and callosal size in MRI. *Neurology, 37*, 1385–1388.

Kinsbourne, M. (1975). The mechanisms of hemispheric control of the lateral gradient of attention. In P. M. Rabbitt & S. Dornic (Eds.), *Attention and performance V* (pp. 81–97). London: Academic Press.

Kinsbourne, M., & Hiscock, M. (1983). Asymmetries of dual-task performance. In J. B. Hellige (Ed.), *Cerebral hemisphere asymmetry: Method, theory and application* (pp. 255–334). New York: Praeger.

Marr, D. (1982). *Vision.* San Francisco: W. H. Freeman.

Marshall, J. C., Caplan, D., & Holmes, J. M. (1975). The measure of laterality. *Neuropsychologia, 13*, 315–322.

Measso, G., & Zaidel, E. (in press). The effect of response programming on laterality effects in lexical decision. *Neuropsychologia.*

Miller, J. (1982). Discrete versus continuous stage models of human information processing: In search of partial output. *Journal of Experimental Psychology, 8*, 273–296.

Moscovitch, M. (1973). Language and the cerebral hemispheres: Reaction time studies and their implications for models of cerebral dominance. In P. Plimer, T. Alloway, & L. Kramer (Eds.), *Communication and affect: Language and thought* (pp. 89–126). New York: Academic Press.

Moscovitch, M. (1979). Information processing and the cerebral hemispheres. In M. S. Gazzaniga (Ed.), *Handbook of behavioral neurobiology* (Vol. 2, pp. 379–446). New York: Plenum Press.

Moscovitch, M. (1986). Afferent and efferent models of visual perceptual asymmetries: Theoretical and empirical implications. *Neuropsychologia, 24*, 91–114.

O'Kusky, J., Straus, E., Kosaka, B., Wada, J., Li, D., Druhan, M., & Petrie, J. (1988). The corpus callosum is larger with right-hemisphere cerebral speech dominance. *Annals of Neurology, 24*, 379–383.

Oppenheim, J. S., Lee, B. C. P., Nass, R., & Gazzaniga, M. S. (1987). No sex-related differences in human corpus callosum based on magnetic resonance imagery. *Annals of Neurology, 21*, 604–606.

Pandya, D. N., & Seltzer, B. (1986). The topography of commissural fibers. In F. Lepore, M. Ptito, & H. H. Jasper (Eds.), *Two hemispheres—one brain: Functions of the corpus callosum* (pp. 47–73). New York: Alan R. Liss.

Purves, S. J., Wada, J. A., Woodhurst, W. B., Moyes, P. D., Strauss, E., Kosaka, B., & Li, D. (1988). Results of anterior corpus callosum section in 24 patients with medically intractable seizures. *Neurology, 38*, 1194–1201.

Radant, A. (1981). *Facilitation in a lexical decision task: Effects of visual field and anxiety.* Honors undergraduate thesis, University of California, Los Angeles, Department of Psychology.

Rayman, J., & Zaidel, E. (1989). *Rhyming and the right hemisphere.* Manuscript submitted for publication.

Reinarz, S. J., Coffman, C. E., Smoker, W. R. K., & Godersky, J. C. (1988). MR imaging of the corpus callosum: Normal and pathologic findings and correlation with CT. *American Journal of Roentgenology, 151,* 791–798.

Risse, G. L., Gates, J., Lund, G., Maxwell, R., & Rubens, A. (1989). Interhemispheric transfer in patients with incomplete section of the corpus callosum: Anatomical verification with MRI. *Archives of Neurology, 46,* 437–443.

Rothwell, B., & Zaidel, E. (1990). Visual field differences in the magnitude of the Oppel-Kundt illusion vary with processing time. *Perception and Psychophysics, 47,* 180–190.

Salamy, A. (1978). Commissural transmission: Maturational changes in humans. *Science, 200,* 1409–1411.

Sergent, S. (1987). A new look at the human split brain. *Brain, 110,* 1375–1392.

Shallice, T. (1988). *From neuropsychology to mental structure.* Cambridge: Cambridge University Press.

Sperry, R. W. (1968). Mental unity following surgical disconnection of the cerebral hemispheres. *The Harvey Lectures, 62,* 243–323.

Spielberger, C. D., Gorsuch, R. L., & Lushene, R. E. (1970). *STAI manual.* Palo Alto, CA: Consulting Psychologists Press.

Stein, R., & Zaidel, E. (1989). *Hemispheric error correction in lexical decision.* Unpublished manuscript, University of California, Los Angeles, Department of Psychology.

Studdert-Kennedy, M., & Shankweiler, D. (1970). Hemispheric specialization for speech perception. *Journal of the Acoustical Society of America, 48,* 579–594.

Thakur, R. C. (1977). Anxiety as a determiner of the effect of distraction on bilateral transfer. *Indian Journal of Psychological Research, 21,* 202–206.

Tulving, E. (1983). *Elements of episodic memory.* Oxford: Oxford University Press.

Turkewitz, G., & Ross-Kossad, P. (1984). Multiple models of right hemisphere information processing: Age and sex differences in facial recognitions. *Developmental Psychology, 20,* 95–103.

Weber, G., & Weis, S. (1986). Morphometric analysis of the human corpus callosum fails to reveal sex-related differences. *Journal für Hirnforschung, 27,* 237–240.

White, H., Banks, W. P., & Zaidel, E. (1989). *Laterality effects in symbolic judgment: The influence of semantic congruity on hemispheric processing.* Manuscript submitted for publication.

Witelson, S. F. (1989). Hand and sex differences in the isthmus and genu of the corpus callosum. *Brain, 112,* 799–835.

Witelson, S. F., & Kigar, D. L. (1987). Neuroanatomical aspects of hemisphere specialization in humans. In D. Ottoson (Ed.), *Duality and unity of the brain: Unified functioning and specialization of the hemispheres* (pp. 466–495). Hampshire: Macmillan.

Zaidel, E. (1976a). Auditory vocabulary of the right hemisphere following brain bisection or hemidecortication. *Cortex, 12,* 191–211.

Zaidel, E. (1976b). Language, dichotic listening and the disconnected hemispheres. In D. O. Walter, L. Rogers, & J. M. Finzi-Fried (Eds.), *Conference on human brain function* (pp. 103–110). Los Angeles: Brain Information Service/BRI Publications Office, UCLA.

Zaidel, E. (1978). Concepts of cerebral dominance in the split brain. In P. Buser & A. Rougeul-Buser (Eds.), *Cerebral correlates of conscious experience* (pp. 263–284). Amsterdam: Elsevier.

Zaidel, E. (1979). On measuring hemispheric specialization in man. In B. Rybak (Ed.), *Advanced technobiology* (pp. 365–403). Alphen aan den Rijn: Sijthoff and Noordhoff.

Zaidel, E. (1983). Disconnection syndrome as a model for laterality effects in the normal brain. In J. Hellige (Ed.), *Cerebral hemisphere asymmetry: Method, theory and application* (pp. 95–151). New York: Praeger.

Zaidel, E. (1986). Callosal dynamics and right hemisphere language. In F. Lepore, M. Ptito, & H. H. Jasper (Eds.), *Two hemispheres—one brain: Functions of the corpus callosum* (pp. 435–459). New York: Alan R. Liss.

Zaidel, E. (1987). Hemispheric monitoring. In D. Ottoson (Ed.), *Duality and unity of the brain: Unified functioning and specialization of the hemispheres* (pp. 247–281). Hampshire: Macmillan.

Zaidel, E. (1989). Hemispheric independence and interaction in word recognition. In C. von Euler, I. Lundberg, & G. Lennerstrand (Eds.), *Brain and reading* (pp. 77–97). Hampshire: Macmillan.

Zaidel, E., Rayman, J., Letai, D., & White, H. (1989). *Modules of the brain: A dual task approach to hemispheric function.* Unpublished manuscript, University of California, Los Angeles, Department of Psychology.

Zaidel, E., White, H., Sakurai, E., & Banks, W. (1988). Hemispheric locus of lexical congruity effects: Neuropsychological reinterpretation of psycholinguistic results. In C. Chiarello (Ed.), *Right hemisphere contributions to lexical semantics* (pp. 71–88). New York: Springer.

Zaidel, E., Zaidel, D. W. & Bogen, J. E. (in press). Testing the commissurotomy patient. In A. A. Boulton, G. B. Baker, & M. Hiscock (Eds), *Neuromethods: Vol. 15. Methods in human neuropsychology.* Clifton, NJ: Humana Press.

DISCUSSION

JÖRG PAHL: I've heard it said that "split brain" is actually a misnomer and that there is something to the exchange of information that the subcortical areas are responsible for.

ERAN ZAIDEL: Yes, anybody who has looked at the split-brain patients for any length of time knows that. In fact, the early papers emphasized information transfer between the two sides over noncallosal routes. There are various possibilities. One is cross-cueing. For example, you flash the picture of a triangle to the right hemisphere, and after a while the left hemisphere is able to say, "that was a triangle." How does it do it? Often the patient does this. He makes the shape with his head and then the left hemisphere reads off the movement and it is able to verbalize it. That's one way. Other forms of transfer apparently involve some relay of semantic affective information subcallosally. This was all well known long ago, so I don't think we're adding anything new here. The more perplexing issues involve the alleged emergence of speech in the right hemisphere in split-brain patients, and I believe those are cases where the left hemisphere was badly damaged early on.

GEORGE OJEMANN: The question I was about to ask has just been led into. In our series of unilateral barbiturate injections on an epileptic population that we have just looked at, about 9% of 225 patients had bilateral speech. I'm wondering whether anything is known about the preoperative lateralization of your population of split-brain patients. I know there are big individual differences in what the right hemisphere can do, and you somehow wonder if that might not be related to what it could do preoperatively in terms of language.

ZAIDEL: There's that famous paper by Whitaker and Ojemann in the *Annals of the New York Academy of Sciences*, which I think correctly addresses the validity of generalization from split-brain patients to the general population. Part of this is on the basis of early brain damage, which may have caused reorganization and therefore atypical representation of language and other functions in the disconnected hemispheres. I actually believe that this is not the correct explanation in the case of these patients. It may be true in some split-brain patients, but not in these for the following reasons. We have looked at various sources of evidence on extracallosal brain damage, and none of them seem to predict the laterality of the result that we get on different tests. Specifically, most recently, I saw an MRI that Joe Bogen obtained, and there is no evidence for extracallosal damage to the language area or anywhere near it that could explain the shift to the other side. More importantly, we correlated the behavioral laterality effects that we observed with performance on various sensory–motor tasks, and it turns out that the only task that predicts laterality of extracallosal damage is a stereognosis task: no visual and no auditory tasks show an association with laterality of extracallosal damage.

OJEMANN: You recognize that the 9% don't have lateralized brain lesions either. This is a population of people who simply have epilepsy and in whom there is fairly high percentage with bilateral speech. My concern is that some of your patients may fall into that group.

ZAIDEL: That's why I always felt that converging evidence and behavioral patterns of performance are crucial. I actually believe that the normal right hemisphere has the capacity for more and better language than the disconnected right hemisphere.

GLENN ROSEN: John Marshall has contended that the deep dyslexic and sometimes the developmental dyslexic are identical in terms of the errors that they make. And therefore the kind of brain damage that you see in deep dyslexia would also explain developmental dyslexia. Your contention is that it's in the right hemisphere. Are you saying then that the possibility could be that developmental dyslexics read or process language in the right hemisphere?

ZAIDEL: I believed that in 1979, and I still think that's a very attractive model in some cases. I think the similarity between an acquired and a congenital dyslexia is limited. It's sometimes there and sometimes not there. Some of us have written about deep dyslexia, arguing that in fact the semantic errors and other symptoms reflect right hemisphere processing. There were many people, especially the British neurolinguists, who objected to the right hemisphere hypothesis on various grounds. About 3 months ago I got a paper from one of them, Karalyn Patterson. She tested three cases of hemispherectomy in children who had tumors relatively late—including one at age 10 and one at age 14. The girl who had the whole left hemisphere removed read very much like a deep dyslexic, so the paper contains a recanting of the original objection. I believe that at least in some acquired alexia the right hemisphere takes over, at least occasionally.

SANDRA WITELSON: Some of my previous work on developmental dyslexia may be relevant here. You may remember a report on developmental dyslexics in which I suggested that the bilateral representation they had for spatial processing plus their performance on a letter manipulation task suggested that they were reading with their right hemisphere. What I find fascinating is the idea of monitoring the nondominant hemisphere. If that is the typical human model, then what would happen in those individuals, let's say in women or left handers, in whom overall brain organization may be different? In a way your model would have profound implications about the kind of mind that those other people have.

ZAIDEL: Yes, indeed. Furthermore, that's not the only way to monitor. We've been trying to think fairly carefully about what it means to detect an error. One way to look at an error is to have a goal, try to accomplish it, to perform the action, and then take note of the discrepancy between the goal and what you're actually accomplishing. How do we correct an error? It seems to me there are two or three different ways. One is to compute the same thing again, as when you add a series of numbers. Now it's bad to add it the same way twice, because I'm going to make the same mistake, so I add it first going from top down and again from bottom up. Doing it twice in different ways is the better way. The best way would be to do it twice in different ways at the same time, so you don't have to wait. Still, you can do it sequentially, so you know there are various ways to monitor, and I suspect that some ways are better for some things and others are better for others.

JASON BROWN: If I understand you correctly, you are postulating a kind of transcallosal suppression with conditioned effect of some sort in the area nearer to the lesion of the left hemisphere. Is that right? A number of people have written about transcallosal issues. I think it explains some clinical syndromes, such as sympathetic apraxia. Inhibition is mirror to the anterior lesion would explain apraxia in the left hand, and that's why you don't get persistent left-sided apraxia in the splits. Would you be willing to speculate a little more about the kind of effect you think is occurring transcallosally, from a more physiological standpoint? Secondly, do you think this is a left–right effect only, or do you think there's a right-to-left effect? The third point that I want to make is that there are some PET studies that look at this phenomenon. There are PET studies that show, during the first 2 weeks following a stroke, some opposite-hemisphere suppression with greater suppression in the mirror area. We have studied only four or five chronic aphasics, and haven't found any right hemisphere suppression. We looked very carefully for focal suppression near the lesion and we haven't found that. We haven't found suppression to correspond to severity in aphasia. You might expect that the milder the aphasia, the more active the opposite area would be, but we haven't found this in our aphasic population.

ZAIDEL: I think that's an excellent suggestion, to look for the physiological mechanism, since we really don't know what it is. The data are very confusing in that regard since it is difficult to separate facilitation from inhibition with a PET scan. The way I think about it is that the corpus callosum can pull it off through different channels of communication. Each channel has its own control code so you can send information through it or not. Maybe something goes wrong with the control code in the channels connected to the site of the lesions. Now, I believe that it goes both ways, no question about it. Certainly, the split-brain data suggest that interpretation of the evidence from unilateral syndromes. For example, there is no neglect in the split-brain patients, which might suggest that in the right parietal patient there is inhibition of the left hemisphere.

OJEMANN: I just want to make a comment in regard to the transcallosal inhibition issue. We have looked now at enough cases of neural activity in nondominant hemisphere during a simple language task. What I thought I was going to see was lots of inhibition, and, in fact, there is significantly more inhibition in the dominant than nondominant hemisphere. So inhibition has not been characteristic of the activity in nondominant hemisphere during a language task in patients whose lateralization we know, and when we know this is not the language-dominant hemisphere. So, it doesn't seem, at least so far, that dominant inhibition is something that's over there.

ZAIDEL: We would not expect cross-callosal inhibition all the time. Moreover, functional inhibition may be accomplished through facilitation of a conflicting module or of incompatible behavior.

OVERVIEW

JASON W. BROWN, MD
New York University Medical Center

INTRODUCTION

One theme that clearly stands out in these chapters that will form the substance of my remarks is the need and the opportunity for a new approach to the study of brain function. We all know the century-old story of descriptive accounts of brain function and dysfunction and the various efforts that have been made to localize function in specific brain areas. But the opportunity has not been there to look at evolving patterns of organization and distributed systems in relation to cognition and specific behavioral tasks. This has changed in recent years with the dramatic advances in metabolic and electrophysiological mapping, permitting a reevaluation and, one hopes, a rethinking of traditional concepts of the neurology of behavior. This chapter takes up the idea of dynamic systems underlying cognitive function and their relation to patterns of growth in phylo-ontogeny.

ONTOGENY

The findings of Diamond and Scheibel (this volume) point to the possibility, indeed the likelihood, of neuronal growth into late life. The richness of the distal dendritic arborization in the left Broca area has been shown to continue into at least early adolescence and probably is sustained into midlife or later. This is consistent with the hypothesis (Brown & Jaffe, 1975), since confirmed (Obler, Albert, Goodglass, & Benson, 1978; Joanette et al., 1983), that changing aphasia type with age, given a constant lesion, implies growth over the life span. Diamond's finding of increasing cortical growth in aged rats with learning, together with the Buell–Coleman (1979) studies in humans, document sustained growth into late life and support clinical evidence for progressive development of the language areas.

Ontogenetic studies demonstrating sustained and perhaps task-dependent growth of neocortex should not be taken to indicate that increasing size is the important factor. There is a qualitative aspect in the growth pattern that needs to be explored. I have argued that this pattern is one of *regional specification*, a type of surround-to-center differentiation. Conceivably, regional specification evolved as a solution to the problem of limitations imposed on a maximally expanded and infolded brain by the size of the maternal pelvic canal. Specification extends processing without increasing volume. In man, this effect would be chiefly for left hemisphere, with a more generalized organization on the right side (see Semmes, 1968). In this view incomplete asymmetry accompanies more diffuse intrahemispheric organization in both hemispheres.

The work on asymmetry of the planum temporale is largely consistent with the specification concept. Witelson finds a larger callosum in non-right-handers, with axonal elimination characteristic of dextrals suggesting that asymmetry is achieved through pruning rather than growth. Rosen, Galaburda, and Sherman (this volume) find in rats that when a region is symmetrical, callosal connections are diffuse—more support for regional specification—and along the same lines argue that planum asymmetry involves reduction, not selective enlargement.

There is considerable evidence for parcellation as a mode of ontogenetic growth, for example, loss of connections in the development of sensory systems, competition for survival at the neuronal level (Edelmann, 1987), even the finding that evoked potentials in maturation become gradually restricted to the stimulated modality and, with pathology, regeneralize. One is reminded of Coghill's (1929) thesis that local, graded reflexes individuate out of mass reflexes; indeed, the whole legacy of clinical and physiological studies point to specification as a central, almost quintessential phenomenon in brain maturation.

The conclusion of these studies, together with the cited morphological findings, is that structure in the brain is a stage in a growth process that is artificially frozen, and the process through which structure is laid down involves the specification of cores out of more generalized surrounds.

PHYLOGENY

Pandya and Yeterian (this volume) review evidence for dynamic patterns in forebrain evolution, extending work by Bishop (1959), Yakovlev (1948), Sanides (1970), and Braak (1980). A fundamental concept that has emerged from this work is that of core specification as a vehicle in evolutionary advance. The process involves a succession of surround-to-center differentiations, leading through planes of limbic, mesocortical, and belt zones toward the "primary" perceptual and motor cortices.

One implication of this finding is that if brain processes underlying cognition correspond with patterns of phyletic growth, the processing is from archaic strata toward the "primary" areas and not in the reverse direction, as is usually assumed. Such work is consistent with studies of vision in astriate humans and animals and a wealth of clinical data (see Brown, 1988) along with a variety of other observations, for example, rCBF and PET studies indicating that "primary" sensory cortices mediate mental imagery as well as perception. Deacon (1988) has shown that the reciprocal pattern of laminar innervation of corticocortical connections from prefrontal to premotor to precentral region corresponds with that from inferotemporal cortex to V-3 to V-2 and V-1. If direction of processing is reflected in these patterns, the series from inferotemporal cortex toward V-1 would represent the "outflow" path in object formation.

There are deep similarities in the process of evolutionary and ontogenetic growth. The building up of phyletic structure through core differentiation of focal regions within more generalized surrounds extends into maturation in regional specification of the language zones, the diffuse to focal gradient in dominance establishment, and the gradual commitment of cortical sites to specific functions. Maturation involves a continuation of the same growth trends that account for evolutionary structure, that is, a single process in phyloontogeny involving the specification of regional cores within background fields. This process may be expressed in various ways, such as parcellation or pruning effects and lateral or surround inhibition. Given a fundamental process underlying evolutionary and developmental growth, one might ask how it relates to patterns of neuronal activity mediating cognitive function and, more deeply, the connection between growth and ongoing brain process.

PHYSIOLOGICAL PARALLELS

Similar effects have been reported in physiological studies. A good example is work on the readiness potential (Kornhuber, 1985) discussed by Schlag and Schlag-Rey (1987). The appearance of bilateral vertex negativity preceding a purposeful movement by several hundred milliseconds and leading to a potential over contralateral motor cortex timed with the motor event can be viewed as a surround-to-center progression. There is progressive restriction of the activation pattern from one that is bilateral and generalized to one that is contralateral and focal. The source of the potential is unclear. Supplementary motor area (SMA) has been suggested (see Goldberg, 1985), and recordings from SMA during limb movement in man reveal bilateral slow activity preceding motor cortex discharge (Chauvel, Bancaud, & Buser, 1985). Preliminary magnetoencephalographic work suggests a deep midline source in the initiation of distal limb movement. In addition to the physiological parallels with the process of core differentiation in phyloontogeny, these studies support the idea that actions unfold in a direction retracing forebrain evolution (in Brown, 1988; Fuster, 1985).

Work on synaptic inhibition in development (e.g., Wall, 1988) may provide a physiological model for the process of regional specification. Wall suggests that the basis of some forms of recovery after brain damage may rest in the disinhibition of latent synapses and the reenlargement of receptive fields. In other words, recovery occurs through the reappearance of a state of more generalized representation through the disinhibition of systems or networks, the inhibition of which accounted for the emergence of the now-damaged functional zone in the first place. Naturally, with diffuse representation there would be qualitative changes in functional capacity, and this would account for the nature and degree of restitution possible in a given case.

METABOLIC STUDIES

To some extent work with rCBF and PET might be expected to throw light on aspects of cognitive processing. Pahl and Gitelman and Prohovnik (this volume) have reviewed these data and pointed to some of the difficulties in methodology and interpretation. Metabolic techniques do provide an opportunity to examine functional systems entrained in given behaviors, but so far most of the interest has focused on local changes in metabolism. In our lab, we have looked at intercorrelational matrices in subjects undergoing resting and language (phoneme-monitoring) activation PET mapping (Bartlett, Brown, Wolf, & Brodie, 1987). A major finding is that of mirror correlations between cortical and subcortical regions at rest, with correlations between left language areas superimposed on the resting pattern during language stimulation. This finding is consistent with the above speculations in that there is a shift from a symmetrical bilateral state to one that is asymmetric and left-biased during language processing.

In other studies, we have found clear behavioral dissociations between language and nonlanguage (timbre-monitoring) tasks in left- and right-damaged patients (Chobor & Brown, 1987), lefts having difficulty with phoneme, rights with timbre monitoring, whereas PET maps show a similar pattern of left greater than right temporal activation for both tasks, a pattern not markedly different from the resting state. Such findings suggest that behavioral testing may in some instances be more sensitive to cognitive change than metabolic studies.

More recently, we have analyzed data in four left-brain-damaged aphasics during language and timbre stimulation. All subjects showed slight right temporal increases on both tasks, but only two subjects showed increase during language but not during timbre stimulation in the right Broca area, and these subjects were the only ones to perform the language task accurately. These findings indicate that metabolic correlates may be task specific in brain-damaged patients. In fact, in a single conduction aphasic 6 months post-onset, the left temporal metabolic lesion was 20–30% larger than the CT lesion during language but not during timbre stimulation, suggesting that even the size of the metabolic lesion may depend on the ongoing behavior.

LANGUAGE AND LATERAL ASYMMETRY

Central to the issue of brain and behavior is the problem of lateral asymmetry. Zaidel, Clarke, and Suyenobu (this volume) argue that the right hemisphere is a type of module incorporating various subroutines or components differing from those of the left hemisphere. Some problems with modularity theory are discussed elsewhere (Schweiger & Brown, 1988). With regard to interhemispheric effects, an alternative view is that a unitary bihemispheric system processes material up to a certain point, with further processing in left hemisphere only (Brown, 1988). In this view, the holistic–analytic dichtomy refers to successive points in a single unfolding system rather than to parallel operations. Recent work on hemispheric sharing in callosal patients supports this idea, including cross-field semantic, affective, and spatial priming effects and task-completion studies.

There is evidence that left Broca–Wernicke areas mediate phonological processing and that this is a (?the) crucial step in the advance from ape to man. The emergence of the Broca–Wernicke zones within anterior and posterior integration neocortex and the finding (see Pandya & Yeterian, 1985 and this volume) that integration cortex is prior in evolution to the primary "sensory" cortices, imply that these zones develop as outcroppings of penultimate phases in forebrain evolution, consistent with the evolutionary idea that new structures develop as branches of early stages, not as terminal additions.

This is not to maintain that these zones are programmed or prewired for phonology or that phonology is encoded in the genome and realized through the language areas. Descriptions of aphasia in the deaf with left Sylvian lesions are sufficient to refute this claim. But sign language involves the segmentation of lexical wholes in a manner not dissimilar from the analysis of lexical representations into their phonological constituents (Bellugi, Klima, & Poizner, 1988), so that the common operation is one that mediates the specification or individuation of lexical wholes into their component parts rather than a unique language function.

What this line of thinking leads to is a theory of language processing in which content is transformed through sequential whole-to-part transitions. This proceeds from conceptual to semantic levels with the isolation or resolution of a lexical representation through a zeroing in on the item within a semantic net or field, followed by the filling in or specification of "slots" in an abstract lexical frame with appropriate segments or phonological elements. According to this view, a serial context-to-item transformation is repeated at multiple levels rather than multiple operations applied to different linguistic or cognitive contents.

The configurations undergoing analysis need not be precisely localized. Ojemann, Cawthon, and Lettich's (this volume) finding of interference with naming at discrete points suggests a mosaic organization, but this could also reflect a tapping into configurational networks at various points or nodes. There is some evidence for a more focal organization of left language areas in relation to intelligence. Gender-specific effects have also been reported (see Kimura & Harshman, 1984; Brown & Grober, 1983). These observations can all be assimilated with the concept of diffuse-to-focal change in maturation, a variant of the core-specification theory.

The concept of a semantic-to-phonological transition in language production and perception mapping on to an evolutionary stratification implies that a deep level of semantic processing is mediated by archaic structures. Using different

methodologies, Halgren (this volume) and Kaufman provide evidence that hippocampus is associated with the P300 and N400 waves related to meaning in the
stimulus. This is consistent with clinical work indicating early semantic processing
linked to limbic–temporal mechanisms (Brown, 1988). What is not so clear is an
interpretation of the EP to reflect serial processing from registration to the
extraction of meaning or information in the stimulus. If the direction of processing corresponds with growth trends in evolution, if meaning is mediated by
ancient rather than recent evolutionary structure, if the processing leads toward
rather than away from the "primary" cortex, one might predict instances of intact
late potentials with flat early EPs. This has, in fact, been reported by Neville,
Snyder, Knight, and Galambos (1979) in cases of pure alexia, and there is considerable evidence in studies of brain-damaged subjects that the initial EP does not
correspond that strongly with behavioral capacity in the affected modality
(Brown, 1981).

What appears to be the case for language is that deep semantic systems
unfold into surface phonological stages through transitions involving context–
item transformations. This series unfolds unidirectionally over distributed systems in forebrain evolution. Moreover, the pattern in language processing corresponds to that in other cognitive domains. Fuster (1985; see also Brown, 1988) has
demonstrated a microgenetic sequence in the temporal structure of unfolding
action representations. There is a progression from axial and postural systems
about the body midline toward the fine distal digital innervation that employs
neural systems in the sequence of their appearance in phylogeny. Moreover, this
transition can be characterized as a progressive specification within a more global
organization. Similarly, in visual perception, the progression from indistinct ges-
talts of shape mediated by pretectal, limbic, and parietal systems toward the
analysis of features through V-1 and V-2 is also one of item specification (Brown,
1988). In both instances, item or core specification proceeds from archaic systems
to those of evolutionary recency.

PROCESS AND GROWTH

Anatomy is a phase in the life-span development of the brain. This development unfolds in patterns that extend phyletic growth into ontogeny. The differentiation of central cores in the evolution of the brain is replicated in regional
specification of neocortex, Phyloontogeny is the application of a surround-to-
center growth process reiterated on each new evolutionary and developmental
formation.

Cognition retraces evolutionary structure each moment in the microtemporal
unfolding through which behavior and mentation are elaborated. This unfolding
proceeds through a reiterated process very much like that of core differentiation.
Contents are selected through the suppression of alternative routes, a type of
growth through inhibition. Theories of figure–ground and gestalt formation,

center–surround, frame–content, or context–item transformation, or concepts of differentiation, individuation, or specification attempt in different ways to capture the same phenomenon.

These observations suggest that growth patterns in phyloontogeny establish lines of development that constrain or determine the cognitive process. In other words, the process underlying cognition involves a rapid, reiterated growth over evolutionary structure. Specifically, transformations mediating the appearance of new layers in the gradual evolution of the brain over the prehistory of the organism form the basis for transformations underlying life-span growth patterns in ontogeny. This same process is then collapsed in cognitive functioning and mediates the microtemporal transition from one level to the next in behavior.

The idea that cognitive processing involves a unidirectional and reiterated unfolding bottom up over phyletic systems rather than an open-ended concatenation or interactive network and that the mode of transition over levels replicates patterns of evolutionary and developmental growth implies that physiological events underlying cognition constitute a type of growth process in miniature. This should not be surprising. We assume that each time a behavior occurs there is an associated structural change in neuronal populations active in the behavior. Presumably, this change impacts on the configurational or network dynamic carrying the behavior and is responsible for learning.

According to this view, behavior unfolds in a wave or field-like transition over evolutionary levels in the brain, with the microtemporal progression (microgenesis) from one configuration to the next involving successive levels of constraint. Ensuing configurations are specified out of preceding ones through a modeling or sculpting effect. This effect is applied at successive levels to populations consisting of innumerable neurons, the series as a whole laying down a track that is the trace of the event.

This means that the trace has neither psychological nor physiological localization but consists of a network of potential synaptic relations. The trace depends on the relative strengths of myriad synapses and includes similar complex networks at all levels through which the behavior occurs. Because a behavior or mental representation can be taken to be the result of a processing series in which the final content (object, word, action) is not retrieved *in statu quo* from a store but differentiates through a sequence of transitions, the trace would embrace a wave of configurational change passing over all of the levels through which the representation develops. A trace, therefore, is not an entity that can be searched for and localized but is the *probability* of the recurrence of a given configuration at a particular stage in the cognitive process. The memory store is the sum of traces so defined or, put differently, the resting state of all *potentially realizable* configurations.

Memory is to the cognitive process as anatomy is to growth. Memory is the static element in process, what is left when the processing is over. In the same way, anatomy is like a snapshot in a moment of growth. When we interpret anatomy in terms of growth, we recapture a dynamic that bridges into process. The process in growth is the basis for memory, which after all is the growth that process undergoes over time. It is no wonder, then, that the growth of structure in the brain and the unfolding of representations in cognition reflect a common process that is grounded in the development of organic form. The deeper understanding of this process and its relevance to fields of neuroscience that seem so disparate and irreconcilable is a crucial challenge for brain theoretical study.

REFERENCES

Bartlett, E. J., Brown, J. W., Wolf, A. P., & Brodie, J. D. (1987). Correlations between glucose metabolic rates in brain regions of healthy male adults at rest and during language stimulation. *Brain and Language, 32*, 1-18.

Bellugi, U., Klima, E. S., & Poizner, H. (1988). Sign language and the brain. In F. Plum (Ed.), *Language, communication and the brain* (pp. 39-56). New York: Raven Press.

Bishop, G. (1959). *Journal of Nervous and Mental Disease, 128*, 89.

Braak, H. (1980). *Architectonics of the human telencephalic cortex.* Berlin: Springer Verlag.

Brown, J. W. (1981). Electrophysiological correlates of language: Studies in aphasia. In G. Adam, I. Meszaros, & E. Banyai (Eds.), *Advances in physiological science: Vol. 17. Brain and behavior.* London: Pergamon Press.

Brown, J. W. (1988). *The life of the mind: Selected papers.* Hillsdale: NJ: Lawrence Erlbaum.

Brown, J. W., & Grober, E. (1983). Age, sex and aphasia type. *Journal of Nervous and Mental Disease, 17*, 431-434.

Brown, J. W., & Jaffe, J. (1975). Hypothesis on cerebral dominance. *Neuropsychologia, 13*, 107-110.

Buell, S. J., & Coleman, P. D. (1979). Dendritic growth in the aged human brain and failure of growth in senile dementia. *Science, 206*, 854-856.

Chauvel, P., Bancaud, J., & Buser, P. (1985). Participation of the supplementary motor area in speech. *Experimental Brain Research, 58*, A14.

Chobor, K. L., & Brown, J. W. (1987). Phoneme and timbre monitoring in left and right CVA patients. *Brain and Language, 30*, 278-284.

Coghill, G. E. (1929). *Anatomy and the problem of behavior.* New York: Macmillan.

Deacon, T. (1988). Holism and associationism in neuropsychology: An anatomical synthesis. In E. Perecman (Ed.), *Integrating theory and practise in clinical neuropsychology* (pp. 1-48). Hillsdale, NJ: Lawrence Erlbaum.

Edelmann, G. M. (1987). *Neural Darwinism: The theory of neuronal group selection.* New York: Basic Books.

Fuster, J. (1985). Commentary. *Behavioral and Brain Sciences, 8*, 567.

Goldberg, G. (1985). Supplementary motor area structure and function: Review and hypotheses. *Behavioral and Brain Sciences, 8*, 567-616.

Joanette, Y., Ali-Cherif, A., Delpuech, F., Habib, M., Pellissier, J. F., & Poncet, M. (1983). Evolution de la sémiologie aphasique avec l'âge. *Revue Neurologique, 139*, 657-664.

Kimura, D., & Harshman, R. A. (1984). Sex differences in brain organization for verbal and non-verbal functions. In G. De Vries, J. P. C. DeBruin, H. B. M. Uylings, & M. A. Corner (Eds.), *Progress in brain research* (pp. 423–441). Amsterdam: Elsevier.

Kornhuber, H. H. (1985). The bereitschaftspotential and the activity of the supplementary motor area preceding voluntary movement. *Experimental Brain Research, 58,* A10–A11.

Neville, H. J., Snyder, E., Knight, R., & Galambos, R. (1979). Event related potentials in language and nonlanguage tasks in patients with alexia without agraphia. In D. Lehmann & Callaway (Eds.), *Human evoked potentials* (pp. 269–283). New York: Plenum Press.

Obler, L. K., Albert, M. L., & Goodglass, H., & Benson, D. F. (1978). Aphasia type and aging. *Brain and Language, 6,* 318–322.

Pandya, D. N., & Yeterian, E. H. (1985). Architecture and connections of cortical association areas. In A. Peters & E. G. Jones (Eds.), *Cerebral cortex* (Vol. 4, pp. 3–31). New York: Plenum Press.

Sanides, F. (1970). Functional architecture of motor and sensory cortices in primates in light of a new concept of neocortex evolution. In C. Noback & W. Montagna (Eds.), *Advances in primatology.* New York: Appleton-Century-Crofts.

Schlag, J., & Schlag-Rey, M. (1987). Evidence for a supplementary eye field. *Journal of Neurophysiology, 34,* 920–936.

Schweiger, A., & Brown, J. W. (1988). Minds, models and modules. *Aphasiology, 2,* 531–544.

Semmes, J. (1968). Hemispheric specialization: A possible clue to mechanism. *Neuropsychologia, 6,* 11–26.

Wall, P. J. (1988). Recruitment of ineffective synapses after injury. In S. Waxman (Ed.), *Functional recovery in neurological disease* (Vol. 47, pp. 387–400). New York: Raven Press.

Yakovlev, P. I. (1948). Motility, behavior and the brain. *Journal of Nervous and Mental Disease, 107,* 313–335.

INDEX